City at the Center of the World

Pitt Latin American Series

John Charles Chasteen and Catherine M. Conaghan, Editors

City at the Center of the World

Space, History, and Modernity in Quito

Ernesto Capello

University of Pittsburgh Press

Published by the University of Pittsburgh Press, Pittsburgh, Pa., 15260
Manufactured in the United States of America
Printed on acid-free paper
10 9 8 7 6 5 4 3 2 1

ISBN 13: 978-0-8229-6166-6
ISBN 10: 0-8229-6166-0

Library of Congress Cataloging-in-Publication Data

Capello, Ernesto.
 City at the center of the world : space, history, and modernity in Quito / Ernesto Capello.
    p. cm. — (Pitt Latin American studies)
  Includes bibliographical references and index.
 ISBN-13: 978-0-8229-6166-6 (pbk. : alk. paper)
 ISBN-10: 0-8229-6166-0 (pbk. : alk. paper)
 1. Quito (Ecuador)—History. 2. Quito (Ecuador)—Population. 3. Quito (Ecuador)—
Historiography—Social aspects. 4. Collective memory—Ecuador—Quito. 5. Historic
preservation—Ecuador—Quito—History. 6. Place (Philosophy) I. Title.
 F3781.3.C37 2011
 986.6'13—dc23   2011021269

Contents

Illustrations

Acknowledgments

This book owes much to the suggestions, advice, and support of numerous people, each of whom deserves recognition. I have been fortunate to have been mentored by extraordinary teachers, beginning at Academia Cotopaxi in Quito, where Arthur Pontes and Eric Little first awoke my interest in history and Matthew Szweda and the late Buddy Burniske taught me the value of clear prose and analytical thinking. At Vassar College, David Schalk and the late Hsi-Huey Liang inspired me to pursue graduate work while Leslie Offutt reintroduced me to Latin America and has proved a tireless advocate and true friend over the years. I especially thank Mauricio Tenorio Trillo, with whom I first discussed this project over a rambling walk through Austin, Texas, that ended with empty coffee cups and a host of fascinating thoughts to be digested. He has continued to be a source of inspiration, a dedicated advocate, and strategic contrarian throughout the many phases of the book's development. I wish to also thank several other mentors, including Jonathan Brown, Ginny Burnett, Jay Byron, Jorge Cañizares-Esguerra, Shane Davies, Susan Deans-Smith, Gary Dibble, Henry Dietz, Seth Garfield, Aline Helg, Peter Jelavich, Christopher Leff, Mitch Miller, Michael Murray, and the late Donald Olsen.

The book has also benefited from the invaluable advice of a number of colleagues in Ecuador and the United States. Guillermo Bustos of the Universidad Andina in Quito proved an invaluable guide as I first began to explore Quito's archives, while Valeria Coronel and Eduardo Kingman of the Facultad Latinoamericana de Ciencias Sociales (FLACSO) have been instrumental in shaping my understanding of Quiteño and Ecuadorian history. Chad Black was a comrade in arms throughout my research and made critical methodological suggestions that first helped me consider the possibility of bridging the colonial and national periods. Nancy Appelbaum, Marc Becker, Lina del Castilo, Consuelo Figueroa, and the late Thelma Foote have read and commented extensively on drafts of chapters for which I thank them. My writing group partners Pablo Bose, Margo Thomson, John Waldron, and especially Ignacio López-Vicuña deserve special recognition. Other valuable suggestions for contextualizing this study within Ecuadorian historiography have come from Xavier Andrade, Christiana Borchardt de Moreno, Kim Clark, Peter Henderson, Ana María Goetschel, Mercedes Prieto, Juan Ramos, Betty Salazar, Mireya Salgado, and Kate Swanson. I wrote the first draft of this book in New York where Pablo Piccato not only facilitated library access at Columbia University but was also a creative listener and friend, while Elaine Carey, Brenda Elsey, Thom Rath, Christoph Rosenmuller, and Mauricio Borrero provided intellectual camaraderie during my tenure in the city. My colleagues in the history departments of the University of Vermont and at Macalester College fostered a collegial working environment and also provided critical feedback in writing workshops. I particularly thank Erik Esselstrom, Sean Field, Jim Overfield, Amani Whitfield, and Denise Youngblood at the University of Vermont and Lynn Hudson, Jamie Monson, and Peter Rachleff at Macalester College. I also thank Ramón Rivera-Servera for his ongoing friendship and for his advice at a crucial moment in the project's development.

This book would not have been possible without much financial and institutional support. Vassar College granted me a Dorothy Evans Fellowship for alumni graduate study while the history department at the University of Texas at Austin provided me with a University Fellowship and a Perry Castañeda Fellowship. My research in Ecuador was funded with the support of a Fulbright IIE Fellowship and facilitated by the impressive individuals who ran the Fulbright Commission, including former director Susana Cabeza de Vaca, Ana Lucia Córdoba, Elena Durango, Karen Aguilar, and Mariangela García. The Universidad Andina Simón Bolívar and the FLACSO in Quito provided institutional support while a critical post-doctoral research trip was funded by the Dean's Fund at the University of Vermont. I wish to thank Mary Helen Quinn, Marilyn Lehman, Anna Marie Manuzza, Kathy Carolin, Kathy Truax, and Herta Pitman for their administrative support as well as the scores of student workers in Austin, Queens, Burlington, and Saint Paul who have photocopied, scanned, bound, and otherwise supported this book in manuscript form, especially Luisa Aya and Ina Rojnic for their help with the index.

Multiple archivists, librarians, and private individuals facilitated access to the sources that shaped this book. At the Archivo Nacional del Ecuador, I thank Grecia Vasco Escudero and Margarita Tufiño. At the Archivo Metropolitano de Quito, I thank Dr. Jorge Salvador Lara, Diego Chiriboga, and Marco Carrera. At the Biblioteca Ecuatoriana "Aurelio Espinosa Pólit" in Cotocollao, I thank its former director, R.P. José Ayerve, who was gracious enough to allow archival access despite the library's closure and also Orlando Bracho. I thank George Weingard, who introduced me to Pedro Durini, who has been extremely generous by not only agreeing to participate in an oral history but also facilitated access to the Durini Collection at the Museo de la Ciudad. Ximena Endara and Andrea Moreno made my working in the Durini archives a pleasure despite the collection not yet being fully catalogued. I thank Gloria Gangotena de Montufar and Carlos Freile for their help in accessing the Cristobal Gangotena y Jijón papers at the Universidad San Francisco de Quito. Perhaps no single archivist has been more helpful than José Vera Vera at the Fondo Jijón y Caamaño of the Banco Central del Ecuador. I wish to also acknowledge the entire staff of the Banco Central libraries, especially Honorio Granja, and of the Biblioteca de la Universidad Andina Simón Bolívar, the Biblioteca de la Pontificia Universidad Católica del Ecuador, the Benson Collection of the University of Texas Libraries, the New York Public Library, the Columbia University Libraries, the St. John's University Library, the University of Minnesota Libraries, and the Library of Congress, especially Ginny Mason who gave me a behind the scenes glance at the library's map collection. I wish to particularly thank the staff of the Bailey-Howe Library at the University of Vermont and the DeWitt Wallace Library at Macalester College, especially the inter-library loan staff.

I must also highlight the extraordinary support that I have received from the University of Pittsburgh Press. I must first thank the Pitt Latin America Series editors, John Chasteen and Catherine Conaghan, for their enthusiasm for the manuscript and also John Beverley for his early interest in my work. The professionalism of the staff at the press has made a complex process incredibly smooth. Special recognition is due to Josh Shanholtzer for his championing of the project and his levelheaded advice over the past two years. I also thank Maureen Cremer Bemko and Deborah Meade for their copyediting advice, Ann Walston for her striking cover design, and also David Baumann, Maria Sticco, and especially Alex Wolfe. I am particularly grateful to the two anonymous reviewers whose suggestions strongly improved the final manuscript and to Kris Lane and Mark Overmyer-Velasquez for their comments.

Writing is in many ways a social enterprise. I particularly thank my friends and colleagues Ellen Arnold, Emily Berquist, James and Kavita Bhandary-Alexander, Karl and Brienne Brown, Daniel Bryan, Amanda Ciafone and Dan

Gilbert, Paul Deslandes, Jeremy Drosin, Jordana Dym, Lauren Fichtel, Mary Ellen Fieweger, Moya Foley, Sally Franklin, Juan García, Aldo García-Guevara, Larry Gutman, Chris and Vicki Hartman, Dan Haworth, Bryen Jordan, Anna Labykina, Pepo Lapaz, Jeffrey Leib, Jason Lowery, Johanna Maron and Ned Schodek, Abby McGowan, Terence Murren, Lara Nielsen, the Ortman family, Mick Ritter, Jeremy Smerd, Leo Sotomayor, Clay Steinman, Mark Stoler, Patrick Timmons, Julio Vargas, Luis Vivanco, Alex Zakaras, and Frank Zelko. I also wish to thank my family, especially Carol Boland, Hazel and Ernie Boland, Napo Capelo, Bernice and E. G. Conklin, Carol and Alan Perlmeter, Jessica Perlmeter and Anthony Cochrane, Lillian and Jack Perlmeter, and Nancy Sullivan and Michael Apicelli. My grandparents Cristina and Alejandrino Capello were among the thousands of midcentury provincial migrants to Quito, and their memory was always an inspiration. My sisters, Cristina and Emily Capello, have been comrades and intellectual combatants for so many years, and I thank them for their emotional support and their caustic humor. I wish to thank my parents, the late Jorge Capello and Kathy Boland Capello, for that foundational decision to raise their children binationally, for their love and encouragement, and especially for ensuring that there were always books upon the table, even in lean times.

Finally, I wish to express my love, gratitude, and admiration for Rachel Perlmeter. Not only did she first suggest that I might enjoy exploring Quito's history, but she has also discussed, read, edited, re-read, and re-edited every word of the dozens of papers, articles, and manuscripts that have culminated in this book. She has patiently endured nightly writing woes, clarified convoluted syntax, and known when to encourage my more fanciful ideas and when to let them dissipate. She is simply the most beautiful, stimulating, and dedicated person I have ever known.

Prelude

On the afternoon of Friday, December 6, 2002, at the Plaza de Toros on Quito's upper-class north side, approximately eighty people gathered to protest bullfights celebrating the anniversary of the Spanish founding of the city. [1] The carnivalesque spectacle, dubbed "Kito Anti-Taurino," wove among a reveling crowd that was rife with Iberian textures—flat-brimmed sombreros, gaily patterned ponchos, and wineskins brought out for the holiday. The protesters unfurled banners challenging the Eurocentric festivities by proclaiming the pre-Columbian origin of the city with a banner on which a broad black line slashed through "1534," the year when conquistador Sebastián de Benalcázar first arrived in the equatorial valley. Ribald clowns with painted faces satirized the ritual violence of the bullfight, using juggling pins to stand in for the beasts' horns and the matadors' sabers while denouncing the "bloodthirsty" practice as antithetical to the deep Andean "respect for life and nature." In the midst of the cacophony, a storm of flyers and broadsides took the battle to an ontological level, arguing that the word *Quitu* stemmed from an ancient Shyri Indian term meaning "center of the world."

Seventy-six years earlier, on May 29, 1936—another Friday—the upper echelon of Quito's diplomatic and administrative corps had gathered near the small town of San Antonio de Pichincha, twenty-seven kilometers north of the Ecuadorian capital. The dusty desert landscape contrasted sharply with the elegant coattails and stovepipe hats of these luminaries, whose presence graced a site where eighteenth-century French geographer Charles Marie de La Condamine had erected a commemorative pyramid, destroyed in 1747 by order of the Spanish Crown due to its inclusion of the French fleur-de-lis. Flanked by mustachioed French colonel Georges Perrier, acting president and sometimes dictator Federico Páez dedicated a new monument, based upon the original, to celebrate the bicentennial of the original mission. Designed by Luis Tufiño, military cartographer and director of the National Observatory, the monument site would become a tourist complex known as the Mitad del Mundo (meaning middle or center of the world) and a key component in the development of a regional tourist industry trading upon the capital's equatorial location.

The previous decade, amateur photographer Guillermo Illescas documented the Chimbacalle train station in Quito's southern environs (fig. 0.1). One of his photographs, most likely posed, is dominated by the outward gaze of a hardened indigenous man who sits on the curb with bare feet outstretched while he carefully clutches a crust of bread in his right hand, which is cradled in his left, as one might receive Communion. The broad brim of his coarse white hat shields his eyes, while a rope emerges from his poncho to advertise his profession as a porter. Women surround him on either side. The older woman, possibly his wife, and the young woman, possibly his daughter, bow their heads as they reach for items from the gunnysacks at their feet while a young boy in a floppy black hat pleads for a morsel from the girl, presumably his mother. Behind the family stand representatives of the city's motley population—an elderly beggar woman hiding under a crumpled fedora, two *chalina*-clad girls chatting over bags of produce, and a light-skinned dandy. This last figure completes Illescas's critique of the city's stagnant inequality; the man's three-piece suit, walking stick, cigarette holder, and apparent pomposity desperately contradict the poverty-stricken scene at his feet. He is a symbol of fashionable modernity in an unchanging society.

The porter and his family, however, also participate as active agents in the city's shifting modern pulse by virtue of their engagement with the loading and unloading of train cars at a railroad station, a little more than a decade old, which connected Quito to the port of Guayaquil and thus to the world economy. The photographer's vision of history belies this dynamism and accentuates stagnation, a stance contradicted by the lived experience of his subject (the porter). This rhetorical (re)production of tradition pregnant with social denunciations itself corresponds to tropes advocated not only by Illescas but also, increasingly, by other activists skeptical of the tenets of modernization and progress trumpeted by elites and state builders. Yet the construct itself also exists as simulacrum in a city far from the global core.

Fig. o.1. Guillermo Illescas, "Untitled" (c. early 1920s). Courtesy Archivo Histórico, Banco Central del Ecuador.

These three images suggest the resilience and contestation surrounding a trope identifying Quito as the center of the world, a conceit with multiple definitions and a complex development that this book seeks to unravel and trace. In particular, I explore a series of manipulations of Quito's history that crystallized between the 1880s and the 1940s, a period of explosive modernization, social upheaval, and demographic growth that paradoxically coincided with efforts to preserve the city's colonial core and to develop a vibrant tourist economy based on the capital's historical legacy. As the seemingly solid firmament of a long stagnant city disappeared, *quiteños* needed to find a definable history, one that would be a psychic anchor and also serve as a spatial framework for engaging a shifting cityscape.

A seminal moment occurred in the wake of the 1895 Liberal Revolution, which traditionally has been interpreted as a signal of the rising power of Ecuador's coastal planter elite, concentrated in the great port of Guayaquil, at the expense of the highland aristocracy, whose fortunes had long been linked to Quito's political and economic hegemony. Of particular importance were radical reforms that challenged corporate privileges, sponsored public works, and committed to the secularization of the state. This interpretation prioritizes an essential political-economic analysis highlighting the nation's expanding access to global markets and national integration, especially after the completion of a railroad between the two cities in 1908. However, because the Liberal Revolution occurred as part of a continuum of positivist reformism across the nineteenth century, it should not be a central focus. Moreover, the traditional dynamics that operated among various elements of society did not prevent change but instead were essentially generative, enabling individuals and collectives from across sociopolitical hierarchies to position themselves in a global and increasingly local marketplace where history could serve as both resource and political tool. By embracing and peddling visions of the city as museum, as phantasmagoria, or as allegorical repository of universal Catholicism, these groups, institutions, families, and communities defined and created a Quito responding to and rooted in a "historic" identity.

These constructions represented modern inventions, to be sure, but not solely of the state-driven form of nationalist political theater tied to official pageantry and invented holidays described by Eric Hobsbawm and Terence Ranger, though these certainly played a part.[2] Instead, the reinventions of Quito's colonial past represent dialogical processes involving re-encounters with tenets sometimes centuries old or only generations removed from their origin. The actors most involved in these discursive formulations primarily came from the city's traditional elite but also included shifting constellations of individuals, families, migrants, and even indigenous communities well aware of the power inherent in controlling history. These salient re-imaginings of the city's past thus demonstrate not only the role of tradition as a generating force in *quiteño* modernity but also the dynamism and resilience of an urban population contending with radical change.[3]

The series of lenses I use to examine this dialogical process are determined by particular narrative configurations of space and time, or what the Russian critic Mikhail Bakhtin calls the chronotope (literally, space-time).[4] Bakhtin argues that chronotopes determine the scope and style of a given literary genre by codifying a means of apprehending and moving through space within a temporal trajectory. For example, classical adventure myths feature a hero traversing multiple landscapes with little attention to a realistic chronology while folktales depend on the irruption of idyllic quietude by the carnivalesque presence of rogues, fools, or buffoons. He adds that these genres concretize social relations by virtue of their repetition, in a manner reminiscent of Maurice Halbwachs's views of collective memory.[5] Like Bakhtin, Halbwachs argues that a group framed by shared encounters depends upon constant (re)affirmation of their collective memories, languages, and codes. Only through reiteration can the collective continue to exist. This process depends on proximity, regular engagement, codifiable terminology, common locales, and dialogue. Memory thus becomes spatial and tangible in its formulation but also contingent upon a discursive and dialogical process.

During the *fin-de-siglo,* Quito became the site and the backdrop to the creation of a number of groups whose articulation as communities helped determine the shape and character of their city, just as they were themselves constructed by their environment. This study addresses the crystallization of six major chronotopes, that is, six critical acts of comprehending, constructing, and explaining Quito's urban milieu that would prove to be of lasting cultural and social import.[6] Each resonates with ancient meaning yet crystallized in the specific historical age associated with the city's twentieth-century upheaval. The book suggests that each chronotope placed the historical experience of a particular group of individual and collective actors at the center of a global metanarrative.[7] The selective deployment of these collective mythologies accentuated the power, economic strength, and versatility of the groups in question, which include elite Hispanist intellectuals, military cartographers, the members of an indigenous commune, and a family of immigrant Swiss-Italian architects. From these various positions, each group claimed the right to reinvent Quito's geographic form and history on its own terms. By tracing each chronotope's origins and reflecting upon their contemporary resonance, the book reveals how the plasticity of history and memory has (re)shaped the spatial and cultural landscape of the city to the present day.

My exploration begins with a chapter providing a panoramic view of Quito's *fin-de-siglo* history that seeks to locate this moment within the context of extended regionalist discourses. Citizenship (*vecindad*) in colonial Spanish America associated local urban identity with belonging to a universal corpus such as the Spanish nation or the Catholic Church.[8] I locate the crucial nature of regionalist politics and poetics in Ecuador's postcolonial history as an outgrowth of this bifurcated formulation of collective identity. There follows a broader discussion of the rivalry between Ecuador's coastal and Andean regions in the nineteenth and early twentieth centuries. I particularly focus on the degree to which aspirations toward universality colored expressions of regional identity that were similar to colonial notions of citizenship. Extending the analysis of Kim Clark, who has argued that the Liberal program in Ecuador was tinged with metaphors equating the coast with progress and the Andes with stagnation, I maintain that the Liberal Revolution proponents' concern with positivist narratives necessitated a rehabilitated image of Quito as a historic center.[9] The stirrings of nostalgic regionalism as national phenomena marked the configurations of actors, identities, and spaces that developed in the wake of Liberal reforms.

I subsequently trace the intellectual and political genealogy that gave rise to *fin-de-siglo* attempts by discrete segments of *quiteño* society to lay claim to the city's essential identity by elaborating universalizing chronotopes. I locate the colonial and nineteenth-century precursors of these totalizing discourses by following an archaeological approach that acknowledges the internal logic of each chronotope while underscoring its contingency. The narratives crafted in the early twentieth century deployed and manipulated these earlier frameworks yet should be considered manipulations and inventions by specific collectives of actors seeking to establish footholds of knowledge, power, or economic vitality within a rapidly modernizing city. I also highlight the traces of chronotope formation and their continued sociocultural import in the contemporary city.

Chapters 2 through 4 focus on institutional formulations of Quito as a historic center ripe for tourism developed by state organizations whose interests at times coalesced with those of other establishment actors but just as frequently diverged. The state did not act monolithically in constituting Quito as a city of memory but instead operated from a confluence of impulses framed by internal organizational logics.

Chapter 2 traces the historic ties between cartographic production and the metaphorical construction of Quito as the *mitad del mundo*. Colonial imagery depicted Quito as a new Rome, and an eighteenth-century Franco-Hispanic mission to measure the arc of the nearby equatorial meridian broadened global scientific interest in the equatorial Andean province. The allegory linking Quito's geographic and scientific centrality continued to flourish during the nineteenth and twentieth centuries. The process of local cartographic production ultimately became institutionalized within the Military Geographic Service (Servicio Geográfico Militar, or SGM), which used mapping to produce a sanitized vision of Quito's touristic predilections during the 1920s and 1930s. Monuments and commemoration have inscribed this chronotope upon the urban landscape.

One of the primary marketing strategies in the development of this tourist economy concerned Quito's renowned colonial architecture. The image of a city defined by its Iberian heritage was cultivated by conservative intellectuals seeking to situate Quito within a global movement called Hispanism, which theorized a common cultural community among Spain and the nations of Spanish America. Chapter 3 traces the role the National Academy of History (Academia Nacional de Historia) played in creating a mythologized Spanish Quito. Allying itself with the municipality, this body succeeded in reifying the racial power imbalance of the capital while justifying the preservation of its colonial city center even as modern structures arose in its environs. These multiple restrictions and the continuing activism of its cultural elite marked Quito as a potential World Heritage Site, an award bestowed by UNESCO in 1978. It was the first urban center to receive the honor.

The invention of Quito as a Spanish city found a major ally in the municipal government during the 1930s, largely as a result of the presence of Conservative activists led by the industrialist and historian Jacinto Jijón y Caamaño and his successor, Gustavo Mortensen. During that decade, the municipal government engaged in a series of political skirmishes with the national government over control of plans for the city's future development, a battle that pitted national party leaders against each other as well as local officials. Chapter 4 situates the conflict as an outgrowth of a century-old tug-of-war between the city government and the national state. It emphasizes the impact of this struggle on urban planning measures between the rise of the Progressive Party at the national level, in 1885, and the adoption of the city's first master plan, in 1942. I argue that the success of the conservative municipality built upon its administrators' ability to harness a "neocolonial" decentralization of local governance nationally while systematically implementing modern measures to centralize Quito's sociospatial order at the local level.

Chapters 5 through 7 move from an emphasis on institutional chronotopes to a focus on individuals, families, and collectives recently incorporated into the urban fabric. Trading on personal identity and communal history provided flexibility for groups navigating the unfamiliar contours of the modern city. These chapters also demarcate strategic manipulations of narratives of personal, local, national, and global history. Groups that were part of the urban fabric not only weathered Quito's challenges but also inverted traditional narratives by situating their own past at the center of the city's chronotopical landscape.

Chapter 5 considers the difficulties of traversing the burgeoning real estate and construction markets that accompanied Quito's demographic boom from the perspective of the Durini family, recent Swiss-Italian immigrants who established the city's premier architectural firm. Extensive research in the hitherto unavailable Durini business archives reveals a family deploying its cosmopolitan heritage and training in order to establish itself in what was originally a relatively "provincial" design market. I argue that the family's sensitivity to their elite clients' desire for modern sophistication helped the firm rise to the pinnacle of the profession, in the process creating a hyphenated vernacular architecture peculiar to the family's adopted city yet reflecting international norms and styles.

Chapter 6 features another series of migrants—a cadre of provincial intellectuals linked by a common antipathy to the mythology of Quito's traditionalist image—that figures into rising hopes for a revolutionary city. Their denunciations of traditional views of Quito originated in nineteenth-century liberalism and were elaborated in the ascetic novels written by socialist nationalists and *indigenistas* during the 1930s. I compare these published portraits to the transcendental imaginaries of the avant-garde, whose ambivalence about the city's present colored their equally bemused view of its future potential and begged the question as to whether modernity had ever visited the ancient Andean citadel.

These denunciations attempted to decenter the protagonistic role ascribed to the capital in institutional historiography, partly by developing narratives featuring elite exploitation of rural populations and incoming migrants. However, they did not incorporate the voices of indigenous peoples themselves, whose engagement with the discourses of Quito's historicity is the subject of chapter 7. This chapter traces the development of a chronotope of indigenous autonomy with an emphasis on the community of Santa Clara de San Millán, in Quito's northern environs, whose struggle with the municipality over communal landholdings had begun soon after the Conquest. Using civil court cases, notary documents, and the community council's minutes, I argue that Santa Clara exploited the political and economic opportunity afforded by urban incorporation while simultaneously manipulating land histories and communal genealogy to sustain both a measure of autonomy and relative internal stability.

My discussion of these parallel chronotopical narratives challenges the traditional historiography of Quito, which has largely considered this moment as a lynchpin in the development of modern class identity. The important works of Lucas Achig and Fernando Carrión, for instance, build on Manuel Castells's influential observation that the modernization of urban form and construction of monumental avenues à la the Champs-Elysées in the *fin-de-siglo* Latin American city demarcated zones of elite hegemony and limited subaltern access to the centers of power.[10] Others, including Guillermo Bustos, Milton Luna, and Manuel Espinosa Apolo, have extended this analysis to questions of cultural or racial identity, again subordinated to class.[11] While my study does not contradict these authors' conclusions that race and class severely constrained an individual's social possibilities, it does suggest that corporate identity was extremely fluid and multivocal. As such, this work has more in common with Eduardo Kingman's exhaustive study of urban hygiene that attempts to situate Quito's spatial alterations between 1860 and 1940 as outgrowths of shifting elite visions of the urban *polis,* in which the identification of place with class is paramount.[12] However, it also questions the continued support Kingman displays for Castells's basic presupposition of collusion among elites and intellectuals hoping to prove their "modern" credentials through urban planning.[13] I maintain that nothing could be further from the truth, as the upper class exhibited a summarily ambivalent attitude toward a movement that fundamentally challenged their traditional prerogatives.

This book also seeks to advance a broader understanding of the dialectical relationship between "tradition" and "progress" in the formation of Latin American cities. Although early analysts of the urban history of Latin America, particularly Jorge Hardoy and Richard Morse, attended to cultural resonance between the colonial and modern cities, the question of the impact of cultural mores did not receive substantive criticism until the late twentieth century.[14] This situation has begun to change; scholars such as Mauricio Tenorio, Marisol de la Cadena, and Mark Overmyer-Velázquez have highlighted the economic and political benefits of adopting a "traditionalist" urban imaginary.[15] My work seeks to build upon the insights of these studies by demonstrating the degree to which "history" proved a tradable commodity that provided a pliable blueprint for the construction of modern Quito. I thus hope to illuminate the degree to which even a quaint polis, sometimes thought of as "backward" and "isolated," reframed the paradigms of modernity and established its right to be considered not only a global capital but, indeed, *the* city at the center of the world.[16]

City at the Center of the World

Chapter 1

The Politics and Poetics of Regionalism

In 1935, as part of an early attempt to develop a tourist economy in Ecuador, the Dirección General de Propaganda y Turismo issued a series of picture postcards designed to advertise the country's charms to the world at large. Printed in Italy by the Instituto Geográfico de Agostini, the series was available in sepia, blue, or green and sold as sets as well as individually.

The pictures on the fifty postcards are equally divided among images of the coastal and Andean regions of the country, with two landscapes from each area and twenty-three shots of each of the country's two largest cities, Quito and Guayaquil, indicating the importance of these two urban centers. Perhaps more revealing of the cities' importance is the rhetorical schema developed throughout the collection. Of the twenty-three Guayaquil postcards, twenty-two feature twentieth-century construction (parks, promenades, and statues of prominent independence heroes) while the twenty-third features a bare-chested young man rowing a traditional dugout canoe by moonlight down the Guayas River. Of the twenty-three Quito postcards, one duly features a poncho-clad indigenous boy herding sheep in the woods of Itchimbia in the eastern environs of the city. Three demonstrate the new building of the Central University (an

Fig. 1.1. Las Colonias Promenade, Guayaquil. Courtesy Library of Congress, Prints & Photographs Division, lot 2779.

Fig. 1.2. Las Peñas, Guayaquil. Courtesy Library of Congress, Prints & Photographs Division, lot 2779.

institution dating to 1651), while the remaining nineteen feature colonial-era churches.

Taken as a set, the postcards serve as a panoramic performance of regional stereotypes. Guayaquil is offered to the modern tourist eager to stroll along a promenade with lovely young girls in spring dresses (fig. 1.1) and represented by a gallant, imported from impressionist Argenteuil, who prepares to launch a yacht at the "tourist paradise" of Las Peñas (fig. 1.2). Quito, meanwhile, seems

Fig. 1.3. San Francisco Convent, Quito. Courtesy Library of Congress, Prints & Photographs Division, lot 2779.

Fig. 1.4. Surroundings of Quito. Courtesy Library of Congress, Prints & Photographs Division, lot 2779.

more like a museum to be admired by the connoisseur of baroque antiquity, adorned as it is by sumptuous colonnades, majestic interior courtyards, priests (fig. 1.3), and, if one passes into the countryside, picturesque Indians (fig. 1.4). The postcards offer an impression of bifurcation, one that equates Guayaquil with modernity and Quito with tradition.

While this binary stems partially from each town's architectural record (old Guayaquil having been largely destroyed in an 1896 fire and Quito boasting one

Table 1.1 Ministry of Tourism sample postcards and captions

No.	City	Image title	Postcard caption*
1	Guayaquil	Las Colonias Promenade	Visit Ecuador, that welcomes you. Enjoy the modern conveniences of our cities.
4	Guayaquil	Bolivar Park	The favorable money exchange makes Ecuador one of the most inexpensive Tourist Countries to visit. The rate of exchange is stabilized at 15 sucres per dollar.
10	Quito	Façade–La Compañía	Visit Ecuador, land of history and tradition, land of ancient and colonial art. See the celebrated churches of San Francisco, La Compañía, La Merced.
25	Itchimbia	Surroundings of Quito	Visit Ecuador, let her enchant you with her clear sky and pleasant climates, with her abundant curative waters and with her many and luscious fruits.

*The captions are the original translations on the postcards.

Source: Library of Congress, Prints & Photographs Division, lot 2779.

of the best preserved colonial centers in South America), the rhetoric also exhibits a more deliberate plan to capitalize on a denial of coevalness.[1] The postcard text, presented in both English and Spanish on the back of each card, crystallizes this schematic (table 1.1). Guayaquil is framed as a favorable business zone, with contemporary architecture and cultivated urban green space, where one receives the "modern conveniences of our cities" and "the favorable currency exchange rate . . . at 15 sucres per dollar." The majesty of Quito, on the other hand, signifies the "land of history and tradition, land of ancient and colonial art" where one can "see the celebrated churches of San Francisco, La Compañía, La Merced."

This presentation of Guayaquil and Quito as the symbolic, political, economic, and social engineers of regional identities by no means expressed the contemporary or, worse, the historical situation of Ecuadorian regionalism. Instead, it displays a particularly banal attempt to profit from conventions that, by the 1930s, had become commonplace in a country that had long sought to overcome the economic and political rivalry of these two centers. These rivalries arose in the politics and poetics of regionalism from the colonial period into the early twentieth century. In the complex relationship between locality, collective identity, and citizenship, there existed a process whereby a multipolar colony dominated by the Quito marketplace became transformed, at least officially, into a biregional nation coalescing around the poles of Quito and Guayaquil. It was this process that necessitated the disputation of Quito's past and that was itself informed by that competition to control the city's frame. Embracing the identification of the city with a now mythologized past made it possible to challenge Guayaquil's preeminence as a national site of modernity. Indeed, this potentiality allowed Quito to claim a global signification dating back to the sixteenth century—a history that could propel the city toward future glories.

Quito as Colonial Capital

The history of regionalism in Ecuador rests on a firm foundation linking urban spaces with citizenship—a system with roots in the colonial era. Beginning in 1501, with Queen Isabella's presentation of detailed instructions to Nicolás de Ovando regarding the design of Santo Domingo, centrally planned urban settlements became the administrative, commercial, and military cornerstones of Spanish rule over a vast rural hinterland. These ideal cities were characterized by the use of a grid plan strongly influenced by Leon Battista Alberti's treatises on urban form, and, as such, they represented the pinnacle of Renaissance modernity. Beyond the grid, the Spanish American city instituted a particular social model based on proximity to the urban center. At the core lay a plaza that determined the hieratic and civic center, characterized by the presence of the *cabildo,* or municipal council, as well as a church. The surrounding blocks housed the chief citizens, or *vecinos,* followed by merchants, artisans, and mestizos. The schematic terminated with poor neighborhoods that abutted semi-autonomous indigenous parishes or towns (*pueblos de indios*) in the nearby environs, the residents of which would labor for their European overlords but ideally remain in their own (rural) sphere. Towns and cities were arranged in an interlocking network, with small towns overseeing the surrounding countryside, larger centers administering the small towns, and so on, up through the viceregal capitals, which answered directly to the Crown.

This spatial map delineated not only the imperial bureaucracy but also a crystallized consideration of citizenship, or *vecindad.* This Castilian concept built upon a complex matrix of legal and extralegal codes that determined one's standing in a community according to a set of norms seldom defined but generally understood. Establishing *vecindad* necessitated verifying customary characteristics such as Catholicism, masculinity, and the intention to reside in a community. Such norms proved flexible enough for foreigners to apply for and achieve *vecino* status and had proven enormously effective during the Reconquista's purging of Moorish and Jewish populations. Similar civic structures were instituted in the Americas but were soon altered due to shifting circumstances—for instance, residence requirements diminished in importance in areas that had been settled by Europeans for only a short time. Instead, racial and at times economic distinctions between *vecinos* became established, even as kinship networks continued to link individuals across regions according to their common origins in Europe.[2]

The structural importance of locating one's belonging in a community of *vecinos* in a particular city first and extending that membership to one's place in a national (Spanish) or universal (Catholic) corpus nevertheless shaped Spanish American considerations of *vecindad*. At times, these sentiments became manifest in panegyrics establishing what Richard Kagan has termed "communicentric" representations of urban communities. These were expressions of belonging in which individuals and corporations qualified the particular characteristics that denoted membership in their community of urban dwellers. Examples include patron saints (of which Mexico City's Virgin of Guadalupe is the best known), urban views featuring prominent citizens, allegorical landscapes, and illustrations of leading economic enterprises such as Potosí's silver mines.[3] Such images are ancestors of the peculiar depictions of Quito that would be adopted and reimagined during the *fin de siglo.* This is particularly true of the Hispanist ones, which directly referenced the colonial heritage in promoting Quito's hidebound character.

The geography of a colonial Spanish American city thus established radiating categories of power and belonging according to spatial, racial, and aesthetic segregation. While this ideal pattern was easily sketched on paper and zealously guarded in newly built centers such as Lima, it was increasingly difficult to administer in areas with existing indigenous populations.[4]

Quito's history serves as a case in point. As a northern Incaic stronghold and the birthplace of the emperor Atahualpa, the Andean citadel of Quito attracted the attention of conquistadors in the midst of the wars of the Conquest. One of Pizarro's original partners, Diego de Almagro, established a charter for the city in August 1534 soon after decisively defeating Atahualpa's lieutenant, Rumiñahui, near present-day Riobamba in central Ecuador. Almagro's envoy, Sebastián de Benalcázar, entered Quito on December 6, too late to save its legendary treasures and the grand imperial palaces from the blaze set by the retreating Incan armies. The conquistador drew the first *traza,* or central grid, among the ashes and consecrated the city to Saint Francis. Despite the monumental possibilities of developing the great Añaquito plains to the north, Benalcázar emulated his Incan forebears by exploiting the military advantages of the steep hills, deep ravines, and narrow approach of the original site. A substantial quantity of raw material for construction also lay among the ruins of the old city. The Franciscan monastery that began to rise in 1535, for instance, incorporated the remains of the great Incaic Temple of the Sun, which had made the city the most splendid in the northern Andes. Thus, from the start, colonial Quito existed as a hybrid space where various elements competed for predominance.

The uneven topography and existing population also altered the spatial and social map of the new city from the Spanish ideal. The grid morphed to conform to the rough terrain and was interrupted in numerous places by rushing creeks. Settlement patterns quickly abandoned the ideal radial structure and instead adopted a pattern reminiscent of the Incaic upper-half/lower-half dichotomy. The parish of El Sagrario replaced the "upper" section that had housed the Inca nobility, the Temple of the Sun, and the palace constructed by Atahualpa's father, Huayna Capac. There, the new symbols of Spanish power congregated, including the Franciscan monastery, the cabildo, the cathedral, the parish seat, and elite residences. To the east, downhill, lay the urban parishes of San Sebastián and San Blas, regions that were reserved for indigenous dwellings and that had previously housed the lower strata of Incaic Quito. Even this socioracial segregation changed over the course of the seventeenth century as the city grew to perhaps as many as fifty thousand inhabitants during the height of colonial power.[5] Indigenous households, for example, began to stray westward to the upper slopes of Mount Pichincha in the parishes of San Roque and Santa Bárbara, drawn by the construction of the Franciscan monastery and its artisan workshops.

A shifting local and regional economy influenced these new settlement patterns. During the sixteenth century, economic development in the Audiencia of Quito had been dominated by gold mining. Major mines lay at Zaruma, in the contemporary southwestern province of El Oro, and at Almaguer, near the northern city of Popayán in present-day Colombia. The Zaruma mines petered out in the 1590s, and, while Almaguer lasted a few years longer, by the turn of the century the Audiencia was facing a potentially grave economic crisis. These economic pressures took on a political dimension because creoles resented the viceregal imposition of an *alcabala,* or sales tax, in 1592. This crisis led to the expulsion of the Audiencia president by a rebellious cabildo, a move that in turn inspired armed intervention by a viceregal militia and the curtailing of cabildo autonomy in subsequent decades.[6]

The region slowly recovered from this crisis after the textile sector began to expand. Local entrepreneurs embraced the *obraje* system, in which sweatshops staffed by indigenous workers produced cheap woolen goods for sale throughout the Andean empire, as far north as Panama and as far south as Chile. The pioneers of this system, such as Chambo-based *encomendero* (labor grant recipient) Rodrigo de Ribadeneira, capitalized on their waning access to free indigenous labor to supply the emerging market at the great silver mines at Potosí, which had become the engine not only of the Spanish imperial economy during the late sixteenth century but would also subsidize the expansion of European enterprise into the huge Asian market of that era.[7] The success of entrepreneurs like Ribadeneira gave rise to a series of other *obrajes* throughout the region, particularly near the cities of Latacunga, Quito, and Otavalo.

Quito's expansion in the seventeenth century was partly due to regional demographic recovery as well as its dual role as an administrative center and as a marketplace.[8] The city's plazas drew merchants from throughout the Andean corridor as well as from the fertile Chillo and Tumbaco valleys to the east, which also were home to important *obrajes.* Another increasingly important industry, the production of religious art, began to develop simultaneously. Quito had been established as a bishopric in 1545, it became the seat of an Audiencia in 1563, and it soon came to house the regional headquarters for both the regular and secular clergy. The Franciscans took the lead in training local artisans devoted to producing icons, sculpture, and painting.

This process began through the efforts of Friar Jodoco Ricke in the 1540s and continued with the introduction of a number of sculptors from Seville and Granada in the late sixteenth century. These trained artisans constructed the largest religious complex in South America, the San Francisco monastery. Its 8.6 acres included a convent six patios deep (see fig. 1.3). The main façade, a masterpiece of Spanish American baroque, emulated Juan de Herrera's majestic fortress of El Escorial while the interior incorporated subtle indigenous motifs in gold leaf.[9] By the end of the century, Quito's artwork began to travel—indeed, the oldest extant American painting is a portrait of three mulatto lords from the Ecuadorian port of Esmeraldas painted in 1599 by the Quito master Andrés Sanchez Gallque and sent to Madrid as a gift for Philip II.[10]

The "Quito school" of polychromatic sculpture exploded during the seventeenth century. In addition to the workshops maintained by the Franciscans, a number of competing concerns arose in connection with the Dominican monastery on the city's southeastern edge. The secular clergy and other orders followed, including Jesuits, Dominicans, and Carmelite nuns, among others. Their myriad churches helped employ numerous artisans, particularly at the Jesuits' convent (1605–1765), which brought the city great renown for its extraordinarily opulent gold leaf adornment of the nave and the retablo. The sculpture itself traveled the extent of the Audiencia's jurisdiction and was soon revered throughout the empire for its delicacy and fine detail.[11]

Thus, by the seventeenth century, Quito had not only become an economic and administrative center but had also crafted a regionally renowned reputation as an artistic haven accentuated by religiosity—a city of God, or even a new Rome.[12] However, the eighteenth century brought a stagnant economy and a notorious challenge to the city's cultured image abroad. The latter had arisen largely due to the Franco-Hispanic Geodesic Mission (1736–1745), a scientific voyage to measure the arc of the Quito meridian to answer a dispute about the shape of the Earth.[13] The French academician Charles Marie de La Condamine and the Spaniards Jorge Juan and Antonio de Ulloa subsequently penned accounts of their travels in the Quito region. La Condamine's accounts of his celebrated trek down the Amazon proved an instant success in Europe, not only because of the exotic nature of the tropical flora and fauna he described but also because of his vivid emphasis on the barbaric qualities of Quito natives. He was particularly critical of the indigenous population—with whom he could not communicate—and also stressed the gory details of a murder he had witnessed in a public plaza in the southern city of Cuenca.[14] Ironically, the geographic study that was to have firmly placed Quito within the corpus of modern cities thus served to undermine its claim to a progressive spirit in keeping with contemporary European social attitudes.

La Condamine's critiques represented a major embarrassment to the Quito elite, who were simultaneously undergoing other troubles due to prolonged economic woes occasioned by the severe decline of Potosí mining. The erosion of the Potosí market made Quito's *obrajes* dependent on Lima's appetite for luxury textiles. Moreover, a century-long process of administrative reorganization collectively known as the Bourbon Reforms opened up American ports to non-Iberian trade for the first time. This restructuring hampered Quito's textile exports as a flood of inexpensive, high-grade French cloth undercut its product in the viceregal capital. While the cheap woolens that were produced in the northern regions of the Audiencia continued to be distributed throughout the rest of the Viceroyalty of New Granada, under whose jurisdiction the Audiencia had been placed in 1739, Quito underwent a serious slump. A series of plagues hit the city in the 1750s, exacerbating its problems. When the viceroyalty attempted to expand the *alcabala* on *aguardiente*—sugarcane liquor—in 1765 following the decimation of the imperial treasury due to the Seven Years' War, a widespread and cross-class rebellion broke out, which anticipated the better-known Tupac Amaru and Tupac Katari uprisings of the 1780s. In addition, the so-called Rebellion of the Barrios affected relations between urban officials and the surrounding indigenous population.[15]

Thus, as the colonial era waned, Quito was entering a period of profound crisis. The uncertainty encouraged widespread migration from the tormented city. Those departing represented all classes and races, and the loss of population virtually froze the city in time as new construction stagnated over the next century. This mass migration also affected the subsequent growth of regional conflicts as Cuenca and the port of Guayaquil boomed due to their embrace of the capitalist possibilities offered by trade deregulation. Cuenca developed as an important center for quinine harvesting and millinery production while Guayaquil's nascent shipbuilding industry fueled the city's rise as a major cacao port. The shift in economic and population concentration bred serious regional competition between the three urban centers over the next century, and this tension soon became inscribed in cultural and political wars that dominated the nation's politics and poetics during the nineteenth century.

Competitive Regionalism in the Nineteenth Century

By the late eighteenth century, the economic and cultural model that had prevailed in colonial Quito had fallen victim to centrifugal pressure. Local critics, however, continued to argue for imperial reform rather than structural adjustments designed to make the local economy more competitive. Perhaps the most strident voice was that of *quiteño* doctor Eugenio Espejo, whose many satirical writings located the contemporary crisis within the scholastic pedagogy of the Jesuit population and the limited development of local medicine. The Quito censors tolerated these works because of imperial antipathy toward the Jesuits, who were expelled from the empire in 1767, but they reacted quickly when Espejo turned his attention to Charles III and José de Gálvez, minister of the Indies, in his polemical tract *Retrato de golilla* (Portrait of a Magistrate). Arrested in 1788 and sent to Bogotá, Espejo and his politics became radicalized. On his return to Quito, he formed the patriotic society Amigos del País, one of several across South America that agitated for greater local autonomy and the extension of the franchise to subaltern groups without challenging Catholic religious dominance.[16] Despite his attention to Quito's particular foibles, however, Espejo continued to conceive of the crisis as one stemming from imperial decadence in the face of a global political, pedagogical, and scientific turn.

Meanwhile, regional economic tensions increasingly affected political relations with the Crown. Guayaquil and Cuenca had been named separate provinces or *gobernaciones* during the mid-eighteenth century, a designation that gave them greater control over internal affairs. Despite Cuenca's larger population, Guayaquil's rising cacao trade with New Spain accelerated its status, inspiring a royal decree that gave the Viceroyalty of Peru authority over the port's economic affairs. The indignity of this measure was a key reason Quito became the site for one of the first resistance juntas in the aftermath of Napoleon's invasion of the Iberian Peninsula. Led by the Marques de Selva Alegre, Juan Pío Montufar, the conspirators behind the junta, proclaimed on August 10, 1809, deposed the president of the Audiencia, Count Ruiz de Castilla. Their call to the other jurisdictions of the Audiencia to join in proclaiming independence was met with ambivalence in Cuenca, Guayaquil, and Popayán, however, which ensured the failure of this first movement, the incarceration of the original conspirators, and their execution in August 1810. A second independence movement erupted in Quito later that month, led by a now disgruntled Ruiz de Castilla in alliance with Archbishop Pedro Cuero y Caicedo. Again, the regionalist divide was made manifest as Guayaquil and Cuenca remained loyalist centers over the next two years, a situation accentuated by the Viceroyalty of Peru's formal annexation of Guayaquil.

On the eve of independence, therefore, severe regional tension already existed among the three major districts of what would eventually become Ecuador. The Guayaquil elite only sought to redress their grievances with the capital after the restoration of Ferdinand VII in 1814 and his subsequent repudiation of the liberal Constitution of Cádiz. In 1815, a group of Guayaquil notables, including the Cádiz delegate and poet José Joaquín de Olmedo, officially petitioned that the district be returned to the jurisdiction of New Granada. Their request garnered strong support in Quito due to the port's extensive customs duties. Despite the Crown's approval of this measure in 1819, Olmedo and his fellows broke decisively with the Crown a year later while his cousin, Vicente Rocafuerte, also a veteran of efforts to establish the Cortes de Cádiz, became a high-profile diplomatic supporter of Bolívar's Colombian experiment.[17] Access to Guayaquil granted a foothold to an army led by Bolívar's lieutenant, Antonio José de Sucre, who marched up the Andean corridor the following year. On May 24, 1822, he defeated the Spanish garrison in the capital city at the Battle of Pichincha, formally ending the independence wars in the Audiencia.

Interprovincial strife grew complicated during the short-lived Gran Colombian experiment. Bolívar's eradication of indigenous tribute threatened the traditional alliance between Cuenca and Guayaquil because the Andean economy depended more heavily on the indigenous poll tax than did that of the coast. Cuenca, which, like Quito and Guayaquil, served as the capital of a district overseeing provincial governments, thus began to serve as arbiter between the port and the capital. This role became even more critical following the establishment of the Republic of Ecuador in 1830, when internal regional conflicts rose to the fore.[18] The leaders of this expanding antagonism were Juan José Flores, a Venezuelan-born general who married into the Quito landed aristocracy, and the aforementioned *guayaquileño,* Vicente Rocafuerte. A brief truce existed in the 1830s as the result of an agreement to have the president come from one city and, the next term, from the other, on an alternating basis, an accord that faltered the following decade because of a fiscal crisis precipitated by a drastic dip in world cacao prices. A spate of civil wars ensued, highlighted by the now exiled Flores's 1844 attempt to reinstall a Spanish monarch in the country.[19]

The progressive general José María Urbina, best known for abolishing slavery in 1852 and eradicating tribute five years later, suggested a solution via electoral reforms designed to limit the centrifugal tendencies of the tripartite district system by granting provincial assemblies the right to elect national deputies. This arrangement had the unintended effect of cementing local power bases at the provincial level, which in turn threatened to split the country apart after its defeat in a border war with Peru in 1858.[20] Instability increased over the next year to the point that four governments (one each in Quito, Cuenca, Guayaquil, and in the dusty southern border town of Loja) each claimed national sovereignty.[21] Order finally returned after the rise of a staunchly conservative magistrate named Gabriel García Moreno, whose extended arguments in favor of greater centralization and bolstering Catholic power provided a potential response to national fragmentation.

A onetime liberal and native of Guayaquil, García Moreno had long been one of the foremost advocates for renewing the national commitment to the Catholic Church. His positions had put him at loggerheads with the anticlerical governments of the 1840s, leading to a period of European exile during which he witnessed the aftereffects of the 1848 revolutions. A return visit to France in 1854 solidified his favorable impression of the autocratic regime of Napoleon III, who would later be invited to annex the Andean nation by his conservative admirer at a moment of particular despair. García Moreno became active in Quito's municipal politics in 1857 and was also selected to be rector of the city's university. Upon ascending to the presidency in 1861 he immediately set about quelling the regional forces that had threatened to split apart the country while enhancing the Catholic credentials of the nation.

García Moreno's reforms resurrected modified versions of a number of structures of colonial life inflected with a centralized autocracy inspired by the French emperor. Like Urbina before him, García Moreno turned to the provincial authorities to tackle the thorny regional divides, expanding the number of provincial administrators and increasing their influence while eradicating the district system altogether. This policy again served local landholding interests, particularly in the Andean corridor, which was granted a majority of provincial delegations. The move also limited the power of the three major urban centers. Cuenca was particularly diminished; its original jurisdiction had included the most populous areas in the country. Henceforth, the city would be marginalized by a central government increasingly dominated by the port and the capital. Paradoxically, García Moreno increased the autonomy of local municipalities in a manner similar to the Spanish Habsburg imperial system of the sixteenth and seventeenth centuries. This move limited the political maneuverability of larger blocs and also supplied an easily mobilized national network that proved particularly useful in quelling indigenous opposition to other new institutions, such as *concertaje* (labor conscription or debt peonage), an institution that would literally work to break down regional divides.[22]

Concertaje not only bolstered the hacienda system by replacing tribute but also fueled national public works projects designed to create a serviceable infrastructure. The system's indigenous conscripts, who often worked without the benefit of even hand tools, built hundreds of miles of roads in the southern Andes that helped integrate the Andean and coastal regions.[23] Their labor also built railroad lines in the coastal lowlands, which soon linked Guayaquil with a navigable river system where paddlewheels began hauling cacao destined for the world market, ushering in a boom that would last until the 1920s. Plans to expand the railway to the Andean slopes, however, remained incomplete due to the harsh mountainous terrain and mudslide-prone jungles.[24]

Fig. 1.5. Alameda Park, Quito (c. 1900). Courtesy Archivo Histórico, Banco Central del Ecuador.

Whereas the coast received infrastructure improvements designed to promote its rise as a global economic player, the capital became García Moreno's site for symbolic construction. His intent was to update the city's façade in hopes of resurrecting its seventeenth-century role as an international leader in the arts. The most ambitious project was a massive gothic basilica, based on the Cologne cathedral, that would rise atop the Pichincha slopes and take more than a century to complete. García Moreno also invited several foreign architects to build temples to the civic religion of positivistic science. These structures included Juan Bautista Menten's Astronomical Observatory—the first of its kind in South America—and, to the south of the basilica, Thomas Reed's panopticon prison, which combined surveillance with interior walls painted a terrorizing black.[25] Menten's observatory doubled as the centerpiece of the city's most fashionable park, the Alameda (fig. 1.5), which also boasted a monumental arch entry, strolling paths, and boating canals.[26]

The patronage of architecture formed one of the pillars of a corresponding cultural agenda to create what Derek Williams terms a modern *pueblo católico*.[27] An alliance with the papacy resulted in the signing of a concordat in 1863, which in turn led to increased clerical involvement in educational and government affairs. Rural schools were the first institutions targeted for expansion, which resulted in a massive construction campaign, again fueled by labor conscription. The effort helped double the rural student population by 1875.[28] The regime simultaneously expanded higher education in the major urban centers, often acting in collusion with the Jesuit order, whose cause García Moreno had championed since his journey to Europe in the 1850s. Quito received the majority of the new institutions, including the Colegio de San Gabriel (1862), the Polytechnic

'd the School of Fine Arts. The state subsidized tuition for
t these institutions and even sent the best of them to study
ase of landscape painter Rafael Salas, whose somber por-
s encircled in fog highlighted their mysterious character
nfluenced by Frederick Edwin Church's depictions of
. ..ountains. These vistas also became the first to be distributed
..y as souvenirs to visiting foreigners.[29]

Despite the global aspirations of the regime and its patronage of science, the arts, and education, the era also featured extreme censorship and the repression of dissidents. Leading opposition figures were exiled, most importantly the essayist Juan Montalvo (1832–1889). Montalvo hailed from the central Andean city of Ambato, where he began penning stark critiques of the regime's censorship in his review, El cosmopolita (1866–1869). These led to his eventual banishment to Colombia, where his vitriolic prose continued to attract further converts. His 1874 book, La dictadura perpetua, accused García Moreno of monarchist pretensions, and it circulated widely in an underground network of associates, liberals, and students across the country.[30] When García Moreno reinstalled himself as president for a third term in 1875, young liberals who had been in contact with Montalvo took matters into their own hands, attacking the president on the steps of Quito's cathedral, where a Colombian native named Faustino Reyes cut him down with a machete.[31]

García Moreno's death not only led to Montalvo's famous quip—"Mi pluma lo mató"—but also inaugurated a period of strife and civil war in which regional caudillos competed to fill the power vacuum. A military dictatorship under General Ignacio de Veintimilla brought a brief period of stability in the late 1870s, but the suspension of civil liberties and Veintimilla's reluctance to give up power in 1882 sparked uprisings by two other military leaders: the moderate Francisco Salazar and a radical liberal from the coastal province of Manabí named Eloy Alfaro, known as Viejo Luchador (Old Warrior) because of his constant insurrections. Salazar's troops managed to defeat Veintimilla and ushered in a renewed truce under the Progressive Party, a new political organ made up of coastal and sierran moderates who touted progress while maintaining the clerical and economic policies of the Garcían era. Alfaro's refusal to bow to a government he characterized as a more benign version of the Garcían dictatorship led to his eventual exile over the next decade until the regionalist fires that had been temporarily banked flared again.

The Liberal Revolution

The Progressive period between 1883 and 1895 ought to be viewed as one of compromise, when regional antagonisms were pacified. While the Church continued to play a major part in the administration, the new government avoided the massive repression of the dictator's earlier rule. Provincial rule continued to define national politics and also began to play a more important role in tightly controlling funds for local development projects, in effect restricting the relative autonomy municipal authorities had enjoyed during the previous generation. The major cities of Quito, Cuenca, and Guayaquil were particularly affected; their budgets were overseen not only by the provincial authorities but also by the national congress. As in the Garcían age, the national treasury bankrolled projects employing new technologies, of which the most important were the stringing of a telegraph line between Quito and Guayaquil, the elaboration of a relatively efficient postal service, and the provision of electrical lighting to the major cities.

Improvements and expansion in the coastal cacao economy accompanied and partly subsidized these innovations in the national infrastructure. While the Garcían steamship networks had increased local production capacity, the introduction of a new bean that flourished in the hitherto underutilized Andean foothills generated soaring harvests that catapulted Ecuador into the position of leading global cacao producer from the 1890s to the 1920s.[32] The growing prosperity did not trickle down to the general population, with more than 70 percent of revenue going into the hands of ten families. Nevertheless, chronic labor shortages on the coast fueled a desire to loosen the traditional landed ties of rural workers in the sierra. A new regional crisis began to develop in the mid-1890s due to the reluctance of sierra landowners to eradicate *concertaje.* Guayaquil again became the center of vigorous opposition, given that the majority of the cacao barons resided there and were linked through trade and fiscal ties to the new banking sector, whose credit also helped fuel speculation and further growth of the export sector. These tensions lay at the heart of the cacao industry's embrace of Eloy Alfaro's revolution in 1895, despite initial reservations about the radical populism of his agenda.[33]

Regional and political tensions also colored the literary flowering of *costumbrismo,* a South American romanticism centered on the portrayal of local color. Conservatives such as Juan León Mera provided idealized images of *serrano* gentility in works like *Cumandá,* a novel featuring a love story between the scion of a landowning family and a virginal Amazonian Indian.[34] Fray Solano (José Modesto Espinosa) expanded the genre with his lampooning feuilletons depicting Quito's provincial quietude and the ironic humor of its inhabitants, for the first time identified as *sal quiteña.*[35] *Costumbrismo* also emerged as an important influence on the plastic arts of the late nineteenth century. The two primary artists to embrace this movement, *quiteños* Joaquín Pinto and José Agustín Guerrero, highlighted their politics in their watercolors depicting daily life in the capital. The conservative Pinto celebrated images of street vendors, festivals, and indigenous dancers while the liberal Guerrero foregrounded the misery of indigenous conditions in a manner reminiscent of Manuel Fuentes's depictions of poverty in Lima.[36]

While Quito's artists embraced *costumbrismo*'s examination of internal traditions, Cuenca and Guayaquil's cultural sphere began to show signs of increasing diversification. The new school of painting inaugurated in 1893 at Cuenca's University of Azuay featured foreign faculty such as Seville native Tomás Povedano Arcos.[37] Guayaquil's cacao elite, many of whom maintained residences in Paris, imported scores of paintings and sculptures from Europe to decorate homes increasingly built on a Parisian model.[38] These diverging attitudes toward art and culture fueled the increasingly acrimonious debate surrounding the nation's participation in the 1889 Universal Exposition in the French capital. Archbishop Ordóñez of Quito condemned Ecuador's contribution to the exposition as an immoral display because it featured images of naked Amazonian Indians. Juan León Mera adopted the archbishop's position and waged a campaign to force Progressive president Antonio Flores y Jijón of Guayaquil into canceling Ecuador's participation in the exhibit. The president refused, arguing that the exposition would not only illustrate the advanced state of Ecuadorian culture before a global audience but would also increase the market for Guayaquil's cacao exports. Following a dramatic attempted resignation by Flores, summarily refused by Congress, the matter was dropped. Flores's success led to Ecuador's later participation in the Columbian Exposition of 1893 in Chicago and a number of other similar events, all in the hope of attracting foreign investment.[39] This linking of business, art, and cosmopolitanism marked the urban development of the port as well, which built the country's first indoor central marketplace just prior to the 1896 fire that destroyed most of Guayaquil's colonial architecture.

By the mid-1890s, an intensifying regional political-economic polarization with cultural overtones was developing in the country. Matters came to a head after a succession of events in 1894–1895 sparked a massive insurrection that put the Radical Liberal Party firmly in power for several generations. The first of these events was a scandal concerning the publication of the fourth volume of a history of Ecuador penned by the bishop of Ibarra, a moderate cleric named Federico González Suárez. The work's treatment of the sexual exploits of seventeenth-century Dominican friars raised the hackles of the conservative establishment and provoked a heated debate regarding clerical participation in politics. More vituperative gossip erupted the following year, when the Ecuadorian navy secretly brokered the sale of a Chilean warship to Japan, then at war with China. This *"venta de la bandera"* (sale of the flag) scandal implicated several officials in the Progressive government and led to the resignation of both President Luis Cordero and the governor of Guayas.[40] Liberals perceived the ensuing power vacuum as a golden opportunity and quickly contacted the Viejo Luchador—Eloy Alfaro—then in exile in Panama.

Alfaro's return was at first embraced by small cacao planters but opposed by the cacao elite until he marched to Guayaquil at the head of an army made up of rural and urban cacao workers, many of whom were of indigenous and African extraction. Though nonplussed, the cacao barons agreed to back his insurrection since it would give them the opportunity to increase their pool of labor. The subaltern army Alfaro commanded caused even more havoc in Cuenca, where the socially conservative elite actively resisted the uprising. In abandoning its traditional alliance with Guayaquil and moving more conclusively into Quito's orbit, Cuenca effectively ended the tripartite regional scheme that had dominated the politics of the nineteenth century.[41] Despite this deepening polarization, the liberal army rapidly defeated the discredited Progressive government and entered the capital in December 1895 with a mandate for change.[42]

There were two main components to the liberal modernization program that shifted the regional power structure. The first sought to curb the power of the Catholic Church, whose alliance with Andean landowners had bolstered their political dominance through most of the nineteenth century. Although continued pockets of conservative resistance hampered Alfaro's ability to introduce secularizing reforms in his first term, the voluntary exile of the majority of the episcopacy limited the Church's ability to mount a serious challenge to the government. By 1900, the Vatican had decided on a pragmatic course and thus endorsed Bishop Federico González Suárez's condemnation of a planned invasion of conservative forces massing in Colombia. Open strife diminished, but jockeying over control of social functions continued under Alfaro's actively anticlerical successor, Leonidas Plaza. The year 1900 saw the institution of a civil registry, followed by civil marriage two years later and the declaration of freedom of worship in 1904. The state confiscated clerical lands that same year, though for the next four years it allowed the Church to keep rental income. In 1906, the Vatican countered the land confiscations by naming González Suárez to the archbishopric of Quito. His moderate politics and national reputation allowed him to advance policies designed to limit the state's anticlericalism, such as rebuilding an episcopacy decimated by exile and death during the previous ten years.[43]

Creating a national economic infrastructure formed the second pillar of the Liberal program. One of the key aspects of this endeavor involved the migration of the untapped labor pool of the Andes to the cacao plantations. *Concertaje* remained the major obstacle to planters' longtime desire to access that labor, and it was therefore repeatedly attacked in the Liberal press. A bill calling for its eradication was introduced in Congress in 1899; however, the landholding classes managed to block its passage until 1918. Thereafter, migration to the coast boomed. By 1950, 41 percent of the national population resided in the littoral as opposed to just 15 percent in 1840 and 30 percent in 1909.[44]

The most important initiative, however, was the building of a railway linkage between the capital and the main port. As Alfaro's signature work, the costly and controversial rail venture transformed the country's spatial dynamic. Interregional cargo shipments increased dramatically after the railway's completion in 1908 as an integrated national market developed for the first time, with agricultural staples traveling down the mountains and imported commodities flowing into the highlands. Internal transportation of agricultural products increased from an annual average of 27,511 tons in 1910 to 158,272 in 1942. Shipments of lumber and manufactured goods also increased dramatically while those of livestock and minerals doubled.[45] These figures represented a marked change from the nineteenth century, when the central highland district's main customer was Colombia and the littoral's need for grains and other staples was fed largely by both Colombia and Peru.[46]

The construction of the railroad transformed Ecuadorian regionalism more profoundly than any other effort since the days of García Moreno. Perhaps its most salient impact was to exclude Cuenca from benefiting from the increased commerce by avoiding the city's orbit altogether. The route planning for the railway effectively marginalized the city and accelerated an increasingly bipolar constitution of the national economy.[47] Liberals rhetorically proclaimed the railway to be a "redemptive work," as Kim Clark has put it, arguing that decades of stagnation would be wiped away with a chug and a whistle. This argument usually featured regionalist metaphors that equated the Andes with insularity, clerical lethargy, and stagnation while the coast was presented as vibrant, mobile, and progressive. The railroad, by opening isolated pockets of the Andes to the wider world, would thus redeem the nation and force it to embrace the progress of the twentieth century.[48]

As the longtime stronghold of the Conservative Party, the city of Quito, with its myriad churches, legions of indigenous laborers, and provincial reputation, was also a ripe target for the liberal establishment. Critics such as Cuencan-born journalist Manuel J. Calle and Juan Montalvo's erstwhile associate, Roberto Andrade, penned a flurry of essays and novels that echoed José Agustín Guerrero's ribald castigation of the city's insularity. Alfaro himself made the transformation of Quito a personal goal, freeing government funds for public works projects. These included a new marketplace modeled on Les Halles in Paris and a national exposition. Construction was paralleled by increased offerings in secular education, beginning with the 1897 establishment of the Instituto Nacional Mejía, a secondary school that by the 1920s had come to rival the Jesuit Colegio de San Gabriel as the foremost educational institution in the country. Among its graduates were major figures of the literary renaissance of the 1920s and 1930s such as Gonzalo Escudero, Jorge Carrera Andrade, Humberto Salvador, and Jorge Icaza.[49] Another key institution was the Escuela de Bellas Artes, founded in 1904, which provided the training for many of the artists, such as Camilo Egas, who came to redefine *indigenista* painting, as well as traditionalists like the portraitist Victor Mideros.

The first phase of the Liberal Revolution devolved into a power struggle between Leonidas Plaza and Eloy Alfaro. It came to an end in 1912, with Alfaro's death and martyrdom. Although the Viejo Luchador remained popular as late as 1910 due to his bold march to the southern border to defend against a possible Peruvian invasion, his attempt to install himself as dictator the next year met stiff resistance. He left for exile but returned after the premature death of President Emilio Estrada, a Plaza ally. Alfaro supported Pedro Montero, a member of the Guayaquil elite, in his bid to succeed Estrada and was arrested in his company in January 1912. The two then traveled by rail to Quito, where they were interned in the García Moreno penitentiary. On January 28, a mob broke into the prison, killed them both, and dragged Alfaro's corpse through the streets to the Ejido—a pastureland on the northern edge of the city. Following the gory incident, Plaza returned to power as the undisputed leader of the Liberal Party, ushering in thirteen years of relative calm and orderly political succession.

The Julian Crisis

The reforms of the Liberal Revolution, particularly the construction of the railroad, provided much-needed national economic and political integration and shifted the tenor of the regionalist strife that had dominated Ecuadorian history since the colonial period. This regional divide, and particularly the rivalry between Quito and Guayaquil, did not disappear following the early decades of the twentieth century. However, conflict between capital and labor that ensued as a result of the modernization of the 1920s began to supersede the regionalist impulse as the dominant force in national politics during this decade.

The crisis of the 1920s and 1930s had its roots in the liberal socioeconomic program. Although large projects such as the railroad had strong government involvement, independent local juntas oversaw hundreds of smaller projects with little regulation, leading to a bloated budget and increasing deficits as most of these projects remained unfulfilled. For example, in 1905, only 55 of the 346 authorized projects were actually under construction.[50] The government's lack of revenue and poor international credit rating led to extensive borrowing from local banks. Matters came to a head with the outbreak of World War I, which led to an international fiscal crisis that caused numerous currencies to rapidly lose value. The hitherto stable Ecuadorian sucre fell dramatically over the war years, from US$0.486 in 1914 to $0.365 by 1917, finally stabilizing in 1920 at $0.20.[51] Simultaneously, cacao prices plummeted as the European market declined during the war years, a situation that also led to greater dependence on trade with the United States. The recession only deepened in the postwar era as the cacao industry crumbled due to a combination of disease, competition from Brazil and British West Africa, and advances in refining techniques that decimated the market for the high-grade bean in which Ecuador specialized. For example, Hacienda Tenguel, the nation's largest producer in 1920, harvesting more than 30,000 quintals of beans, was forced to cut its workforce in half as production declined steadily, reaching a low point of 883 quintals in 1925.[52]

The onset of economic turmoil helped swell the nation's major cities. Guayaquil grew the fastest, its increase being first due to an expanding cacao market and then improvements in public health, which included inoculation campaigns and the efforts in 1919 of the Rockefeller Yellow Fever Commission, which finally eradicated this deadly disease from the port.[53] Quito's population remained a close second until the 1950s, with its population expanding from 51,858 in 1906 to 80,702 in 1922, passing 100,000 in the early 1930s and doubling again by 1947.[54] The eradication of *concertaje* in 1919 freed rural indigenous workers to cut their traditional ties to highland haciendas. In droves, they headed to the southern environs of Quito, where they joined the burgeoning industrial communities that had begun to grow due to the Liberal administration's support for manufacturing and the formation of local banks such as the Banco del Pichincha, which offered credit to enterprising industrialists. The arrival of the railroad in 1908 had accelerated this process, particularly with regard to textile factories such as La Internacional or Jacinto Jijón y Caamaño's Chillo-Jijón industries in the Chillo Valley to the east of the city.[55] Local artisans at first kept pace by expanding the size of their concerns, but, by the 1920s, they were hard pressed to compete with the industrial sector—a reprise of the eighteenth-century demise of the *obraje* system.[56]

Slowly but surely, the industrialization of Quito and the cacao crisis in Guayaquil led to the onset of modern labor strife. Workers' groups had begun to organize in the late nineteenth century, beginning in 1892 with the Sociedad Artística e Industrial de Pichincha (SAIP), an artisan society in Quito allied with conservative groups. Although temporarily shut down in 1896 following the Liberal Revolution, the SAIP returned as a potent force and eventually adopted a socialist stance in the 1930s.[57] Another important group in Quito was the Centro Obrero Católico (COC), founded in 1906 by the tailor Manuel Sotomayor y Luna and a group of elite youths, including future conservative politician Jacinto Jijón y Caamaño. Plagued by miscommunication between its student leaders and the rank-and-file artisans, the COC ceased operating in 1909 but was reestablished as a supporting arm of Jijón's reconstituted Conservative Party following the 1925 Julian Revolution.[58] The Guayaquil labor movement, on the other hand, developed a radical bent in the 1890s, largely through the influence of Manuel Albuquerque Vivas, a Cuban tailor and activist who helped found the Confederación Obrera del Guayas in 1896. A strong anarchist sentiment also infiltrated the first major trade union in the city; *cacahueros,* or workers who dried and transported bulk cacao, formed their union in 1908.

The Ecuadorian labor movement came of age in the early 1920s, driven to collective protest by the steady inflation and decline in the value of the sucre after World War I.[59] In 1922, railway workers and *cacahueros* organized a general strike in Guayaquil that was brutally repressed by the military, resulting in at least several dozen and perhaps as many as a thousand casualties.[60] The massacre discredited the reigning Liberals, who resorted to fraud in the 1924 elections and thus set the stage for increased worker involvement in politics. The Right struck first, however, as Jacinto Jijón led a failed coup attempt with support from the Centro Ecuatoriano del Obrero Católico (CEDOC). Jijón then went into exile in Colombia, and a group of leftist intellectuals led by the economist Luis N. Dillon agitated against the corrupt administration and its close ties with Guayaquil's Banco Comercial y Agricola, the state's largest creditor. Magazines from across the political spectrum, such as the military review *El abanderado* and the socialist *La antorcha,* joined in criticizing the government. In July 1925, a group of disaffected army lieutenants allied with Dillon's leftist supporters and overthrew the government.[61]

The Julian Revolution installed Ecuador's first government with socialist tendencies. However, once in power, the *tenientes* abandoned their calls for social reform and instead resorted to regionalist politics, placing the blame for the current crisis squarely on the shoulders of the Guayaquil banking aristocracy. This rhetorical castigation deepened under the government of the liberals' hand-picked president, Dr. Isidro Ayora, a former mayor of Quito. Ayora's prioritizing of fiscal reform led him to invite the "money doctor," American economist Edwin Kemmerer, to visit in 1926. Kemmerer advocated establishing a central bank, leading Quito and Guayaquil's elites to wrangle over the location of this institution the following year. Although the economist favored establishing the bank's headquarters in the capital, a larger subsidiary was simultaneously built in the port city to calm local jealousies.[62] Ayora's government also adopted a progressive new constitution in 1928 that was the first in Latin America to grant women the right to vote. These reforms, however, could not overcome the Great Depression. Amid more social unrest, Ayora fell in 1931.

Despite ongoing attempts to paper over national social tensions by evoking regionalist pretensions, the 1930s saw increasing militancy from both the Left and the Right as well as concomitant clashes with the state. The most critical conflagration involved the military and the Falangist-inspired Compactación Obrera Nacional (CON) in August 1932 over the presidential succession to Ayora. The CON supported the candidacy of Neptalí Bonifaz, a conservative and former president of the Banco Central who, though legally elected, turned out to be ineligible for the presidency because he had been born in Peru. After weeks of demonstrations by both sides, several military squadrons from the greater Quito area engaged CON brigades, igniting the capital's bloodiest battle since independence, a four-day skirmish known as the Guerra de los Cuatro Días. Elections held the following year confirmed the growing importance of labor when populist candidate José María Velasco Ibarra, a highly skilled orator, won his first term. He would be elected to the presidency five times over the next three decades, though he managed to serve a full term only twice. Labor was not the only sector of society becoming more militant, however. The younger intelligentsia increasingly joined the ranks of the Socialist Party in the aftermath of the Julian Revolution. Many of these progressive intellectuals entered the bureaucracy within the Ministerio de Previsión Social (Ministry of Social Welfare) with hopes of establishing a welfare state and expanding their organization.[63]

Chronotopes of Nostalgic Regionalism

In addition to this mounting chaos, the 1920s also saw the explosion of popularly consumed nostalgic columns, stories, theater, and art emulating the *costumbrista* portraits of the nineteenth century. These chronicles of "traditional" ways were particularly popular in Quito and Guayaquil, the cities undergoing the greatest change during these years. One school emulated the *tradición*, a *costumbrista* variation developed by Peruvian historian and critic Ricardo Palma in the 1870s that consists of a vignette depicting a colorful aspect of the national past, often tinged with irony and satire.[64] The genealogist Cristóbal Gangotena y Jijón crafted scores of Quito chronicles whose picaresque friars and wily gentlemen recalled the *sal quiteña* elaborated by José Modesto Espinosa a generation earlier. Guayaquil's great *cronistas* (chroniclers), Modesto Chavez Franco and Gabriel Pino Roca, on the other hand, substituted heroic soldiers saving the port from pirates by day and seducing young girls by night. Another school embraced the rogues of society, highlighted by the port's José Antonio Campos, who published under the confrontational pseudonym of Jack the Ripper. A somewhat stiffer embrace of colorful deviants appeared in the guided city tours of Quito's Alejandro Andrade Coello, art critic and literature professor at the Instituto Nacional Mejía, who joined the *cronista* fray in the mid-1930s.[65]

It is among these rhetorical constructions of the old city that the postcards with which we began this chapter truly belong. As such, they form part of an ongoing tradition attempting to develop a sense of regional distinctiveness dating to the colonial period but that had come to the forefront in the late nineteenth century. While these tensions had themselves sparked extensive strife, economic rivalry, and political dysfunction, the growing class division of a shifting society made affirming regional specificity a nostalgic, whimsical, and apolitical enterprise. In the case of Guayaquil, this desire was a longing for the world's largest cacao port, a place peopled by elegant bankers, a place of romantic moonlit strolls and prosperity. In the case of Quito, it was a desire for the certainty of the city of *vecinos* safely removed from the indigenous rabble that labored for them, for a city of priests whose exhortations to their flock consisted of gently mocking the local boor who discovered the image of the Virgin Mary in the lard remains on his empanada, as described in one of Gangotena's fables. In short, this desire was a nostalgic constitution of regionalism that had little resemblance to the historical record but that had gained credence amid the chaos of the present.

This book is not about a series of postcards but instead about the evolution of this specific form of nostalgic regionalism. While the Ministry of Tourism embraced particular visions for Guayaquil and Quito, there were many other such reconstitutions of the past framed by a particular reification of the regional distinctiveness of each city. Such distinctiveness had begun to disappear under the onslaught of modern class conflict, but this phenomenon should not detract from the popular resonance of these images, which persisted into the 1930s and endures today. This study considers the genesis and methodology behind the construction of Quito's portraits. Like the postcards produced by the Ministry of Tourism, the six acts of constructing Quito space-time represent a particular juxtaposition or constellation of historical actors who embraced a unique framework to attempt to hold fast and situate themselves amid a changing city that no longer resembled itself. The ballast provided by the embrace of the past diminished the challenge of Guayaquil's increased preeminence as the nation's economic engine by establishing Quito's legitimate role as the historic center of power and culture. This proclamation, regionalist to the core, also hoped to ground the city's credentials as a global capital for a presupposed international audience whose gaze these actors sought to shape through their own commemorative acts. As such, these chronotopes answered the challenge of modernity through a reconfiguration of the past framed by power relations at the local, regional, national, and international levels.

Chapter 2

Mapping the Center of the World

Through the study of Geography a people animates, awakens, develops and progresses, as only it constitutes today's living science; the elevation of views, as one says, and pecuniary benefits—what are they but the real fruits of exact knowledge describing all we see and observe on the surface of the territory of our planet?

Luis Tufiño, 1911

Between 1903 and 1909, four new maps of Quito appeared, a small number, to be sure, but one that equaled the number of city plans drawn over the course of the previous century. This period marked the onset of a pronounced expansion in local cartographic projections designed to facilitate urban planning, conduct censuses, or promote tourist vistas. The authors of these charts included a motley assortment of amateur geographers, architects, foreign commercial hires, and military personnel. Over the course of the first decades of the new century, normative tropes slowly emerged in their works, dominated by a symbolic lexicon considering Quito as a legible space framed dialectically by its colonial core and a modern frontier displacing the underdeveloped and "barbaric" countryside. Underlying this process lay a consensus that maps represented "fruits of exact knowledge," as military geographer Luis Tufiño put it. His elaboration not only served utilitarian aims but also provided a vehicle for patriotic progress.

The contention that maps act as neutral representations of objective reality has been subject to criticism in recent years. As J. B. Harley first pointed out, maps often serve as tools for justifying and obscuring power relations through their incorporation of symbols, the eliding or inclusion of populations, and the creation of focal points by the highlighting of specific aspects of the physical landscape.[1] Denis Wood and John Fels, among others, have extended Harley's analysis by highlighting the subjectivity of the cartographic projection itself, most recently arguing that maps may best be understood as a series of "propositions" rather than as mirrors of reality.[2] Similarly, John Pickles has elucidated a variety of approaches to understanding what he terms the "cartographic gaze," that is to say, the set of practices and techniques that together brand maps with the authenticity of science and the veneer of objectivity.[3] These reconsiderations of mapping practices have given rise to an ever-growing number of studies documenting how maps have served the goals of colonial states and commercial interests through the territorialization of space, that is, the process of naturalizing the claims of states and businesses to control space without regard for the contours of the landscape or the interests of its inhabitants. Crafting this "God's-eye view," however, can no longer be considered a process bereft of contestation from the subjects of the cartographic gaze. As Raymond Craib has argued with regard to nineteenth-century Mexico, state attempts to locate and cartographically delineate "fugitive landscapes" both articulated hegemonic power relations and demonstrated the limits of state domination over outlying populations that engaged in a selective dialogue with national cartographers in order to defend and articulate local interests subject to elision through mapping processes.[4]

The constitution of urban maps bears a general resemblance to the national, imperial, or colonial processes of territorialization described above. However, given the particular importance of the city as a marker of citizenship in Spanish America, urban views should also be considered an expression of what Richard Kagan has termed the "communicentric" ideal. As such, urban maps not only act as a tool for use in implementing crude exploitation and control over territory but also express a more subtle articulation of collective identity (what Kagan terms *civitas* or civic-communal identity) that can at times be divorced from cartographic accuracy (*urbs* or constructed space).[5]

The maps of Quito discussed below denominate particular elite constitutions of the city's character. A review of their communicentric imagery helps illustrate the complexity of the hegemonic project involved in the representation and production of Quito space. Despite a general consensus as to the legitimacy of cartography as a direct topographic reflection, Quito maps also showcase shifting and conflicting considerations of social legitimacy and visions of community. Of particular importance is the alteration of the dominant city view, from one characterized by insular religiosity to that of a tourist destination at the center of the world, with a monumental colonial core, sophisticated northern districts, and bountiful environs.

This process intersected with two colonial discourses that evoked the city's universality. The first of these stemmed from a millenarian vision identifying the city as a new Rome that would lead the continental crusade to convert indigenous peoples to the Catholic faith. The second touted Quito's secular role as the site of the eighteenth-century Franco-Spanish Geodesic Mission that set out to measure the arc of the equatorial meridian. Each of these allegorical and inherently cosmopolitan vistas came to be enshrined cartographically while being reframed for the modern consumer. Elided in these representations were the indigenous populations, haciendas, and small towns of the rural periphery, which was now reconsidered as a periurban space open for chalets of the elite, factories, or tourist-friendly day trips. Quito cartographers thus helped consolidate state and commercial interests in the development of the city's environs while also crafting a moral justification for its imperial expansion through chorographic images. As such, they served as brokers between the state and the business community, a role cemented in the 1930s with the centralizing of cartographic practices within the Servicio Geográfico Militar. This specialized corps of engineers, cartographers, and geographers reified and mass-produced the topographical mythologies of Quito-space developed over the previous half century.

There was thus a process of institutionalization, commodification, and codification of the city's cartographic lexicon from the colonial period through the 1940s. In this genealogy of Quito's cartographic production, the intersection between colonial discourses, technological innovation, state-driven commemoration, and military professionalism is of central concern. The maps produced in the name of these vectors celebrated the city's equatorial position and prestigious contributions to world science, particularly after a second French geodesic mission, the staff of which visited Ecuador between 1901 and 1906. These tropes combined under the chronotope marking the city as the *mitad del mundo,* the center of the world.

Colonial Cartographies and Universal Aspirations

The growing assemblage of maps in *fin-de-siglo* Ecuador represents one of the later chapters in a global expansion of cartography originating in the sixteenth century. Beyond providing advantages for Western imperial powers exploring the globe and navigating as they went, maps, particularly cadastral maps, expanded the potential surveillance of local and colonial populations by the early modern state. Perhaps the most ambitious harnessing of cartography in this vein was the chorographic-geographic survey of the Spanish Empire initiated by Phillip II's royal cosmographer, Juan López de Velasco, in the 1560s. By 1580, this endeavor had led to the completion of the Escorial atlas, which was upheld as the first systematic and comprehensive representation of every inch of the Iberian Peninsula. The simultaneous attempt to extend these *relaciones geográficas* to the Americas, however, met unexpected obstacles in the alternate mapping practices of indigenous populations in the New World. In New Spain, for example, maps produced for this survey often incorporated native glyphs or featured distended geography incommensurate with European practices.[6] The subsequent imposition of planar geography and the "God's-eye view" of orthogonal projections have been interpreted in recent scholarship as a direct assault on native cosmographies by a nascent imperial power.[7] Simply put, the deploying of cartography's potent scientific gaze served as a means of justification for the self-appointed civilizing mission of the Iberian power.

While world maps provided an extensive argument for European centrality, an ambiguity pervaded the urban views, which alternately reified and subverted this implicit geopolitical hierarchy. On the one hand, the development of the orthogonal city plan and the imposition of a monotonous grid upon preexisting cities bolstered claims of Western scientific superiority. As often as not, however, the city view incorporated iconography demonstrating its communal character, thus opening the possibility of a distinctly creole sensibility interrogating the preeminence of the European core.

This situation partly developed from the paradoxical constitution of urban collective identities as emblematic of micro- and macropatriotism implied in *vecindad.* Local identities began to coalesce over the course of the sixteenth and seventeenth centuries, and, while not excluding simultaneous participation within the Spanish Empire, they began to challenge exclusive identification with one's peninsular origins. This sense of uniqueness intensified during the seventeenth century, particularly with the increasing presence of peninsular immigrants and the subsequent rise of what David Brading has called creole patriotism.[8] The articulation of this distinctly American consciousness developed slowly and depended on the elaboration of rituals and images that performed and bolstered a sense of communal distinctiveness.

Maps and urban views constituted some of the most visible means of illustrating a city's civic values in both Spain and in Spanish America, yet, by the seventeenth century, imperial policy had forbidden their elaboration due to security issues after raids on Spanish American cities by pirates and competing European powers. The constitution of allegorical images standing in for chorographic representations of urban landscapes grew in the wake of the ban on city maps in 1632. The seventeenth century thus saw the expansion of symbolic visual culture often focused on Marian cults and Old World allusions designed to identify local *civitas.* Mexico City, for instance, not only became identified with the Virgin of Guadalupe but was also construed as a new Jerusalem. Lima, proclaimed *"la ciudad de los Reyes"* by Pizarro upon its founding, was similarly conceived as a Western paradise, a new Eden, by its secular and clerical population alike.[9]

Like its fellow American capitals, Quito also adopted an Old World referent to highlight its central role in the formation of a millenarian world, in this case the holy center of Rome. The label appears to have originated following the discovery of the Amazon by Francisco de Orellana in 1541 on an expedition that departed from Quito and provided justification for considering the city as the starting point for a new crusade. The subsequent constitution of Quito as a pilgrimage site bolstered this contention and led to the development of no fewer than three major Marian cults by the end of the seventeenth century, of which the nearby Virgin of Guápulo and the Virgin of El Quinche are the best known. Moreover, the city garnered a reputation for miracles, including the celebrated seventeenth-century "divine" intervention to save the city from plague at the request of a young martyr, Mariana de Jesus.[10]

As Carmen Fernández-Salvador has argued, these cults inspired attempts by the city's Jesuit and Franciscan communities to brand the city as a new Rome, from which continental conversion would emanate.[11] For instance, one seventeenth-century Jesuit, Pedro de Mercado, devoted his account of the city almost exclusively to the "miracles" performed by its inhabitants, implying a contrast between their "saintly" lives and the vice-ridden lives of the rest of the province's inhabitants.[12] Quito's Franciscan monastery provides an image-laden example of the process of relocating Rome to the slopes of Pichincha.

Fernández-Salvador notes the presence of two sets of depictions of Roman pilgrimage sites that follow the sequential order recommended in seventeenth-century Italian guidebooks. She posits the existence of a virtual tour of the historic capital of Christendom organized by the liturgical calendar, and she bases this theory on the series of murals found in the church choir and in the adjoining Cantuña chapel, named for a well-to-do seventeenth-century indigenous blacksmith who was active in the local cult of the Holy Cross (Veracruz) and who, legend holds, made a pact with the devil by offering him the lost treasure of the Inca Atahualpa to complete the chapel in a day.[13] This circuit begins with Saint John the Baptist, representative of the Lateran Basilica within the city walls of Rome. Rather than proceed according to the city's geography, the next stops are the basilicas of Saints Peter and Paul, outside the historic walls but next up on the liturgical calendar. The next three paintings continue this trajectory by depicting Our Lady of La Antigua (referencing the basilica of Santa Maria Maggiore) and then Saints Lawrence and Sebastian. Finally, in the most elaborate work in both the chapel and the main choir stands Saint Helen, an image that likely references the Church of the Holy Cross in Jerusalem because its relics were brought to Rome by Emperor Constantine's mother, Helen. Fernández-Salvador reads the emphasis on the Holy Cross within Cantuña's chapel as an expression of the devotion of the indigenous *cofradía,* or lay brotherhood, that met within its walls. Like Rome in the previous millennium, the Andean citadel would inherit the task of spreading Christian doctrine to a new continent.[14]

During the eighteenth century, the conceit of Quito's messianic character was reborn due to its role in the development of the secular religion of geographical science. As the need for cartographic secrecy receded, an adherence to Enlightenment principles helped persuade Philip V of Spain to participate in the Franco-Spanish Geodesic Mission to measure the arc of the equatorial meridian in Quito and thus answer a dispute concerning the shape of the Earth. While the measurements taken by French academician Charles Marie de La Condamine and his Spanish counterparts, Jorge Juan and Antonio de Ulloa, clearly confirmed Newton's hypothesis of an equatorial bulge, much of the expedition's notoriety lay in its members' subsequent travels and activities. La Condamine's journey down the Amazon brought European science to the tropical rainforest. Juan and Ulloa, on the other hand, not only duplicated La Condamine's efforts in Quito but also ended Spain's long-standing absence from cartographic endeavors by producing the *Relación histórica del viaje a la América meridional* (1748), which provided extensive maps of Spanish American cities, from Quito to Riobamba to Lima. The mission also encouraged *quiteño* science as Riobamba native Pedro Vicente Maldonado, who had already developed a close friendship with La Condamine, built on these urban maps and his own measurements of the northwestern coast to craft the first provincial map of Quito, which was received with great accolades during a 1746–1747 trip to Europe.

Conflicts between the French and Spanish members of the expedition developed rapidly as each group sought to take authorial control over the results of the expedition. La Condamine, for instance, sought to memorialize his contribution not only through his eventual writings but also by erecting pyramids in the plains of Yaruquí to the east of the Andean capital and decorating the structures with the French monarchy's fleur-de-lis. Juan and Ulloa sued him in local courts for this obvious slight to the Spanish Crown, yet La Condamine was able to escape imprisonment by noting the symbol's presence in the Iberian coat of arms. The pyramids themselves, however, were razed a few years later. La Condamine's attempts to claim exclusive proprietary rights over the expedition's findings continued in his 1745 treatise, in which he repeatedly described the activities of his Spanish counterparts as ancillary. Naturally, Juan and Ulloa rebutted this portrayal in their own work, which contained extensive accounts of their mathematical calculations—descriptions designed to highlight the best of Spanish science as well as their crucial role in measuring the arc of the meridian.[15]

The two maps of Quito that resulted from the expedition's measurements embody the conflicting authorial drama of the general texts. The maps represent the first internationally mass-distributed images of the city and coincide in depicting a small mountain citadel from which contemporary science would emanate. Each offers an orthogonal projection with Mount Pichincha at the map's summit, ignoring the cartographic convention of placing north atop the image and instead emulating the local tradition of painting the city view from the vantage of the Itchimbia peak in the eastern environs of the city. Both maps also highlight the expeditionary mission by depicting the arc of the meridian, albeit in slightly different ways. La Condamine's meridian emerges from the city's coat of arms on the lower left corner of the map and travels unimpeded across the urban grid until reaching a cartouche at the upper right (fig. 2.1),

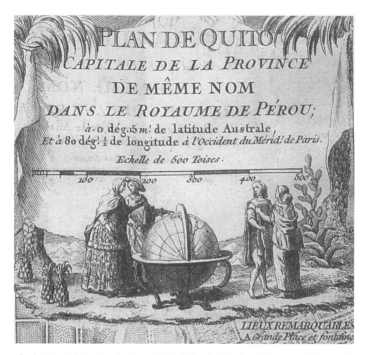

Fig. 2.1. Charles Marie de La Condamine, detail of *Plan de Quito* (1751). Courtesy Library of Congress.

which identifies the city as Quito and provides its coordinates in reference to the Parisian meridian. The cartouche also includes a detailed image of two couples, one European and one indigenous, who stand on either side of an enormous globe, which the white male is showing to his partner. Surrounding the figures are exotic equatorial flora, including cacti, pineapples, and palm fronds (atop the cartouche). Taken together, the images present a vision of a culture about to emerge from its primitive existence, indeed, to become literally the center of the globe, through the potency of European science. The map's toponymy furthers the exotification of Quito, subtly erasing the previous two centuries of colonial rule.[16] Thus, the Panecillo, a small hill on the city's southern edge, is identified by its pre-Columbian title of Yavirac while the Alameda pastures in the northern environs of the city are identified as the site of the battle between Gonzalo Pizarro and Viceroy Blasco Núñez Vela in 1546.

If La Condamine presents a noble but primitive Quito, Juan and Ulloa's map (fig. 2.2) emphasizes the strength of the Spanish monarchy and furthers the case for their personal prominence within the scientific expedition. As in the earlier work, by La Condamine, the arc of the meridian in the Spanish map travels from lower left to upper right, ending in a cartouche identifying the plan of Quito, complete with its location vis-à-vis the Paris meridian. The Iberians break with La Condamine by foregrounding the city's built environment, which interrupts the meridian's progress until it emerges in the "vacant" countryside on the upper

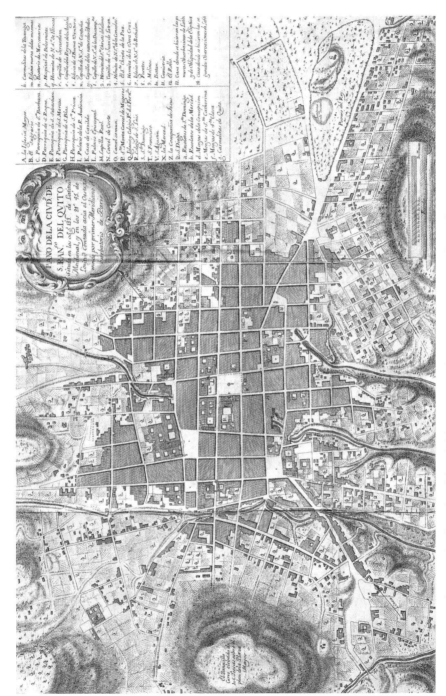

Fig. 2.2. Jorge Juan and Antonio de Ulloa, *Plano de la ciudad de San Francisco de Quito* (1748). Courtesy Library of Congress.

31

right. Here it encounters another cartouche, one that deemphasizes the pastoral landscape present in the Frenchman's iconography, instead presenting a simple scroll decorated only with the royal lion echoed by the nearby presence of the Alameda, identified as "*potrero del Rey.*" Similarly, the work's toponymy limits references to nature, with the exception of the Panecillo—once again identified by its Iberian name—and instead foregrounds the city's religious association by highlighting Catholic landmarks. In a list of fifty-two public buildings, all but ten are sacred structures, including churches, chapels, parish seats, and nunneries. The few secular buildings collectively emphasize municipal authority, but among them are two houses where the scientists conducted measurements of the Quito meridian. As such, the map ultimately merges traditional symbols of religiosity and power with a new sense of the city's scientific prominence.

The Franco-Spanish expedition ultimately had little impact on the production of local cartography, partly as a result of Pedro Vicente Maldonado's demise shortly after his arrival in Europe. However, it placed the city and Audiencia of Quito at the center of an international coterie of experts and intellectuals in a way that has rarely, if ever, been duplicated. La Condamine's colorful description of his exploits brought notoriety even as he dismissed the land as fundamentally backward. While the nationalist Jesuit Juan de Velasco expressed his dissatisfaction with La Condamine's condemnation of Quito's barbaric indigenous inhabitants, the region's international prominence grew as a result. Its equatorial associations expanded following the celebrated travels of naturalist Alexander von Humboldt, whose *Personal Narrative of Travels of the Equinoctial Regions of the New Continent during Years 1799–1804,* published in French, German, English, and Spanish over the first decades of the nineteenth century, firmly cemented Quito's global reputation as a fascinating tropical landscape.[17] When the province joined Bolívar's Gran Colombia in 1824, enterprising leaders hoping for quick international recognition renamed the Quito department Ecuador after its geographic location, a decision that may also have reflected Guayaquil's developing autonomist spirit. The appellation stuck following the separation of the Quito, Guayaquil, and Cuenca departments from the Colombian republic in 1830 and has remained the name of the nation ever since.[18]

The cult of the Geodesic mission continued to develop in the aftermath of independence. Indeed, the nascent Rocafuerte government celebrated the 1836 centennial of La Condamine's arrival by rebuilding the very pyramid at Oyambaro that had caused such consternation a century earlier, this time without the offending fleur-de-lis at its apex. While budgetary constraints continued to retard the development of national cartographic production, this effort bespeaks the importance the event had acquired in the local and national imagination of a country seeking to define its character. Ultimately, however, it would be the universalizing doctrine of a city of God that drove the expansion of local cartographic production during the García Moreno administration.

The Garcían State, or a Marriage of Technology and Religion

García Moreno came to power in 1858 in the wake of a flare-up of the perennial border conflict between Ecuador and Peru. The boundary dispute originated in the transfer of the Audiencia of Quito in 1739 to the jurisdiction of the newly created Viceroyalty of New Granada. The subsequent shuffling of Quito (and especially the prosperous port of Guayaquil, with its substantial customs duties) in between the two viceroyalties led to repeated conflicts and confusion over rightful territorial sovereignty. In 1828, the new republics of Peru and Gran Colombia (of which Ecuador was still a part) clashed in a vicious war that ended with Colombian victory at the Battle of Tarqui in 1829. Three separate agreements were negotiated between 1829 and 1832, yet, in the 1850s, the dispute emerged again when Ecuador was trying to transfer ownership of disputed territory to settle its debts to British and U.S. interests. The resulting 1858 skirmish contributed to the national destabilization that gave rise to García Moreno's administration in 1861.

The new president quickly set out to expand the national educational system in alliance with clerical instructors, actions that built on his former career as rector of the University of Quito. The majority of his energies went into the formation of rural schools designed to help incorporate isolated regions into the national body politic. Technical education, though, was a secondary interest. García Moreno sponsored the formation of the Escuela de Artes y Oficios in Quito for artisanal training, along with a tuition-free polytechnic designed to accelerate the growth of scientific activity in the nation. As with many of his other endeavors, this venture was managed by Jesuit recruits imported from Europe, the first of whom reached Quito in August 1870. The arrival of the Jesuits coincided with the resumption of negotiations between Ecuador and Peru, which made the study of cartographic drafting and geodesic surveying a growing imperative. Although the university was forced to close its doors temporarily after García Moreno's assassination in 1875, it had a direct impact on the growth of future cartographic studies.[19]

Perhaps the most important contributor was the Jesuit mathematician Juan Menten, best known for his later role as director of Quito's observatory, whose building in the heart of the Alameda he also designed. At the polytechnic, Menten was responsible for courses in geodesy, mathematics, and drafting. By 1875, the priest and his students had completed enough local measurements to compile the first map of Quito since the colonial era to employ updated measurements. Menten's projection not only sought to document the slight growth that the city had undergone over the previous century but also challenged the traditional horizontal orientation of Quito maps, using a vertical orientation with north at the top of the view. This normalizing of European mapping conventions continued in the subsequent efforts of Menten's colleague, Teodoro Wolf. A geologist of German origin, Wolf's career at the polytechnic ended prematurely due to a scandal in 1874 over his teaching of Darwinian evolution. Despite the nationalist overtures of this pedagogy given the importance of Darwin's visit to the Ecuadorian Galapagos Islands to his theories, Wolf was branded a proponent of a heretical theory and ultimately defrocked. García Moreno, loath to lose a technician of Wolf's skill, rehired the former priest to complete a national chorographic survey updating the eighteenth-century studies of Maldonado, La Condamine, and Juan and Ulloa. Wolf soon compiled a plan of Guayaquil, conducted extensive studies of the southern coastal plains, and began a national survey to support Ecuador's case in the ongoing territorial conflict with Peru, a project he completed in 1892. Like Menten, Wolf also chastised local practices as out of touch with European scientific norms; for instance, he criticized most Ecuadorian maps because they featured the Quito meridian as the longitudinal reference rather than the Paris or Greenwich meridians then in vogue in Europe.[20]

Menten's and Wolf's lasting contributions as brokers of cartographic modernity can best be seen in the career of one of their students, the civil engineer and architect J. Gualberto Pérez. Pérez was himself from a humble family and benefited from a government scholarship while at the polytechnic. There, he excelled at drafting until the school closed in 1876; he then completed his secondary studies at the Jesuit institution, San Gabriel, graduating in 1882.[21] Pérez then attended Quito's university following the inauguration in 1883 of a science faculty run by former polytechnic students, and he graduated with a degree in civil engineering in 1887. He soon secured a position as a municipal engineer, beginning a long-standing relationship with the city government that would include several architectural and cartographical projects. One of the first was the completion of a cadastral map that Pérez had begun drafting in 1885 while still at Quito's university. This map would become the primary image of the city for the next two decades (fig. 2.3).[22]

Pérez's 1888 cadastral map re-imagines earlier tropes in a view consciously meant to be mass produced. The crux of the map's rhetorical imagery hinges upon a merger of the clichéd vision of Quito's Catholic identity with an emphasis on strict scientific accuracy. Unlike Menten, Pérez returns to the colonial convention of placing Pichincha at the top of the map—the first of several choices that recall Juan and Ulloa, whose emphasis on the city's religiosity is also echoed in the list of public buildings and monuments. Of the eighty-five structures on the map highlighted in dark red in a style introduced by Menten's 1875 plan, sixty-five have a religious affiliation; they include churches, schools, and parish seats. Unlike his predecessors, however, Pérez details the plans of individual homes throughout the city, a cadastral convention in keeping with one of the map's stated goals. He also includes the elaborate gardens of the Alameda

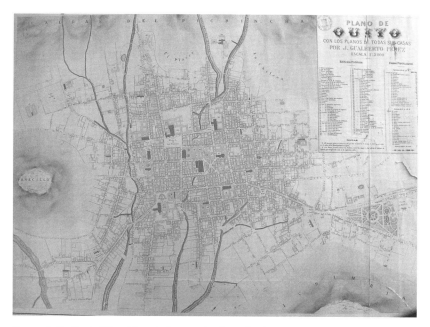

Fig. 2.3. J. Gualberto Pérez, *Plano de Quito con los planos de todas sus casas por J. Gualberto Pérez* (1888). Courtesy Biblioteca Ecuatoriana "Aurelio Espinosa Pólit," Quito.

and the paths and fountains of plazas such as those of Santo Domingo and the Plaza Grande, thus conveying a sense of the lived experience of the city's public and leisure spaces.

Although the map was probably not originally commissioned by the municipal council, as Pérez was still angling for the terms of his payment when he presented his draft to the council in 1887, it was indelibly marked by its potential for administrative functionality. For example, street names are clearly labeled on every block, facilitating cross-referencing. Moreover, the total number of houses on each street appears in a list next to that of public buildings. Plotted empty lots on the eastern edges of the city transform the map into a working cadastre that the municipality could use to track ongoing growth and to facilitate taxation. The outlying areas remain nameless, identified only by their proximity to larger avenues, such as "Calle NE de la Carrera de Guayaquil," which runs near Alameda Park between Calles Guayaquil and Vargas. The inclusion of these barely traced arteries reifies the municipality's territorial designs upon its outlying communities, illustrated most clearly by Pérez's appending of a blank sheaf of papers on which to record further construction. The future is clear: soon the city would expand into the "vacant" environs, rolling over its haciendas and indigenous communities. The map would shape the territory.[23]

Pérez construed his map as Quito's first cartographic commodity. When presenting the work to the council, he articulated a well-tuned sales pitch high-lighting not only its administrative uses but also the difficulties he experienced during the drafting process. He particularly emphasized the tumultuous na-ture of the cadastral measurements due to "the opposition of most household-ers who did not allow me to take the necessary measurements" as well as the considerable amount of time he committed to the project. He argued that these travails justified a fee of twelve hundred sucres for the completion of the work, a figure he characterized as modest compared to the three thousand sucres that Wolf had received three years earlier for his less detailed map of Guayaquil.[24] These arguments resonated with the municipal council, which not only agreed to pay his fee but also presented him with a gold medal for his "patriotic" ser-vice, an action that symbolically conjoined the cartographer and the cabildo as co-producers of the map.[25] This alliance was further cemented with the one hundred reproductions produced by Erhard Frères, a Parisian firm that had previously produced several Mexican and Argentine maps. Again, the cabildo highlighted its authorial role by incorporating a notation indicating that the idea for the project and its scope originated with the council. Upon arrival in October 1889, the copies of the map were distributed for display in offices and classrooms as the public face of the city.[26] When Teodoro Wolf subsequently reproduced this map alongside his own of Guayaquil in his 1892 geography text, the map rhetorically reached the pinnacle of its power in a work funded by the national government.

The repeated utterance of authorial ownership over a map establishes legiti-mate claim to the image and, through the image, to the domination of the land-scape it describes. The case of Pérez's map demonstrates an attempt by a young engineer to inscribe his own authority as a cartographer while also serving the interests of a municipality eager to consolidate its control over its outlying regions. The regular replication of this rendering in subsequent decades illus-trates the degree to which the fusion of religious, civic, and scientific authority resonated as the primary qualities of Quito late into the nineteenth century. Despite appearing more than a decade after the end of García Moreno's rule, the Pérez map crystallized the Garcían paradigm. The relevance of this framework declined soon thereafter as a new public sphere and visual culture came to local prominence.

Progress, Commemoration, and the Liberal Map

The global *fin-de-siglo* has been characterized as a moment in which nation-alism began to be ritualized in mass spectacle. Governments adopted commem-orative gestures that performed a teleological construction of nationality wed-ded to new or "invented" traditions. States adopted national anthems, produced pageants with actors in native costume, or held parades that helped disseminate these symbols to a wide audience. Some were older images reconfigured for modern times, such as the reintroduction of the French *tricolore* during the Third Republic. Others were brand new yet attempted to adorn themselves in the trappings and weight of the historical past, such as the adoption of highland dress by some members of the British nobility. These ubiquitous new symbols produced a legible cascade of allegorical imagery that itself inspired a simplified view of national identity, one that omitted the participation of those who existed outside these mythscapes.[27] These increasingly commodified images appeared on a dizzying variety of ceremonial and functional goods, including maps and urban views. From route maps to road atlases to tourist guides, the number of commercially available maps increased exponentially, often incorporating new graphic symbols illustrating national metaphors. The map was thus re-imagined as a mass-produced commodity, consumed by tourists and locals alike, that reified power relations while encouraging the development of specific industrial, commercial, or tourist economies.[28]

Ecuadorian visual culture engaged these international tropes, reconfiguring and re-imagining them in dialogue with local conditions and power relations. The desire for a primordial, authentic, and romanticized *folk* so prominent in European nationalist imagery produced a local conundrum due to the perceived degradation of the Ecuadorian indigenous population. As in Peru or Mexico, the Ecuadorian state solved this problem by ignoring the contemporary situation of indigenous communities while embracing pre-Columbian cultures in the abstract.[29] This effort involved the production of laudatory portraits of the Incaic sovereign Atahualpa and his lieutenant Rumiñahui, personages doubly removed from contemporary indigenous peoples as a result of their Incaic (Peruvian) roots. A similar object of fascination was found in contemporary Amazonian tribes only recently "encountered" by civilization. The examples of Juan León Mera's novel *Cumandá* and the controversial inclusion of Amazonian nudes at the 1889 Universal Exposition in Paris initiated a fascination with the visual pomp of an idealized indigeneity. These images were carefully disassociated from the laborers of the highland haciendas or cacao plantations, characters portrayed as "degenerate" in lettered circles. Instead, nostalgic maquettes and photographs of the Incaic ruins of Ingapirca were duly displayed at the nation's pavilion at Madrid's Exposición Hispano-Americano in 1892, as was a life-size sculpture of an Amazonian Shuar warrior (a tribe better known at the time as the Jívaros).[30] At the 1893 Columbian Exhibition in Chicago, these "heroic" icons gave way to the weavers of the contemporary Otavalo tribe, whose "industrious" entrepreneurship proved an exception to the rule of indigenous barbarism, as Brooke Larson has eloquently noted.[31]

The intersection of this nationally produced visual culture with internationally accessible geographic and cartographic iconography also began in Chicago. On the occasion of the 1893 exhibition, a consortium of Guayaquil-based bankers tied to the daily *Diario de Avisos* collaborated with the government to produce an English-language commemorative tome, titled *Ecuador in Chicago,* documenting Ecuador's participation in the fair. The volume included several views of the national pavilion but also provided its foreign audience with vivid descriptions of the nation's geography, its political and economic history, and investment opportunities. Airbrushed portraits of the directors of the *Diario de Avisos* and several local banks, socialites, government ministers, the president, and other notables introduced Ecuador's high society to the world. Photographs of Guayaquil's port facilities and Quito's churches, along with yet another reproduction of both the Wolf and Pérez maps of the two major cities, served to illustrate a picturesque country ripe for investment and friendly to foreigners. Commerce, not religion, would be at the center of Ecuador's future role in the world.[32]

Ecuador in Chicago, taken as a whole, anticipated the ethos of the modernization program adopted after the 1895 Liberal Revolution and also sounded the death knell for Gualberto Pérez's view of a sacred yet insular capital. The possibility of developing an alternative map increased when the construction of the Guayaquil-Quito railway brought an influx of technically adept engineers and surveyors into the nation. One of these "experts," the American engineer Henry Grant Higley, was enlisted to craft just such a vision of Quito. Higley's reputation rested on previous cartographic experience in Nicaragua, where he had completed a map of the Mosquito Coast (1888) as part of an endeavor to bolster investment in the Bluefields development. Like his later work in Ecuador, the map of Bluefields was distinguished by an engaging multicolor scheme and advertisements for local businesses placed in the margins and aimed at an international audience. Soon after arriving in Ecuador, Higley completed a simple plan of Guayaquil (1899) that appears to have been used by railway workers, and he followed it up with a more elaborate portrait of Quito subsidized by local businessman Julio Esau Delgado (fig. 2.4).[33]

Higley's *Quito en 1903* plan, unlike the works of Pérez and Menten, avoids the austerity of an orthogonal projection in favor of a bird's-eye view or panoramic map. The perspective emulates the traditional landscape views from Itchimbia's slopes yet was most likely designed for a foreign audience. Panoramic maps had become a vibrant industry in Higley's native United States during the nineteenth century because they presented an open and inviting image. Many of these panoramic designs exaggerated the features of prominent structures or natural monuments, making such maps more accessible as tourist guides.[34] The panorama-type view would therefore have been familiar to American or European travelers or investors, who appear to have been the audiences. An inset map of the proposed route of the Guayaquil-Quito railway, labeled in English, also appears directed at these groups, as do the myriad advertisements for "cosmopolitan" import businesses placed on the map's border. Moreover, the projection's flattening of the city's irregular topography would have made it easier to discern the various landmarks and features, thus making the map a more inviting text.

Fig. 2.4. H. G. Higley, *Quito en 1903* (1903). Courtesy Library of Congress, Geography & Map Division.

An iconological analysis of the map reveals a city at once traditional and modern—a beacon of progress ripe for foreign investment yet appreciably historic. The city's monumental character is advanced by the elongation of the spires of San Francisco, Santo Domingo, and the National Observatory as well as by the incorporation of eight photographic vignettes adorning the city's outskirts. The subjects of these vignettes include modern structures such as the Teatro Sucre and the Military Quarters and, in a cluster atop the diagram, the city's best-known colonial monuments: the Santo Domingo and San Francisco monasteries, the cathedral, and the Government Palace. The merger of tradition and modernity continues in the top right section with portraits of Ecuador's sixteen presidents surrounding the national coat of arms, with the liberal caudillos Plaza and Alfaro receiving places of honor at the top and bottom. In the upper left corner, a swirl of red flags rounds out the patriotic imagery with a flourish by marking the spot of the 1822 Battle of Pichincha. The entire map is framed with evocations of cosmopolitanism in the railway map and in advertisements for goods such as liquor, photographs, and imported clothing.

Higley's panorama challenged the communicentric ideals of an earlier era by partially secularizing the city's monumentality within this global visual culture of commemoration and commerce. This concatenation deepened over the remainder of the century's first decade due to the parallel collaboration between the Ecuadorian and French militaries that followed a call in international geodesic circles to refine La Condamine's measurements using modern surveying instruments. Both the French and Ecuadorian governments recognized the public relations benefits in bankrolling such a scheme, and, after an exploratory trip by French delegates in 1899, the two nations initiated a second calculation of the arc of the equatorial meridian in 1901 under the leadership of Captain E. Maurain and Lieutenant Georges Perrier. Generous financial support for commemorative festivities celebrating the eighteenth-century legacy went with the binational mission on its travels through the country, and the first volume of a lavishly illustrated series of reports appeared in 1910. Much to the delight of the governments of Plaza and Alfaro, archaeological studies conducted by the mission's chief medical officer, a dashing intellectual named Paul Rivet who would later found the Musée de l'Homme, received great international acclaim.[35] When Rivet's research gave rise to his controversial theory that the South American coast had first been settled by Polynesians, it appeared as though the nation had once again risen to the forefront of the scientific imaginary.

The mission also provided a practical benefit in training local military personnel in modern surveying and drafting measures, which proved particularly crucial as the early twentieth century saw a renewal of Ecuador's simmering border conflict with Peru. This strife additionally led then-president Alfaro to reach out to a moderate Dominican friar named Enrique Vacas Galindo to conduct a study of national borders during a journey to Spain. Vacas Galindo's findings appeared between 1901 and 1903 in exhaustive state publications designed to make the case against Peru. An abridged version was bankrolled in 1905 by an organization called the Junta Patriótica Nacional (JPN), which counted liberals, conservatives, and several clerics—including both Vacas Galindo and Federico González Suárez, then bishop of Ibarra—among its membership. Each of these publications argued for a "Greater Ecuador" that bordered Brazil and whose territory included the headwaters of the Amazon. When outright hostilities broke out in April 1910, the junta quickly circulated a separate pamphlet that included six maps vividly illustrating the relevant colonial and nineteenth-century treaties. Among these views was one arguing that Peru considered Ecuador's territory to end just off the eastern edge of the Andean spine. This claim proved particularly effective in rallying the Ecuadorian populace to Alfaro's side, and the map was reprinted in various newspapers across the country.[36]

Alongside this collaboration with the Church, the military and civilians cooperated in the formation of a purely secular body called the Sociedad Geográfica de Quito (SGQ) that included prominent military officers such as the president's brother, Olmedo Alfaro, as well as Gualberto Pérez and Luis Tufiño, director of the National Observatory in Quito's Alameda Park. The group successfully lobbied the government for funding in March 1910 and was charged thenceforth with expanding local cartographic study in support of national security. Gualberto Pérez quickly engaged in a survey of the southern regions under dispute while the body advocated splitting the vast Oriente province into two districts in order to better administer the Amazonian region. The group also embraced the stock liberal measure of creating a civil registry.[37] Most importantly, they called for the inauguration of a military geographic corps organized along the French model so as to create a national topographic map. As articulated by Luis Tufiño in a letter to the Ministry of Public Works, which was later circulated as a pamphlet, this corps would lead teams of university students into the field to conduct the necessary surveys, thus enhancing the students' practical knowledge while accelerating the mapping process. Tufiño argued that such a move would not only help national defense but would also increase the potential for tourism and international investment.[38]

Tufiño's pamphlet proved to be a blueprint for the future development of a geographic corps, yet the endeavor had to be postponed after Alfaro left office in August 1911. However, the SGQ proved more successful in challenging the clerical vision of Quito as a sacred city by cementing its own secular markers in key locations within the city. This process began when Alfaro bequeathed the group the former Japanese pavilion from the 1909 National Exposition (held to commemorate the centennial of Ecuadorian independence) to use as a permanent headquarters. The exposition had helped develop the old Dominican horse pastures (known as the Recoleta) into a fashionable park ringed by "modern" structures such as the building in question. A more significant event, however, occurred when Archbishop González Suárez approved the razing of a pyramidal observation station erected by the Geodesic Mission on the Panecillo with the

Fig. 2.5. Paul Loiseau-Rousseau, Geodesic Monument, Alameda Park, Quito. Photograph by the author.

intention of replacing it with a new church overlooking the capital. The Socie-dad Geográfica de Quito erupted in fury, denouncing the proposed structure in the press as an "*atentado de lesa civilización*" (uncivilized attack). The archbishop, himself an avid archaeologist who had collaborated with Paul Rivet on digs, soon backed down and destroyed the already laid foundation of the new church, promising to build a commemorative pyramid on the site—a pledge that earned him laudatory accolades and honorary membership in the SGQ.

The decision to build the commemorative pyramid on the Panecillo was the first of several attempts to celebrate the Geodesic Mission's journey in the Quito area. By the end of the year, the planned site for the new pyramid had been changed to Alameda Park, in the shadow of the National Observatory, a decision that symbolically identified the fruits of national scientific pursuits as the legacy of the French missions. A new transnational collective, the Co-mité Franco-Ecuatoriano, collected funds for a splendid monument to the two missions, and President Alfaro laid the cornerstone that April. The structure (fig. 2.5) was designed by Frenchman Paul Loiseau-Rousseau and erected by the Swiss-Italian architect Francisco Durini, who was developing a local reputation as an architect of eclectic tastes.[39] It featured an elongated square pyramid deco-rated by the names of the members of both missions as well as of French and Ec-uadorian donors. The iconographic elements included an angel of wisdom writ-ing the ongoing history of national science upon the pyramid's southern face. At its summit, in place of the fleur-de-lis that had created such problems two

Fig. 2.6. J. Gualberto Pérez, detail of *Quito actual y del porvenir* (1912), photostat. Courtesy Library of Congress, Geography & Map Division.

centuries earlier, an Andean condor was perched with a globe upon its wings, an image that cemented the capital and nation's embrace of its planetary centrality.

As the monument went up in Alameda Park, the Sociedad Geográfica laid claim to its third significant site within the city in under two years, with the first being its inhabiting of the Japanese pavilion and the second, its successful attempt to take control of the Panecillo. Each of these sites existed within an inhabited symbolic landscape. Alameda Park and the Recoleta each lay on the outskirts of town near the largest swaths of new construction in the modernizing city. The SGQ thus inserted itself into modernizing territory, an act underscoring the need to plan for colonizing the environs of the Turubamba and Añaquito plains. The uproar over the pyramid on the Panecillo not only linked the society with the Liberal assault on the Church but also allowed it to claim a site whose panoramic view of the capital had eclipsed the eastern view from Itchimbia as the most "accurate" point of reference, given the suitability of its position for surveying the southern plains and its proximity to an orthogonal projection.

The first urban map created by a member of the SGQ makes this civilizing and expansionist gaze explicit. The work in question, Gualberto Pérez's *Quito actual y del porvenir,* presents a utopian design intended to guide the city's future development. The blueprint is based on a regular grid frequently interrupted with broad diagonal avenues ending at circular plazas in a manner reminiscent of Haussmann's plan for Paris, likely from the influence of contacts within the French mission (fig. 2.6). However, Pérez avoids Haussmann's incisions on the traditional city by enshrining the built environment at the center of the future city. An unaltered version of his cadastral map (the original map had recently been updated to include new construction, at the behest of the municipality) thus is the basis for the capital's core: the Quito "*del porvenir*" begins only in the outer environs. No such consideration for preservation, however, is given to existing communities on the northern and southern plains. These are colonized by the grid in a manner reminiscent of the "frontier expansion" that Mauricio Tenorio Trillo has identified for Porfirian Mexico City.[40] As in Mexico, Pérez's proposed suburbanization of Quito shifted new development away from a preserved center and flattened outlying haciendas and Indian villages, all in the name of an ill-defined "*del porvenir*" that embodied a set of practices identified with the legitimation of the orthogonal gaze and the commemoration of Quito's place within a pantheon of capitals.

Pérez's design did not immediately come to fruition, although one could argue that it anticipated the dominant orientation of the Plan Regulador de Quito drawn up in 1942 by Guillermo Jones Odriozola. Of more immediate importance was its expansion of the audience for cartographic treatments of urban development. The map circulated widely, appearing in major newspapers across the country and whetting the public's appetite for a commercial strain of cartographic imaging.

This phenomenon paralleled a rise in local tourism and the beginnings of Quito's transformation into an international destination. The city's elites had long maintained secondary residences in the nearby countryside, but, as the new century began, even families of modest means began to engage in temporary excursions. For instance, the poet Jorge Carrera Andrade, whose family occupied a small house on the slopes of the Panecillo near the homes of indigenous laborers, in his memoirs speaks of childhood summer days spent at his family's "*refugio campestre*" at their small *quinta* (country house) near El Batán hacienda in the early 1910s.[41] Those with lesser budgets rented automobiles and luxury carriages for day trips to nearby destinations such as Cotocollao, Sangolquí, or Guápulo as early as 1908, when the tourist agency "La Central," on Carrera Venezuela near the Plaza Grande, first opened its doors.[42] With the arrival of the railroad that same year, many of its passengers would have been both domestic and international travelers enticed up the Andes by the speed of the locomotive.

Statistics on tourists traveling to Quito are hard to come by for the early part of the century; however, an increase in publications specifically designed as commemorative booklets or guidebooks demonstrates their growing numbers. Local photographer José Domingo Laso, for example, published two albums in concert with the 1909 centennial of the declaration of independence.[43] These volumes showcased an idealized cityscape featuring majestic colonial structures (mostly churches) and streetscapes in which undesirable elements (most likely Indians) were casually excluded.[44] Laso, having himself purchased advertising space on Higley's map, returned the favor for local businesses. Those who bought ads included prominent concerns such as the Botica Aleman, the oculist L. E. Troya, various clothing importers, and several hotels. Proudly standing in their Sunday best before cabinets and shelves stocked with the best national and foreign wares, these merchants displayed a contemporary cosmopolitanism that augmented the city's colonial monumentality.

Laso's publications, however grandiose, imparted little practical knowledge about the city, and, despite their hefty price, they appear to have been more suitable as souvenirs. Less expensive options for the national or foreign traveler began to appear in the 1920s, of which Humberto Peña Orejuela's *Guia de Bolsillo de Quito* was the most widely distributed. Basically a directory providing addresses and listings of local businesses, Peña's pocket guide was reissued several times.[45] Its conspicuous lack of a map was balanced by the simultaneous expansion of locally produced and commercially available plans of the city that could have served as a cross-reference for a newcomer. This abundance of maps was partly the result of the formation of a local lithographic service run by the Estado Mayor General (EMG), a body affiliated with the military that began to offer topographic courses in 1917–1918 under the direction of Luis Tufiño, one of Pérez's colleagues from the SGQ.[46] One of the first commercially sold maps appeared in 1920, the same year as Peña's guide, and it was produced with an eye toward Latin American tourists. Its author was a colorful Colombian travel writer named Froilán Holguín Balcázar, whose career as a correspondent had begun in 1905 with an ill-fated trip to Guayaquil, where the self-described penniless gypsy was forced to drink water from the city's public fountains. His first foray into mapping Quito came with the 1920 *Plano comercial de Quito,* which included a street diagram listing the locations of major businesses while touting recent infrastructural advances such as sewers and water tanks, presumably in an effort to boost development as well as cater to tourists.[47]

The use of maps to promote investment intensified during the buildup to the 1922 centennial of the Battle of Pichincha, in which Quito had been liberated from Spain. With state support, the municipality and a new planning commission called the Junta de Embellecimiento de Quito stepped up their efforts to provide infrastructural improvements and services. One of their first moves was to organize a census of the city and county. The 1921 chart of population centers (fig. 2.7) produced for census workers indicated both a spatial and a rhetorical embrace of the imperialist design that had been featured in Pérez's 1912 map. Like *Quito actual y del porvenir,* the city's limits extended far into the Turubamba and Añaquito plains. Because of its function, the map necessarily represented habitations on the city outskirts yet used a color scheme that perpetuated the dismissive gaze of a civilized city toward the wild countryside. Fully traced city blocks are represented as pink squares, covering even the sparsely inhabited areas on the southeastern edge. Outlying communities, however, received full colorization only if, as in the case of a few blocks in the La Magdalena district south of the Panecillo, they had buildings on all sides. Otherwise, only the streets are shaded with a lighter pink. The map distinguishes between two forms of ostensibly equivalent individual structures on the periphery: *casas sólidas* (represented as black squares) and *casas no-sólidas* (represented as white squares). The common practice of using squares to represent all structures on such maps levels difference between these buildings; however, the choice of white for the "non-solid" houses correlates to the color used for the undeveloped plains—one imagines these "homes" as potential sites for more solid future construction. The iconographical colorization further correlates the non-solid with the rural realm, suggesting these blank, "empty" squares represent *chozas*—rude indigenous huts. As with the division between the two types of city blocks identified ("constructed" and "in progress"), the houses (and presumably their inhabitants) seem to come from two different worlds. The identification of some of the larger haciendas as structures with clearly drawn plans furthers a conception of *civitas* that includes the *hacendado's* home but not the peasant's *choza* as a part of the built urban territory.

The 1921 census map was the first of three that the EMG reproduced and then sold in honor of the 1922 centennial. Its second venture featured a map of the city's parochial districts that had been prepared for the municipality and presented to it in January 1922 in anticipation of the centennial festivities in May. Lieutenants Luis Herrera and Ezequiel Rivadeneira drafted the work,

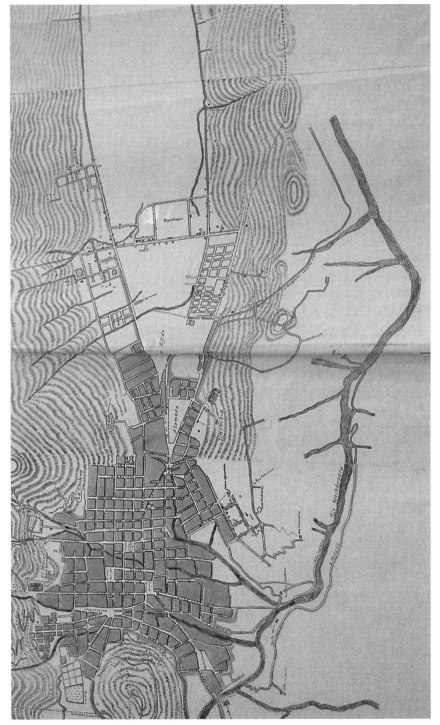

Fig. 2.7. Detail, *Plano de la ciudad de Quito para los trabajos del Censo* (1921). Courtesy Biblioteca Ecuatoriana "Aurelio Espinosa Pólit," Quito.

which the city adopted as its official standard. From the start, the city council saw the map not only as an educational tool, as in 1888, but also as a possibly marketable commodity, and it ordered reduced wall-size copies in February.[48]

As with the various maps of Quito, beginning with that of La Condamine, one of the crucial features of the Herrera-Rivadeneira map (figs. 2.8 and 2.9) is the establishment of authorial legitimacy. The title of the map provides a summary of its history, identifying not only the general who ordered the map but also his intention to donate it to the municipality precisely for the purpose of celebrating the centennial. General Don Rafael Almeida's signature figures prominently beneath the title, flanked by the autographs of the two cartographers. A second claim to legitimation lies to the left of the title, in the form of a reproduction of the municipal ordinance thanking the EMG for its fine work.[49]

The image of the ordinance appears as if etched on an ancient scroll, a nostalgic evocation echoing the climate of historicism of the 1922 celebrations that was also manifested in the production of a commemorative volume penned by Isaac Barrera of the National Academy of History, as well as *tertulias* or seminars dedicated to discussing the city's history, essay competitions, and newspaper articles on the independence wars.[50] Rhetorically, the map's authority thus results specifically from this appreciation of the city's glorious past along with the author's technical prowess. Individual claim to authorial legitimacy, however, has receded in the face of increasing institutional (military) authority.

Chorographic details incorporate not only the built environment but also engage municipal planning designs in a communicentric statement that again reinforces class, spatial, and racial divisions. A color-coded scheme delimits the city's parochial divisions. As with earlier maps, the southern working-class and mixed-race districts of La Magdalena and Chimbacalle are not presented as fully developed parts of the city, and only the main streets are highlighted. In the north, however, the area of Santa Prisca parish that was targeted for transformation into the upscale Mariscal Sucre suburb is presented as if already completed, with full colorization in dark green. Its street outlines belie this designation, as they are identified by dotted lines representing their status as planned rather than completed construction. The district thus represents a paradoxical duality as a "fully urban" area as yet unbuilt. Its status as part of Quito's aristocratic *civitas* starkly contrasts with the obscuring of working-class and rural districts. However, this inclusion was not extended to the entirety of the Benalcázar *parroquia* (civil parish); its outer edges received the same colorization as the southern parishes, in a gesture similar to the representation of *chozas* in the 1921 census map.

As with prior maps, featured buildings also provide great insight into the image's communicentric values. To begin with, abstract lines replace building plans throughout, with the exception of public buildings colored red. There is no table listing all the structures, but analysis reveals the further diminishment of religious markers and a corresponding growth in markers of civil administra-

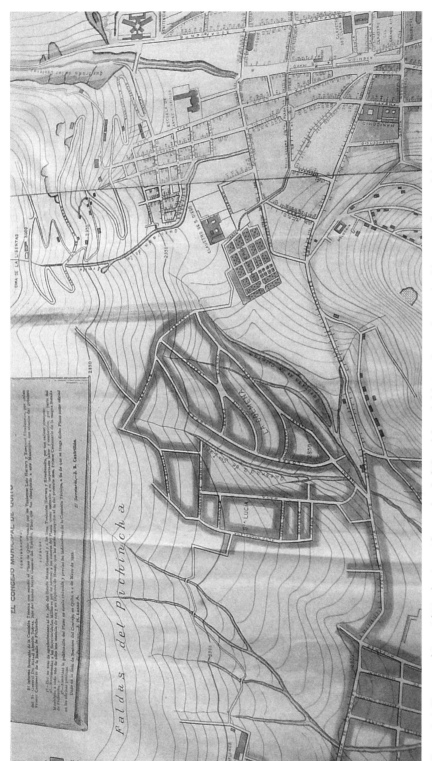

Fig. 2.8. Luis Herrera and Ezequiel Rivadeneira, mid-range detail of *Plano de la ciudad de Quito levantado por orden del Sr. General Don Rafael Almeida, S., Jefe del E.M.G., y obsequiado al Ilustre Concejo Municipal de Quito en Homenaje al Centenario de la Batalla de Pichincha* (1922). This view shows the scroll used to document municipal acceptance of the map. Courtesy Biblioteca Ecuatoriana "Aurelio Espinosa Pólit," Quito.

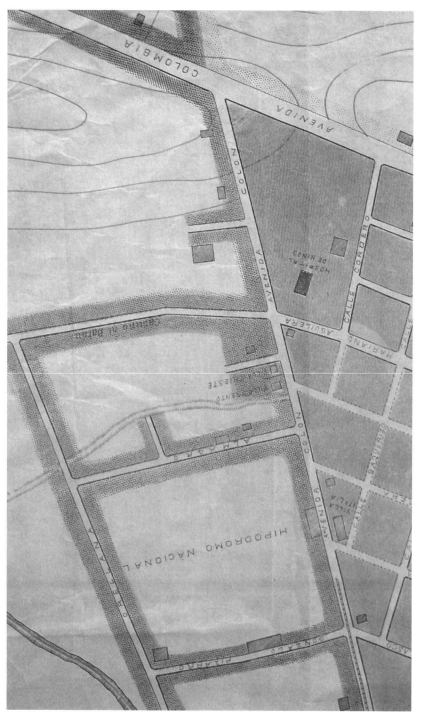

Fig. 2.9. Luis Herrera and Ezequiel Rivadeneira, close-range detail of *Plano de la ciudad de Quito levantado por orden del Sr. General Don Rafael Almeida, S., Jefe del E.M.G., y obsequiado al Ilustre Concejo Municipal de Quito en Homenaje al Centenario de la Batalla de Pichincha* (1922). This view highlights the contrast between the depiction of the Mariscal and *parroquia* Benalcázar. Note the dotted lines on the western blocks. Courtesy Biblioteca Ecuatoriana "Aurelio Espinosa Pólit," Quito.

tion. One of the most interesting facets of the map, however, is the inclusion of numerous private buildings, shaded in gray, which collectively declare the actualization of industrial and residential districts even if they are still under construction. To the south, for instance, nascent industry appears represented by the El Retiro mill and a textile plant. To the north, this image is mirrored by well-known elite chalets such as Francisco Durini's Villa Trento and Villa Trieste as well as La Circasiana, the residence of conservative politician Jacinto Jijón y Caamaño. The spatial dynamics of the city's subsequent zoning divisions into a southern industrial belt and the northern suburbs are therefore anticipated by the map's iconography.

This map also became the object of the third of the EMG's commemorative commodities when poster-sized, red-tinted reproductions appeared in local bookstores and newsstands that May. These reprints incorporated a thick border highlighting local businesses, following the lead of Higley and Holguín Balcázar's embrace of the map as advertising space. Unlike the edition given to the municipality and other institutions, this version did not feature the municipal ordinance and the extended title summarizing the map's history. Instead, it had the simple title "Plano de la Ciudad de Quito en el Centenario de la Batalla de Pichincha." Public buildings appear as on the earlier version, but this time there was an accompanying list that would make them easily identifiable to a tourist or business traveler. This emphasis on legibility, combined with a smaller size— the reprint was approximately one-third the size of the earlier map—increased their accessibility and practicality.

The commercial success of the Herrera-Rivadeneira map marked the greatest level of military cartographic preeminence to this point; however, its production would expand exponentially over the rest of the decade. The arrival later in 1922 of an Italian military mission, invited to help Ecuador modernize its armed forces in response to a similar French advisory trip to Peru, accelerated this process. The Italian commanders encouraged the development of military engineering and persuaded President José Luis Tamayo to inaugurate a course in topographical studies under the auspices of Lieutenant Colonel Luis T. Paz y Miño, who would subsequently rise to prominence as an administrator and cartographic historian.[51] Other Italian initiatives included courses on the study of cartography, geodesy, and topography that led to extensive surveying of border regions. Through the political turmoil of the mid-1920s, calls for a national atlas became commonplace both in the military and in the press. One of President Isidro Ayora's first decrees upon coming to power following the Julian Revolution ordered that such a map be created under the auspices of many of those involved in cartographic studies over the past decades, including Paz y Miño, Luis Tufiño, Ezequiel Rivadeneira, and the Italian colonel Giácomo Rocca. Extensive cartographic training took place in 1927 as efforts intensified to form the special corps that Tufiño had first called for in 1911. On April 11, 1928, Ayora finally inaugurated the Servicio Geográfico Militar (SGM), which would dominate cartographic production in Ecuador through the rest of the twentieth century.[52]

More broadly, one can argue that the maps of the Liberal era illustrate a transformation in the conceit of cartography. Besides eroding the expertise of the individual in favor of the institutional might of the military, the maps produced between 1903 and 1922 demonstrate a marked tendency to use cartography as a tool for justifying the imperial expansion of the city. The relationship between color and the built environment shifted as well to designate a socioracial division of space that anticipated the class and racial segregation that would eventually mark the city's twentieth-century schematics. The era also saw the onset of the map's commodification and the initiation of an alliance between business (especially those businesses catering to tourists), the municipality, and military cartographers. This relationship would deepen over the next two decades as the transformation of Quito's socioeconomic spatiality would become concretized.

These changes paralleled a culture of public commemoration that was indivisibly bound to the production of urban views. The technical advice of the French Geodesic Mission heavily influenced the expansion of mapping in the early years of the century, and that growth accelerated further in the wake of the 1909 centennial of the first call for independence from Spain. The claiming of sites specifically identified with both the spread of geodesy and the modern fringes of the city established the legitimacy of the Sociedad Geográfica de Quito while its successors in the EMG expanded the cartographer's gaze. With the institutional framework offered by a separate geographical military corps, the 1930s would afford the opportunity to consolidate the disparate strands of cartographic production under a single roof. The new maps produced would once again build on the culture of commemoration and help expand the city, both for business and for the growing tourist trade.

Institutionalization, Tourism, and the Pleasure City

The formation of the SGM constituted one of the most important events in the history of Ecuadorian cartography. For the first time, an institution specifically geared to the study of national geography gathered together surveyors, cartographers, and administrators. Its leadership represented the cream of military geographers, led first by Italian military advisor Giácomo Rocca and then by Ezequiel Rivadeneira, now a lieutenant colonel. Continuing Italian influence also led to the modernization of many of the techniques used in geodesic surveys, which had hitherto been based mainly on simple ground-level surveys and triangulation. Photogrammetric techniques debuted in Ecuador with the onset of a campaign to compile a national atlas. The use of photography sped up the research phase, which was completed by 1930.[53]

One of the first of the new maps was another plan of Quito, completed in 1932.[54] Once again, the military chose to unveil and present the finished work to the municipality on a national holiday, August 10 (Independence Day). The map represents the first conspicuous attempt to provide a full topographical description of the city. Earlier maps had tended to end contour lines at the edge of the constructed area, which had the effect of making mountains like Pichincha, Itchimbia, and the Panecillo appear as small rises that suddenly ended. The SGM's map, however, weaves topographical lines in between the major constructed areas and preserves the landscape's irregularity. This approach accentuates the difficulty that constructing the city must have presented, as can be seen very clearly by examining the alteration between peaks and flattened city blocks in areas like El Tejar, for example. The contour lines, however, also bespeak the continued presence of an elite vision of the city due to selective interruptions along upscale areas such as the Mariscal while continuing unbroken through the working-class housing districts north of El Tejar.

A similar understanding of Quito's sociospatial divisions appeared in the national atlas completed later that year. On a page dedicated to the capital, the SGM chose not to include the entire city but to eliminate the now solidly working-class districts of La Magdalena and Chimbacalle just south of the Panecillo while including the northern Añaquito plains. This decision not only symbolically laid claim to the northern environs but also presented a particular constitution of the city's public image as formed by its colonial core, the upscale residential north, and a landscape unspoiled by industrial production. The decision to return to the colonial custom of using the Quito meridian as the main coordinate of the graticule reinforced this identification of the city with its Spanish, white, and elite past. It also supported a growing movement by the local and national government to encourage day trips to the north.

As noted earlier, state propaganda designating Quito as a city of striking colonial churches had been in vogue since at least the days of the *Ecuador in Chicago* commemorative volume and was echoed in the various maps produced through the early 1920s. The government began to target a foreign audience of business leaders and leisure travelers as early as 1923, when it began to edit a publication titled *El Ecuador Comercial.* The magazine focused on the potential for international investment but also featured portraits and panoramic views of the country's major attractions, beginning with the capital and then proceeding through the other major cities and monuments. Restaurants, department stores, bookstores, and other establishments purchased advertising space in the magazine, often including photographs of their proximity to the city's major plazas or colonial architectural monuments. In the late 1920s, Ayora's government produced targeted publications such as *Ecuador: Revista de Propaganda y Turismo,* which was targeted to a Venezuelan audience and overseen by the diplomatic mission in Bolívar's homeland. The serial included statistical information on the nation's economic production while also featuring vignettes, picturesque imagery, and laudatory travelers' accounts of visits to Quito, Guayaquil, or Cuenca.

The growing number of Latin American business and pleasure travelers, to which these texts catered, also meant an expanded market for cheap maps of the capital without the busy trappings typical earlier in the century. Works such as the Editorial Chimborazo's 1931 *Plano de la ciudad de Quito hecho para actividad* targeted the visitor unfamiliar with the city and therefore emphasized legibility. Its simplified plan eliminated major topographical features other than the labeling of the slopes of Pichincha and Itchimbia, printed the names of streets in a large typeface, and had a clear legend identifying the best-known monuments.[55] The possibilities expanded in 1934, when the SGM inaugurated a printing press in order to more easily produce and distribute the national atlas.[56] One of the first tourist maps published by the new press was the 1935 *Plano indicador de Quito* (fig. 2.10) drawn by the aforementioned Froilán Holguín Balcázar. Holguín's patented map, popular on the Latin American business circuit, showed a city enclosed by a circle surrounded by advertisements and names of local landmarks. Codes delineated in the central circular area referred to buildings, businesses, or landmarks listed on the right-hand side of the map and easily located by aligning a pointer with the corresponding numeral. Quito's inclusion among Holguín's exclusive circuit, which included European capitals like Berlin and Paris along with Mexico City, Buenos Aires, or Caracas, cemented its growing international visibility.[57]

This map's publication coincided with that of the series of picture postcards (discussed in chapter 1) that presented Quito as a city of churches with inviting environs easily accessible for day trips and joy rides. The map echoes this perception of the city's outskirts, including as it does imagery showcasing the forests outside the city and the depiction of bathing establishments, restaurants, and breweries all located within a short distance. These ranged as far north as Tulcán on the border with Colombia, as evidenced by Plutarco Paz's advertisement for a branch of his currency exchange establishment, which, significantly, included images of American dollars as well as Colombian pesos as available denominations. The map even included several ads from automobile vendors on the off chance a visitor wished to purchase or rent a car. Also significant were the myriad ads of tire manufacturers catering to the motorist with a flat, a ubiquitous occurrence to this day on Andean roads littered with potholes due to uneven paving and heavy tropical storms.

The year after Holguín Balcázar drew his map, the state expanded its involvement in the development of regional tourism with the inauguration of a monument at the Equator in time for the 1936 bicentennial of the original Franco-Hispanic mission that had given the city, and the nation, its first taste of international notoriety. The plans for an equatorial structure dated back to the original truce between González Suárez and the Sociedad Geográfica de Quito in 1911 following the church's razing of the second mission's observation stations

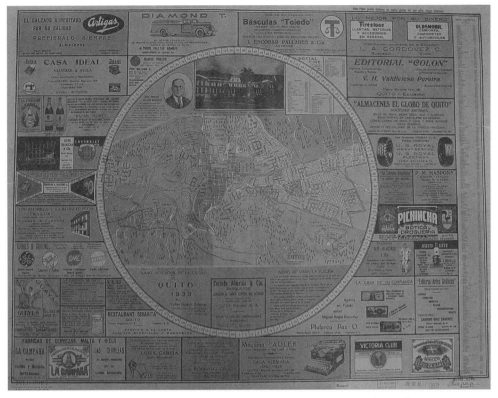

Fig. 2.10. Froilán Holguín Balcázar, *Plano indicador de Quito* (1935). Courtesy Library of Congress.

on the Panecillo. Besides establishing the need for a monument in Quito itself, the parties hoped to restore the pyramid of Oyambaro, which had been built according to La Condamine's original designs (fig. 2.11) the century before but that had since fallen into disrepair. Moreover, they hoped to build a second replica at Caraburo, a site near the town of San Antonio de Pichincha, twenty kilometers north of Quito, near the Equator.[58] This latter pyramid represents the first significant attempt to create an equatorial destination on the city's outskirts.

The anniversary provided an opportunity to certify Ecuador's identification with the geographic advances of both the first and second missions. A bicentennial steering committee was formed in November 1935 and consisted of government and cultural functionaries, representatives from the Servicio Geográfico Militar, and several members of the Comité France-Amérique, an organ of the French foreign service that sought to increase ties between American nations and France. Presiding over the committee was art historian José Gabriel Navarro, who strongly embraced Ecuador's Spanish cultural heritage. The events the group planned for May 1936 included an assortment of galas, lectures, and pageants, with primary events occurring in both Quito and Riobamba, birth-

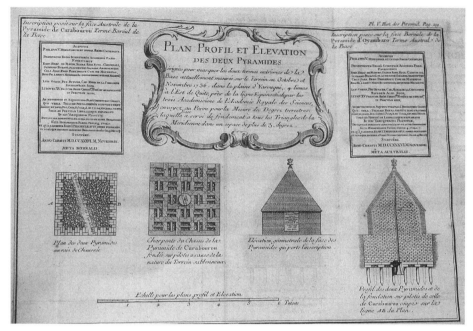

Fig. 2.11. Charles Marie de La Condamine, *Plan Profil et Elevation des deux Pyramides*. Courtesy Library of Congress.

place of Pedro Vicente Maldonado. These events involved the participation of General Georges Perrier, the French envoy who was the second mission's commander. He not only penned a detailed history of his previous visit to the equatorial nation but also laid the cornerstone for a new monument celebrating the two journeys. This structure, designed by Luis Tufiño, director of the National Observatory and longtime cartographic advocate, would rise precisely at 0° latitude.[59]

Tufiño's design referenced both La Condamine's original plans and Paul Loiseau-Rousseau's monument in Alameda Park. The new structure (fig. 2.12, lower left) featured the simple lines of the eighteenth-century pyramids with an abstraction of the global motif atop the later work. While the figurative condor with its nationalist associations was significantly absent, in its place Tufiño substituted variegated steps that are reminiscent of pre-Columbian architecture and that lead to a single point at the apex upon which the world was balanced. This subtle indigenist touch significantly incorporated an allusion to Ecuador's native peoples for the first time since La Condamine's eighteenth-century map. Although Tufiño may have meant this as a show of solidarity, it more likely referenced the notoriety that Paul Rivet's archaeological studies of pre-Columbian Ecuadorian peoples had received worldwide and that was prominently cited in most concurrent publications.

Fig. 2.12. Servicio Geográfico Militar, detail (photograph of monument, lower left) from *Plano de la ciudad de Quito* (April 1946). Courtesy Biblioteca Ecuatoriana "Aurelio Espinosa Pólit," Quito.

The aesthetic value of the monument can be considered as secondary to its impact in providing a defined destination on the Equator that could be exploited by the nascent tourist industry. In a series of booklets it produced during the early 1940s, the Servicio Geográfico Militar prominently included photographs of the structure that consolidated the trends of growing secularization and the embrace of the surrounding landscape evident during the previous decade.

The guides present a topographic projection of the full extension of the city on one side, with city blocks colored in peach, parks in green, and public monuments in red. Red capital letters clearly label the main neighborhoods and parks, while a listing of plazas appears in the lower-left corner. In keeping with the broader secularization trend, only the primary churches are highlighted in the list of monuments, sharing space with leisure establishments such as the bullring. On the other side appear a flurry of images that clearly indicate a tourist-friendly city and region. At the center lies an inset map of the capital that shows the primary roadways along the Andean corridor reaching up to the Equator itself. Photographs of restful spas frame this route map on four sides, underscoring the pleasant climate of the city's environs. Surrounding this central depiction of a city at peace with its environs are two rows of images and advertisements. The latter cater to the international luxury traveler and include airlines, travel agencies, and luxury hotels such as the Colón Majestic. Local travel needs are also represented, with ads for Michelin tires, car rental companies, banks, museums, the national railway company, and Luigi Rota's radio and electronics store.

In keeping with the growing association of site-specific photography with cartographic production, the images in these two rows of photos and advertisements define a communicentric identity that combines various tropes developed over the previous several centuries. The first of these identifies Quito's religious missionary impulse, symbolized by a photograph of the city's cathedral. The second concerns its cosmopolitanism, as represented by a shot of the recently erected statue of Simón Bolívar, a national symbol despite his Venezuelan origin. The third, involving portraits of the nearby mountains of Iliniza and El Altar, for the first time incorporates a countryside whose "barbaric" indigenous populations had been successfully tamed and elided. Last, but not least, is the 1936 monument raised at San Antonio de Pichincha (see fig. 2.12). Flanked by advertisements for hotels, a travel agency, and even a development bank, the monument in this production crystallized the chronotope of the city's global centrality that had been developing for centuries yet which could now be defined through a shorthand identifying a specific locale: the site now known as *mitad del mundo.*

The Chronotope of *Mitad del Mundo*

Maps have proven to have power as a planning instrument and as a tool of the state, the municipality, and business. Mapmakers operated as knowledge brokers who legitimated the transformation of Quito-space according to a legibility wedded to social control. By portraying the possibilities of urban expansion, maps helped the state steamroll over the northern and southern environs of Quito in the name of progress, modernity, and suburbanization. This was not always a seamless process, as the indigenous populations elided in the blank landscapes targeted for development attempted, at times successfully, to slow the city's imperial intrusion. More insidious, perhaps, was the colonization of those "vacant" landscapes as destinations for tourists seeking an authentic encounter with nature or an escape from the cacophony of Quito or their hometowns in North America or Europe. However, the most important achievement of the city's cartographers with regard to Quito's modern economy was to codify and sharpen the long-standing metaphor of Quito's global centrality. By presenting the city as a locus of modernity, an artistic haven, and a site of scientific progress, maps bolstered the city and its inhabitants' claims to worldwide preeminence.

The clearest expression of this dynamic was the elaboration of an invented chronotope of the city as the *mitad del mundo,* or center of the world. This framework built upon the idealization of Quito's geographic proximity to the Equator, its cultivated image as a new Rome, and a reconsideration of the eighteenth-century Geodesic Mission. At the beginning of the twentieth century, an iconology developed that would manifest itself monumentally across the city and its environs. The minuscule geodetic pyramid, used as a surveying instrument in the 1730s and again during a second French mission from 1901 to 1906, has become the ubiquitous symbol of Quito's place within the global corpus of universal science. Today it can be found in a plethora of consumer goods, from key chains to T-shirts and even a fruit liquor called Spirit of Ecuador, whose pyramid-shaped bottle can be found throughout the city and ordered online as far afield as New Jersey.

Most famously, the symbolic pyramid has become enshrined in a complex, also known as Mitad del Mundo, that was erected in 1978 in concert with Quito's designation as a World Heritage Site. At that time, Tufiño's monument was replaced by a thirty-meter-high replica located at the end of the so-called Avenue of the Geodesics, an extended walkway flanked by busts of the preeminent geographers from both French missions along with their Spanish and Ecuadorian counterparts.[60] The complex, as evidenced by its extraordinary commercialization, represents the logical extension of a chronotope delivered by its maps and mapmakers. Despite its obvious commemoration of the great study of the eighteenth century, the complex also maintains its ties to the early colonial idealization of Quito as a new Rome or city of God. Besides a restaurant, a planetarium, and a hotel, the complex boasts a replica of a small Spanish town built on the central design first approved by Nicolás de Ovando in 1502, complete with central plaza, church, the homes of *vecinos,* and even a bullring. These features signal an association of the complex with the pillars of Hispanic culture and as such present a refracted and anachronistic vision of the early claims of global centrality sparked by a missionary zeal. Simultaneously, however, it engages with a separate chronotope, that of Quito as a quintessentially Spanish city.

This vision has also proved extraordinarily pliable as constructions of national and local identity have shifted with the times. The monument houses an anthropological museum that features maquettes depicting the nation's pre-Columbian past. Their embrace of the quiescent indigeneity referencing Paul Rivet's pioneering research presents a jarring image removed from the ethnic struggles that have characterized the decades since the early 1980s, yet could be referenced as a multicultural icon by embattled national governments.

Globalization has also placed its mark on the region by virtue of a gargantuan convention center erected to host the 2004 Miss Universe pageant virtually on the Equator itself. In coming years, the city's mythical associations with this chronotope will introduce foreign visitors to the new international airport, whose main hall will feature a grandiose mural celebrating La Condamine's voyage. Ironically, this structure will be located on the Yaruquí plains themselves, the site of the commemorative pyramid adorned with the fleur-de-lis that caused such trouble three centuries ago. Needless to say, the contested nature of this chronotope will be conspicuously absent.

Chapter 3

Hispanismo
Site, Heritage, Memory

The city of Quito is a precious jewel and spiritual fountain, a witness of the linkages between Ecuador and the renewal of Latin culture. Quito, without Gothic art, born for the future, must never let itself be defrauded by pressing modernity and must conserve for posterity the purity in which Latin America was formed and the spirit in which it was born.

Julio [Giulio] Aristide Sartorio, 1934

Visitors to Quito in the 1920s and 1930s increasingly commented on the city's majestic colonial architecture. This represented a marked change from nineteenth-century accounts, which often decried the city's insularity or stressed the physical prowess of its indigenous population or the lack of basic services.[1] This shifting discourse stemmed from a variety of causes. To begin with, activist municipal authorities vastly improved the city's services and infrastructure during the early twentieth century, making it easier for tourists to look beyond the dusty streets and poncho-clad Indians to note the buildings and plazas through which they walked. Another crucial factor was an evolving global sensibility in the aftermath of World War I. Rather than seeking the energy of the teeming city centers of nineteenth-century progress, Western travelers began to embrace the primitive, the pastoral, the vibrancy of cultures unencumbered by the weight of modernity in such places as Mexico, New Orleans, or Italy. Quito, with its picturesque churches, red-tiled roofs, and unique location nestled in the heart of a dramatic inter-Andine valley, appeared as the quintessence of traditional Spanish America—a quaint idyll sought by nostalgic tourists eager to find traces of a simpler past.

The rhetorical association of Quito with Spain simultaneously drew upon a twentieth-century global movement known as Hispanism, which identified a common cultural *raza* between Spain and its former colonies; adherents of Hispanism believed that *la raza's* spiritual purity would redeem the world from its current materialistic morass.[2] By conceiving the city as a spiritual, administrative, and artistic center grounded in its Spanish heritage, Ecuadorian *hispanistas* attempted to situate the city's history on the world stage, particularly with respect to its glorious artwork. The movement also sought to transcend local political differences through a unifying rhetoric that might supersede the traditional liberal-conservative and class divides. These political and social divisions were especially sharp during the economic and political crisis of the interwar years, an era that coincided with the greatest expansion of the myth of Quito's Hispanic character. During this time, Quito's Hispanists built upon an intellectual legacy with roots in the colonial period but that found its modern formulation in the historical and religious philosophy of the city's archbishop, Federico González Suárez. Working with the institutional support of the National Academy of History, González Suárez's students put aside regional and political debates to advance a scholarly vision of Quito and Ecuador firmly grounded in its colonial heritage. In so doing, they not only sought to heal the wounds of the Liberal Revolution but also attempted to limit the active expansion of the socialist and indigenist movements. Quito, as the local symbol par excellence of Spanish culture, became their canvas and their museum, a city to be revered and celebrated because of its redemptive qualities. By rehabilitating the city center, identifying and protecting its architectural marvels, and elaborating a complex web of Spanish cultural iconography, the city's Hispanists invented a tradition of a whitened and legible Spanish city that, paradoxically, contrasted with its social reality as a burgeoning mestizo and indigenous space as the elite fled to chalets and villas on the outskirts.[3]

Postcolonial Diplomacy and Anxieties

The early modern Spanish conceived the discovery and conquest of the Americas in biblical terms, seeing the hand of divine Providence in the glorious rise of the house of Habsburg. Millenarian visions of the new rule of Christ, foretold by the book of Revelation and by medieval scholars of renown such as Joachim de Fiore, likewise abounded. Hardened by the wars of the Reconquista, Iberians were emboldened by the feats of Cortés and Pizarro and clamored to participate in the great battle between the forces of good and evil. As Jorge Cañizares-Esguerra has written, the Americas were viewed as a territory in the grip of the forces of Satan, whose conquest, while difficult, could lead to the establishment of a terrestrial paradise.[4] This was to be a long and difficult slog due to the entrenchment of the devil's minions, who soon began to cor-

rupt even the Spanish themselves, as famed Dominican Bartolomé de Las Casas
articulated so clearly in his treatises about the excesses of the Conquest. As a
result, the battle was joined by increasing numbers of Catholic militants hoping
to bring a swift end to the conflict with extensive conversion and diligent action,
including the vast campaigns against indigenous idolatry in the late sixteenth
and seventeenth centuries.[5] Peninsulars, or those born on the Iberian Peninsula,
continued to view Spanish America as a wilderness during the eighteenth century, while creoles, born in the New World, maintained their stock in Western
civilization even as they continued to denigrate the savagery of indigenous and
subaltern populations. These tensions contributed to the eventual separation
between colony and metropole in the nineteenth century.

The imperial crisis that developed following Napoleon's invasion of the
Iberian Peninsula offered the first chance for American creoles to participate
in imperial governance at the Cortes de Cádiz (1810–1814). Initial patriotic
fervor slowly turned to disillusion for many of the new delegates due to their
marginalization at the Cortes and as a result of Ferdinand VII's authoritarian
repudiation of the liberal Constitution of 1812 upon his return to the throne.
The career of Guayaquil-based poet and Cádiz delegate José Joaquín de Olmedo
epitomizes this stage of relations. He first learned of the Napoleonic invasion
while traveling in Lima and, in response, wrote a passionate poem titled "El ár-
bol," which stressed the sacred friendship between colony and metropole.[6] The
poet's nationalist fervor began to diminish during the Cortes, however, as his
impassioned pleas for social reform fell on indifferent ears.[7] By the second round
of independence wars, Olmedo was a confirmed republican, leading the junta
that liberated Guayaquil and, on October 9, 1820, even writing the city's declaration of independence. His enmity toward Spain continued after the port city
joined Colombia, a feeling captured in his most famous poem, "Canto a Junín."
This extensive ode to the republican victory over Spanish forces at the Peruvian
town of Junín in 1824 denigrates the colonial past as barbaric while celebrating
Bolívar's glory and even Peru's Incaic heritage.[8]

Jaime Rodríguez has argued that the negative experiences of Cádiz not only
inspired national resistance movements but also helped cement transnational
alliances that would bear fruit in the series of defensive alliances set up in the
aftermath of independence.[9] Beginning with the 1826 Panama congress, attempts to form a unified front against the threat from Spain developed among
the new American republics. Undaunted, Spain attempted to retake Mexico in
1829, only to be driven back by the forces of Santa Anna. Given the unpleasant
prospect of ongoing conflict, the possibility of commercial incursions by other
European powers, and the continued importance of trade between the Iberian
power and its former colonies, Spain initiated discussions to normalize relations with the American republics in 1832, an effort that, by the decade's end,
had led to the establishment of diplomatic ties with Mexico and Ecuador.

Clashes between Spain and its former colonies continued to flare up from time to time, particularly in 1846, when it was revealed that Queen María Cristina had been plotting with former Ecuadorian president Juan José Flores to reestablish a monarchy in the Andean republic.[10] These tensions briefly paled in light of the imminent threat posed by the United States, whose triumph in the 1846–1848 war with Mexico inspired a newfound sense of Hispanoamericanism voiced at the second transregional congress in Lima.[11] However, antipathy resumed following Spain's 1864 invasion of Peru's Chincha Islands in an attempt to restrict British access to the lucrative Peruvian guano trade. The incursion led to a display of hemispheric solidarity by the nations of Spanish America, which broke off relations with Spain as a bloc in order to support Peru.

Nevertheless, the 1860s also saw progress in cultural dialogue through the efforts of institutions like the Real Academia Española de la Lengua. Following extensive restructuring in 1858, the once exclusively peninsular organization began offering corresponding memberships to Spanish American intellectuals.[12] Although the Argentine Domingo Sarmiento famously refused membership, six prominent intellectuals, including Peruvian Felipe Pardo Aliaga and Mexicans Bernardo Couto and Joaquín Pesado, had joined by 1865.[13] In 1871, the Real Academia moved to thaw relations, iced by the Chincha invasion, by calling for corresponding national chapters in the former colonies—the first time that American linguists had been treated as cultural equals by the mother country. The overture soon bore fruit as first Colombia and then Ecuador embraced the initiative, followed by the other republics over the next several decades.[14] After 1885, the Real Academia's efforts received support from the Unión Iberoamericana, an organization seeking greater commercial and cultural unity and headed by Iberian senator and former Cuban intendant Mariano Cancío Villaamil. As a consortium of liberal persuasion, the group advocated opening up trade barriers between Spain and its colonies. While its more fanciful notions, such as the call for a new transatlantic state, were doomed to failure, it succeeded in fostering closer ties with the former colonies. For example, its membership successfully lobbied for the participation of most American states in the 1892 Madrid Historical American Exposition celebrating the quadricentennial of Columbus's voyage.[15]

These Iberian appeals for transnational political and cultural structures coincided with calls for national regeneration in the wake of decades of civil war. These considerations built upon a metanarrative celebrating an eternal Spain whose civilizing force had transformed the world. However, Spain's own regionalist divisions and a general suspicion of Madrid's centralizing tendencies led many to espouse a hybrid nationalism building upon medieval notions of *vecindad* in which each province or kingdom of Spain had a stake in national identity. Barcelona-based conservatives like Manuel Mila y Fontanels or Joaquín Rubio, for instance, sought the roots of Spain's glory in its local customs, particularly the vibrancy of Catalan Catholicism.[16] These precepts were taken up by one of the most influential figures of late nineteenth-century Spanish letters, Marcelino Menéndez Pelayo, whose *Historia de los heterodoxos españoles* (1880–1882) lauded Spain's divinely inspired role as leader of the eternal, natural, and Catholic spirit while also underscoring the heterodox community that made up its people. Other fervent believers in the possibility of Spanish regeneration followed a politically liberal line in which Catholicism was replaced by nature as a unifying force. Intellectuals such as Leopoldo Alas (Clarín) or Fernando del Río moved away from the Church to embrace the teachings of German philosopher Karl Krause regarding nature's fundamental spirituality. Similarly, the historian Rafael Altamira noted the possibility of science reflecting national reality but held that local personality animated the national body.

The localist strain in these appeals to a higher conceptualization of the Spanish people helped build a bridge to the American republics and to their reconsideration as vibrant partners who could regenerate the former mother country. Figures such as Menéndez Pelayo delved into Spanish American poetry, even editing an anthology of American works, while Altamira publicly extolled the energy that cultural reunion with the Spanish American republics could offer an aging peninsula. These ideas of global redemption built upon the founding mythologies of Iberian conquest as well as the stark appreciation of economic disaster represented by Spain's loss of its last colonies in 1898.

The "*desastre del '98*," as the Spanish-American-Cuban war was known on the peninsula, also propelled Spanish American intellectuals to declare their solidarity with Spain. At times, this position manifested in virulent antipathy to the colossus of the north, as in Nicaraguan Rubén Darío's famous warnings to Theodore Roosevelt about the specter of "a thousand cubs of the Spanish lion" to the south. Perhaps most influential was Uruguayan José Enrique Rodó's monumental essay *Ariel* (1900), which provided an intellectual defense of anti-Americanism by contrasting the spiritual vitality of pan-Hispanic youth with the material decadence of the United States. *Ariel* became a rapid international best-seller, as popular on the peninsula as in the Americas. Intellectual giants like Miguel de Unamuno or Rafael Altamira echoed Rodó by allowing that peninsular regeneration would come through collaboration with the vibrancy across the ocean. Altamira's extensive praise of the book led to its embrace across the political spectrum, by intellectuals as varied as the aging liberal Clarín and the conservative Antonio Goicoechea.[17] Over the next two decades, Arielismo and pan-Hispanism became increasingly important movements across the region, and they would begin to determine state cultural policies in the 1920s.

The movement grew more pervasive. In Spain, the Primo de Rivera dictatorship adopted a Hispanist policy focused on developing a role as a cultural leader of the Hispanic world. Annual celebrations of Columbus's discovery, now renamed "Día de la Raza," played a large role in this endeavor. Populist governments in Spanish America also embraced the holiday, while simultaneously inserting *hispanista* tenets into nationalist discourse. Attempts by the Augusto Leguía regime in Peru to bring King Alfonso XIII to the centenary of independence in 1921 represent a particularly ironic example of the depth of reconciliation. Although the Spanish monarch canceled at the last minute, he sent a congratulatory letter reprinted in all local newspapers praising Lima as a "valuable fruit of the civilizing and Christian force of the Hispanic race."[18] This form of expanded cultural communication came to an early zenith in 1929 at the Ibero-American Exposition in Seville, which featured exhibits from all the Latin American republics and a shared glorification of the discovery of America as well as the future possibilities for the Hispanic world.[19]

This form of state-sponsored integration suffered an extended challenge during the Spanish Civil War, which politicized pan-Hispanism. Most Spanish American governments sought to remain neutral, given the intensity of local class conflict. The notable exceptions included Argentina, which supported the Nationalists, and Mexico, which welcomed scores of refugees and sold arms to the Republic. It is worth noting that each of these states had extremely strong detractors among the Argentine Left and Mexico's fascist elements, such as the Golden Shirts.[20] Following the decline of fascism after World War II, collaboration with Franco's regime became inscribed in cold war politics.

Hispanism's global reach also expanded in the 1920s as intellectuals outside the Hispanic world incorporated its lexicon. Somewhat strangely, one of the burgeoning centers for this pro-Spanish and Spanish American sentiment was the United States. The surge began in the early twentieth century with an increase in academic studies of the history and culture of the region.[21] The greatest exponent of American support for pan-Hispanism came from Waldo Frank in his works *Virgin Spain* (1921) and *América Hispana* (1930), which embraced the poetry and vitality of Hispanic culture.[22] Frank's career and travels through the region forged bridges between leading intellectuals with whom he maintained an extensive correspondence, including José Carlos Mariátegui and Mexican essayist Alfonso Reyes. He also translated numerous Spanish American novels, such as *Don Segundo Sombra* and *Martín Fierro,* into English.[23]

Despite Hispanism's worldwide reach, local circumstances played a significant part in attracting many intellectuals to the movement. While concerns about American imperialism strongly influenced Rodó and Darío, for others this issue was not a determining factor. Jeanne Delaney, for instance, argues that for Argentine Manuel Gálvez, his experience as a rural gentleman confronting secular Buenos Aires gave rise to *El Solar de la Raza* (1913), his influential panegyric to the Spanish provincial town.[24] Similarly, the embrace of Hispanism in Ecuador became embroiled within the regional and political divides of the *fin-de-siglo,* particularly in the aftermath of the 1895 Liberal Revolution.

"Transcending" Regionalism

Spain's attempts to overcome its regionalist divisions through an appeal to a hybrid trans-Atlantic cultural community had a strong resonance in Ecuadorian politics. The regionally biased strife of the nineteenth century had exposed severe divisions along ideological, cultural, and geographical lines. Nostalgia for the colonial period found early adherents among conservative politicians and clerics, of which former president Juan José Flores is a vivid example. As mentioned earlier, his disillusion with the state of the nation after his exile in the 1840s led him to embrace the idea that only a monarchy could restore the republic to some modicum of stability. After visiting the courts of Europe, he found a sympathetic ear in Spanish queen María Cristina, who flirted with the idea of outfitting an expeditionary force to retake the former Andean province. Out of desperation following the 1859 civil war, even García Moreno, whose personal antipathy toward all things Spanish was well known, invited Napoleon III to make Ecuador a Gallic protectorate. When that failed, he installed a neocolonial regime built upon the old pillars of church and landowner.

To nurture this alliance, García Moreno held his nose and approved the formation of a local chapter of the Real Academia Española de la Lengua (RAE) in 1874. This action paved the way for diplomatic rapprochement, bolstered his support with conservatives, and expanded cultural ties between the two countries. The Quito chapter of the RAE worked to reestablish formal diplomatic ties over the next decade, a goal achieved in February 1885, which was earlier than most of Ecuador's neighbors were able to accomplish that feat. The group also provided a local forum for Hispanophilic cultural events, including public discussion of linguistics and readings of current and classical literature. Two of the RAE's members, Julio Castro and the amateur historian Pedro Fermín Cevallos, expanded the reach of its activities when they founded the Quito chapter of Unión Iberoamericana in 1885. Local chapters in Guayaquil and the southern city of Machala followed. In 1889, the group inaugurated a newspaper that published laudatory portrayals of Spanish culture and called for a Hispanic trade communion.[25] Despite the group's obvious energy and initial enthusiasm from the public, financial difficulties resulted in the newspaper's early demise, though the center continued its activity.

The growth of Hispanophilia soon permeated liberal ranks as regard for the nation's Spanish heritage expanded. Even Juan Montalvo, staunch opponent of Spain's colonial occupation of Cuba, began to underscore the vitality of the Spanish spirit and the heroic deeds of the conquistadors in his later writings. This reverence for the rigor and independence of the Spanish spirit was most vividly depicted in his posthumously published *Capítulos que se olvidaron a Cervantes.* More than simply an appreciation of Spanish culture, this satire channeled the lampooning spirit of Cervantes in its depiction of the knight-errant's travels through small "Spanish" towns with an uncanny resemblance to those of Ecuador's Andean corridor. The corrupt politicians, stodgy priests, and greedy landlords Don Quixote encountered in Montalvo's depiction of the tour through La Mancha also spoofed contemporary Ecuadorian leaders.

Significantly, the dominant figure in the *fin-de-siglo* boom in Hispanist literature was Federico González Suárez.²⁶ González Suárez was also a prominent historian, and it was primarily in this capacity that he influenced the development of Ecuadorian Hispanism. His early work included essays on the ecclesiastical history of Ecuador and an archaeological study of the indigenous Cañari tribe, but it was his *Historia general de la República del Ecuador* that made his name as a scholar. The young priest conducted his research in Spanish archives between 1884 and 1886, years González Suárez spent in Spain under the wing of his mentor, Bishop Ordóñez of Cuenca. He even cajoled his way into the restricted Archive of the Indies in Seville. He also traveled throughout the country, meeting prominent intellectuals such as Marcos Jiménez de la Espada and Menéndez Pelayo. He developed a cordial academic friendship with the latter following their meeting in Madrid the summer of 1885 and sent him copies of the multiple volumes of the *Historia general,* not all of which reached their destination. Their communication ceased in the early years of the century, only to be re-ignited through the intervention of a Madrid-based bookseller, Gabriel Sánchez, who in 1907 offered Menéndez Pelayo a copy of *Historia de las Mohedanos* so that he could write the introduction to the Iberian edition of González Suárez's *Hermosura de la naturaleza y sentimiento estético de ella.*²⁷

Menéndez Pelayo's intellectual impact is readily apparent in González Suárez's *Historia general,* particularly in the Ecuadorian's shared embrace of Augustine's conception of history as the measure by which Providence would judge humanity.²⁸ History thus represents a *ciencia moral* in which the historian, by interpreting the past, facilitates national development in accordance with divine law.²⁹ The desire to recount the national past from the pre-Columbian era to the present engages this philosophy. In this context, the extensive archaeological studies of indigenous cultures serve as a backdrop when accentuating the civilizing mission of Spanish colonization. González Suárez argues against any significant indigenous contribution to national development following the initial struggle for supremacy.³⁰ Since the Spanish predominated, it was their institutions and culture that created Ecuador, and the indigenous cultures so painstakingly documented for the pre-Columbian era fade in the rest of the work. Equally striking is the resistance to documenting the struggle for independence and the national period, a choice that reflects González Suárez's Hispanist belief that Spanish culture formed the core of national identity.³¹

González Suárez's retreat from a racially hybrid constitution of national identity also takes on regionalist overtones, as the seven volumes of the *Historia general* display an overwhelming focus on the administrative and clerical development of Quito. This bias can be explained at least partially by the greater availability of documentation on the city, which, as the capital of the Audiencia, continues to overshadow scholarship on the colonial era. However, his minimizing of crucial events that occurred outside the city's purview, such as the rise of Guayaquil and Cuenca as alternative power centers in the eighteenth century, demonstrates the degree to which the prelate considered the capital to be a synecdoche for the nation. One of the most glaring examples of his Quito-centric approach occurs in a chapter, ostensibly devoted to the founding of the capital, in which he dispatches the establishment of Guayaquil and Portoviejo in just a few concluding paragraphs. While these were indeed lesser cities during the sixteenth century, the symbolism of this decision would not have been lost on contemporary readers. In snubbing Guayaquil—the economic base of the Liberal Party—and Portoviejo—the birthplace of its most charismatic leader (Eloy Alfaro)—González Suárez undercut the party's claim to a substantial portion of the national metanarrative.[32]

Despite this slight, liberals embraced the prelate's work after it raised conservative hackles as a result of his moderate views on social issues. The first few volumes inspired some criticism due to his treatment of the excesses of the Conquest. However, denunciations erupted in 1894 upon the release of the fourth *tomo,* in which he recounted the sexual misbehavior of seventeenth-century Dominican friars.[33] The work created an overnight scandal, and González Suárez, then archdeacon of Quito, was labeled an anti-Catholic, heretical liberal seeking to destroy the power of the Ecuadorian church. The loudest detractors were fellow clergy members, particularly Reginaldo Duranti, a Dominican prior, and Pedro Schumacher, the German-born bishop of Portoviejo. Duranti published a pamphlet challenging the veracity of González Suárez's research and the skewed treatment of the Dominican order while Schumacher circulated a letter condemning the work's educational value.[34] The scandal colored González Suárez's subsequent appointment to the empty bishopric of Ibarra, a position afforded him due to his international scholarly reputation and the Vatican's desire to place an Ecuadorian national in the post. He refused the appointment three times due to the controversy, only to be overruled by Rome. The triumph of the Liberal Revolution and exile of the majority of the national episcopacy by the end of 1895 led him to reconsider, and he was ordained that December, three months after Alfaro took Quito.

The Liberal government looked favorably upon the man whose supposed liberalism prompted rampaging mobs to clamor for his appointment as archbishop during the battles of 1895. In office, González Suárez would prove to be more of a moderate, using his reputation as leverage to challenge the erosion of church prerogatives during Alfaro's and Plaza's first presidential terms. He took a pragmatic approach and sought to avoid the charge of partisanship, an attitude that served him well during such volatile times. For instance, in 1900, he publicly condemned a planned invasion by conservative forces massed at the Colombian border, arguing that patriotism was a Christian virtue that over-ruled partisan affiliations. While this statement engendered another round of reactionary criticism, it helped defuse a potential civil war by delegitimizing the insurgency. In addition, it bolstered his standing with the Liberal government. The Vatican recognized a star in the making and elevated him to archbishop of Quito in 1906. The prelate used his leverage to mitigate anticlerical reforms and rebuild the episcopacy. He also turned his attention to pedagogy, passing the torch of historical criticism to a new generation of scholars who would crystal-lize his vision of a nation rooted in local mores, Hispanist pride, and Catholic universalism. These students would eventually become the founders of a new and critical institution in the development of Ecuadorian Hispanism.

The National Academy of History

Although he consistently avoided embracing a political party, González Suárez was mindful of the political role that historical study played. The scan-dal surrounding the publication of his history, after all, had precipitated the fall of a government and demonstrated the power that the past had on the con-temporary mind. While he had remained silent when attacked by Duranti and Schumacher at the time, in a posthumously published treatise on his method-ology he defended the decision to include the scandalous material in order to levy the judgment of history upon the development of the nation. The uproar, however, convinced him that the sores of independence and nation building re-mained too raw to be analyzed impartially, as much by himself as his audience. This lack of critical distance, despite almost a century having passed, made the continuation of his general history "inopportune." He therefore brought his opus to a truncated close on the eve of independence and shifted his energies to his clerical responsibilities, which had increased dramatically after the Liberal Revolution.[35]

The historian's perspective does not completely drop out of the sermons and political tracts he penned furiously during the early twentieth century. Many of these pieces reveal the analytical line he would probably have followed regarding the national period and reflect his embrace of Catholicism as the primary boon from Spain and best hope for national redemption. This is well summarized in a 1908 encyclical entitled "De la actitud que conviene a los católicos seglares en el Ecuador en las circunstancias presentes." In this essay, González Suárez reviews the trajectory of nineteenth-century politics and its relationship with religion. He argues that liberals avoided anticlericalism prior to 1860 because they found their definition in a strictly antidictatorial stance. While García Moreno briefly managed to unite politics and religion, his administration has been criticized because of the partisanship subsequently grafted onto spiritual matters. In his essay, González Suárez seeks an end to this muddle by advancing Catholicism as a path to national unity, noting that even the most rabidly anticlerical members of the Radical Liberal Party were closet Catholics. He also exhorts the bishops and priests of the land to disengage from the political squabbles of the day to accelerate this process of unification.[36]

The intellectual roots of the pleas made in this 1908 essay are varied and deep. There is a clear resonance with the calls for national and transnational regeneration typical of the Hispanist vernacular. An additional influence, which would prove a bridge to the new generation, was the endorsement of Catholic social action advocated by Pope Leo XIII in his encyclical *Rerum Novarum*, a text that González Suárez regularly cited in sermons and writings. These ideas inspired a short-lived attempt to form a Catholic workers' organization led by a local tailor, Manuel Sotomayor y Luna, and a number of students at the Colegio San Gabriel, Quito's premier Jesuit secondary school. Although the Centro Obrero Católico devolved into squabbling between the organization's membership of artisanal laborers and elite, largely conservative teenagers, the experiment served to cement a friendship between González Suárez and some of the country's future intellectual leaders, including the important figures Jacinto Jijón y Caamaño and Julio Tobar Donoso.[37] The architects of a restored Conservative Party in the 1920s that also built alliances with labor, these two individuals would be among the leaders in crafting a consideration of local and national identity that stemmed directly from González Suárez's theory of history.

González Suárez began to promulgate his conception of Ecuador's Hispanic roots with Jijón and other young intellectuals at *tertulias,* or literary salons, concerning historical and archaeological studies that he began hosting in 1908. The following year, in part to draw Jijón's mind away from the recent death of his mother, the archbishop formalized the group as the Sociedad Ecuatoriana de Estudios Históricos Americanos (SEEHA). The membership also included the art historian José Gabriel Navarro, Jijón's cousin and genealogist Cristóbal Gangotena y Jijón, and Carlos Manuel Larrea. Though mostly of conservative political orientation, with Gangotena's moderate liberalism tempered by his obsession with aristocratic lineage, the group sought to avoid partisan historical writing in deference to their mentor, who circulated his methodological treatise among his charges. More moderate liberals joined in 1915 with the addition of Celiano Monge and a literary critic from Otavalo named Isaac Barrera, best known for his enthusiasm for avant-garde literature and for his well-regarded biography of liberal founding father Vicente Rocafuerte. When González Suárez died in 1917, Jijón took the helm and expanded the society's activities to include the publication of a bulletin he bankrolled. Their self-proclaimed professionalism, based largely on a penchant for extensive citation and their contention that previous work was mired in legend and hyperbole, received national acclaim. Their reputation as the premier school of historical research encouraged Congress to declare them the National Academy of History (Academia Nacional de

Historia, or ANH) in 1920, just in time for the centennial festivities marking Guayaquil and Quito's liberation from Spain, events that invited extemporaneous panegyrics to national greatness. This prestigious title as a national academy provided a platform from which to make their ostensibly impartial view of Ecuador's Spanish and Catholic roots the official national saga.[38]

Perhaps the defining work of this era is a Jijón essay published in 1919 that challenges the eighteenth-century claims of Jesuit Juan de Velasco concerning the existence of a pre-Incaic Kingdom of Quito. Following the earlier writings of González Suárez, Jijón disputes the notion of an autochthonous, proto-national polity or economic confederation. He dismisses Velasco for having based his claims on oral legend rather than on archaeological evidence. Jijón also critiques a contemporary study by Paul Rivet (who had hosted the precocious youngster a few years earlier in Paris) reporting that bronze tools had been in use prior to the arrival of the Incas, another controversial statement hinting at the possibility of a civilizing impulse among the "barbaric" Ecuadorian indigenes.

The obvious politicization of Jijón's article drew complaints from the Left—particularly from the pen of the Loja socialist Pío Jaramillo Alvarado, whose polemical El indio ecuatoriano inspired future indigenist writings.[39] The ongoing controversy propelled Jijón to the forefront of the Conservative Party, for which he stood as presidential candidate in 1924. His loss in this disputed election led to a failed coup attempt, a short exile in Colombia, and his official distancing from the ANH. In the aftermath of the Julian Revolution, Jijón returned to Ecuador as the undisputed leader of the Conservative Party. The platform he engineered from this position gave rise to a two-volume ideological treatise titled Política conservadora (1929). Besides delineating the party's positions on economic and social matters, the text presented a historical account of the formulation of national identity arguing that the Conquest and Christian devotion transformed the American continent and brought its aboriginal inhabitants into the cradle of civilization.[40] Jijón viewed Quito as the epicenter of this civilizing Catholic nation because of its ability to evolve beyond its provincialism by becoming an artistic and spiritual fountainhead for the rest of the Hispanic world during the seventeenth century.[41]

Jijón's articulation of Quito's unique cultural merits deployed a trope that originated with González Suárez but was largely popularized by his former colleagues in the National Academy of History. Jijón's fellow conservative, Julio Tobar Donoso, for instance, wrote a series of essays describing the Catholic sensibility of the Ecuadorian nation along with biographical sketches of outstanding members of the colonial creole elite.[42] Isaac Barrera suspended his modernist leanings to contribute a panegyric to Quito's eighteenth-century cultural development. Published in honor of the centennial of the Battle of Pichincha, this volume recounted the celebratory events and documented the beautification measures pursued by the Junta del Centenario, an independent committee that Barrera led.[43] He also included an extended rumination on the artistic glory of the city's colonial monuments—the churches and palaces that Barrera claimed overshadowed its modern façade. Perhaps the most ardent Hispanophile was Jijón's cousin, Cristóbal de Gangotena y Jijón, who compiled genealogical studies of the city's original *vecino* families, including the Fernandez Salvador clan, the Icazas, and the Borjas. Published in the National Academy of History's bulletin, these works were intended to form the basis of an unfinished magnum opus providing a comprehensive history of "*la raza blanca*" within Ecuador.[44]

Gangotena is best known, however, for a popular work that grew from his self-described "antiquarian mania." This was a collection of *tradiciones*—satirical *costumbrista* vignettes pioneered by Peruvian Ricardo Palma in the 1870s—that heightened the nostalgic qualities of colonial and independence era Quito. Gangotena's *Al margen de la historia: leyendas de pícaros, frailes y caballeros* (1924) presents an idealized and nostalgic portrait of the city, a community of courteous and pious people whose troubles seemed far from the burgeoning social chaos of the present day. This is a picaresque world in which colonial officials might discover images of the Virgin Mary in a spot of lard on their empanadas, hot air balloons might land in the middle of nunneries, and ghosts could offer chivalric greetings to women, the elderly, and the infirm. In the end, these rambunctious antics come to a close, order is restored, and a romanticized Quito endures.[45]

Gangotena and his colleagues coupled their popular appeals to Hispanist sensibilities with activist calls for historic preservation couched as necessary for the survival of *la raza*. Again, this was an endeavor pioneered by González Suárez, who, in his discussion of colonial arts in the *Historia general,* had already espoused protecting the stone façades of local churches from the late nineteenth-century practice of whitewashing.[46] The primary advocate in this endeavor was art historian José Gabriel Navarro, one of the original members of the Sociedad Ecuatoriana de Estudios Históricos Americanos and an enthusiastic exponent of the Hispanic origins of Quito's architectural monumentality, whom we have already met due to his role in the Comité France-Amérique's commemoration of La Condamine's eighteenth-century visit.

Born in 1881, Navarro was a young prodigy who studied with the greatest *quiteño* painters of the late nineteenth century, Rafael Salas and the *costumbrista* Joaquín Pinto. He was among the first students to register at the newly created Escuela de Bellas Artes in 1905, eventually joining the faculty and then becoming its director for fifteen years. In 1925, he published the first volume of an extensive history of colonial art titled *Contribuciones a la historia del arte en el Ecuador.* He followed it up with *La escultura en el Ecuador (siglos XVI al XVIII),* which won the grand prize in the 1927 Concurso de la Raza hosted by the Real Academia de Bellas Artes in Madrid. On the strength of this résumé, he was appointed consul general to Spain in 1928 and resided in Madrid and Seville for the next three years. He acted as Ecuador's cultural representative at the 1929 Ibero-American Exposition and helped organize a Madrid exhibition dedicated

Fig. 3.1. The façade of San Francisco in Quito alludes to the towers of Spain's Patio de los Reyes at El Escorial. Courtesy Library of Congress, Prints & Photographs Division, lot 2779.

to Spanish art in the Indies and held in May and June 1930. He was named minister of foreign relations in 1933 and represented Ecuador at various pan-American summits throughout the decade.[47] His political activity decreased in the 1940s, but he continued to travel and publish widely through the 1960s.

Navarro's main argument, reiterated in numerous books, articles, and speeches, claims that colonial Quito stood as an artistic center rivaled in the Americas only by Mexico.[48] He attributes this phenomenon to the quickness with which Quito's indigenous inhabitants were able to absorb the teachings of European artists, especially the able sculptors who developed the polychromatic sculpture for which Quito was famous. In so doing, however, Navarro minimizes the artistic contribution made by these artisans. He highlights the city's Spanish roots by emphasizing the role of Franciscan training schools and the use of Spanish construction practices. He underscores Spanish and Moroccan features in Quito's colonial monuments, such as the obvious debt the bell towers of San Francisco (fig. 3.1) owe to those on the western façade of El Escorial abutting the Patio de los Reyes (fig. 3.2).[49] The influence of indigenous artistic traditions in features such as the gold leafing adorning San Francisco's interior columns he dismisses as minimal and incidental. Although the colonial architecture of Quito exhibits fewer traces of indigenous iconography than that of other regional centers, Navarro exaggerates this aspect to support a view of Spain as a civilizing force.[50]

The image of Spain as a benevolent patron not only addressed Ecuador's race problem but also responded to a concurrent movement battling the Black

Fig. 3.2. In addition to the bell towers, elements from the entryway of the western façade of the royal monastery of El Escorial in Spain, shown here, appear in Quito's San Francisco. Courtesy Library of Congress, Prints & Photographs Division, lot 7736.

Legend, which originated in the work of Las Casas and concerned the merciless Iberian conquistadors. The Dominican friar's castigations had long inspired Anglo-Saxon antipathy to Spain while Spanish American intellectuals saw Las Casas as an early advocate of imperial reform. However, as Christopher Schmidt-Nowara has demonstrated, figures like Cuban José Antonio Saco and Honduran Carlos Gutiérrez referenced Las Casas not only to demand social reforms but also to assert the generosity of a Spanish civilizing mission based on conversion and fraternity between Spain and the Americas. While jingoistic nationalists continued to view Las Casas as a traitor, some intellectuals such as conservative Antonio María Fabé and Madrid philosopher Emilio Castelar began to propose a countervailing "White Legend" along these lines.[51] Menéndez Pelayo helped popularize this approach, which began to grow increasingly bellicose after 1898. This version of the argument was most succinctly expressed in Julián Juderías y Loyot's 1914 work, *Leyenda negra y la verdad histórica,* which held that Spain's devotion to religion and art made it the greatest civilizing force the world had ever known.

Navarro embraced this strident version of the White Legend and elevated Quito as a symbolic pillar of the defense. For example, he delivered a speech in 1929 suggesting that Quito, with its "splendid edifices, convents and churches of rare magnificence, paintings and statues, formidable amounts of civil and religious furnishings, jewels with delicate silverwork, etc. . . . was a mute witness advocating [in Spain's defense]."[52] The following year he extended this emphasis on the value of Spanish construction in a testament to municipal organization. For Navarro, the founding and construction of cities like Quito, "the most Castilian in America," displayed the superiority of a *raza* whose focus on cultural development elevated it above the economic view of colonization prevalent in other powers, such as Britain or France.[53]

To promote this vision of Spanish cultural superiority, Navarro highlighted specific examples of Quito's high baroque architecture. Most commonly, he maintained that the city's churches, especially those of San Francisco and La Compañía, embodied the spiritual artistry of the city. Emphasizing church architecture not only gave a religious resonance to the identification of Quito as Spanish but also served to pinpoint the spatial location of Spain's presence in the old center. Navarro also contrasted the emblems of colonial architecture with modern styles. Although he stopped short of outright criticism of contemporary trends, he deplored the alteration of traditional construction and the many modernizing face-lifts given to colonial structures. He thus advocated strict conservation of Quito's treasures, arguing that doing so would have practical benefits by encouraging tourism.

A good example of Navarro's critique of modern architecture can be seen in a 1926 article titled "De cómo Quito sería siempre un centro de turismo." In this text, he recalls the Italian painter Giulio Sartorio, who had praised the city as the Athens of the New World. Navarro argues that Quito is owed a place in the pantheon of world arts next to Florence, Venice, or Constantinople despite the recent onslaught of an avalanche of modern vulgarity that threatened the city's distinctive Andalusian portals, Castilian porticos, and monochrome green-tile patios. Navarro suggests "*quiteño* unity in the cult to the past" to arrest this process, calling on the state to help preserve the disappearing traces of the past, such as the fountains that once adorned the city's plazas but had been removed following the introduction of potable water. Through active conservation, Navarro hoped that "Quito's extraordinary beauty will promote its preservation, since the devotion of curious strangers will ensure that the city is always a center of tourism."[54]

Navarro's project to defend Quito's artistic heritage had few adherents in the 1920s, as modern eclectic styles that avoided Spanish colonial architectural tropes remained popular. However, his fellows in the ANH began to follow his lead, first through studies of other colonial monuments, such as Juan de Dios Navas's writings on the chapel of Guápulo in the city's eastern environs. Julio Tobar Donoso also echoed Navarro's plea for conservation in his speech inducting Navas into the ANH, claiming that modern architecture threatened to destroy "el genio peculiar de la ciudad" unless checked by conservation efforts.[55] The identification of Quito with Spain and in particular with the artistic glories of its colonial architecture, however, got its greatest boost in 1934, when the city celebrated the four-hundredth anniversary of its Spanish founding.

The Invention of *Seis de Diciembre*

Travelers who visit Quito today during the month of December can experience the elaborate festivities held to celebrate the city's founding. Wine, beer, and *aguardiente* flow in abundance as revelers in Spanish costume gaily cavort across the city in open-air buses called *chivas* while singing the city's anthems. Until bullfighting's abolition this year, matadors from across the world would descend on the capital for a weeklong series of *corridas*, where they were met by performative protests by defenders of animal and indigenous rights seeking a national platform in which to advance an alternative vision of local history. The party that has become both a national holiday and a defining moment in Quito's civic calendar, however, has its origins in a gimmick promulgated by the National Academy of History—with the support of then–municipal council president Jacinto Jijón—which hoped to popularize its Hispanist vision of local and national identity.

The 1934 commemoration of the quadricentennial of Quito's Spanish founding on December 6 was the first time the anniversary was officially celebrated. The largest public holidays of the nineteenth and early twentieth century remained religious festivities, especially the myriad costume balls held between Christmas and Epiphany and even the Carnival water fights. The main civic holidays included the anniversaries of August 10, 1809 (Independence Day) and of the Battle of Pichincha, when Quito was liberated from the Spanish on May 24, 1822. Civic holidays grew more important in the early twentieth century, as the state held national expositions to celebrate the first centennials of these independence holidays in 1909 and 1922. These celebrations anticipated the politicization of 1934 as they provided a rationale for state and municipal beautification and development projects in the capital. The new December 6 holiday thus represented the continuation of a trend but with a slightly different orientation. Instead of producing a mythscape highlighting the city and nation's modernity and liberal cosmopolitanism, as had earlier centennials, the new celebrations elevated the past to a position of honor and proclaimed Quito a fundamentally Hispanic city.[56]

A key issue in this project concerned which date to celebrate. Although Benalcázar had first entered the city on December 6, 1534, Diego de Almagro first ordered the creation of an administrative center on the ruins of the pre-Columbian citadel on August 28 of that year. Beginning with González Suárez, historians had focused on the earlier date because, under Spanish law, the installation of a cabildo determined the legal autonomy of an urban settlement. The August date was still favored by ANH president Celiano Monge in a June 1931 communiqué to the municipality suggesting they plan a celebration worthy of the city's four-hundredth birthday.[57] However, a study published in the *Gaceta Municipal* the following year by José Rumazo González, assistant to the municipal archivist, favored the celebration of Benalcázar's entry. Rumazo challenged the traditional prioritizing of the administrative framework by arguing instead that it was the grid that Benalcázar had traced upon his arrival that had determined the future shape of the city. Implicit within this contention was a dismissal of the lasting importance of the Incaic settlement in the Quito valley, a position that expanded traditional Hispanophilia beyond the civilizational arguments usually advanced.[58] A slightly expanded version of the article was republished in August 1933 in the Quito daily *El Comercio,* fueling ongoing controversy. In January 1934, the municipal council attempted to address the issue by asking its newly appointed president, Jacinto Jijón y Caamaño, to prepare a report establishing the proper date of the centennial.[59] Jijón presented his opinions two months later.

Jijón's report agrees with González Suárez's selection of August 28. Ever the archaeologist, Jijón begins the study with a brief introduction to the various pre-Columbian tribes that lived near Quito, concluding that, prior to the Spanish arrival, Incan invaders incorporated the city in a frontier zone between two established populations. He thus acknowledges that it is improper to speak of the "founding" of a new conurbation in 1534 because an existing population had already settled the area. He therefore prioritized the administrative step as had his forebears, arguing that the establishment of the first municipal council marked the initiation of the Spanish era for the city and the nation.[60]

Despite Jijón's scholarly position, the municipality opted to celebrate both dates while emphasizing Benalcázar's arrival, in effect advancing Rumazo's claim that a new city and civilization began with the physical arrival of the Spanish and their spatial colonization of the territory.[61] The national government followed suit, declaring a civic holiday for both dates, noting that "the founding of the city of Quito has to be considered the beginning and even the basis of the Ecuadoran nationality."[62] Months of celebratory events ensued, including daily parades, pageants, and parties during December. Although many of these events consisted of secular celebrations, such as interprovincial football games or charitable balls, celebration of the city's Spanish heritage dominated the social calendar. Several of these memorials extended the identification of the city's religious monuments as the key to its Hispanic spirit. On December 5, for instance, the city government placed six plaques displaying the names and coats of arms of Quito's first 240 *vecinos* not on the presidential palace or the municipal hall itself but on the cathedral's façade. An exhibition of the artistic treasures of San Francisco, La Merced, and San Agustín opened on December 6 with special papal permission, while the day's celebrations were capped with the unveiling of a massive stone statue of a stern González Suárez overlooking the cobblestones of San Francisco's plaza. Other events held during the month included the dedication of a plaque to Jodoco Ricke, the city's first Franciscan

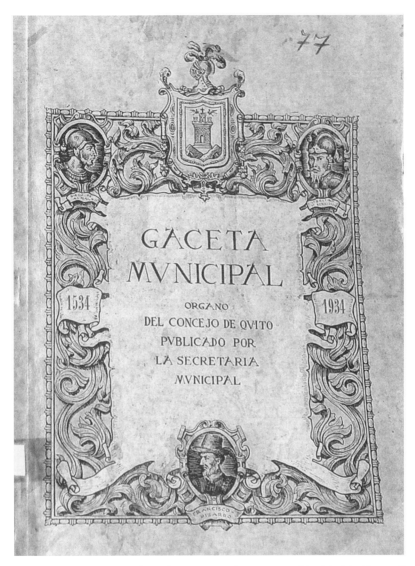

Fig. 3.3. Cover, *Gaceta Municipal* 19:77 (August 28, 1934). Courtesy Archivo Histórico Metropolitano, Quito.

friar, and a design contest to produce colonial architecture "using modern construction techniques."[63]

Perhaps the most impressive element of the centennial, however, concerned the sheer amount of material published to commemorate the anniversary. It ranged from special issues of literary journals to the six-section edition of the Quito daily, *El Comercio,* to collections of historical essays by schoolchildren. The municipality, however, outpaced the others in its celebratory zeal.

For example, it initiated a series of reprints of historic documents that continues today. The first four volumes appeared in 1934 and reproduced the "Libro Verde," which contained the earliest records of the city cabildo.[64] Besides these collectors' items, the *Gaceta Municipal* printed commemorative editions for the August and December anniversaries in which the Hispanist bias of the municipal council, then led by Jijón, can be easily noted. The cover of both editions, for instance, replaced the magazine's earlier minimalist format with a baroque design, framed by an ornate border, with the city's coat of arms surrounded by inset portraits of Almagro and Benalcázar. An image of Francisco Pizarro at the bottom edge completes this tribute to Quito's Spanish heritage, which was retained over the next two decades before the municipality suspended publication of the gazette altogether (fig. 3.3). The content of the two volumes, one for the August anniversary and one for the December anniversary, also exhibits a strong desire to identify the city with its Spanish heritage.

The August issue focuses exclusively on the city's colonial past.[65] It includes essays on Jodoco Ricke, the first minutes recorded by the colonial cabildo, and González Suárez's account of his research trip to Seville. Tributes to the conquistadors by prominent intellectuals such as literary historian Isaac Barrera, the conservative essayist Remigio Crespo Toral, and the director of the National Library, Zoila Ugarte de Landívar, round out the volume.

The illustrations and photographs included throughout confirm the emphasis on the city's colonial monuments and Spanish heritage.[66] A pictorial essay on San Francisco begins with a reproduction of a 1785 painting depicting the city's first Franciscan friar, Jodoco Ricke, baptizing an indigenous family in an evocative reference to Navarro's advocacy of the White Legend. Portraits of the church's celebrated architecture follow, including both a street-level image of the oft-photographed main façade and a somewhat more unusual overhead shot of the circular stairwell off the plaza. The next image, which depicts the yet-to-be-erected statue of González Suárez, furthers the square's identification with the heroism of the city's Hispanist intelligentsia. Similar spotlights on the architecture of the nearby churches of La Merced and Santo Domingo come next. The photographs conclude with portraits of the monarchs who ruled from Iberia during Quito's colonial era, from Charles V to Ferdinand VII.[67]

While the *Gaceta Municipal* from August 1934 emphasized the colonial era, the December issue attempted to draw a bridge between that past and the modern present. This effort began with the introductory remarks, in which the editor notes his intention to evaluate whether the city had advanced far enough over its four hundred years. The issue includes a multitude of essays, photographs, paintings, and other items that attempt to reference the past but also elevate the present. The juxtaposition can seem strange, such as the interruption of an essay about the famous colonial painter Miguel de Santiago with photographs of recently erected worker housing in the Barrio Obrero, on the southern edge of the city.[68] Nevertheless, the issue posits a continuum between the splendors of the city's golden age and its future, suggesting an active engagement with the Hispanist tenet that redemption comes by way of embracing history. In effect, the issue theorizes tradition as the redeeming force behind genuine national growth, a stance articulated by Jijón in *Política conservadora* and one that formed the basis for his administration's social policies. Quito's centennial thus became a rallying point for the pursuit of a regenerating tradition in accord with a *hispanista* conception of the past and the possibilities for future glory.

Many other commemorative publications followed a similar structure. *El Comercio,* for example, introduced its special issue with a Navarro essay elaborating his perennial call for preserving the city as a relic of colonial architecture.[69] The editors bolstered his contention with a series of images picturing the jewels of the *centro* and the growing architectonic segregation of the city. The first set depicted "Quito tradicional" and juxtaposed some of the first nineteenth-century photographs of Quito with contemporary images. Significantly, the editors buried only an occasional shot of modest modern buildings among the more grandiose and numerous shots of colonial structures. A second set of photographs titled "Quito nuevo" complemented this edited vision in reverse—by including contemporary structures on the northern and southern edges of the city.[70] The one exception to this rule was a rather lovely shot presenting the intersection of García Moreno and Sucre streets as a mixture of the old and new. Four centuries are represented in this photograph: an early colonial home belonging to R. Vásconez Gómez and probably from the seventeenth century, the edge of La Compañía (completed in 1765), Rosa Chiriboga's nineteenth-century neoclassical mansion, and Francisco Durini's Banco Central headquarters. This last structure, despite being the only twentieth-century edifice represented, was the exception that proved the rule, for Durini had paid loving tribute to La Compañía in his façade, using the same andesite stone and abstracting its ornamentation.[71]

El Comercio also highlighted the civilizing force of the Spanish conquistadors in its commemorative volume, echoing the framework utilized in the *Gaceta Municipal* publication from August. Guillermo Bustos has highlighted the particular significance of a dramatization of Benalcázar's entry into Quito drawn by contemporary artist José Yépez and reproduced on the front page of the newspaper's second section, which was devoted to the centennial.[72] The foreground features the conquistador astride a horse, which is flanked by fellow soldiers and a friar, presumably Ricke. The inclusion of a pair of Amerindians kneeling on the ground to offer food and drink to the Spaniard clarifies the message of the artwork as a reification of the civilizing narrative typical of Ecuadorian Hispanism. As Bustos notes, its prominent placement in the special section of the newspaper crystallizes the innate superiority of the Spanish portion of the nation's character.

The Chronotope of Hispanic Heritage

Despite the merits of his analysis, Bustos mistakenly argues that the celebrations of 1934 represented an isolated commemoration with minimal connection to contemporary celebrations of December 6.[73] Over the next two decades, the Hispanist membership of the National Academy of History and the conservative leadership of the municipality systematically codified their interpretation of the city's role as the repository of the Spanish center of national identity even as the celebrations dropped from the public consciousness. This systematic effort started in the late 1930s as the council began to hold an annual "*sesión solemne*" to commemorate the founding. The cult to Benalcázar's memory accompanied this ritual, beginning with Jijón's publication of the first volume of his exhaustive (and unfinished) biography in 1936.[74] In November 1942, the city inaugurated a special decoration named the Orden de Honor de Caballeros de Quito Sebastián de Benalcázar, which was given annually to citizens who had contributed in an outstanding manner to the city's development in the previous year.[75] In 1949, the city unveiled a statue in Benalcázar's likeness in front of an eighteenth-century neoclassical structure built on the site where the conquistador's own house had once stood, with the journalist, diplomat, and *hispanista* Gonzalo Zaldumbide presenting the introductory remarks at the unveiling.[76] In subsequent years, this so-called Casa de Benalcázar would become a pilgrimage site for local Hispanists, and today it houses the Instituto Ecuatoriana de Cultura Hispánica as well as a museum of colonial sculpture.[77] By 1959, the identification of Quito with this recently invented holiday had become so strong that the afternoon newspaper *Últimas Noticias* published a call for the entire city to celebrate the anniversary, which it did, with riotous merrymaking in the streets.[78] The popular celebrations that ensued never abandoned the stately embrace of a Hispanic sensibility, as evidenced by the yearly bullfights, Iberian garb, and political strife that continue to mark the holiday in its present form.

The vision of Quito's *centro* as a living museum promulgated by Navarro, Jijón, and others garnered extensive institutional support. The postcards discussed in chapter 1 and maps from chapter 2 represent some of the earliest efforts by the national government to apply this idea but certainly not the last, as the movement to promote the city's tourist potential continued. By 1938, the foreign press had so internalized Quito's Spanish identity that the *New York World-Telegram* presented a photograph of the Plaza de la Independencia highlighting the cathedral (fig. 3.4), with San Francisco's towers in the background, and an accompanying caption encouraging American tourists to experience this "colorful" city where "the camera virtually shows a bit of Spain transplanted in Quito."[79] Two years later, the priests of San Francisco emerged from the cloister

Fig. 3.4. "Bit of Spain in South America," *New York World Telegram*. Courtesy Library of Congress, Prints & Photographs Division, NYWTS

to authorize a visitor's guide that marketed the quaintness of their monastery, previously off limits to all but its residents.[80]

This international profile dovetailed with an expansion of preservation laws adopted by the city and national governments and overseen by figures such as Navarro and Gangotena y Jijón. By the end of the 1930s, the municipality required special permits to build in the *centro,* even from clerical groups repairing or altering their structures.[81] Perhaps the most important moment in the history of the old city center's survival happened when Navarro wooed a young Uruguayan architect named Guillermo Jones Odriozola to provide a comprehensive zoning plan for the city, which was formally adopted in 1942 and enshrined the colonial core, or *casco colonial,* as a protected zone. Although the district later became a lower-income neighborhood and many of its monumental structures deteriorated, the integrity of the colonial city remained unmatched among South American capitals. As a result, this architectural showcase hosted an international gathering in 1967 to bolster Latin American monuments, which in turn gave rise to the so-called Charter of Quito calling for rehabilitation of colonial centers. The Ecuadorian government followed this move with the formation of a committee to study the potential for rehabilitating the historic center. UNESCO funding subsidized the group after the global agency's 1972 summit establishing the World Heritage program. By 1977, the group's efforts led to the Coloquio de Quito, a meeting at which the *centro* was declared a national heritage site along with several other sites of interest in the surrounding regions. In addition, officials at the colloquium adopted the "Plan piloto de Quito" as the blueprint for a new cycle of preservation. UNESCO capitalized on the city's name recognition and the following year honored Quito as the first city to be named a World Heritage Site, finally actualizing Navarro's desire that it achieve global recognition as one of the architecturally great capitals of the world. The city government has slowly embraced further preservation over the last thirty years, including a major push since the early 1990s under a series of progressive municipal administrations that have persuaded many local and international businesses to reinvest in Quito's core.

This history of preservation has continued to reinforce the chronotope marking Quito as a Spanish city. Historians such as Ernesto de la Orden Miracle and José María Vargas took up Navarro's art historical work through the 1970s. These intellectuals conferred with architectural preservationists, such as Toledo's J. M. González de Valcárcel, who drew up the volume accompanying the 1970s restoration pilot plan.[82] The Spanish government has continued to support these sorts of efforts, especially during the 1990s. Together with the municipalities of Andalucía and of Quito, the Spanish produced a series of studies of the monumental core's history, structural problems, and the possibilities for its long-term conservation, echoing the work that Navarro began in the 1920s.

The conservation of the city advocated by the city's Hispanist intelligentsia would have been impossible without the active collaboration of the municipal government, which represented the effort's single most important institutional advocate. This support was partly due to the fact that many prominent Hispanist preservationists also sat on the council, particularly during the 1930s, when figures such as Gangotena, Navarro, and Jijón served multiple terms as cabildo members, with Jijón acting as president during the 1934 quadricentennial celebrations. The embrace of city politics by these intellectuals, though informed by a desire to protect architectural treasures and manipulate the cultural mythology of Quito's Hispanic character, also grew out of a detailed political program espoused by Jijón's Conservative Party. This agenda advocated the restoration of municipal prerogatives over local planning and resource management across the nation. The Conservatives' program launched a new incarnation of a tug-of-war between the Quito cabildo and the national government that started in the nineteenth century but grew increasingly urgent with the burgeoning real estate market in the city's environs.

Chapter 4

Governance and the Sovereign Cabildo

In September 1895, the day after his victorious entry into Quito, the new president, Eloy Alfaro, penned a letter to Carlos Freile, the newly appointed governor of Pichincha, bemoaning the capital's lack of basic services. Bristling at the city's underdevelopment, he declared his immediate intention to authorize up to fifty thousand sucres for the construction of a central market. The Viejo Luchador also pledged future funding for other badly needed public works, arguing that "this capital has been quite badly maintained."[1] The bluster of this communiqué, intended to discredit the Progressive governments of the previous decade, obscured Alfaro's equally important commitment to building an alliance with the municipal council. Each promised reform had been requested yearly by the city council during the previous decade only to be refused by a state bereft of funds. In offering to support the realization of these reforms, Alfaro hoped to establish a loyal following among members of the local government of a city long known as a conservative bastion.

The cabildo benefited from the patronage of the Liberal state, but this alliance did not last. The pressures and potential profits occasioned by the capital's growing population, expanding real estate market, and developing sociospatial segregation instead led the Concejo Municipal de Quito to play a lone hand as it attempted to safeguard its autonomy over urban planning. This prerogative had been guaranteed under the Spanish Crown but slowly eroded during the nineteenth century as part of state centralization efforts. In attempting to restore its previous privileges, the city government sought to develop a narrative recasting local governance as a quintessential value of national identity and universal progress. This chronotope engaged international debates regarding urban form and planning that were reconsidered and revised to conform with and respond to local political, economic, and racial conflicts.

The quest for autonomy achieved its zenith under the auspices of revamped Conservative leadership during the 1930s. During a moment of national political and economic chaos, leaders like Jacinto Jijón y Caamaño and Gustavo Mortensen successfully engineered Quito's emergence as an autonomous regional center. Their program offered both a reconsidered vision of the municipality's historic role as caretaker of national fortune as well as sustained paternalist engagement with the pressures of emerging class conflict. Their resulting clout allowed not only for the achievement of long-sought municipal autonomy but also the crystallization of a hierarchical sociospatial order harkening to the racial and class segregation of the colonial era. Their crowning achievement, the 1942 Plan Regulador de Quito drafted by Uruguayan architect Guillermo Jones Odriozola, provided a blueprint for the city's future development along these lines.

Quito's planning process has long been understood as a political struggle. Most of the studies that have appeared since 1980 have built upon Manuel Castells's contention that urban planning systematically operated as elites colluded to limit subaltern access and opportunity in the modern city. Lucas Achig and Fernando Carrión, for example, maintain that real estate speculation in the city during the 1930s successfully enabled elite incursions into the northern environs and set the stage for racial segregation across the city.[2] Eduardo Kingman follows sociologist Pierre Bourdieu to charge that the creation of an internationally legible constitution of an urban *habitus* bolstered by considerations of hygiene and beautification diminished public consideration of indigenous and subaltern contributions to Quito's social milieu in the early twentieth century. Like Achig and Carrión, he considers the municipality a natural ally with elite developers and the national state in this endeavor.[3] Demarcating shifting power arrangements—in which the city government regularly clashed with its supposed collaborators—demonstrates that the municipality followed an institutional logic that transcended partisan affiliations in which the search for autonomous control over planning was paramount.

The success of this effort depended on articulating a specific vision of both history and modernity that placed the municipality at the center of a broader metanarrative of global import. Quito's displacement by Guayaquil as the dominant political and economic center of the country complicated this task, as it necessitated the negotiation of an identity and politics commensurate with Quito's simultaneous status as "capital" and "second city." In this regard, Quito ought to be considered a relatively unique specimen among Latin American capitals. Unlike Mexico City, Buenos Aires, or Lima, the Ecuadorian metropolis never had hegemonic primacy. Indeed, its particular brand of tradable historicity can be more fruitfully compared to the positioning common to secondary centers whose economic and political import has largely faded, for example, Cuzco or Oaxaca.[4] These cities, however, never experienced the simultaneous responsibilities and opportunities that accompanied the status of national capital, which provided greater state impetus for sustaining local development.

Several factors affected the success of this balancing act, including the relationship between the city and national governments, access to and control over planning funds, and, perhaps most importantly, the ability to articulate the municipal council's dual nature as a bastion of both modernity and heritage. These three factors had a collective impact on the process of urban planning during three distinctive epochs. During the late nineteenth century, Progressive local governments strained against both state-imposed budgetary limits as well as an internal ambivalence as to the value of "progress" in the isolated Andean polis. After 1895, the Liberal Revolution's sustained modernization program affected the relationship between city and state. Despite the great advances fostered by collaboration between the two levels of government, the state utilized public works to accentuate its own prestige at the expense of urban autonomy. By the late 1910s, this nepotistic system had bankrupted the city council and led to the inauguration of an independent but congressionally brokered planning commission that crippled urban self-governance. During the late 1920s and 1930s, a moment in which a weak national government suffered from the ill effects of the Great Depression, municipal governments sought to restore their control over planning. This struggle came to fruition under a series of activist municipalities dominated by a resurgent Conservative Party that deployed a selective reimagining of the city's colonial history and fomented fears of unregulated real estate speculation to justify a paternalist reorganization of urban space under their control. The crowning event in this program, the adoption of Jones Odriozola's master plan in 1942, codified a new sociospatial and political order in the city that would dominate Quito's subsequent twentieth-century story.

The Rise and Fall of the Cabildo

The empire that Spain built in the Americas linked a series of urban outposts ruling over vast rural holdings, the survival of which depended on the stability of the municipal government, or cabildo. The conquistadors were the initial members of the cabildo, but membership soon expanded to include major landowners and entrepreneurs. Cabildos thus functioned as key cogs in the interlocking chains of colonial bureaucracy, with posts that were highly coveted for their influence and power, particularly among the cabildos of major cities like Mexico City, Lima, or Quito. Kinship networks typically helped determine the shape of these spheres of influence, which often extended beyond the immediate hinterlands to link together elites at the regional, viceregal, and imperial level.[5]

In the case of Quito, the cabildo's strength stemmed from its control over land grants, or *mercedes,* in the city and its five-league hinterland. The largest beneficiaries were the monastic orders and the upper echelon of the city council, including the Pérez Guerrero, Arias, and Sancho de la Carrera families. Municipal members amassed huge fortunes through their acquisition of lands and the purchase of the cabildo's institutional holdings, which were sold at regular intervals throughout the seventeenth century. Membership in the cabildo thus became a crucial step toward the consolidation of personal power, and that local governmental entity became synonymous with the interests of the local elite.[6] This dynamic remained largely unchanged throughout the colonial period. Indeed, even the Bourbon attempts to consolidate royal control across the empire ultimately expanded municipal power in the Quito region following the Rebellion of the Barrios in 1765. This uprising consisted of a massive cross-class protest over new royal taxation measures. To restore order, the president of the Audiencia was forced to ally himself with the cabildo, which began to enjoy greater autonomy as a result. The 1781 eradication of the *corregimiento* (an administrative unit responsible for collecting indigenous tribute) also effectively elevated municipal power, as no replacement subdelegate was named under the new taxation system. Instead of reverting to the president of the Audiencia, control over rural tribute and administration passed to the cabildo.[7] By the eve of independence, the city council not only controlled land distribution but also dominated regional taxation. These responsibilities continued to be exercised following independence, allowing a modicum of institutional stability during the transition to the republican era.[8]

However, the second half of the nineteenth century represented a period of state consolidation of power in Ecuador. The process involved curtailing municipal economic leverage, beginning with the eradication of indigenous tribute in 1857. The replacement for tribute, the so-called *contribución subsidiaria,* allowed for uncompensated indigenous labor drafts but simultaneously eliminated the collection of specie. Government oversight expanded during García Moreno's push to overcome Ecuador's regionalist politics following the chaotic 1859 civil war. Although the conservative caudillo's investment in the power of provincial governors did little to halt regional divides, granting these authorities budgetary powers crippled local initiatives.[9] García Moreno's initiatives were expanded in an 1878 legal code (the first *Ley de régimen municipal*) that severely restricted urban fundraising powers by only allowing direct taxation of luxury items, entertainment, and animal slaughter.[10] Although the newly renamed Concejo

Municipal could still set indirect fees for services such as public lighting, other former privileges were revoked. These included the ability to buy and sell land-holdings—still the greatest revenue source for most cities—without the prior approval of the national legislature.[11] These constraints created rifts between the state and municipalities across Ecuador but were particularly acute in Quito and Guayaquil, neither of which felt its share of national tax revenue was sufficient given the cities' status as the nation's two largest economic centers.[12]

The main source of conflict concerned the amounts of money destined for modernization of urban infrastructure. García Moreno's public works projects and those he inspired in the mid-nineteenth century, which had substantially improved the national transportation network, had done little to upgrade urban services. Even monumental edifices such as Quito's Astronomical Observatory and the panopticon prison had little practical effect on daily activities. This fact was not lost upon the city council. Indeed, Quito's municipal government desperately hoped to upgrade the urban fabric and throughout the 1880s and 1890s presented yearly petitions to the national government for a variety of public works. The most critical needs were a central market, a cattle bypass, and public services such as sewers, tramways, and electric lighting. Although these appeals were summarily rejected or underfunded, the projects reveal a great deal concerning the city government's conflicted relationship with the state and its internal ambivalence regarding modernization. Technological advances and hygienic regulation fascinated many council members; however, others viewed these innovations with suspicion, arguing in favor of maintaining a traditional organization of social space.

Attempts to regulate commercial space as part of a broader sanitation campaign demonstrate the complexity of this process. On the one hand, as Eduardo Kingman has argued, these programs sought to displace subaltern spaces of socialization and economic exchange. The cattle bypass, for example, was intended to eliminate the presence of rural indigenous merchants (and their livestock) in the central urban grid. A parallel endeavor arose with the slow eradication of *chicherías,* which were popular establishments serving corn beer and catering largely to an indigenous population.[13] In so doing, the city government helped encroach upon periurban spaces that could then be transformed by "progress" into arenas stripped of their premodern elements. However, these attempts frequently met with sustained opposition from traditionalists, the state, or subaltern entrepreneurs themselves.

The case of the marketplace epitomizes this complex process. The municipality couched the project as necessary to bring Quito in line with other South American capitals, each of which boasted an indoor market, along with Guayaquil, which had just completed its own.[14] President Antonio Flores y Jijón, himself a *guayaquileño* and member of the Progressive Party, approved this request just after taking power in 1888, perhaps in a bid to quell regional envy. Flores earmarked the municipally owned Santa Clara *plazuela* as the site for the new building and passed on the request for congressional approval. The legislature, however, balked at the expropriation of the lots surrounding the tiny square, delaying approval for two years until the municipality was charged with raising the necessary monies.[15] Given its inability to levy a direct tax or sell unwanted property, the council had few options other than taxing the vendors who regularly gathered before the San Francisco church, a measure that had first been raised in 1887 but abandoned because the lack of fixed stalls in the market would make regulation difficult.[16] The idea gathered renewed traction following congressional approval of the market in 1890, eventually resulting in a modified proposal that responded to the problem of implementation. The new measure called for building a series of kiosks to house the larger merchants in the informal markets found in Plaza Bolivar (a new name for the plaza in front of San Francisco) and Plaza Mejía on the eastern edge of town. These would be rented out for up to a two-year period with the possibility for future renewal, with the proceeds earmarked toward the eventual purchase of the private homes surrounding Santa Clara.[17] Vendors, however, balked at occupying these kiosks, which ultimately led the municipality to attempt to entice them to agree to permanent stalls by offering a month free of rent and taxes.[18] Once they began to be occupied, further conflicts arose in 1894, when a local meat merchant tried to bypass the municipality by building his own kiosk, arguing that he was thus exempt from rents or taxes. The city magistrate wanted the rest of the council to declare this kiosk a threat to public hygiene, but the group's worry that this would necessitate outlawing all meat sales in public plazas led them to reject his petition.[19]

Subaltern resistance to these efforts to restructure commercial space also took advantage of traditional conceptions of social and spatial order designed to appeal to conservatives on the council. A clear example of this process can be seen in an 1892 case involving soap makers from the low-income San Roque neighborhood on the southwestern edge of the city. Women dominated the field, cooking the rank mixture on the patios of their houses. Soon after the municipality passed a law relegating the industry (and the smell) to the outskirts of town, a number of San Roque *jaboneras* sent a firm refusal to obey an ordinance they considered tantamount to the destruction of their livelihood. They couched their claim in both spatial and historical terms. Alleging that the industry had been critical to the local economy since the days of Queen Isabella of Spain, they cited two objections to the proposed transfer. First, they argued that the law did not expressly call for the removal of all soap manufactories but only for those within the *recinto* (enclosure) of the city, which they defined as meaning "the city center itself." Since San Roque lay on the southwestern edge of the city, they argued that moving the workshops was unnecessary. Second, they cited the extreme difficulty of transporting their operations, noting that their heavy kettles necessitated sedentary conditions, unlike candle manufacture.[20]

The municipality categorically dismissed the second argument proffered by the *jaboneras* as an example of retrograde underdevelopment. The precise spatial

argument of their charge, however, inspired heate͏
cil members seriously considered approving the so͏
logic rested upon the traditional understanding of lo͏
which the central parishes received distinctively diffe͏
taxes). The municipal attorney, Diego Román, ultim͏
missing the claim of residence since the days of Isab͏
that Ecuadorian territory had not been explored unt͏
importantly, he noted that sanitary measures could

due to the need to protect the entire urban population. This argument carried
weight and led to a consensus that the bill referred to the entire city, a decision that represents the first conscious attempt to radically alter the prevailing
spatial hierarchy by incorporating the outskirts into the defined territory of the
city. Implementation of the considered opinion of the *concejo*, however, continued to be a problem. As late as 1900, city inspectors still encountered the pun-
gent odors of underground soap manufactories in their traditional locations.[21]

The ambiguity surrounding urban spatial dynamics colored conflicts with
wealthy entrepreneurs as well, particularly with regard to the increasingly vague
distinction between urban and rural parishes under the cabildo's jurisdiction.
Despite the city's extension into its environs, these outlying areas were nevertheless governed under separate legal codes. An incident from 1886, involving
aguardiente manufacturer Antonio Herrera, highlighted the stakes involved.
Herrera resided in the ostensibly rural parish of Santa Prisca in Quito's northern environs, which had recently received a spate of construction on its southern
limits abutting Alameda Park. Arguing that Santa Prisca could no longer be
considered part of the rural hinterland, he complained about paying a one-peso
tax for introducing liquor into the city. The debate concerning this measure
lasted more than a month as the council tried to establish the merits of Herrera's
view of urban limits. A special study by the municipal attorney agreed with
Herrera's characterization, yet the majority of the council fervently disagreed
that Santa Prisca was an urban neighborhood, due to the preeminence of farms,
meadows, and forests outside the few blocks immediately north of Alameda
Park. Detractors also noted that granting Herrera's request would effectively
remove any taxation on his liquor, as the distillery was not charged the regular
urban indemnities, which, in any regard, were lower than the duties levied on
imported spirits. As the request would therefore have called for the complete
reworking of the tax code, Herrera's request was ultimately denied.[22]

Like the case of the *jaboneras,* Herrera's request for an urban tax base demonstrates the degree to which the city's expansion had begun to contest traditional spatial organization at both the social and economic levels. One of the
most extensive debates sparked by these ambiguities arose with an attempt to
introduce a tramline into the city. Like the marketplace issue, the introduction of a tramway had been approved by Congress (1883) but languished due to
underfunding. After vigorous lobbying by newly appointed council president

Andrade Marín—a prominent lawyer and moderate liberal who had
...ged the council's lethargy for years—Congress finally released the funds
...88, pending a detailed study regarding implementation. The project proved
...o be a more difficult venture than originally expected as the council divided
sharply over the scale of the tram network. Again, the key issue concerned the
relationship of the city to its hinterland. Many council members hoped that
the trains would not be limited to urban parishes and could therefore serve to
integrate commerce at the county level. Then the council attorney, Julio Paz
y Miño, charged that trains that traversed only the city's 174 hectares would
be merely recreational vehicles, given the ease of navigating the city on foot.
His arguments included a convoluted discussion on the etymology of the word
tranvía, which he considered to mean a road (*vía*) that knows no limits (*trans*).
Andrade Marín and others, however, noted that the original authorization had
specifically called for *ferrocarriles urbanos,* which necessitated restricting the
trains to the country's urban zone, an argument that persuaded his fellow council members.[23]

As with other projects, the trams were eventually cut due to financing issues—one of the reasons many viewed modernization with disdain. The roots
of this fiscal crisis lay in Andrade Marín's taste for expensive projects as well as
in the ongoing national political strife. After years of challenging the council's
lethargy, he finally succeeded in securing election only after offering a virtual
bribe in which he promised to donate a parcel of land he owned behind the cabildo headquarters to build a small plaza. The active modernization agenda
he followed led to the initiation of tramways, electrical lighting, and the cattle
bypass road as well as the cobblestone paving of central streets and substantial
repairs on the decaying aboveground sewers.[24] However, a simultaneous economic slide led to the contraction of government funds, fiscal decline, and the
council's rejection of Andrade Marín's bid for reappointment as president in
December 1889.[25] The government's failure to repay a ten-thousand-sucre advance that had been used to suppress an insurrection the year before aggravated
the crisis and led to the revocation of almost eight thousand sucres' worth of
expenditures budgeted for the marketplace, trams, debts, and public lighting.[26]

Again, the council responded to this further erosion of its planning prerogatives with compromise measures, which can be seen most clearly in the
drawn-out saga to improve nocturnal lighting. Both the council and the Congress viewed the city's continued use of candlelight as unbefitting a nineteenth-
century capital and thus authorized an illumination property tax in 1883, with
lots levied at one-thousandth their value. This levy (unsurprisingly) proved
insufficient to raise the funds necessary to install the centralized gas or electric
system the municipality had in mind. Furthermore, Congress granted exclusive
development rights to the expensive Vinuesa-Ontaneda firm, thus excluding
bidders from less costly outfits.[27] An interim solution suggested by local entrepreneur Pedro Manuel Pérez Quiñonez and supported vocally by council mem-

ber Juan José Narváez, a landowner from the nearby town of Tumbaco, was to adopt tubular kerosene lanterns manufactured by the R. E. Dietz Company in New York.[28] These lamps used a process developed by John Irwin in 1869 in which kerosene vapor and air pumped through a series of tubes combined in a central chamber. The resulting combustion allowed for a flame that was easily four times brighter than a single candle, more efficient, and, best of all, afford-able.[29] Eighty lanterns were thus ordered as a stopgap measure in 1887.

The city did not entirely abandon the possibility of instituting centralized public lighting. Although most European and American capitals still used gas lighting because of the potential for centrally located regulation, Quito's municipal government was intrigued by the prospect of electricity. Edison's perfection of the lightbulb in 1879 and the opening of the first central power stations in London and New York in 1882 inspired many council members.[30] The most aggressive push came in late 1888, when a commission headed by then–vice president Andrade Marín seriously reviewed Vinuesa-Ontaneda's proposal for illuminating the blocks surrounding the Plaza de la Independencia with twenty-two electric bulbs. The commission's report, which recommended adopting the measure in order to bring Quito to the forefront of global technological modernity, sparked a tense discussion. During the debate, Andrade Marín squared off with Narváez, who interrogated the utility of the new technology given that not even Paris had adopted electric lighting. As he put it, "Our town is poor and does not need to be bothered by such luxurious contributions. Later, when the invention is perfected, it will come to our land on its own, without our having to thrust ourselves into conjectures."[31]

Narváez's call for patience and opposition to adopting an as yet untested technology articulated a widespread concern among members of not only the council but also the legislature. Given the city and state's limited means, what was the harm in waiting until more ambitious cities abroad had perfected the new invention? Andrade Marín's enthusiasm could not overcome this pragmatic objection—so he backed down. However, he attempted to save face before agreeing to the proposed alternative—more Dietz lamps—by noting that the number of bulbs from the Vinuesa-Ontaneda proposal would not allow for the citywide illumination that he hoped Quito would soon enjoy.[32]

The institution of kerosene lighting, while forestalling electricity, had a broader impact due to a subsequent challenge to congressional control over urban taxation policies, perhaps the greatest limitation on any modernization program. Instead of retaining the flat tax on property slated for illumination, the municipality had long advocated a variable levy based on the length of a building's street frontage. Following the city's refusal to pay back its ten-thousand-sucre loan in 1889, Congress offered an olive branch by agreeing in principle to this measure. It took another two years of frequent haranguing and the return of Andrade Marín to the council presidency for this change to be implemented. Nevertheless, the ensuing system demonstrated an increasing sense of the utility of urban security and the need for the local and national public to share the financial burden of modernizing the capital.

However, this new tax system also revealed the continuation of the traditional radial construction of social power. Unlike the measure to eradicate soap manufacture, the duties that paid for public lighting were set on a sliding scale, with the highest levels (eight centavos per meter) in the eight blocks surrounding the Plaza Grande and the lowest (two centavos) on the outskirts of town.[33] The proceeds went to purchasing ever more Dietz lamps, the placement of which radiated outward from the central plaza. Finally, in 1894, the council could boast that the entire city's dim candlelight had been replaced with a warm kerosene glow.[34]

The process of implementing the new lighting system demonstrated the obstacles that needed to be overcome to achieve sustained progress in an era of budgetary constraints. The biggest barrier concerned the limits set forth by the central government, but equally important was the ambivalence regarding modernization itself. Although improvisation and compromise allowed for some advances, major programmatic alterations stalled without state support. This dynamic shifted with the advent of the 1895 Liberal Revolution but was not fundamentally transformed. The increased support for local development projects initiated by Eloy Alfaro and Leonidas Plaza allowed for the realization of major projects that had been considered, debated, and quashed during the Progressive era. However, the municipality continued to depend on the central government, with major advances only occurring during moments of heightened state concern about the shape of the national capital. This included the immediate aftermath of the 1895 revolution, when the new government sought to legitimate its authority, as well as during the 1909 and 1922 celebrations of the centennials of the declaration of independence and liberation from Spain, respectively.

Liberal Spending

One of the crucial pieces of the Liberal Party program concerned its support for fiscal decentralization of public works projects. The ensuing system established independent juntas empowered to organize development programs according to local needs. Although plagued by inefficient oversight and bloated budgets, the Liberal era strengthened municipal power in collusion with the state rather than at its expense.[35] Quito, as the capital and the city most visibly in need of modernization, was a particular target, which, as noted previously, Alfaro had addressed immediately upon entering the capital in 1895. With the support of the new national government, the city would be transformed in the next two decades.

It would be a mistake, however, to view this alteration as unqualified support for local autonomy. Rather, the Liberal era perpetuated political partisanship even as Liberals sought to disturb the historic regional bases of the Conservative and Progressive parties. As Kim Clark has noted, new initiatives such as the national railroad were proclaimed as redemptive works that would rescue the nation from decades of stagnation, corruption, and inefficiency.[36] The city government wholeheartedly embraced its role in this struggle, adopting the motto "*Querer es poder*" (Desire enables).[37] While it would take longer for major reforms such as the building of the marketplace, the new cabildo rapidly completed a series of symbolic gestures underscoring its commitment to progress and the transformation of society. One of the first actions was the relaunching of *El Municipio*, the council's weekly that had been interrupted during the battles of 1895. A number of changes to the publication proclaimed a symbolic shift, including a banner reading "*Nueva Era*" that appeared beneath the title, the addition of page numbers, and the resetting of issue numbers.[38] Another act concerned new landscaping for the damaged gardens of the Plaza de la Independencia, which a local newspaper had termed "*un potrero gratis*" (a free horse pasture).[39] The council also encouraged private citizens to actively engage the new era through in-kind donations to rebuild civil society, an improvised measure calculated to spur support for the new government. Those who did so included former council engineer and cartographer Gualberto Pérez, who completed his embellishment of the Plaza Sucre, begun in 1893, for free, and local elite Juana Naranjo, who donated extra piping to carry water from Alameda Park's fountain to homes nearby.[40]

The new cabildo also sought to match its rhetoric with more substantive reforms, particularly with regard to modernizing the city's infrastructure. These programs largely echoed the desires of municipal governments controlled by the Progressive Party in the 1880s—after all, the city's needs had not changed. Not surprisingly, given Alfaro's early endorsement of the proposed marketplace structure, the council began with that long-desired project. The first step involved securing an additional hundred-thousand-sucre loan to match Alfaro's pledge and to fund a second market on the city's north side.[41] Advertisements calling for designs appeared in *El Municipio* beginning in late 1895, and a special commission began reviewing the proposals the following April.[42] By September, the finalists had been selected and presented to President Alfaro, who worked with the commission to select the design presented by a recently arrived German émigré named Francisco Schmidt. Schmidt's attractiveness as a candidate stemmed from not only his impeccable credentials but also his recent partnership with Gualberto Pérez, whose pro bono labor on the Plaza Sucre was fresh in the minds of the council members.[43] The loans were approved in February, a contract with Schmidt and Pérez signed in April, and by May 2, 1897, construction had finally began on a project first approved fourteen years earlier.

The new cabildo meant for the proposed structure to be quite imposing. Its outer masonry walls took up an entire city block and supported a vaulted glass-

and-iron ceiling that rose to a height of 32.5 meters and reflected the design of Les Halles in Paris. Four massive doors opened onto the ground floor, which was dominated by a central octagonal plaza. Eight corridors led from this space to the second floor, where 156 individual stalls housed merchants. Each stall took up 4 square meters and was separated from the next by wooden panels framed in iron. The facility also boasted 32 warehouses, indoor plumbing, and restroom facilities. The project had a total cost projected at S/.73,500 and an estimated completion time of 28 months. The completion date ultimately had to be pushed back because of ongoing conservative uprisings and delays in delivery of the imported iron and woodwork.[44]

Expensive projects such as the marketplace depended on firm government backing and financial support, which came in the form of state grants, loans, and new taxes following the restoration of local fundraising prerogatives. The Quito municipality celebrated the realization of its longtime goal by passing a flurry of new fines, duties, and other revenue-producing devices. These included sales taxes, other commercial levies, and increased rates on popular diversions such as theaters, pool halls, and cockfights. Perhaps their most important new source of income came from the restoration of control over municipal property, which had been the primary means for raising revenue prior to the mid-nineteenth century. In exultant glee, the council resolved to sell all its property in 1897, regardless of whether it was occupied. Although the council ultimately did not divest itself of all these holdings, the body took steps to do so, ordering an audit to determine the extent of its assets in preparation. Public auctions of several of the more lucrative properties were held in ensuing years and provided significant cash flow.[45]

Over the next two decades, the municipality was able to use this massive influx of resources to begin providing an impressive number of urban services that radically altered the fabric of the city. Completed a few years behind schedule, in 1904, the Santa Clara marketplace created a centralized commercial zone that could be easily regulated, both as a source of revenue and in terms of hygiene and safety. An improved communication network arrived with the organization of a municipal postal service in 1899 and the introduction of telephones the following year. Electric arc lighting appeared on the *centro's* streets between 1900 and 1901, followed by domestic electrical lighting service in 1904. The new Junta de Agua Potable y Canalización inaugurated piped potable water service in 1905 while also organizing a drainage system that ran alongside the Quebrada Jerusalén, a creek that lay at the foot of the Panecillo and divided the city in two. The group also oversaw the development of sewers in the central part of the city in 1906 and eventually turned to a citywide drainage system in 1919. Transportation advances included the arrival of the railroad from Guayaquil in 1908, which inspired the final development of electric trams by 1914. The beginnings of widespread automobile usage during the end of the 1910s also led to asphalt pavement in the central parts of the city by 1919. Both the drainage and paving projects were completed by 1922.[46]

The improvements in urban infrastructure altered the pace of *quiteño* life, afforded the possibility for growing suburbanization, and formalized systems of public commerce by eliminating the need for casual markets and water carriers. These changes have led numerous analysts to consider the Liberal Revolution a transformative moment in the city's history. This analysis, however, downplays the continuity between the alterations of this era and the intentions of the Progressive municipalities of the 1880s and 1890s. Several major players from the Progressive period, indeed, returned to service soon after the revolutionary triumph. These included staunch modernizers like Andrade Marín, who returned to his role as municipal attorney in early 1896 and later reclaimed the council presidency, as well as more cautious bureaucrats, such as Juan José Narváez and Domingo Gangotena.

The stability in council membership across time paralleled continuity in sociospatial outlook, at least through 1910. As in previous decades, poorer regions of the urban periphery, such as El Tejar, on the upper slopes of Pichincha, the mostly indigenous settlements south of the Quebrada Jerusalén, and the still developing mixed-income housing east of Santo Domingo, received scant attention. Instead, modernizing reforms tended to be restricted to central streets and plazas along the traditional centers of power. For instance, an 1897 law requiring the installation of gutters was restricted to the forty-two blocks surrounding the Plaza de la Independencia, a zone demarcating the old colonial city center of churches and elite residences, and to a single artery leading northward from the Sucre Theater along Carrera Guayaquil that presaged subsequent suburban development along the same route.[47] Projects undertaken by the municipality's *brigada ambulante,* or mobile workers, paved those same areas with cobblestone and instituted a centralized street-sweeping program funded with a tax similar to the street frontage levy used for kerosene lighting a decade earlier.[48] The same rationale lay behind the map of the electric arc lighting instituted in 1900–1901, which divided the city into four sections, each charged according to its proximity to the Plaza de la Independencia.[49]

Nevertheless, the growing population in the city's environs made a shift in administrative order necessary. Of particular importance were the emerging suburbs along Carrera Guayaquil to the north and near the Recoleta, the former horse pasture affixed to a solitary convent on the city's southeast. These valuable Belle Époque chalets on the city's outskirts necessitated a shift from the radial orientation of urban services and property tax codes. The possibility of making this change was first raised in 1904 in a short-lived contract with local developer Luis Felipe Carbo to build urban trams. Although the agreement fell apart the following year because Carbo had underestimated the costs, the council for the first time agreed that any urban system would be incomplete without pushing into the ostensibly rural parishes of Chimbacalle on the south and Santa Prisca to the north, where much of the new construction was located.[50] The advent of Ciudadela Larrea, the first planned community erected in Santa Prisca, intensified debates about extending modern services to the parish. In 1906, as a result of these discussions, the parish was chosen to receive canalization for potable water along with the rest of the urban grid.[51]

The southern environs of the city began to receive greater state and municipal attention around the same time, largely because of outbreaks of typhoid fever and bubonic plague in isolated pockets on the coast. The council authorized several measures designed to minimize sanitary risks, including continued attempts to restrict commercial ventures, such as outlawing milk vending in the central districts. A number of these efforts, including a move to deputize the police as a temporary street-sweeping force, targeted impoverished neighborhoods on the south side.[52] The most important issue, however, concerned the fate of the Quebrada Jerusalén, the last of the creeks that had once crisscrossed the Quito valley. Its deep ravine ran along the Panecillo and had for centuries divided the indigenous townships of La Magdalena and Chimbacalle from the southern reaches of the city and had also served as an informal dumping ground. For the health-conscious council, the gorge thus represented a cesspool of stagnant water, refuse, and excrement that desperately needed clearing.[53]

However, as with other public service ventures of the early twentieth century, the successful draining of the Quebrada Jerusalén depended on the whims of the national government. The state had mandated the need to provide a drainage canal as early as 1899 as part of its program to beautify Quito, doing so upon the recommendation of municipal health inspectors. Continued conservative uprisings in 1900 as well as a split between Alfaro and his successor, Leonidas Plaza, delayed the securing of congressional funding until 1902. Despite President Plaza's strong backing, it took three more years for the funds to be freed.

The approval of funding in 1905 stemmed partly from the state's preoccupation with the plague scare along with the continual advocacy of Francisco Andrade Marín, who had returned to the council presidency the previous year. While strongly promoting the importance of the work due to public health concerns, Andrade Marín also stressed its implications for the city's modernization agenda and the potential benefits for securing foreign investment in the capital. He diverted funds earmarked for other projects toward the canal's completion, such as monies remaining after the completion of the ring road bypass for cattle bound for the slaughterhouse.[54] His energetic support for the project continued after his appointment as inspector general of health and hygiene in 1908, the same year in which the plague spread to Guayaquil and Alausí, a critical transfer point on the nearly completed Guayaquil-Quito railway.[55] Besides making progress on Jerusalén drainage, Andrade Marín took advantage of the public health fears to conclude a series of other sanitary advances, including the organization of wastewater collection in the *centro,* paving the *centro* with cobblestones, and improving air circulation in public gathering spaces such as the military barracks and restaurant kitchens.[56]

The transformation of the southern edges of the city did not stop with the Quebrada Jerusalén. One of the key factors in this planning trajectory concerned the decision to locate the central terminal of the Guayaquil-Quito railway in the town of Chimbacalle just across the Machángara River from the capital. This decision was made in September 1906, when Archer Harman, director of the Guayaquil-Quito Railroad Company, met with municipal officials and Eloy Alfaro, who had just returned to the presidency. Prior to that date, a station closer to the city, abutting Santo Domingo or in the northern Ejido, had been favored. However, the cost of circling the city to reach the Ejido made the northern choice problematic, while the need to expropriate urban property to place a train station right in the middle of the colonial city made the Santo Domingo location financially unfeasible.[57] New construction followed alongside the Carrera del Sur, a highway that connected Chimbacalle with Santo Domingo, and intensified once the new station was completed in 1908. Alfaro also promoted the region by resuscitating a defunct plan for an international exposition to celebrate independence, which would be held in the Recoleta in August 1909.[58]

With a budget of more than a half million sucres to pay for lavish items such as imported ironwork for the kiosks and exposition palace, the exposition both bolstered real estate speculation in the southern environs and provided a chance to give the capital a symbolic landscape.[59] The grand event responded to the international fascination with world's fairs, which had engaged Ecuador since the 1889 Universal Exposition in Paris, but it also furthered the Liberal desire to dramatically transfigure Quito. The first of these commemorative symbolic gestures, a column by Swiss-Italian immigrant Lorenzo Durini, appeared in 1906, anticipating better-known centennial monuments, such as Mexico City's Angel of Independence (1910) or Buenos Aires's Obelisk (1936, erected to celebrate the quadricentennial of the city's founding). Like its peers, Durini's column in Quito created a historicist allegory that both responded to and critiqued European considerations of global centrality. However, the monument to independence did not represent a crowning jewel visible for miles along a monumental avenue like Mexico City's Paseo de la Reforma, Buenos Aires's Avenida 9 de julio, Paris's Champs-Elysées, or Vienna's Ringstrasse.[60] Instead, it resided smack in the middle of the Plaza Grande, surrounded by icons of the colonial age, from the cathedral to the archbishopric to the Government Palace. The decision to place the monument there arose from the financial limitations, but it meant the creation of an allegorical scene that celebrated Quito's hybrid nature: colonial grandeur with modern accoutrements.

Durini's column featured a golden winged Victory heralding Quito's cry for independence at its apex, while at the base sat a bronze sculpture of a retreating Spanish lion, wounded in the flank by an arrow shot by an Ecuadorian condor perched halfway up the pillar. Ironically, the design had been the work of a

Salesian priest named Juan Bautista Minghetti, who had drafted it for the Progressive government prior to leaving for exile in 1895, and Durini modified that design only slightly. Nevertheless, its execution underscored the Liberal ability to efficiently complete projects where others had failed (thus echoing their chosen motto, "*Querer es poder*").

This monumental semiology, in which Liberal progress contrasted with stagnant (Conservative) coloniality, also influenced the decision to locate the Exposición Nacional in the Recoleta. Although the square lay at the center of a developing modern neighborhood and near the Chimbacalle station, it had previously housed the Dominican order's stables. The state's transformation of the old *potrero* into a finely landscaped park was a triumph of Liberal anticlericalism, further underscored by the renaming of the square as Parque Rocafuerte, after the first great hero of nineteenth-century Ecuadorian liberalism. The landscaping began with the surrounding streets, which were leveled and paved to provide easy access for the national and foreign notables attending the exposition. These dignitaries would reach the pavilions by strolling through sculpted gardens, one of which featured an artificial waterfall. The largest pavilion was the Palace of the Exposition, which housed the Ecuadorian, Peruvian, and French exhibits. Framing the southern entry to the park, the palace was an elongated neoclassical structure with two wings and, rising in the middle, a domed tower that featured a patriotic icon at its pinnacle—the flying condor from the national coat of arms. To the north and east of the palace were pavilions erected by other nations, including the United States, Chile, Japan, Spain, Colombia, and Italy. The government also constructed a fine arts pavilion, a music kiosk, and a concert café. The last piece was one of the highlights of the fair because of its elaborate art nouveau designs.[61]

This symbolic landscape not only cemented Liberal designs on the capital but also heralded a shift in the city's sociospatial order along a north-south axis. For example, a January 1910 ordinance that reorganized street cleaning procedures divided the city into two administrative zones for the first time, one for the northern half and one for the south.[62] A number of decisions to incorporate the immediate environs into the urban jurisdiction followed this break from the traditional radial organization of the capital. The first of these decisions was to include the hitherto rural parishes of Alfaro (Chimbacalle's new name, given the former president's enthusiasm for the railroad), La Magdalena, and Santa Prisca for a special tax on *chicherías* passed in late December 1909.[63] A more important measure followed in January 1910, when the final contract for tram construction with American businessman E. Hope Norton called for the building of a citywide rail network that would run from the Chimbacalle station to the new Avenida Colón in the heart of "rural" Santa Prisca.[64] Finally, in February 1910, the three parishes were formally incorporated into the city.[65] Santa Prisca's periurban and rural expanses, however, were reorganized as a rural parish, and, in answer to criticism since the 1880s for its inclusion within the urban fabric, officials renamed the parish Benalcázar.

Although the projects pursued by the municipality in the 1910s continued to focus on the city center, they also increased the possibility of future developments beyond its cloister. For instance, the new cadastral map commissioned from Gualberto Pérez in 1911 was to include both existing construction as well as recently planned areas such as the Larrea and Urrutia *ciudadelas* (suburban developments) on the northern borders. Consolidating interparochial infrastructure also remained a concern, with the tram system finally completed in 1914 and improved canalization implemented across town. These changes prompted increased investment in the development of the capital's environs, particularly on the readily available Añaquito plains to the north. Foreign investors began to enter this market in 1913, when a British group called the Anglo-French Syndicate granted a power of attorney to Claude Waterhouse Taylor to purchase plots in Quito.[66] However, it would take until the end of the decade for the northern regions to see major investment. As in 1909, this phenomenon also derived from extensive government intervention.

The main reason for this slow development was an ongoing budgetary problem. The lack of central oversight during the early Liberal years had led to excessive borrowing to complete works such as a municipal chemical laboratory and the tramlines. The latter project was especially expensive given the need to widen the narrow streets of the colonial core enough for trains to pass. By 1915, the council found itself more than S/.240,000 in arrears, and therefore it drastically reduced spending.[67] Infrastructural improvements stalled in subsequent years as construction halted on works such as the Eugenio Espejo Municipal Hospital and the new avenue over the infamous Quebrada Jerusalén.

The upcoming centennial of General Sucre's 1822 victory over the Spanish at Pichincha, however, persuaded the state that these were necessary beautification efforts that could not be allowed to languish. Rather than support the nearly bankrupt municipality, however, Congress opted to create a temporary institution to oversee urban embellishment for the upcoming centenary. Its reputation in tatters, the council was forced to accede to the creation of the Junta del Centenario, as the new body was called.

With the firm backing of the state and free from mundane tasks such as street cleaning or policing, the new group successfully usurped the planning prerogatives of the city government. Its leadership included current council members, local architects, and developers, along with prominent intellectuals and politicians, including the historians Isaac Barrera, Cristóbal Gangotena y Jijón, and Jacinto Jijón y Caamaño. The group's first tasks included establishing a stable urban grid along the old Ejido on Quito's northern outskirts in order to facilitate the exposition.[68] Independent urbanizing efforts soon followed, beginning in 1919 with C. A. Alvarez's proposal to build the Ciudadela América in the city's northeastern environs. Two years later, the Anglo-French Syndicate and the government reached an accord on the company's plan to develop the region just north of the Ejido, in between Avenida 18 de septiembre and Avenida Mariano Aguilera, to form the Barrio del Centenario.[69] Under the terms of the contract, the British firm would not only establish a street pattern but also be in charge of installing a working sewer system and preparing the neighborhood to receive existing municipal services.[70] These successes led the national government to amplify the junta's powers to allow it to expropriate lands, dictate regulations concerning urban aesthetics, impose fines for violations of these rules, and approve plans for any new construction.[71] Each of these had historically been the responsibility of the municipality, which, weakened by its fiscal mismanagement, made little fuss over the changes.

The most impressive project completed by the Junta del Centenario was the infilling of the Quebrada Jerusalén, which had continued to be used as a dumping ground despite the introduction of sewerage in 1908 and some decorative facelifts (mostly the addition of neoclassical lintels) on nearby buildings. The project involved filling the gully with hundreds of tons of dirt brought in by truck, dumped by mechanical shovel, and spread by manual labor—an epic effort that took several years to complete. The clamorous process fascinated the city's residents, many of whom congregated to gaze at progress in action. On at least one occasion, however, an onlooker ventured too close to one of the monster machines, which accidentally dragged him to his death in the depths below. Thus consecrated by technology, sweat, and blood, the completed boulevard over the once stagnant creek represented the greatest triumph of local engineering to this point.

The new thoroughfare consisted of two lanes for vehicular traffic interrupted by an expansive median that served as a promenade. Rows of trees flanked the divider, which led uphill toward a graceful column designed by Francisco Durini and dedicated to the unknown heroes of 1822. The statue allegorically linked the Battle of Pichincha to the recent cataclysm of World War I, which had spawned Westminster Abbey's "Unknown Warrior" memorial in 1920 and the Arc de Triomphe's famed "Tomb of the Unknown Soldier" the following year. It also dialogued with the pillar Durini's father Lorenzo had erected in the Plaza de la Independencia a decade earlier. As in the prior work, a defiant condor with wings outstretched gazed to the east toward a defeated foe. Rather than the imperial Spanish lion, the vanquished in this case was the erstwhile creek—a hideous environmental eyesore.

The monuments to heroic sacrifice did not end at the summit of the grand avenue but also made an appearance just above, at the Cima de la Libertad on Pichincha, where Sucre's forces had engaged the Spanish a century earlier. At this site, the junta erected a vast obelisk, following plans drawn up by Sucre's victorious but cash-bereft regiment. The monolith followed the nineteenth-century design in minute detail, including plaques dedicating the structure to

Bolívar and to the vanquishing troops.[72] Most conspicuously, at the base they included a special decoration honoring Captain Abdón Calderón, a hero of local mythology. Wounded multiple times in the battle, Calderón perished days later at the San Juan de Dios Hospital, possibly of complications from dysentery. Sucre's praise of the young officer in a letter to his grieving mother, however, transformed the memory of this fiery Ecuadorian patriot into the stuff of legend. Retelling his tale had become a staple in Quito's anniversary celebrations in the nineteenth century and was codified into popular form in a children's book of historical legends penned in 1906 by Liberal journalist Manuel J. Calle. Calle's melodramatic story, in which the wounded captain races ahead of the charging army with his sword clamped firmly in his teeth before a cannonball takes his legs, would have been the best known version of the tale in 1922, as it is today.[73] As a symbol of regional valor, Calderón was unrivaled and thus received his position of honor.

The Junta del Centenario's successful rehabilitation of the city led Congress in October 1922 to appoint the junta members to head a permanent planning commission. The new Junta de Embellecimiento de Quito acted as a shadow government. Its responsibilities consisted of augmenting Quito's commemorative statuary with a major monument to Simón Bolívar while continuing its labors in beautification and planning. In addition to its earlier powers, the new junta earned the right to charge a fee for approving new construction blueprints and to levy a limited amount of independent taxes, half of which would be turned over to the *concejo* for day-to-day operations.[74] In effect, this decision signaled the end of the alliance between the municipality and the state that had characterized the first two decades of the twentieth century. Henceforth, the two institutions would remain at loggerheads, with the council once again in a defensive role, as it had been in the late nineteenth century. Somewhat paradoxically, however, the later restoration of municipal privileges would come as a result of sustained action by those conservative and moderate reformers who had cut their teeth as members of the Junta del Centenario. As members of the establishment, figures such as Jacinto Jijón y Caamaño and Gustavo Mortensen sought to reestablish local control over Quito's development during the 1930s.

Conservative Regeneration and Municipal Autonomy

The massacre of perhaps hundreds of striking cacao workers in Guayaquil five months after the 1922 centennial shocked the nation and consecrated the nascent workers' movement in blood. As rural migrants freed from their conscript duties increasingly moved to the cities, new political possibilities emerged. The growing conservative and leftist movements each sought to capitalize on the growing presence of the recently arrived, engaging them in their varied attacks on the reigning liberals. These matters came to a head following the 1924 election and the subsequent triumph of the 1925 Julian Revolution, which brought an end to unmitigated Liberal hegemony through a military revolution loosely tied to a socialist agenda. Perhaps the most important reformist measure was the introduction of a graduated income tax aimed at decreasing the power of Andean landowners and coastal bankers. As a sign of the new government's commitment to social change, salaried workers with annual incomes under twenty-four hundred sucres, such as day laborers, transportation workers, and domestics, were exempt from this new tax.[75]

Equally important efforts at reform, though, were attempts to curtail wasteful government spending and trim the number of autonomous public works projects. The new government identified the popular Junta de Embellecimiento as an example of Liberal excess and suspended its efforts in September 1925. This move led to an uproar in the local press but little else. As early as November, planning functions such as expropriation rights and oversight of construction blueprints had been returned to the domain of the *concejo*.[76] Rather than an altruistic act for municipal benefit, the shift, together with decrees centralizing fundraising, advanced state domination of the planning process. By the end of the year, municipal levies on new buildings, public spectacles, billiards, telephones, public lighting, and the sale and slaughter of cattle had been eradicated. In their stead came a series of new, centrally controlled property taxes, registration fees (for example, for automobile registration), municipal service duties, and entertainment and luxury taxes.[77] In addition, the national government promised to provide a yearly dispersal of funds for public beautification, which for Quito meant an additional one million sucres per year, a sum that the government began to distribute in 1926.[78]

Ironically, this new regimen of expanded state control was put into place by Isidro Ayora, a prominent Quito physician and former council president who was named acting president of the country following the restoration of civilian rule in February 1926.[79] A native of Loja, Ayora first came to Quito in 1897, in the wake of the Liberal Revolution, to study medicine at the university. He followed this program with advanced degrees from Berlin and Dresden, returning to Quito in 1910 to head the state's new maternity hospital before inaugurating his own medical practice the following year. Ayora's shimmering modernist clinic on the city's outskirts catered to the well-to-do and elevated his local prestige. His election to the municipal council in 1918 and subsequent service paralleled the decline of its local control, though as council president from 1924 to 1925 he did push through the expansion of drainage and sewerage service to hitherto marginalized neighborhoods—progressive measures that endeared him to the revolutionary junta. Once in power, he instituted policies that combined social liberalization (e.g., the extension of the franchise to women in 1928, before any other Latin American government did so) with centralized fiscal policies. His program led to the formation of the Central Bank on the Kemmerer model, which had already been put in place in Colombia, and was also evident in the June 1929 municipal code.[80] The new code's comprehensive delineation of municipal responsibilities paradoxically affirmed municipal control over daily tasks while strengthening government oversight.

The tasks outlined generally corresponded to standard duties that municipalities had been performing for centuries, such as administering local taxation, cleaning the streets, and overseeing law and order. However, the code also stipulated that the types of modernizing reforms that the Quito council had embraced the previous forty years needed to be adopted by all of the nation's cities. These included the stock liberal platform of sanitation, rational street layout, improved transportation, and the construction of electrical grids. The code also demonstrated the growing legislative strength of the extreme Left and Right, with provisions such as calling for the preservation of historic monuments (courtesy of the conservatives) or tax breaks for worker community developments (backed by the socialists).[81]

The planning measures themselves were not particularly controversial and would indeed be implemented by most cities during the 1930s. More problematic was the massive expansion of government surveillance. Ostensibly, the council enjoyed autonomy over the procedures determined by the national state to be its raison d'être, that is, planning, sanitation, and security. However, the law also created a new ministry expressly devoted to oversight, both facilitating communication with the national government and challenging local authority to make independent planning decisions. Since the government also controlled the purse strings, many local officials viewed the code with suspicion. Coupled with the economic disturbances of the Great Depression, this resentment offered the chance for alternative political projects.

Ultimately, it was the Conservative Party that benefited most from the discontent. Widespread distrust of the new social legislation, especially income redistribution, naturally disposed many in the growing urban middle and professional classes toward a less centralized system. These disaffected groups gravitated toward the Conservative Party as a result of its staunch opposition to state expansionism at the expense of local autonomy. At the urging of conservative ideologue Jacinto Jijón y Caamaño, the party had adopted a platform calling for municipal autonomy in October 1925.[82] Jijón hoped that the creation of a constellation of conservative municipalities could lead to an opportunity to challenge the revolutionary junta for national supremacy. While an attempt to oust Ayora in 1927 (Jijón's second coup attempt in three years) failed miserably, the party's fortunes rose during the Great Depression. Unlike the national state, which entered a period of intense upheaval, Conservative Party–ruled municipalities throughout the country provided a modicum of stability during this period.

One of the greatest strengths of the new conservative program was a sound theoretical justification for local bases of power, which Jijón had based on the writings of contemporary Spanish urban theorist Adolfo Posada. In works such as *El regimen municipal de la ciudad moderna,* Posada argued that the contemporary city's size and complexity necessitated that the municipality be granted exclusive control over its own affairs, a move that he argued would lead to greater national health and prosperity. A critical component of the Spaniard's argument stemmed from his understanding of the premodern cabildo as a rational agent that had tempered monarchical autocracy in the same way that he hoped the contemporary municipality could temper the overweening central bureaucratic apparatus of the state.[83] Jijón's polemical tract *Política conservadora* (published in two volumes, in 1929 and 1934), merged Posada's urban historical analysis with paternalistic labor policies growing out of the work he and fellow conservative academics Carlos Manuel Larrea and Julio Tobar Donoso had been engaged in since 1906.[84]

Jijón's extended essay on the subject ruminates on the importance of the municipality to the formation of the Ecuadorian nation. Echoing Posada, Jijón argues that the municipality represents more than a piece of local territorial administration and should be understood as a critical building block of national identity. He bases this claim in a historical review of the development of the Spanish cabildo, which he portrays as a civilizing agent organized according to a variegated structure built upon the European model—"de blancos y para blancos"—in which local politics engage harmoniously with a national center.[85] Elsewhere, he clarifies that the founding of the Quito municipality in 1534 not only "engendered" a new nation but also provided an administrative axis giving shape to a variegated association of semi-autonomous cities.[86] Jijón laments the nineteenth-century disappearance of this system due to aspirations for a central bureaucratic structure, itself the antithesis of a supposed natural Ecuadorian embrace of self-governance. In particular, he rails against contemporary state budget centralization, a measure that he feared would perpetuate bureaucratic responses to urban problems without regard for local conditions.

Jijón's worries derived from his observations of Quito's long-standing struggle with the state over resources, particularly during his service on the Junta de Embellecimiento. The onset of the Great Depression confirmed his worst fears as the state decreased funds earmarked for local development. In 1931, for example, Quito's budget was slashed from one million to a mere three hundred thousand sucres. The following year, the city saw its federal funding disappear altogether. Capitalizing on the situation, the Conservatives pointed to this fiscal crisis across the nation as evidence that their analysis was accurate, and they then initiated a sustained propaganda campaign that quickly affected city governments. As early as 1931, for instance, Quito's *Gaceta Municipal* ran a series attacking the national government while pressing for local control over planning allocations, a policy identified for the first time as a proposed "Ley de autonomía municipal," a designation that parroted the Conservative platform.[87] The subsequent Conservative triumph in the 1933 municipal elections gave the party the right to name a new council president who would fight for more extensive financial independence. Not surprisingly, the individual they chose for this preeminent position was the loudest local advocate on this issue, the newly elected council member Jacinto Jijón y Caamaño.

The activities of the Jijón-led council aimed to restore public faith in municipal control over local administration while encouraging a heroic vision of the colonial city's autonomy—strategies designed to build leverage for a return to local governance. The celebrations of the city's quadricentennial not only proclaimed the city's Spanish character but also sought to expand personal and partisan loyalty among the working class. As Ana María Goetschel has pointed out, measures such as the building of worker housing on the city's south side echoed Jijón's earlier paternalistic construction of barracks at the Chillo-Jijón textile mill in the Chillo Valley to the city's southeast.[88] The housing initiative also had the secondary goal of cementing support among middle- and upper-class moderates with growing fears of working-class violence.

This disquiet had been increasing as thousands of migrants moved from the tumultuous countryside due to a deepening agricultural recession. The squalid conditions in the periurban *suburbios* in which many of them resided were featured in the mainstream press in the late 1920s. This coverage began in the moderate socialist daily *El Dia,* an example being a 1925 editorial contrasting the streets recently widened by the Junta de Embellecimiento with the poor hovels on deserted side streets that lacked even an "idea of good manners."[89] Other newspapers followed suit once the Universidad Central's resident hygienist, the sociologist Pablo Arturo Suárez, began conducting research forays into the city's slums in 1930.[90] Suárez's condemnation of these abysmal habitats appeared frequently in the capital press after the Guerra de los Cuatro Días, a four-day riot in 1932 that pitted the military against worker cells from both the Left and the Right following a disputed presidential election. As more and more editorials expressed horror at the violence and disgust at the living conditions that had sparked it, an opportunity for publicly funded housing arose.

The Conservatives moved quickly to capitalize on this situation. Scores of editorials appeared in 1933 as the party made its push to win seats on the Quito municipal council. Jijón's ally, Luis A. Páez, gave an impassioned plea before Congress that emphasized the wide variety of international responses to social inequities. Páez underscored the nonpartisan nature of his challenge, citing efforts made by the socialist mayoralty of "Red Vienna" along with a more traditional panegyric to planning commissions in Spain, France, Argentina, and Uruguay.[91] Once in power, Jijón wasted no time introducing a resolution to construct new housing blocks for workers. After the measure passed in January 1934, he even hosted an open house at his mansion in order to display a selection of blueprints for the proposed construction. The design ultimately chosen featured single-level white stucco buildings graced with red-tile roofs that evoked the neocolonial paternalism embraced by Jijón and his fellow *patrones.*[92]

The commitment to the Barrio Obrero also strengthened the Conservative hand in its campaign for municipal autonomy. Two events in particular demonstrate the party's growing power. The first concerned the restrictions placed on municipal fundraising in the 1929 legal code, which the council sidestepped in early 1934 by securing a loan for S/.320,000 from the Banco del Pichincha. Mindful of public opinion and crippled by its now chronic instability, the state turned a blind eye. Similarly, Congress avoided a potential confrontation in October 1935 concerning the council's commitment to selling the new houses directly to workers. This policy conflicted directly with Article 17 of the municipal code, which called for city properties to be sold at public auction. As in 1934, the state quickly approved Jijón's request that an exception be made.[93]

The city government then turned its eye squarely on the question of real estate development in the burgeoning northern suburbs and its lucrative business potential. The 1929 code had required municipal approval of any new construction in the city, but private firms and entrepreneurs regularly ignored this provision. The city had attempted to enforce the regulations in 1931 by challenging a plan that local mogul Damián Miranda had drawn to construct a new neighborhood over the grounds of the old Jockey Club off Avenida Colón, just a few blocks down from Jacinto Jijón's residence. The council alleged that Miranda's expansive development required him to lay down urban infrastructure, such as water pipes and drainage canals, and it issued an order to that effect. Miranda ignored their order, however, and fought the case to the Supreme Court, arguing that the tasks required of him were municipal responsibilities.[94] The high court agreed with this characterization, noting that the city government was not authorized to require individuals to update urban infrastructure but only to approve aboveground blueprints.[95] Although incensed with a decision that diminished the degree to which the council could set the course of the city's development, it was forced to comply.[96]

Jijón and his successors Carlos Andrade Marín and Gustavo Mortensen began a steady campaign to expand public support for municipal control over planning in order to combat this form of evasion by business in 1934. Mortensen, who was also the rector of the Universidad Central, organized a series of public lectures on urban revitalization by national and international experts, discourses reprinted in the *Gaceta Municipal* and *El Comercio*. The gazette also reprinted well-known treatises on planning measures, including writings by Peruvian architect Emilio Harth-Terre and Chilean engineer Daniel Zamudio's work on modern urbanism.[97] These articles were often deployed strategically, as in the case of J. Benítez's summary of zoning laws and modern planning from Haussmann to Le Corbusier, which appeared in January 1938.[98] The piece argued that local control over urban development allowed for sanitary and harmonious development, and new council president Carlos Andrade Marín cited it when he petitioned reformist dictator General Alberto Enriquez in 1938 to approve a new master plan to rectify the scattered nature of the capital's growth over the previous quarter-century. This frame of reference helped persuade Enriquez, as did Andrade Marín's savvy decision to drop the oft-repeated call for municipal fiscal autonomy in favor of reinstating the government-funded million-sucre allowance to underwrite this plan. Enriquez summarily issued an August 1938 decree calling for a new master plan for the capital and reaffirming the council's control over parceling out lands for urbanization.[99]

The next year saw increasing public fascination with the new master plan. By January 1939, only four months after the presidential decree had been issued, the first reports on the north's comprehensive urbanization were under way in the university and in municipal headquarters. The council itself invited two notable Uruguayan urbanists, architect Armando Acosta y Lara and Américo Ricaldoni, the director of Montevideo's Plan Regulador, to come study Quito's future needs that June.[100] Although Ricaldoni declined, Acosta y Lara spent three weeks in the Andes during the onset of the dry season that September. He met with local planners, gave a lecture at the university, and provided a comprehensive recommendation suggesting that a "Garden City" approach would be most efficient, given the strong equatorial sun and the lack of shade trees (one wonders what his opinions would have been had he come during the rainy days of April). The address also commended the city's staunch preservationists, such as José Gabriel Navarro, and insisted that the design of the new city ensure the sanctity of the colonial monuments of the *centro*.[101]

These public events did not immediately lead to the inauguration of a new plan; however, they did help forestall a subsequent challenge to Enriquez's decree. Local real estate speculators had interpreted the new regulations as an attack on their ability to freely exploit the real estate market. Mindful of Miranda's success in petitioning the Supreme Court in 1931, they took their case to the new Congress soon after the dictator restored democracy in early 1939. The Senate opted to hear their petition in late September. This decision came so soon after Acosta y Lara's successful visit that it prompted a mass outcry. Editorials supporting the municipal right to determine the course of Quito's future urbanization appeared in each of the city's main newspapers, some penned by council members and some by professors at the Universidad Central. The *Gaceta Municipal* collected and reprinted each of these opinions in a special November issue devoted to the controversy. A reproduced graphic, which had earlier appeared in *El Comercio* and *El Dia*, contrasted the ordered progress of growth overseen by the municipality during the previous four centuries with the haphazard nature of the newest neighborhoods. The accompanying text disdains the capricious speculators whose indiscriminate greed created serious technical and social problems for a municipal government seeking the cultured, civilized, and hygienic growth of the city, all of which were qualities that had been promoted by the city government for the previous half century. This uproar persuaded the Senate to drop the matter, thus tearing down the last barrier to city control over the urbanization process.[102]

The city government's insertion of itself into national and international genealogies of urban planning, which had successfully trumped the opposition of first the state and then private enterprise, continued to drive the creation of the master plan that followed. The director of the new project turned out to be Acosta y Lara's young protégé, Guillermo Jones Odriozola, who had just won the 1939 Grand Prize of the Montevideo Architectural Factory to study in Europe. When his proposed trip was canceled by the outbreak of war, Jones opted to tour South America instead and contacted José Gabriel Navarro, whom he had met at a conference in Brazil in 1937. Upon Jones's arrival in Quito in 1941, Navarro introduced him to Gustavo Mortensen, who had heard of the young architect from Acosta y Lara. Mortensen, who had been elected president of the municipal council, saw Jones as a potential director of the new master plan and invited him to take part in the university's lecture series on urban planning. The Uruguayan prepared a detailed talk on functionalism in urban planning and its potential application to Quito. In a moment of enthusiastic "spontaneity," a member of the audience, council member Eduardo Pólit Moreno, suggested that Jones work on a draft of a regulating plan for Quito. Mortensen quickly acted upon Pólit's recommendation and persuaded the council to hire Jones, who began to work on the new plan in March 1942. Nine months later, the first draft was completed.[103]

The basic precepts behind Jones's plan concerned the functionalism of each urban zone, ideas that he had articulated in his university speech the previous year. This speech noted the need to expand Quito's recreational space so as to achieve a harmonic environment. This effort would involve practical measures such as easing traffic flows and writing zoning laws on the one hand and enhancement of the city's spiritual core on the other. The latter included both extensive attention to parks and other green space and a provision to maintain the city's monumental colonial buildings, again demonstrating a hybrid sense of Quito's spirit as modern and historical.[104] The crux of the resulting blueprint lay in dividing the city into three main zones. To the north would be a largely residential area dominated by the upper classes and characterized by broad, tree-lined avenues. Public green space would be provided by a massive park (today's Parque Carolina) to be built over the makeshift Quito airport, the operations of which would be shifted northward into what was still undeveloped farmland. The south would become a largely working- and middle-class region, chosen to coincide with the already developing industrial belt. In the colonial center, Jones foresaw a mixed-income neighborhood dominated by administrative functions and potentially by tourism. In essence, the plan submitted in 1942 imagined a modern city segregated by race and class with a cloistered museum devoted to administration, finance, and tourism at its center.

Spatial analyses of Quito's planning history at the macro level tend to consider the Jones Odriozola plan as the codification of existing tendencies—namely, the growing sociospatial segregation and the emerging longitudinal orientation of the city.[105] Its importance as a political statement, however, has not often been considered. The plan's adoption came following a decade-long struggle spearheaded by conservative municipal governments seeking to restore the city's control over planning. Their success owed much to the social dislocation of the Great Depression, in particular the state's declining legitimacy and middle- and upper-class concerns regarding worker dissatisfaction. However, given that periods during the previous century had also been marked by chaotic politics, other factors need to be considered in evaluating the success of this campaign. The conservative reconceptualization of the municipality as an alternative center of power and national identity may be compared with the uneven embrace of progress earlier city governments followed. Such a comparison underscores the radical nature of this challenge and its synchronicity with the reworking of history already identified in other institutional chronotopes.

The Chronotope of Municipal Sovereignty

From the mid-nineteenth century to the adoption of the Jones Odriozola plan in 1942, the Quito city government attempted to wrest control over public works and planning prerogatives from the state and private enterprise. The ability of the municipality to control these processes depended on both its relationship with the state and its ability to craft a public image of itself as a local and national engineer of order and progress. While the past provided leverage for urban planning initiatives, only the reconstituted Conservative governments of the 1930s successfully crafted a narrative locating the Quito cabildo at the heart of national identity. Why was this the case?

As noted earlier, municipal control over planning decisions faded as a result of the strong-arm tactics of the Garcían state during the mid-nineteenth century, particularly the elimination of cabildo-controlled budgets. While Quito continued to receive some financial backing from the national government, the legislature routinely reneged on proposed funding for critical infrastructure improvements. This budgetary shortfall severely limited the potential for urban modernization, led to unsuccessful yearly protests, and resulted in a variety of small-scale measures, at times enterprising and at times improvisational. One of the critical problems with city control over infrastructural change developed from severe cleavages among the city's ruling council members, who were divided over how much to push the Congress and how necessary the "advances" were. Disagreements concerning urban limits and spatiality, for example, tended to create open strife, which would then be resolved by delaying difficult decisions concerning the city's incursions into formerly rural zones or the efficacy of its traditional radial socioeconomic map.

The Liberal Revolution of 1895, while providing state support for many of the projects that were outlined during the Progressive era, did not ultimately resolve these more fundamental challenges. In essence, the capital's cabildo controlled local development projects; however, in practice, the state continued to dominate the allocation of funding and to determine the pace of reform. At moments of intense interest in showcasing the capital, such as during the centennials of 1909 and 1922 or during the public health crises of 1905, the national government loosened the purse strings for a variety of modernizing ventures. Otherwise, the main interest appears to have been largely in limited symbolic gestures (such as the construction of the indoor marketplace) that echoed the distinct lack of attention to infrastructure that characterized the nineteenth-century state.

This dynamic shifted slightly with the state's bankrolling of the Junta del Centenario (later the Junta de Embellecimiento de la Ciudad), which can truly be considered Quito's first relatively independent planning commission. However, as noted above, this body itself represented the most strident government attempt to curtail the power of city government, operating as a shadow cabildo with the right to determine the shape of the city, pass new legislation, and impose its own taxes. It should thus come as little surprise that Isidro Ayora, former council president, rapidly eliminated the body as redundant excess. But the new government's adoption of the 1929 municipal code, which detailed the specific responsibilities of the city government, undercut its control over alternate policies and ultimately increased its dependence on state funding. When this budget was later eradicated, the door opened for the alternative proposed by the Conservative-dominated council of 1934 and its subsequent crusade to restore urban autonomy.

At this point, it behooves us to recall the importance the Conservatives placed on taking control over the Quito council in 1934, particularly the special role played by Jacinto Jijón. This was the first time Jijón stood for local office, but it was not his first experience with city planning; he had been working with the Junta de Embellecimiento since its inception, even acting as its head in 1923. This experience decidedly influenced the Conservative platform and would also have attuned him to the mobilizing power of public commemoration. The subsequent public campaign to not only erect substantive public housing but also reframe the city, *and its cabildo,* as the instigator of national identity ought to be seen as a necessary first step in attaining national political power. While Jijón himself retreated from active political life in the next several years, he furthered the intellectual justification for this conception of the capital by penning the multivolume biography of Quito's Spanish founder, Sebastián de Benalcázar. Simultaneously, figures like Gustavo Mortensen built a bridge between the cabildo and an educated public versed in the virtues of urban planning. This network strengthened the city government, which capitalized on the state's ongoing struggles to refashion Quito's planning organization, restore its budget, and move toward the adoption of the Jones Odriozola plan. These results came at the expense of both private enterprise and the national state, which had been eclipsed by the municipal council as the driving force behind

Quito's development by 1942, a situation justified precisely by Jijón's restorative nostalgia.

On the national level, however, the ploy ultimately backfired. In 1941, the Quito cabildo did manage to bring together a national conference of municipalities that successfully called for coordinating planning improvements. However, the hoped-for network of conservative municipal governments did not propel national dominance.[106] The largest problem appears to have been a miscalculation as to the importance of the urban masses, whose support Jijón and Tobar Donoso had long courted but who defected to populist orator José María Velasco Ibarra during the 1930s. Following a disputed 1939 election in which Liberal Carlos Arroyo del Rio topped both Velasco and Jijón, the populist emerged as the most viable national alternative to the reigning Liberals. The Conservative movement suffered further humiliation when Tobar Donoso, then minister of foreign relations in a compromise cabinet Arroyo had constructed, suffered the ignominy of signing the 1942 Protocol of Rio de Janeiro, in which Ecuador ceded half its territory to Peru following a disastrous 1941 border war.[107] President Arroyo del Rio deflected one coup attempt in 1943 but fell to Velasco Ibarra the following May. The triumph of the so-called Glorious Revolution of 1944 marked the consolidation of populist dominance in national politics and the onset of a decline in the associative framework that Jijón and his fellow council members had envisioned.[108]

However, the chronotope linking the historic nature of municipal autonomy and its role in the restoration of urban order continued to hold sway in local politics and to influence the future shape of the city. Jijón himself took advantage of the new political reality and became the city's first mayor in 1945, a new popularly elected post that replaced the old position of president of the *concejo.* From this position he oversaw the creation of the new grid of radial avenues and parks that traversed the Añaquito plains in the first manifestation of Jones's plan—one that has remained largely intact for almost seventy years. Subsequent revisions to the basic schema emulated Jijón's coordination of major planning initiatives with public commemorations of the city's legendary historicity, even during an era suspiciously bereft of centenaries. Thus, the 1967 Plan Director de Quito, which rezoned the Mariscal, making it a financial center, but otherwise largely upheld Jones's plan, arrived on the heels of the United Nations call for sustained attention to preserving historic centers. UNESCO's 1978 designation of the city center as a World Heritage Site unleashed a surge of commemorative planning, beginning with 1980s Plan Quito (largely relegated to preservation efforts in and around the city) and leading to major initiatives from the city government on the twentieth and twenty-fifth anniversaries of the UN's designation, which have seen the colonial city center approximate the "museum city" first envisioned by art historians but concretized by Jones Odriozola. The contemporary Plan General de Desarrollo Territorial appeared in 2006. One of its major concerns is the suburban expansion into the Chillo and Tumbaco valleys that began during the 1980s but has been "characterized by uncontrolled expansion and speculation in residential arenas."[109] While this new document appeared poised to rectify this "disastrous" situation in time for the 2009 bicentennial of independence, perhaps its most direct ancestor was the city campaign to arrest just such growth back in 1934.

The three chronotopes establishing Quito as a site of official historical memory are essentially visions—that of the city as touristed global center, as redemptive Spanish center, or as autonomous city-state—and each played a role in crafting the formal face of Quito according to an institutional framework. There is also the question of land speculation itself. Both the Durini architectural family and the Santa Clara de San Millán indigenous commune crafted personal genealogies that enabled them to navigate the shifting spatial orientation of the city and, in particular, the burgeoning real estate market on the city's north side. Like their institutional counterparts, the Durinis and the commune members had to recognize that this navigational exercise depended on the articulation of collective histories at once *quiteño* and universal.

Chapter 5

The Durini Cosmopolis
Crafting a Hyphenated Vernacular Architecture

In an undated photograph, attributed only to "Pazmiño" (fig. 5.1), a mustachioed man attired in a dark suit and straw boater, brandishing a cane, poses in profile, gazing past two similarly clad figures deep in conversation a few feet ahead of him. In his hands is a small parcel, wrapped in white paper, which suggests that he has just emerged from the great arcade beyond. The majestic arch rising above him provides a window into this grand commercial space filled with bustling shoppers illuminated by the sunshine streaming through the vaulted glass-and-iron roof. A police officer and his daughter animatedly focus on the shops beneath the sumptuous three-story colonnade that frames the hall. A middle-aged man in black homburg and rumpled suit clutches his own package near a women's clothing store, perhaps deliberating over the Edwardian costume of a mannequin by the door. Many simply stroll, ignoring the camera. Not so a lad immaculately dressed in knickers and eight-quarter cap halfway down the hall; he stares, transfixed. Even more intrigued are the several porters loitering near the entryway, ready in an instant to help a gentleman or lady whose purchase might be too large to carry home unassisted. Two in decent attire lean jauntily against the pillars of the great arch; however, tucked behind those col-

Fig. 5.1. Pasaje Royal, Quito (early 1920s). Courtesy Archivo Histórico, Banco Central del Ecuador.

umns on the left, a shabbier pair—including a poncho-clad Indian—is almost invisible in the fading light. One can almost hear the photographer ordering them to move out of the frame. After all, this was to be a portrait of the Pasaje Royal, the triumphant masterpiece of Swiss-Italian émigré Francisco Durini Cáceres, and the one-time center of Quito chic.

Like few other buildings in Quito, Durini's *passage* (1912–1914) articulated a scenography of modernity and consumption located a scant block from the

Plaza Grande, the heart of the colonial city and home to state and city bureaucrats. Customers strolled on a mosaic constructed of North American ceramic tile en route to the central landing, which boasted gardens, a marble fountain, and a kitschy mural of Venus alighting upon a veranda in the Italian countryside. The doors nestled in the delicate colonnades were themselves elegant confections crafted from luxury woods prepared in Durini's own workshop and outlined in shimmering copper trim. The display cases and counters inside the shops echoed this décor, while the lighting fixtures featured stripped copper reminiscent of the Secessionist stirrings that had invaded Vienna, Prague, and Turin over the previous decade. These stores boasted imported fashions, haberdashery, and eyeglasses straight from Hamburg and London. After a busy afternoon shopping, businessmen, socialites, or dandies could relax by sampling the Gallic delicacies of the Pasaje Royal restaurant (whose menu was even printed in French) or taking in an evening of theater, dance, or cinema at the Teatro Eden.[1] Some even went so far as to relocate to the building's spacious apartments on the third floor while the city's best firms rented berths down the hall.

One of those companies was that of the building architect himself, whose offices overlooked Venezuela Street from the central archway. Like his grandiose structure, Francisco Durini Cáceres profited from an aura of consummate modernity. Along with his father, Lorenzo, and brother Pedro, Durini built the largest architectural concern in the capital at least partially based upon their ability to promote a worldly image of European gallantry coupled with exquisite technical expertise. This persona afforded the Durinis their first commissions; however, the firm's lasting power rested upon Francisco's ability to integrate himself and his architecture into the cultural sphere of his adopted home. The Pasaje Royal epitomizes these two characteristics: not only did it afford elites an opportunity to perform cosmopolitanism *a lo italiano* but it also reflected Francisco's personal ties, as the site belonged to the Palacios family, who happened to be the architect's in-laws. Later works continued to reap the rewards of personal connections but also introduced a search for an Andean vernacular modernism. This transition reflected Francisco's developing hybridity, which advanced without eliminating his Old World élan. As such, the Durini oeuvre can be viewed as an attempt to link an ecumenical personal history with the spirit of national renewal that suffused Quito's political and cultural landscape in the early twentieth century.

The Durini firm's business practices mirrored this aesthetic development, which can be seen through an analysis of its correspondence, workbooks, sketches, drafts, and the firm's library. These documents have only recently been donated to the Museo de la Ciudad in Quito by Francisco Durini's children, and this study is the first to utilize them. They demonstrate both the tenuous nature of architecture as enterprise as well as the multiple strategies the Durinis employed to overcome the difficulties of building in a peripheral city. Along with the firm's urbane image and the principal architects' constant refinement of their technique, three other factors proved invaluable in producing a vibrant firm. The first concerned the aforementioned drive to permeate the inner sanctum of the *quiteño* upper class. Each of the three Durinis diligently cultivated relationships with members of the city's upper classes, both socially and aesthetically. Second, they persistently sought to develop local sources for the fine woodwork, metals, and marble sculpture adorning their structures in order to eliminate their reliance on foreign artisans, a strategy that allowed them to significantly undercut their competition. Perhaps most important, however, was their willingness to experiment so as to fulfill the whims of an eccentric elite with at times exotic tastes.

This analysis of the firm's successful cultural integration efforts focuses first on the elements of mimesis and hybridity in colonial and nineteenth-century Ecuadorian architecture. It also homes in on the Durini family's development of a cosmopolitan vernacular architecture. The story begins with two brothers, Lorenzo and Francisco Durini Vasalli, who immigrated to Costa Rica from their native Switzerland, where Lorenzo had befriended exiled Ecuadorian politician Leonidas Plaza during the 1890s. Seduced by Plaza's offer of patronage, Lorenzo migrated to Quito in 1904. Plaza's commissions largely evaporated after Lorenzo's arrival, leading to the formation of a new company with his sons, Pedro and Francisco Durini Cáceres. Lorenzo died prematurely, in 1906, likely due in part to exhaustion and overwork, but the business practices of his new firm and the importance that the performance of cosmopolitanism played, both personally and professionally, in its success is worthy of study. Francisco's development of an Andean vernacular modernism unified his personal heritage and historicist training, and his handling of Italian *stile floreale,* the city's colonial palate, and the universal aspirations of his clientele are of particular interest.

Historicism and Mimesis in Quito's Nineteenth-Century Architecture

Nineteenth-century Western architecture reflected a romantic embrace of history and a nationalist search for origins. The fascination with progress advocated by Hegel and Comte inspired a stylistic language in which architectural form displayed patriotic teleologies. The historicist ethos boisterously transformed European and American capitals into allegorical landscapes, as in the famous examples of Haussmann's Paris or the Viennese Ringstrasse. As noted by Carl Schorske, among others, Vienna's Rathaus quarter perhaps exemplifies the ideal vision of architectural style as "the embodiment of history," with an ideational mosaic including neo-Renaissance (learning) for the university, neo-Gothic (emergent burgher identity) for the municipal headquarters, and baroque (artistic patronage and elegance) for the theater.[2]

The historicist pageant also appeared in great American capitals as elites and state actors attempted to display their national pride and glory in a manner similar to that of the old continent. The earliest examples of such centralized display occurred in former viceregal capitals such as Mexico City and Rio de Janeiro. The latter was a special target of monumental construction following the 1808 arrival of Portuguese emperor João VI, whose exile during the Napoleonic wars was largely spent transforming the Brazilian capital into a "tropical Versailles" (curated by a French commission) whose botanical gardens can still be enjoyed.[3] These didactic constructions and reconstructions of symbolic urban centers reappeared in Pierre Charles L'Enfant's plan for Washington, DC, the Belle Époque reconstructions of Buenos Aires and Rio de Janeiro, and the allegorical statuary along Mexico City's Paseo de la Reforma, which served as a veritable pageant of nationalist history during the Porfirian period.[4] As in Vienna or Paris, these state monuments anticipated nearby haute bourgeois housing enclaves, which also embraced a formal language rooted in historic revivalism. The widespread nature of these positivist spectacles led to Jorge Hardoy's influential formulation claiming that no autochthonous architecture developed in Latin America until experimentation with modernism began there in the 1930s.[5] Hardoy's argument has been echoed in the popular notion that the *fin-de-siglo*'s historicism ought to be viewed as a moment of intense cultural dependency driven by a state acting as stylistic interlocutor in alliance with modernizing elites, who had gained traction in the majority of urban histories written about the *fin-de-siglo*. Of particular import was the eradication of "any trace of Spanish or colonial origin . . . as a reminder of a past of shame and backwardness," as one contemporary scholar has put it.[6]

While one can indeed identify a broad translocation of styles—at times even of buildings, as in the celebrated case of the iron mansion Gustave Eiffel sent in pieces up the Amazon to Iquitos for the Peruvian rubber baron Anselmo del Aguila—this interpretation oversimplifies the process of cultural exchange represented by historicist and eclectic architecture. Roberto Segre has maintained that the consideration of Latin American eclecticism as inherently mimetic obscures its beneficial impact as an opportunity for local architects, European immigrants, and legions of workers and artisans. He also notes the palpable potential for aesthetic innovation offered by the utilization of historic styles as a template for a wide variety of stylistic combinations while calling for relational unity with the stylistic palate of the surroundings.[7]

The development of Quito's architecture during the nineteenth century echoes the dialectic between mimesis and hybrid innovation. The earliest advocates for modernizing the city's architectural palette had frequently traveled in Europe and recommended adopting French and Italian styles.[8] Nevertheless, few alterations occurred during the first half of the nineteenth century with the exception of the neoclassical remodeling of the Palacio de Carondelet, previous seat of the Audiencia president, following the split from Gran Colombia in 1830. Change came about suddenly in 1868, when a devastating earthquake left many buildings badly damaged and destroyed the towers of the San Francisco church.[9] President Gabriel García Moreno, whose penchant for public works has been noted, took advantage of this situation and not only funneled state funds into the reconstruction of the church but also took steps to develop a local infrastructure for modern construction and design. As such, his administration's efforts ought to be considered both an importation of European know-how and the establishment of a local cadre of trained architects and artisans heralding the expansion of modern historicist construction in the last third of the century.

One of the first steps in the effort was the establishment of the Polytechnic University in 1870. Its Jesuit professors not only revolutionized cartography but also taught drafting and architectural design. Juan Menten's impact was particularly instrumental given his role as chief architect for the National Observatory, the first built in South America. García Moreno invited not only the university's Jesuit professors but other European architects, including Englishman Thomas Reed and the German Francisco Schmidt, to participate in state projects. Reed, though a transient, produced several monumental works in the early 1870s, including the panopticon prison, the garden paths of Alameda Park, and the imposing stone La Paz Bridge crossing the Machángara River at the city's southern entry.[10] Schmidt, who began his stay in Quito by erecting the Escuela de Artes y Oficios, an artisan school run by the Catholic Church, became one of the critical figures of *quiteño* construction over the next several decades, eventually joining forces with the engineer, architect, and cartographer Gualberto Pérez in one of the city's most important architectural concerns of the *fin-de-siglo*. Schmidt's historicist roots are reflected not only in the Romanesque of the Escuela de Artes y Oficios (and its incorporation of Gothic arches) but also in his choice of a neoclassical ethos for the Teatro Nacional Sucre, perhaps his most important project of this period. Begun in 1879, yet not completed until the centennial of independence from Spain in 1922, the work's main entry incorporated the original arches of the slaughterhouse that had previously dominated the square.[11]

Although both Reed and Schmidt offered classes at the Polytechnic University, architectural studies and monumental construction stagnated during the Progressive era as the national government moved away from urban revitalization. The few changes to the city's architectural landscape came in the form of modernizing face-lifts for the aging structures of the colonial city center. Few and far between, they nevertheless preoccupied the municipality, which passed an early zoning law (as part of an 1890 ordinance) seeking to encourage regularity among new and extant buildings by preserving horizontal continuity, requiring whitewashed or painted façades in sensible colors, and rounded corners.[12] Attempts to create new monuments did occur, notably when a statue of Marshal

Antonio José de Sucre was commissioned to adorn Santo Domingo Plaza. Other ventures were begun but not completed, such as a proposed column celebrating the birth of independence that was first proposed by the Congress in 1888. The project languished until 1894, when President Luis Cordero appointed Juan Bautista Minghetti to design the monument. Although Minghetti drafted plans, the Liberal Revolution stopped the project.[13]

The new Liberal government that came to power in 1895, however, strongly supported the creation of monumental architectural works reflecting contemporary trends, of which the most famous is Schmidt and Perez's Mercado del Sur, which was the first structure in the city to make substantial use of glass and iron in its roof. These efforts by the Liberal government grew exponentially during Leonidas Plaza's administration, particularly after the establishment of the new Escuela de Bellas Artes (EBA) in 1903, which provided a training ground for new local architects and draftsmen along with painters, musicians, and sculptors. The school's organizing force was the author, landscape portraitist, and liberal ideologue Luís A. Martínez. Martínez secured the Italian architect Giácomo Radiconcini to head a fledgling program that trained a number of students in neo-Renaissance aesthetics. Radiconcini had mixed results in developing local expertise; however, he did encourage an embrace of historicism that fostered the careers of other foreign architects. These included the Russo brothers, Pablo and Antonino, and the German priest Pedro Huberto Brüning. The Russo Hermanos firm, for instance, was particularly successful in residential building, eventually winning the municipality's Premio al Ornato in 1920 for the Renaissance revival Gangotena-Mancheno house on San Francisco Square.[14] On the other hand, Brüning, who arrived in 1899, when relations between the Liberal state and the Church normalized, transformed sacred space throughout the country by incorporating an unadorned neo-Gothic style, usually in brick, that contrasted with the famous examples of high baroque churches that are so common in the Ecuadorian Andes.[15] By 1910, this imported historicism had become the dominant school in *quiteño* architecture, with a particular emphasis on French and Italian styles.

The Durini family represented one of these early architectural imports whose technical knowledge and masterful work on the Costa Rican National Theater attracted Leonidas Plaza during his exile in the Central American nation. Unlike their peers, however, the Durinis shifted their approach from academic historicism to eclecticism, showing a strong influence of Italian *stile floreale* considered in dialogue with Quito's colonial monumentality. Moreover, the development of a hybrid vernacular architecture represented not only an aesthetic innovation but also a response to the potential pitfalls of a tight market in which representation of one's cosmopolitanism and local commitment proved necessary to navigating Ecuadorian elite society and attracting clients and patrons.

Lorenzo Durini and *"el arte del martillo"*

The crucial element of hybridity, which eventually appeared in the Durinis' architecture, stemmed from a dynamic family history that had thrived on both sides of the Atlantic since the mid-nineteenth century. The patriarch of the family, Giovanni Durini (normally referred to as Juan in existing documentation) was born in Lombardy but relocated to Tremona in the Italian section of Switzerland as a result of his involvement in Risorgimento uprisings.[16] There, the youth met his future wife, Elizabetta Vasalli, with whom he had two sons, Lorenzo and Francisco (the Elder). Juan Durini garnered some renown in Tremona for his sculpture. However, a regional recession led him to join the legions of masons, sculptors, and architects immigrating to the Americas at the height of the export boom. Most of those emigrating from Europe to Latin America settled in the great commercial entrepôts of Argentina, Brazil, or Mexico. Durini was an exception, instead migrating to Lima, during its moment of guano prosperity, where he profited from the whims of the freewheeling local sophisticates. He soon saved enough money to send his sons back to Genoa to complete their own training before returning to Lima to collaborate with their father.[17]

Lorenzo, Juan's elder son, married a *limeña,* Juana Cáceres, during this interlude, and the couple returned to Tremona in the late 1870s. His two children, Francisco Manuel and Pedro, were born in the old country but would spend their formative years in Costa Rica. The family's move to San José stemmed from the activities of Lorenzo's brother, Francisco the Elder, who left Lima for the possibilities afforded by the Central American republic's coffee boom. There, he developed a niche as an importer of high-quality statuary and mausoleums from Italy. Lorenzo, himself an accomplished sculptor, contributed pieces but increasingly farmed out contracts to associates in Genoa and Switzerland. Once this system was established enough to work independently, he moved to Costa Rica. There, the brothers formed a new firm named Durini Hermanos, whose rapid turnaround of high-quality efforts garnered them a local reputation, particularly among Lorenzo's contacts in freemasonry circles. Their greatest renown, however, came as a result of their fortuitous involvement with the Costa Rican National Theater.

The theater proved a staging ground for the business techniques the Durini family would later employ to great success in Quito and is therefore worth discussing in detail. The project originated as a result of a series of earthquakes in 1888 that destroyed the capital's elegant Teatro Mora, also known as the Municipal Theater, a spot frequented by the urban elite. The event coincided with a national election during which presidential candidate José Joaquín Rodríguez stressed the imperative of rebuilding a structure that could symbolize the nation's commitment to arts and culture. Upon taking office in 1890, Rodríguez

Fig. 5.2. Lorenzo Durini, San José National Theater, stairwell (1897). Courtesy Durini Collection, Museo de la Ciudad, Quito.

appointed his son-in-law, Secretary of War and Mining Rafael Iglesias, as manager of the project. A nominally independent commission selected a composite Italianate plan incorporating aspects of several designs submitted by local architects. However, Iglesias preferred to incorporate Beaux Arts decorative elements and challenged the plan upon his own ascension to the presidency in 1893. This

position bred sustained conflict with the director of public works, Nicolás Cha-
varría, who ultimately resigned from his post, the first of three such resignations
over the next two years. In 1895, the exasperated administration finally looked
abroad, inviting Italian engineer Ruy Cristóforo Molinari to repair the damage.

The Durini brothers took advantage of this power vacuum to increase their
profile. The firm had been engaged with the project since 1890, when portions
of Francisco the Elder's design had been incorporated into the initial Italianate
proposal. Durini Hermanos secured a subcontract in 1893 to provide stairwells
for the main foyer of the theater (fig. 5.2), but, without a central overseer on the
project, Lorenzo's role steadily increased. These new responsibilities included
building dressing rooms and providing ever more statuary (including one piece
that had originally been destined for a private mausoleum and accidentally got
wrapped into the budget). By the time Molinari arrived, Lorenzo had become
de facto director of the project and was hoping to be able to continue working
on the interior. Indeed, the Durinis submitted a proposal to finalize their efforts; however, their insistence on continuing payments to Italian vendors when
products had yet to be received poisoned the public to their case. The contract
ultimately went to Molinari's more established firm, but the Durinis had successfully raised their national profile.[18]

Another by-product was the growing attention that Lorenzo Durini received
from a fellow mason and prominent Ecuadorian exile, General Leonidas Plaza
Gutierrez. Plaza was a member of Eloy Alfaro's Radical Liberal Party who had
left Ecuador for exile in San José in 1884 after a failed uprising. His fascination
with Lorenzo's statuary led to conversations concerning vast public projects, including a magisterial Legislative Palace, that he hoped to erect when he finally
returned to Ecuador. When Plaza received news of the Liberal Revolution in late
1895 and returned to his homeland, Lorenzo and Francisco Durini expected to
soon follow their friend to transform the Andean capital.

This large-scale project languished during the first years of the Liberal Revolution, however, due to continuing political strife in Ecuador and a growing
rift between Plaza and Eloy Alfaro over the speed with which the separation
of church and state should be instituted. Plaza's victory in the 1901 presidential elections not only accelerated the passage of anticlerical laws but also led to
his extended patronage of the arts. Besides establishing the EBA and recruit-
ing the conservative academicist Giácomo Radiconcini to head its architectural
program, Plaza hoped to make a dramatic mark on the capital by keeping his
pledge to Lorenzo Durini. Plaza soon invited him to submit blueprints for a vast
new Legislative Palace.

Lorenzo's blueprints, which were completed by Plaza's inaugural in 1902,
met Radiconcini's preconditions by virtue of his strict adherence to neoclassical
idiom while also bowing to Plaza's desire for a monument to secular society.
However, the split in Liberal ranks meant that securing congressional approval
would take time, regardless of the design's merit. Plaza opted to introduce his

protégés to the capital's powerbrokers through a back channel in 1902 by inviting Francisco the Elder to submit a proposal for a new waterworks the municipality had decided to construct. Despite the deadline for proposals having passed, Durini's assurance that he could find an American partner to partially cover the cost, coupled with Plaza's support, persuaded the council to accept the Durini application that December.[19] In January 1903, Francisco the Elder traveled to Quito to sign the contract, and during this journey Plaza introduced him to several members of the traditional and Liberal elite. The visit secured the commission for the waterworks; however, it also appears to have left Francisco convinced that Plaza had been exaggerating local support for the Legislative Palace project and the availability of liquid capital for future commissions. Indeed, he warned Lorenzo of this potential difficulty soon after departing. Nevertheless, his older brother opted to trust in the president's friendship, and he embarked for Quito in June 1903.[20]

When Lorenzo arrived in the Ecuadorian capital, however, he soon came to rue his decision. Although he admired the exquisite sculpture of the anonymous indigenous craftsmen evident in the city's fine colonial churches, Francisco the Elder's assessment of the city's problems appeared accurate. Modern façades graced isolated buildings damaged during the 1868 earthquake that had also demolished the bell towers of San Francisco, yet the majority of private homes still had their crumbling colonial features.[21] The few new structures mostly ignored basic tenets of the EBA's historicist ethos, with which Lorenzo was intimately familiar; most obviously flouted was the tenet of architectural cohesion within a single structure. The municipality had attempted to regulate this situation in 1890 with a zoning ordinance that called for whitewashed exterior walls, rounded corners, and the inclusion of chimneys rather than the open fires that typically graced the interior patios of colonial homes as well as informal indigenous *chozas*.[22] The majority of the population could not afford the luxuries decreed by a state fascinated with the prospect of a unified architectural framework, however, and thus routinely ignored these strictures. The few exceptions, which included Francisco Schmidt's still unfinished neoclassical Sucre Theater and Manuel Jijón's mansion in the northwestern environs, appeared as isolated jewels, underscoring the difficulty of making a living as a society architect.

Lorenzo expressed his deepening anxiety in a series of letters, penned over the course of the summer of 1903, in which he bemoaned his dwindling bank account and the lack of a new commission.[23] He wrote his son Pedro as early as July 30, 1903, complaining of his fear that he would need to return to stonemasonry, which he termed "*el arte del martillo*," which inspired only excruciating headaches. This striking admission suggests his later illness was both psychological and physical. His early September hospital stay after spitting up blood furthers this interpretation, considering that his first correspondence upon exiting, which was to his father, highlighted not the pain but instead the medical bill of S/.273

Fig. 5.3. Commemorative photo of the Plaza de la Independencia on the occasion of the 1906 dedication of the monument. Courtesy Durini Collection, Museo de la Ciudad, Quito.

that he could not afford.[24] Indeed, by the end of the month, he considered moving to Lima to work near his father since no opportunities had yet opened up in Quito.[25]

A growing rift with Francisco the Elder, who had yet to find an American partner for the waterworks, exacerbated the situation. Angry confrontations between the siblings ended with Francisco storming out of Lorenzo's house during one of his periodic visits to Quito and embarking for Costa Rica, vowing to dissolve the partnership.[26] These challenges finally inspired Lorenzo to enact a plan he had long contemplated, one that involved forming a partnership with his sons to compete for the scant commissions available in his adopted home. This idea appears to have occurred to him as early as July 1903, when he exhorted Pedro to quickly liquidate the company in San José and join him in Quito as soon as possible.[27] Pedro's business background would provide welcome relief from the daily grind for Lorenzo, yet the key to the endeavor concerned his older son, Francisco Manuel, who was then a student at the Instituto Tecnico di Milano. As Lorenzo explained in a letter to his father that October, forming the company would allow "Manuelito," who was making rapid progress through his program in Milan, to supplement his income with side projects and gain valuable experience as both a drafter and as a liaison with Lorenzo's Italian contacts.[28] Unspoken was the simple consideration that the move would drastically

Fig. 5.4. Detail of commemorative photo of the Plaza de la Independencia from the centennial celebrations of 1909. Courtesy Durini Collection, Museo de la Ciudad, Quito.

decrease Lorenzo's overhead by minimizing the need to hire a representative in Italy, a critical issue given the family's uncertain finances.

The opportunity to implement this plan came with the revival of the long-dormant municipal project to build a heraldic column celebrating Quito's 1809 declaration of independence from Spain. Congress had first approved the effort in 1888, and Minghetti, the Salesian priest, had completed his design in 1894. In addition to its winged Victory, Spanish lion, and Andean condor, Minghetti's design featured bas relief panels depicting the heroic martyrs of the massacre of August 2, 1810 (figs. 5.3 and 5.4). Minghetti joined the myriad clerical exiles who left Ecuador following the Liberal triumph, but after stability returned at the dawn of the new century, Plaza pulled strings to allow a Durini project to be considered by the municipality in the summer of 1903. Lorenzo immediately shipped Minghetti's diagrams to Milan for his son Francisco Manuel to review. The latter reworked the original project into a classical model, softening several of the figurative features after consultation with Adriático Froli, a Milanese sculptor with whom Lorenzo had previously collaborated. He also altered several elements to dialogue with the surrounding square. These changes included transforming the central pillar into an assortment of four Corinthian columns, whose orientation toward the corners of the plaza helped accentuate the monument's symmetry despite its figural emphasis on the east. The shift also amplified the piece's cultural specificity by incorporating a repeating global motif along the base's perimeter, thus both reinforcing the balance between the monument and the plaza and also trading upon the nation's and the city's equatorial associations. The global motif was repeated at the apex, where it served as a base for the winged Victory herself. Both of these elements might have been Lorenzo's suggestion, given the recent arrival of the second French Geodesic Mission, which had reintroduced the idea of the city's global centrality into the national public sphere.

Given the conceptual strength of Francisco Manuel's final design for the project, Lorenzo persuaded him to visit Quito to present the plans in the name of L. Durini & Hijos, the new company he hoped would replace the disintegrating Durini Hermanos. Francisco made the trip from Milan, making a strong pitch to a closed-door session of the municipal council in March 1904. Surprisingly, given the inclusion of proposals by the likes of Frédéric-Auguste Bartholdi, famed designer of New York's Statue of Liberty, Durini's scheme emerged victorious, partly as a result of its moderate price tag.[29] Another important facet appears to have been the burgeoning friendship between Pedro Durini and the young entrepreneur Genaro Larrea, who recently had taken the reins of the committee in charge of the project. A contract followed in May, which appeared to secure the first link in a number of future endeavors.[30]

The new company proved to be more successful than Durini Hermanos, partly because of Plaza's continued support but also because of a symbiotic business model. Despite worsening stomach illness, Lorenzo operated as the chief sales representative, given his contacts in the upper echelon of the government. For example, in 1905, he secured congressional support for his designs for the new Legislative Palace and also a new commission to erect a small municipal market on the north side of the city, in the San Blas neighborhood. These works were accentuated by Francisco Manuel's finishing touches, sent from Milan, where he had returned to continue his studies. There, he acted as a liaison with local artisans, purchased luxury materials such as marble and iron elements, and continued to refine his drafting techniques. For example, he collaborated with Froli on the revision of the design for the interior of the Legislative Palace that was finally accepted by the Congress, in the process accentuating ornamental elements to take advantage of the sculptor's idiom. Back in Quito, Pedro provided logistical support for the coordination of material transport within the country and courted influential young people, involving them as a resource for the design team. A case in point can be seen in an expedition he organized to hunt an Andean condor with the objective of embalming it to send to Adriático Froli, who had a poor grasp of the physiognomy of the bird. Although no condor was found, the expedition helped cement Pedro's local contacts and reputation as a sporting aficionado, which would later prove advantageous.[31]

But the spirit of collaboration could not help the firm contend with the grave political situation that developed in 1906. Plaza's term in office ended in September 1905, when his hand-picked successor, Lizardo García, came to power. Alfaro's wing of the party had nothing but contempt for this new leader and soon staged a local insurrection. By January 1906, the support for García had diminished, leading to Alfaro's successful coup. His return to power led to the exile of his opponents, including Leonidas Plaza. For the Durinis, these events abruptly removed their primary patron, whose backing had secured their most lucrative contracts. The new administration quickly pulled the funding for the Legislative Palace, by far the most exorbitant of Plaza's promised commissions. By April 1906, the state had defaulted on its payment for even the initial studies, and the firm faced a serious fiscal crisis.[32]

These pressures took their toll on Lorenzo, whose stomach ailment, which was probably cancer, worsened to the point that he finally acceded to familial requests that he return to Italy for medical treatment. Francisco Manuel opted to interrupt his studies again and return to Quito to oversee the final elevation of the monument while his father prepared to travel to Milan for treatment and to manage the Italian connections. Lorenzo's weakened state did not, however, stop him from continuing to offer his son suggestions for future projects, including a lengthy epistle concerning a project to enclose a park in Riobamba honoring the eighteenth-century cartographer Pedro Vicente Maldonado, the design of which was also tied to the commemoration of La Condamine's voyage.[33] His trepidation concerning the journey and commitment to the independence monument led to a clandestine stay in Guayaquil following Manuel's arrival. Only when the monument was dedicated on August 10, 1906, did Lorenzo Durini finally embark for Milan. He died there the following October.[34]

Cosmopolitanism as Commodity

Lorenzo's death presented a major challenge for the Durini firm. Faced with the prospect of diminishing returns, given the tight architectural market, the brothers spent the next several years attempting to diversify operations, with mixed results. Pedro, who had long been charged with coordinating the firm's finances, attempted to develop a store specializing in luxury and imported goods, particularly sporting accessories. Although his contacts among the capital's playboys did not garner enough income for this endeavor to succeed, they did bring him several commissions for mausoleums, which proved a relatively profitable but enervating venture, ultimately abandoned.

Francisco continued to stress the technical expertise he had gained in Milan when wooing clients, but, unlike his brother, he sought local, hybrid means of nourishing his business. This involved deepening his relationships with the municipality, the national government, and the elite, whose ranks he unequivocally joined following his 1908 marriage to Rosa Palacios. He also developed an artisanal workshop to produce lesser-grade statuary and woodwork in order to curb the costs associated with the highly transnational operation that Lorenzo had favored. Eventually these decisions would lead to shifts in his architectural sensibility, which developed a hyphenated Andean-Italian vernacular. The techniques that each of the Durinis deployed to scrape together commissions in a tight market thus built upon cultivated personas as cosmopolitan artists and technicians. A Durini structure represented more than a building—it represented a way of life defined by a modern sensibility that was constructed with modern techniques.

Pedro Durini, in particular, tended a reputation as a detached cosmopolite with a flair for adventure that dovetailed with his commercial interests in importing luxury goods. As a youth of sixteen he had left Costa Rica to develop an import store in Guatemala, which summarily failed. Undeterred, as the century dawned he traveled to Hamburg—then one of the world's largest ports, with shipping companies trading with South America, Africa, and Asia—to perfect his business acumen. He studied at its university, took advantage of the city's sporting culture, and perfected his linguistic skills (he could competently speak and write French, German, Italian, Spanish, and English). He also appears to have engaged with the architectural innovations developing among the Wagner school in Vienna and was most likely the source of a series of magazines on this work that ultimately found their way into Francisco Durini's private library. Upon his return to San José in 1902, Pedro successfully acted as business manager for the family firm while also dabbling in ready-made construction materials purchased from Europe and the United States.[35] His small inventory of marble and iron ornaments, paint, and woodworking tools followed him to Ecuador in early 1905, and they became the basis for a store that was soon an important side venture for the firm.[36] As early as September 1905, L. Durini & Hijos was filling orders for extensive interior remodeling. A particularly adventurous client, Miguel Páez, decided to outfit his entire home, including a dining room, various sitting rooms, and a music room (with piano). Páez picked the desired items out of a catalog featuring the products of distributors as far-flung as Paris, Hamburg, and New York but that were deliverable within a scant seven months.[37]

The store operated largely as a sideline for Pedro, who appears to have devoted most of his time to sport and leisure. These activities, however, expanded his social contacts and eventually led to his first independent commissions. Soon after arriving in Quito, he helped organize and found the Polo Club at the Hippodrome in the city's northern environs. There, he and his fellow playboys, including his brother Francisco, incongruously demonstrated European flair with overly long polo mallets ill suited for use with minuscule Andean horses (fig. 5.5). Pedro also fenced, hiked, and, in April 1907, founded the Andes Tennis Club, which today is the oldest country club in the city.[38]

Fig. 5.5. Pedro Durini, one of the founders of the Polo Club at the Hippodrome, with his long European mallet and minuscule Andean polo pony. Courtesy Durini Collection, Museo de la Ciudad, Quito.

Pedro Durini's style appears to have endeared him to the *quiteño* upper crust and made him one of the rising stars of a widespread movement geared toward adopting a sophisticated culture of leisure. The new leisure class provided a source of amusement and a natural clientele for the lavish mausoleums Pedro designed. The earliest and the best known of these projects came to him through his debonair colleague Genaro Larrea, whose important role in the realization of the independence monument has already been noted. After Larrea's father, Teodoro, perished while visiting Cannes in 1905, the young man persuaded his mother, Teresa Valdivieso, to hire Pedro to build a final resting place in San Diego cemetery, home to the remains of Quito's best families.[39]

Pedro had already established his credentials as a producer of mausoleums when, following his father's illness, he completed another San Diego resting place that Lorenzo had designed for the Palacios family. Pedro now worked diligently on the Larrea commission in the hope that he would be able to set up an independent operation specializing in these elaborate monuments. He presented more than a thousand drawings to Mrs. Larrea, who proved to be a particularly finicky patron. She finally chose a particularly lovely plan featuring a winged angel resting by a cross, her head propped up by her left arm, her

Fig. 5.6. Pedro Durini, Larrea Mausoleum (1908). Courtesy Durini Collection, Museo de la Ciudad, Quito.

right arm lying still against her body, holding a garland (fig. 5.6). By January 1907, Pedro had sent the designs to his brother, who had returned to Milan, to share with his schoolmate, Pietro Capurro, who had become the firm's primary sculptor following Lorenzo's illness and death. Last-minute additions by the Larreas arrived in a number of other letters, including two on January 16, and the clients' numerous specifications and fears that the piece would be less than adequate began to frustrate Pedro.[40] When the family decided that they wanted

The
The Du
134 |
ther had
worksh
on f
p

the mauseoleum project completed earlier than origir
to panic. He thus exhorted Francisco to energize Ca
the sculptor to take particular care with this piec
Quito of his former rival, Carlo Libero Valente,
to tarnish Capurro's local reputation. More disa
of the angel's wings broke off during packing—
Although it took until the following April for the thn ,
work to reach Guayaquil, they arrived safely in Quito by May , ,
quickly assembled.[41]

Pedro's difficulties managing the whims of his patrons and designers illuminate several of the obstacles that needed to be overcome in order to successfully
manage the type of transnational operation the Durinis ran. Chief among these
were the frequent hindrances to the shipping of building materials, statuary,
ornament, ironwork, and so forth. While these often stemmed from unavoid-
able transportation problems, they resulted in production delays. To forestall
impatient clients like the Larreas, the company took precautionary measures to
avoid defaulting on their contracts or running over budget. These precautionary
practices began during Lorenzo's era as a result of the problems that had cost
Durini Hermanos the commission on the National Theater but became codified when it appeared that his frequent collaborator, Adriático Froli, would not
be able to complete his work on the independence monument on time. With
Pedro's help, Lorenzo compiled a copybook reproducing the entire series of contracts and correspondence with the sculptor in preparation for possibly suing
him for breach of contract, which was ultimately unnecessary in that instance.[42]

A more problematic situation developed with regard to Capurro, Francisco's
intimate friend from his days studying in Milan. The two had first collaborated
on a monument to the poet, Juan Montalvo, in the central Andean city of Ambato. The design featured a bronze statue of the liberal writer atop a pedestal,
quill in hand, with a marble Apollo secretively crouching over his lyre below
so as to share his intimate knowledge only with the genius himself.[43] Even at
this early stage, a mild conflict developed as Capurro's payments were delayed
during the 1908 fiscal crisis. The friends continued to collaborate over the next
three years until Capurro submitted his own design for a monument that was
to be erected in Latacunga to honor a deceased philanthropist named Vicente
León. The fact that the design was submitted through the Ecuadorian consul in
Genoa, Leonidas Pallares Arteta, whom Francisco had introduced to Capurro,
compounded his sense of betrayal. Francisco thus quickly drafted his own design, along with an extensive letter to the head of the committee explaining
his philosophy as an architect. The cultivation of the client worked; Francisco
was granted the commission. However, the breach with Capurro delayed other
projects until an adequate replacement was found the following year (1912) in
another Italian, Ricardo B. Espinosa.[44]

Francisco's response to this ongoing difficulty built upon a solution his fa-

initiated soon after arriving in Quito, which was to develop his own shop. At first, this enterprise was dedicated to woodworking, with a focus furniture making, but it ultimately developed into a more rounded enterprise. Francisco's development of this workshop was facilitated by the growing availability of trained masons and artisans who studied at the Escuela de Artes y Oficios. Some of these individuals became long-term collaborators, such as the stonecutter Pedro Cóndor, who would become best known for his work in the 1920s on the Círculo Militar, a social facility bankrolled by the armed forces and featuring an ornate stone façade and interior décor with Andean motifs, such as the repeated image of a condor, evoking the national coat of arms.[45] These skilled workers contributed greatly to diminishing the reliance on foreign artisans except for the most delicate of tasks. Moreover, Durini took advantage of his own technical skills as an engineer to limit his expenditures. He had acquired this technical knowledge during his studies in Milan, where the Instituto Tecnico represented the only institution in Italy where one could simultaneously learn the craft of the designer and that of the *capomaestro,* or master builder. This multifaceted expertise allowed Francisco to build a reputation as an engineer as well as an architect, which expanded his opportunities in the Andean citadel.[46]

One of the most important clients Francisco courted as an engineer was the Quito municipality, which respected his talents as a result of his efforts with the column to independence but which still harbored some resentment toward the family following the waterworks debacle. The city government hoped to beautify Quito for the 1909 centennial and as a result engaged in a number of improvements to the local infrastructure and recreational space. Francisco Durini's Milanese experience working with iron helped persuade the municipality to hire L. Durini & Hijos to build monumental gates enclosing the Plaza de la Independencia as part of the park's reconstruction in 1905. Following his father's death, Francisco took the lead on this project and also persuaded the body to grant him and his brother other small jobs, such as leveling the streets around the plaza and quickly building a modest marketplace in the northern neighborhood of San Blas. Francisco completed the latter ahead of schedule and under budget as a result of a successful negotiation of a 50 percent reduction in the transportation costs of materials from Guayaquil to Quito.[47]

These minor contracts began to pay off in November 1906, when Francisco was hired as a consultant to ascertain the possibility of renovating the municipal headquarters. In his report, Durini argued that any attempt to simply provide a modernizing facelift would fail because the walls could not support an additional story and because the proportions of the façade were unbalanced and did not follow "*el estilo que ostenta*" (the style it purports). As such, he recommended razing the Casa Municipal, expropriating some adjacent land, and immediately initiating a contest to design an appropriate venue for the august body. The budget would be substantial: S/.120,000. Although there was initially some resistance to his suggestions, an impassioned speech by the *procurador síndico* (prosecutor) associating Durini's recommendation with the advent of modernity and the necessary transformation of Quito in accord with the advancement of humanity persuaded the council of the need for urgent action.[48] Their first move was to hire Durini as municipal engineer to oversee the implementation of public construction and plans for a new palace, which Durini executed according to a neo-Renaissance model that was in line with the ideal of urban order and governance. Although the building's cost proved to be prohibitive, it remained one of Durini's favorite designs and opened up private interest in his workmanship and expertise.[49] As early as 1907, he was consulted to approve plans for Ramón Barba Naranjo's house on the Plaza Grande, which featured interior patios and an iron-and-glass roof and also provided a facelift to a villa belonging to Carlos Alvarez.

While Francisco appears to have cemented his position as an established architect by 1907, Pedro's design program languished over the next two years. He did receive another commission for a mausoleum in Ambato, but his travails persuaded him to diversify his entrepreneurial activities, still his greatest strength. In April 1908, he began importing samples of photographic equipment from Dresden, taking advantage of his German contacts. This was followed with a flurry of luxury sporting goods, including billiard supplies from New York, tennis balls and tennis shoes from New Orleans and London, and, randomly, cardboard boxes, also from New Orleans. New construction materials such as bulk cement came next, along with typewriters and ever more paraphernalia for the rapidly expanding Andes Tennis Club.[50] In the midst of this flurry of commercial planning, for reasons not fully clear, Pedro opted to return to Costa Rica in 1909 to establish his new store. Francisco the Elder, however, had begun to operate more extensively in other Central American republics and in Mexico, which limited Pedro's prospects in San José and forced him to return empty-handed to Ecuador in 1911. His arrival in Guayaquil coincided with a military uprising against President Alfaro, whose term was just coming to a close but who was not willing to give up power peacefully. The impulsive Pedro joined the militias attempting to overthrow the president. In the ensuing coastal campaign, he caught yellow fever, perishing in February 1912 at the age of twenty-nine.

Ironically, Pedro's rootless and erratic final years ultimately led him back to Quito as a result of Francisco's integration within the *quiteño* elite. The Palacios family, one-time patrons whose mausoleum Pedro himself had completed in 1906, offered their son-in-law the option to have his brother share the family crypt. Pedro's remains were dutifully transferred to Quito and buried in the San Diego cemetery in close proximity to his most accomplished architectural work.[51] Henceforth, Francisco's developing hybridity would become the watchword of Durini construction in Ecuador's capital. Increasingly, his engagement with the city's culture would impact his architectural experiments as well as his commercial exploits.

Beyond Historicism

When the Durinis arrived in Ecuador, they faced many commercial challenges—difficulties that they were able to overcome by convincing clients of the quality of their technical training and by cultivating an air of modern cosmopolitanism. They also had the advantage of being able to insert themselves seamlessly into the mainstream of Ecuadorian architectonic circles by virtue of their facility within the academicist style then in vogue in the capital. The popularity of this academicist style was partly due to the prevalence of positivist philosophy within state circles as well as to the presence and influence of Giácomo Radioncini in the Escuela de Bellas Artes. Lorenzo's extensive experience working within historicist traditions had served the Durinis well in this regard, as did Francisco's training in Milan, a city well known for its conservative architectural climate. However, by the early 1910s, Francisco had begun to alter his tectonic language to take more advantage of the possibilities of modern construction techniques, including the use of poured concrete and an altered formal language that began to be influenced by art nouveau elements. These changes would be incorporated into the Pasaje Royal and developed further in his mature eclectic works, particularly in commercial buildings such as the Círculo Militar and the Banco del Pichincha headquarters along with the many residential villas that dotted the Mariscal and other parts of the old city.

Although Francisco Durini never fully abandoned the formal language of European historicism, these later structures marked his increased desire to form a seamless integration with existing buildings in the case of those in the *centro* and a growing interest in ever more elaborate and imaginative ornamentation in the new villas. This gradual change was partly a result of his personal interests but largely developed from his deepening involvement within the social circles of his adopted homeland. Over the next two decades, therefore, Durini emerged as a practitioner of what ought to be considered a hyphenated architecture that incorporated his roots in European historicism and sensitivity to the whims of his new compatriots and clientele.

The projects that Lorenzo Durini had arranged for his sons had run their course by 1912, a year that must have been traumatic for Francisco due to not only Pedro's death but also the recent alienation of Pietro Capurro. Francisco emerged from this crisis with help from the Palacios family, who acceded to his request to build on their land a massive shopping arcade, the Pasaje Royal. The piece was indebted to the great nineteenth-century *passages* and in particular responded to Milan's Galleria Vittorio Emanuele II, with which Francisco would have been quite familiar from his school days. At the same time, however, its scale and approach to ornament marked a great departure from Francisco's earlier historicist work. It was by far the largest commercial establishment in the city, with dozens of stores, a theater, restaurants, and cafés—a place to see and be seen. For a time, the Pasaje was Quito's tallest building, with its four stories outstripping the horizontality of a city whose proximity to several fault lines still limits its potential for a vertical cityscape. In addition, it incorporated aspects of contemporary movements in its use of art nouveau's decorative language in the floral designs affixed to the entrance archway and first-floor lintels along with the use of Secessionist-inspired display cases and lighting fixtures in the interior.

The move from a conventional historicism toward an eclectic approach referencing the early modernist movements probably had been brewing for some time but been delayed by the need to fulfill Lorenzo's commissions. Pedro Durini may have been an early source of interest in the revolutionary formal language of the Jugendstil, as his studies in Hamburg (1899–1902) coincided with the movement's beginnings, and he was most likely the procurer of the several early issues of *Der Architect* that became part of the Durini library. These journals featured a variety of designs from the Wagner school, including works by Josef Hoffmann and Jože Plečnik among others. By the time of his arrival in Milan the following year, Francisco would have been well aware of the innovations occurring in Europe.

Moreover, he came to the Lombard metropolis immediately after the 1902 Turin exposition of decorative art, which established the Italian presence of art nouveau, known locally as *stile floreale* or *stile Liberte.* Although it is unlikely that he experienced the exhibit firsthand, he would surely have been exposed to its repercussions within the Milanese architectural establishment and been familiar with the vanguard production that figures such as Raimondo D'Aronco, Joseph Olbrich, and Charles Rennie Mackintosh unveiled that year. He would certainly have experienced the Milanese experimentation of Giuseppe Sommaruga's Palazzo Castiglione (1901–1903), with its flamboyant three-dimensional floral decor.[52] Over the next several years, Francisco appears to have continued reading about the new style in magazines such as *L'Édilisia Moderna* and to have secured the commemorative issue of *L'Árchittetura Italiana* dedicated to the 1911 world's fair in Turin. He also procured a copy of Emerich Fellinger's *Das moderne Zimmer* (1907), which featured Secessionist furniture and interior decoration and which could be shown to clients wishing to partake of the most contemporary innovations.[53]

Durini's venture into a hybrid blend of historicism and the stirrings of a modernist aesthetic reflected these influences, introduced a new formal language into the city, and established him as an independent voice expanding the possibilities of local architecture beyond the academicism of the Escuela de Bellas Artes. The municipal council members, with whom Durini still enjoyed close contacts, reified this position by presenting him with an award in 1915—the re-

Fig. 5.7. Francisco Durini, Círculo Militar under construction (1920s). Note also the pilaster adornment on the crumbling colonial next door. Courtesy Durini Collection, Museo de la Ciudad, Quito.

cently approved Premio al Ornato. The popularity of his arcade as a nexus for the performance of modernity also persuaded other patrons to place new projects in his hands. The earliest contract came from the Círculo Militar, a social club organized in 1916 by officers from the armed forces. President Alfredo Baquerizo Moreno granted the group the exclusive use of an existing structure to develop as a gathering space, a project that the group's director, General Moisés Oliva, opted to grant to Francisco Durini. As in his 1906 negotiations with the municipal council, the architect maintained that the extant structure would be unable to bear the load of a third story. This time, the building was promptly razed to the ground—a reflection of the growth in his reputation over the intervening decade.

Although the plans for the new structure were approved in 1917, it took until 1926 for the building to open for public functions, while final touches were implemented as late as 1936. The resulting facility was the most dramatic expression of leisure space in Quito and soon became a favorite spot not only for the military but also for private galas and state balls. The ground floor boasted spacious reception halls and a fine restaurant while amenities such as a library and guest rooms were to be found on the second story.

The Círculo Militar (fig. 5.7) represented the first of Durini's structures to extensively feature regional materials and the craftsmanship of local artisans; it was a strategy that anticipated the incorporation of autochthonous materials by architects like Mexico's Juan O'Gorman in his search for an alternative modernism during the 1930s.[54] Its façade evoked the city's colonial architecture through the incorporation of andesite, a light-gray stone used extensively in La Compañía and in the central nave of San Francisco but which had fallen into disuse until a new quarry in Latacunga was inaugurated in the early twentieth century. Durini had already experimented with this stone in the base for a statue of Antonio José de Sucre that still sits before the Santo Domingo monastery, and he chose it for its relationship to the city's monuments. While the main thrust of the façade thus referenced the past, its tectonic and decorative elements addressed the present and future. The frame as well as the roof incorporated the first local usage of reinforced concrete, which was left untreated on the roof. The lintels and capitals of the second floor included three-dimensional floral ornamentation typical of *stile floreale* while the main iron-and-glass door was based on a design by Joseph Trier, a furniture manufacturer then residing in Darmstadt, home of the famed Jugendstil colony and Technical University.[55] This door, however, was not an elaborate import, as would have been the case only a few years earlier, but was instead the product of local sculptors Segundo Ortíz and Manuel Ayala, who also cast the letters identifying the building above the central arch and the bronze condors on the interior stairwells. The latter, a late addition to the plan, expanded the building's stylistic mélange by evoking art deco's geometric abstraction. The lush interior palate in golds and browns accentuated the bronze ornamentation while an iron-and-glass cupola provided a dance of natural light typical of a Durini structure.

This merger of autochthonous materials and nationalist symbology with a dynamic eclecticism incorporating art deco and *stile floreale* motifs also permeated Durini's other major commercial structure from this era—the Banco del Pichincha headquarters (fig. 5.8). Founded in 1906, the bank had been waiting to build a central location for some years and had conducted preliminary talks with Durini as early as 1916. Ultimately, regional competition with the Guayaquil-based Banco Agrícola, which completed its headquarters in 1920, gave the project greater urgency and led to Durini's being hired. The building was to rise at the corner of García Moreno and Sucre streets, adjacent to the

Fig. 5.8. Francisco Durini, Banco del Pichincha (1920s). Courtesy Durini Collection, Museo de la Ciudad, Quito.

ancient Compañía de Jesus church. The narrowness of the lot and surrounding streets necessitated an irregular design that Durini sought to deemphasize so as to relate to the symmetry of the façade of the Jesuit monument next door. He ultimately selected a neoclassical plan that was folded along the intersection so as to provide a monumental entryway that would exist in dialogue with the convent. As in the Círculo Militar, Durini chose to use andesite as the primary tectonic element, which deepened its relationship with the temple.

The dominant entrance from the corner of García Moreno and Sucre streets begins with an elegant stone stairway leading to a doorway flanked by two Doric columns supporting the entablature. Angular condors evoking an early art deco aesthetic flank the curved architrave, guarding a pair of free-standing caryatids that hold aloft electric torches illuminating a metope (initially planned to identify the banking establishment) that was left blank until the building passed to the Central Bank in 1929. An orientalist theme, perhaps inspired by D'Aronco, can also be identified in the minaret-like turrets on the northern façade. As in the Círculo Militar, these elements responded to continental trends, as did the interiors, which were dominated by a curved stairwell in granite, marble, and andesite. The vast lower level comprised tellers' windows framed in iron, again the workmanship of local artisans, while the second floor comprised offices and meeting spaces. As in 1916, the completion of the building and its respectful attitude toward the venerable Jesuit church, La Compañía, won the city's highest architectural prize upon its completion in 1924.[56]

These prominent accolades expanded Durini's visibility at precisely the moment in which private commissions began to balloon as a result of the city's northward push in the 1920s and 1930s. Durini quickly engaged the new market, completing two Italianate villas, the Trento and the Trieste, by 1922, correctly gauging the shift in demand. His prominence was accentuated by his ties to the military and municipality; these two structures appeared as beacons of modernity on the Battle of Pichincha commemorative map elaborated by these groups. The lower prices associated with Durini's mature structures as a result of his growing use of local materials and craftsmen (many of whom worked in his woodworking studios) also attracted clients desiring to advertise their sophistication at home as well as at entrepôts like the Pasaje Royal.[57]

Stylistically, Durini's villas corresponded to a trend in Italian domestic construction toward a greater emphasis on the vernacular; this trend coexisted with futurism and the decorative *novecento* movement during the 1920s. While his colleagues in Italy based their structures on local vernacular forms, Durini continued to emulate European models even as he adopted the principle of utilizing local materials and skills. He was not alone in this practice, which has given some critics cause to decry the architectural development of areas such as the Ciudadela Mariscal Sucre as an exercise in the importation of styles with little grounding in local customs or indigenous forms. In the 1940s, American travel and children's writer Ludwig Bemelmans lambasted the neighborhood as the product of "a pastrycook of an architect who . . . has carefully assembled everything that is bad and awful."[58] The more recent evaluations of figures such as Manuel Espinosa Apolo, Paul Aguilar, or Eduardo Kingman have also lamented the lack of authenticity within the neighborhood as a result of its separation from the "indigenous" culture.

But these charges simplify the point behind the visual language and adoption of the foreign vernacular by "pastrycooks" such as Francisco Durini. His buildings, which included Italianate villas, Basque cottages, French chateaus, and even an Andalusian Arabesque palace, corresponded to a particular vision of the search for origins that framed Quito's entry to modernity and dovetailed with the coveted vision of cosmopolitanism as both playfully exotic and demonstrably rooted—qualities that Durini embodied both personally and aesthetically. His grounding in Mediterranean vernacular, coupled with the malleability of his stylistic embrace, afforded clients the ability to transpose their desire for the "cultural transvestism" of cosmo-modernity without leaving home or

Fig. 5.9. Francisco Durini, Gemma Durini House (1940s). Photograph by the author.

abandoning a respectable status in society.[59] A Durini villa thus displayed a modern sensibility grounded in historical precision within a society and landscape of global and local reach.

As might be expected, patrons facing this wide choice of styles reacted with energy. Standard local practice dictated that design work begin with a session in which a series of stock drawings, photographs, or plates be presented as potential models. Durini chose to pique the interest of a prospective buyer in a familiar language first; only afterward would he begin to discuss the possibility of architectonic experimentation. For that purpose, Francisco Durini, like his competitors, kept a number of catalogs, magazines, and classic texts in his office because they could collectively speak to the variety of vernaculars within which he felt competent to work.[60] As would be expected, many of these models featured neoclassical and Renaissance forms but also myriad alternate styles. Modernism was represented by the Secessionist literature already noted and was later supplemented by magazines documenting modernist Spanish American trends. These publications included the several editions of the Cuban review *Arquitecto* from 1928 and of the Argentine publication *Casas y Jardines* from a decade later.[61] Other possibilities included a wide assortment of contemporary Spanish villas, which featured popular Castilian and Basque examples—the latter was even selected by Francisco's sister Gemma for her own Mariscal villa

Fig. 5.10. Francisco Durini, Villa Villagómez, 1932 (restoration, 2007). Photograph by the author.

in the early 1940s (fig. 5.9). An orientalist sensibility, first explored in the minarets of the Banco del Pichincha, echoed not only D'Aronco's Istanbul-influenced *stile floreale* but also the Andalusian villas in Durini's stock catalog. This flavor dominated a 1930s design for a bullring but was most dramatically realized in the Villa Villagómez (fig. 5.10), a testament to Andalusian styles featuring a wide variety of mosaic tiles, intricate woodwork in the stairwells and lighting fixtures, and an extraordinary array of playful natural lighting coming in from the glass roof. This was perhaps the pinnacle of Durini's experimentation and the best expression of the desire for localizing a cosmopolitan vernacular. The project once again garnered him the municipal Premio al Ornato in 1932.[62]

More recently, the Villa Villagómez has earned the contempt of Paul Aguilar in his comprehensive survey of *quiteño* architecture. As an example of the "*gran desconcierto*" (great disorder) of the eclectic 1930s, Aguilar maintains, a profound dissonance lies in a contemporary assertion in *El Comercio* that the structure reflects architecture that was "*verdaderamente nuestro*" (truly ours).[63] However, the claim that an Arabesque chalet truly represented an autochthonous Ecuadorian spirit squares with the local elites' ambitions to showcase their own cosmopolitanism while seeking their origins in a distant European past. In realizing this work, which reflected owner Jorge Villagómez's recall of a journey to Andalucía, Durini produced fantasy, thus serving as an enabler buoyed by his own hybrid eclecticism. Such was his stock in trade.

The Chronotope of a Hyphenated Vernacular

The most virulent opponent of the new architecture developing during the 1920s and 1930s was the art historian José Gabriel Navarro, whose embrace of a Hispanist aesthetic and moral code has been discussed previously. Curiously, this champion of Quito's colonial monuments was close friends with Francisco Durini and regularly invited him to lecture for his architectural history classes at the Universidad Central.[64] This pedagogical collaboration of the conservative Hispanist and the modern eclectic at first glance appears ironic. However, as has been discussed, Durini's embrace of a cosmopolitan vernacular could easily coexist with the preservationist ethos of his colleague. In works such as the Banco del Pichincha and the Círculo Militar, for instance, Durini consciously sought to place modern structures into a city known for its colonial monumentality. This attempt to integrate his architectonic language into the existing cityscape would have no doubt appealed to Navarro. Moreover, Durini's embrace of vernacular architecture with origins in contemporary Spanish villas and even the inculcation of an Andalusian style would also have appealed to the venerable art historian, who frequently lauded the Moorish origins of the ornamental details of many of Quito's religious icons. In a similar manner, Durini most likely understood and possibly applauded the city's architectonic shift toward a colonial revivalist style in the 1940s, even as it limited his own productivity. After all, his work and possibly his lectures had helped spark the very interest in the vernacular that was now returning to a local formulation of cosmopolitan principles.

The creation of a hyphenated architecture that could exist as simultaneously Ecuadorian and cosmopolitan stands as the primary emblem of the Durini family's oeuvre, particularly Francisco's mature works. The success of this endeavor stems from two primary causes. The first is the tectonic incorporation of local materials to inflect and redefine a European modernist aesthetic existing in dialogue with the monuments in Quito's historic center. As noted above, this strategy anticipates the highly touted modernist experiments by figures like Juan O'Gorman, Oscar Niemeyer, or Roberto Burle Marx. As Valerie Fraser has emphasized, these architects' deployment of native plants, volcanic stone, or colonial *azulejo* (glazed tile) facilitated their transformation of functionalism from an architecture rooted in Le Corbusian theory to a particularly Mexican or Brazilian statement, indeed, an alternative modernism.[65] While Durini never fully embraced functionalism or indigenous revivalism, as did the giants of Latin American modernism, his mature works ought to be considered in the same vein.

The second reason the Durinis successfully negotiated a tight market and in the process built lasting works marked by their hybrid nature stemmed from the very business model they followed. As a family, the three Durinis collaborated in producing not only works of art but also a public image. Each facet of their private and public lives helped develop this conception, from Lorenzo's Masonic contacts to Pedro's leisurely lifestyle to Francisco's focus on craft and technical expertise. The cultivation of these personas represented more than just sensibilities; they served a practical function in the development of relationships with prospective clients eager to display their own modernity. The subsequent diversification of the establishment, and Francisco's eventual move toward incorporating local elements and artisans, grew out of a material need as much as an interest in contemporary architectural trends.

In evaluating the impact of the Durinis on Quito's cultural framework, one need only point to the extensive recent renovations to several of their best known works, including the Villa Villagómez, the Círculo Militar, and Gemma Durini's villa. In the globalized present, their restoration has become a critical facet in the constitution of a romanticized view of Quito's past. The hands of the municipality and the state lie heavily upon this measure, as is probably to be expected. No matter the potential impact of the Durini oeuvre on local interest in vernacular architecture, the fact remains that theirs was a decidedly elite project despite the broader development of local artisanal production. The Mariscal Sucre itself, as has been noted, represented the pinnacle of the imperial designs of the expanding city, eager to swallow up the surrounding countryside.

Their elite centrality, however, does not mean that they have not become an inextricable part of the city's urban fabric. Even in the cases of buildings that no longer exist, such as the Pasaje Royal, their production stands as the image of an era while, in at least one case, they continue to mark the popular culture of today. The piece in question is a statue of a large globe held aloft by two powerful Atlases—exquisitely crafted stone figures that once guarded the entrance to the Banco de Préstamos, another of Durini's 1920s commercial establishments. Today, they hold aloft an image of Ecuador's equatorial position and greet the thousands of revelers who pour into the Estadio Olímpico Atahualpa, the great fortress where Ecuador's national football team has secured its recent runs to the World Cup and an enduring cosmopolitan arena for the display of local culture on a global stage.

Chapter 6

A Phantasmagoric Dystopia

Eloy Alfaro's 1895 arrival in Quito as leader of the triumphant Liberal Revolution inspired the relocation of scores of partisan journalists, intellectuals, and politicians clamoring to build a new society. The migrants included a young satirist from Cuenca named Manuel J. Calle, known for his lampooning portraits of conservative ideologues.[1] Upon the appearance of Calle's magazine, *Revista de Quito,* in the Andean citadel, however, the publication turned its attention to the banal provinciality of Calle's adopted home. His chronicles challenged the cherished notion of Quito's traditionalist image by describing it as a veneer for an outmoded way of life at odds with the demands of modernity and progress. Calle's caustic pen rendered *quiteños* gullible fools ignorant of the outside world, as stated in an 1898 column about a swindling matador who persuaded the superintendent of police to establish an impromptu bullring, where the vagabond never appeared. Instead, the city's bumbling citizens piled into the makeshift clearing to try to fight the bulls themselves, with "*un cholo de los nuestros*" (one of our mestizos) receiving warm accolades and a broken arm for his troubles. As Calle put it, Quito remained "*el país de los chinos*" (the land of Chinamen), impoverished and bereft of the hallmarks of progress necessary to attain the oft-invoked status of nostalgic world capital.[2]

Calle's tales of the city's failings form part of a broader theme in liberal and socialist fiction that labeled Quito's traditionalism a phantasmagoria that masked its recalcitrance and underdevelopment. Inverting the heritage paradigm, these radical authors—first liberals and then socialists—instead accentuate the capital's social tensions and estrangement from global progress. Their partisan portraits elaborate an urban guide that recasts the cityscape as a hypocritical necropolis of misogyny, racism, and economic exploitation rather than a testament to earlier glories and future development, a situation generally attributed to constrictive, conservative mores.

Beyond simply casting the city's failures within the broader scope of global revolutionary processes, these novels feature the city's relationship with its rural surroundings, inverting the Ibero-American convention of an enlightened city and barbarous countryside. Instead, they recast these pastoral landscapes as a space where redemption of urban decadence is possible. This trope appeared sporadically during the colonial era, particularly in denunciations of the city's rebellious nature by colonial or clerical officials. However, its modern manifestations began with Juan León Mera's counter-cartographic national epic, *Cumandá* (1879), which lamented the passing of García Moreno's conservative project. Liberal novelists like Roberto Andrade and Luís A. Martínez inverted Mera's politics while refining the conceit of a redemptive countryside he introduced. Later generations evoke the implicit elevation of the rustic experience by focusing on the role of the city as the engine of provincial exploitation, a motive particularly present in the *indigenista* writings of Jorge Icaza or the social realism of Humberto Salvador. A secondary theme concerns the insularity and alienation of the city, which is largely developed through a naturalistic obsession with sexual trauma and exploitation.

One useful way to encounter the generic framework that dominates these denunciatory writings can be seen in a chronotope Bakhtin refers to as the idyll. Bakhtin considers the idyll to be a setting characterized by a humdrum existence that is dominated by cyclical continuity over generations, thus expanding the term from its common pastoral associations. However, he adds that this cyclical time appears largely "as an ancillary time, one that may be interwoven with other noncyclical temporal sequences or used merely to intersperse such sequences that are more charged with energy and event."[3] Similarly, in a world shaped by liberal positivism and Marxist dialectics, the idyll represents a foil of positivist, cosmopolitan, or revolutionary desires. As such, these denunciatory dystopias not only challenge the encomiums circulating through the public sphere but also elaborate anticipatory images of a revolutionary era of redemptive potential.

Idylls and Polemics

In spite of the conceit of Quito's loyal and messianic role, the city was a frequent site of insurrection during the colonial period. It was of course in the plains of Añaquito that Gonzalo Pizarro defeated and decapitated Viceroy Blasco Núñez Vela in 1546. In 1591, cabildo resistance to royal tax policy inspired the Rebellion of the Alcabalas, which not only resulted in increased viceregal oversight of the city's cabildo for more than a century but also extended Quito's rebellious reputation. Seventeenth-century commentators as diverse as Ayacucho noble Guamán Poma de Ayala and the Jesuit Pedro de Mercado highlighted the city's iniquity while Jorge Juan and Antonio de Ulloa reported on pervasive tax evasion and abuse of indigenous communities in their 1748 work, *Noticias secretas*. These charges inspired a series of reforms meant to minimize the perceived corruption of the city and its hinterland, which in turn fostered increased instability. As Martin Minchom has noted, the city hosted a score of insurrections over the long eighteenth century, of which the most important are the 1765 Rebellion of the Barrios and the 1809 declaration of independence, each of which would have continental repercussions.[4] However, perhaps more instructive, given its resonance in later revolutionary writing, was a 1747 clash inspired by the first direct attempt by the Crown to clamp down on the city's tax evasion.

This conflict emerged after the establishment of a royal monopoly over the sale of *aguardiente* in 1746, a decision likely informed by Juan's and Ulloa's observations of tax evasion during their sojourn in the Audiencia.[5] The next year saw a *visita,* or inspection, by Gregorio Ibánez Cuevas, an Aragonese friar and commissary of Lima, whose presence provoked opposition among local church officials, who had probably been selling the liquor illegally. Ibáñez arrested the mission's leadership upon arriving in Quito; however, the Audiencia hierarchy conspired with the Dominican monastery to free the prelates, leading the *visitador* to rally a group of plebeians from the San Roque neighborhood on Quito's southwestern fringe to stage a symbolic protest. The commissary and his band donned hangman's nooses as they promenaded the city's breadth, from San Francisco downhill to the Dominican monastery, where they took several turns around the plaza while chanting a hymn based on the psalm, "In exitu Israel du Egipto." The group followed this ritualistic association of Quito and Hebrew enslavement with an "exodus" to the Franciscan sanctuary of San Diego, located at San Roque's southern extremity high on Pichincha, where they bunkered for the next month. Tensions rose anew during the celebrations of New Year's Eve, when a *zambo* (mixed African-Indian racial type) tailor named Manuel de la Parra assaulted a city guard patrolling the San Roque outskirts. The ensuing riots saw a determined band attacking the house of the president of the Audiencia and vandalizing the local prison. Citywide carousing spread, as crowds publicly pronounced their faith in the Franciscan friars, their antipathy to the peninsular Audiencia leadership, and their pride in the barrio of San Roque. The disturbances came to an end only when armed soldiers dispersed the crowds along the deep ravines of the aptly named Quebrada Jerusalén.

The millennial fervor inspired by Ibáñez Cuevas's inversion of the traditional image of Quito as a new Rome slumbered after this incident but would be periodically reconfigured by reformist movements. In 1771, for example, Jesuit Mario Cicala decried Quito's rampant gambling and theft, which had reduced the city to poverty and misery so egregious it had led to demographic collapse.[6] No less a personage than the famous physician Eugenio Espejo frequently satirized the city's miserable health conditions and its mistreatment of the poor and indigenous in pasquinades, essays, plays, and sermons while advocating for autonomy or even independence.[7] Even the great nineteenth-century champion of Quito's artistocratic landowning class, Gabriel García Moreno, got his start as the reformist rector of the city's university and dedicated himself to purging its hidebound professoriat.

However, this tenet failed to take root, perhaps as a result of the particular relationship between Quito and its immediate indigenous hinterland. Instead, it took the fall of the Garcían autocracy to develop its reconceptualization. Paradoxically, this revamping emerged in the writings of García Moreno's staunch ally, Juan León Mera. Although known primarily in his age as a poet—indeed, he authored the lyrics to Ecuador's national anthem—Mera is best remembered today for his romantic novel *Cumandá* (1879). This melodramatic piece has often been hailed as the first Ecuadorian national epic; however, its importance for the phantasmagorical chronotope stems from its perennial deconstruction by radical authors seeking to inform an alternative national image paradoxically indebted to Mera's own interrogation of urban civility.

Written after García Moreno's assassination, Mera's novel features the doomed love story of a white Andean named Carlos and the beautiful Amazonian princess Cumandá. The pair first encounter each other following a decision by Carlos's father, Orozco, to found a missionary station in the Amazon. Their mutual attraction notwithstanding, they are soon separated when Cumandá's father travels downriver to pledge his allegiance to the violent Jívaro chief Yahuarmaqui. Carlos saves Cumandá from marriage to Yahuarmaqui but cannot ultimately defend her from the headhunters, a tragedy compounded by the melodramatic revelation that she is in fact his sister, kidnapped years earlier. The traditional scholarship on the novel highlights the themes of incest and racial tension in the book while underscoring the lyricism of Mera's depiction of the Amazonian rainforest. Recent work by Ricardo Padrón and Fernando Balseca, however, emphasizes the regional cartography at the center of the novel. Padrón in particular has stressed the "counter-cartography" developed by the course of the Andean core's failed evangelization of the periphery, a motif that reflects Mera's despair at the end of the Garcían reign.[8]

Mera's vision of Andean impotence represented a critique of the Liberal intelligentsia, yet his counter-cartographic stance would be appropriated during the heady triumph of the Liberal Revolution. As Kim Clark has emphasized, the government counterpoised Andean stagnation with coastal movement in an attempt to promote its positivist social program.[9] Liberal activists argued that Quito's insularity reflected both economic isolation and the constrictive power of an outmoded social structure dominated by the Church—a trope first developed locally by Eugenio Espejo.[10] Despite the patriarchal attitude of many of these reformers, their worries regarding the constriction of women's economic and social activities underlay the state's concern with providing female educational facilities and opening access to labor markets.[11] A similarly paternalistic and economic argument underlay the concomitant opposition to *concertaje,* the land tenure system based on peonage ties to Andean haciendas that basically prevented indigenous people from entering the market economy.[12]

Whereas each theme formed part of the broader Liberal modernization program, the attention to what Francine Masiello terms the "perversity of gender relations" evoked the tenets of *fin-de-siglo* melodrama across Latin America. As in works like José Martí's novel *Amistad funesta* (1885), Ecuadorian liberals argued that insular jealousies and rivalries among the highland elite hampered national progress while echoing the obsession with gossip in works such as Cabello de Carbonara's *Blanca sol* (1889).[13] In the Ecuadorian case, liberal activist writers like Roberto Andrade and Luís A. Martínez upended Mera's counter-cartographic tradition by juxtaposing the themes of urban depravity and the liberating potential of nature in order to argue against the Conservative cause Mera had strongly advocated. In the process, they bolstered the image of a dystopic Quito whose redemption could come only through reconciliation with its rural hinterland and an embrace of the destiny of progress and development.

Roberto Andrade, a longtime liberal pamphleteer notorious for his peripheral involvement in the plot to assassinate García Moreno, presented his indictment in *Pacho Villamar* (1900), a semi-autobiographical novel that depicts the title character's coming of age in Garcían Quito. Its central conflict concerns the stifling of impoverished Pacho's courting of the beautiful Magdalena Gutierrez by the city's conservative orthodoxy. Although she returns his affections, her parents arrange a marriage to a wealthy landowner from Latacunga. Pacho's subsequent challenging of his Jesuit teachers lands him in exile, where he meets the liberal icon Juan Montalvo in Colombia. Magdalena's cloistered existence thrusts her into Pacho's arms following his dazzling return. They have a child that Magdalena abandons to a monastery, where the boy is taught to abhor his father's libertine values. Learning of his son's existence years later, Pacho seeks him out, only to be rejected by the conservative lad, who then escapes to Guaya-quil accompanied by a Jesuit mentor. Pacho follows but is arrested and executed as a would-be assassin by a firing squad acting on the priest's fabrications.

The novel dovetails with a regionally charged metaphorical cycle linking Magdalena's spiritual emptiness to her isolation in Quito whereas Pacho's ad-venturous spirit stems from his regular encounter with rural climes—an inver-sion of traditional associations of urbanity with civilization. There is a racial tinge to this inversion, as the countryside appears as a vacant and virginal land-scape despite its harboring the majority of the nation's indigenous population. Andrade instead transposes Indians onto the squalid cityscape as part of a de-graded panoply, including "a barefoot and disheveled mestiza, an elderly man of ruinous appearance, some whistling rascals and . . . two petty bureaucrats with long, frayed frock coats, torn old boots, and hats that had known several heads."[14]

Although marred by uneven passages of polemical invective and layers of overt melodrama, *Pacho Villamar* set forth a basic pattern repeatedly emu-lated in liberal fiction. One of the earliest examples was by Luís A. Martínez, a landscape portraitist and Liberal bureaucrat involved in the establishment of the Escuela de Bellas Artes. His novel *A la costa* (1904) features the trials of the respectable but impoverished Ramírez family.[15] This work expands An-drade's condemnation of the misogynistic violence perpetrated against women in insular Quito, invoking the naturalistic sensibilities of nineteenth-century Spanish American melodrama, in which "sex-crimes [underscore] the corrup-tion of national values."[16] As in *Pacho Villamar,* class difference dooms a short-lived romance between Salvador's sister, Mariana, and his wealthy classmate, Luciano. This restriction exacerbates Luciano's covetous desire for the nubile Mariana, who is blatantly exoticized for her erotic charms (round breasts, full lips, and rumored ancestors from the largely Afro-Ecuadorian Chota Valley).[17] Luciano abandons the deflowered girl after satisfying his lust. She then retreats into a desolate loneliness until revived by the sermons of a young priest named Justiniano. The corrupt cleric then lures the girl to his boudoir, a rendezvous that leaves her the disgraced mother of an illegitimate child and leads her to prostitution.

For Martínez, the most tragic consequence of Mariana's fall can be seen in her family. The second half of the novel features Salvador Ramírez's attempts to escape the capital's obsession with the stigma of his sister's corruption. The sub-sequent journey *a la costa* begins with his joining the opposition to one of Eloy Alfaro's earliest campaigns. Besides landing on the wrong side of history, the battle reunites him with Luciano, who still hides his culpability for Mariana's decline. He then joins the scores of *serranos* (highlanders) relocating to the cacao fields of the littoral, described in lush passages reminiscent of Mera's tropical fixation, aided by Martinez's experience as a travel writer, mountaineer, and *paisajista* (landscape artist).[18] There, Ramirez finds satisfying employment and even a loving romance with Consuelo Gómez, the comely daughter of a fellow highlander who lost his money and lands in the stock market. Their happiness is short-lived, as a rival suitor assassinates Consuelo's father and a snake bites Ramírez, who re-encounters Luciano when rushed to find medical treatment in Guayaquil. Luciano confesses to his role in Mariana's dishonor during this encounter, which inspires Salvador's final realization that his friend's betrayal pales before the crushing codes of *quiteño* society.

Both of these novels displayed melodramatic tendencies; however, they also argued for the Liberal modernization program, as would befit party stalwarts like Andrade and Martínez. However, the split in the Liberal Party following Plaza's ascendancy to the presidency in 1902 drove a wedge into the heart of the movement. Alfaro's coup in 1906 encouraged a brief alliance between conservatives and *placistas,* who backed uprisings in Cuenca and Loja. These unlikely bedfellows broke ranks in 1907 due to ideological differences and *placista* sympathy for the Alfaro government's strong management of public health crises that year, including the outbreak of bubonic plague and typhoid on the coast.[19]

These turbulent times fueled a turn toward radical political and aesthetic alternatives among students seeking to transcend the obsessive polemics of the previous generations.[20] Conservative secondary students like Jacinto Jijón y Caamaño and Julio Tobar Donoso, mentored by Archbishop González Suárez under the aegis of the Sociedad Ecuatoriana de Estudios Históricos Americanos, founded the Centro Católico de Obreros as early as 1906 in a bid to build alliances with the growing workers' movement.[21] Socialist-inclined University of Quito students simultaneously developed ties with the artisanal Sociedad Artística e Industrial de Pichincha (SAIP), whose leaders strongly endorsed Plaza's secularist agenda. Bolstered by deepening anarchist activity in Guayaquil, scores of students and artisans marched across Quito on April 25, 1907, to challenge the legitimacy of Alfaro's new government. In a harbinger of a century of conflict between the state and the Universidad Central, the military met the marchers in a bloody confrontation that left three students dead and scores more wounded.[22]

These conflagrations alienated the most innovative writers of this era. Disaffected by what Cathy Jrade terms the "spiritual and aesthetic vacuum" left by declining capitalism and the rise of positivist hegemony, these detractors sought to transcend vitriolic polemic through *modernismo,* a Spanish American aesthetic revivalist movement personified by José Martí and Rubén Darío.[23] These poets owed their public platform to an impoverished scion of the Otavalo creole class named Isaac Barrera, who parlayed a scholarship to Quito's conservative Colegio de San Gabriel into a career as essayist. One of his pieces, an *El Comercio* column published in 1910, provided a genealogy of *modernismo* and also cemented his career. His passionate defense of experimental writing endeared him to a cadre of wealthy creole poets whose patronage facilitated the publication of a review titled *Letras* (1912–1914). This magazine published the first verses of figures like Arturo Borja, Humberto Fierro, Ernesto Noboa y Caamaño, and Medardo Angel Silva—artists who evoked Verlaine, Poe, Baudelaire, and Rimbaud, along with Darío and Martí. Poetry turned to practice as melancholic afternoons at the Alcocer tavern soaked with beer and *aguardiente* bled into evenings at the swanky Club Pichincha. Ultimately, their abuse of ether and morphine accelerated a series of early demises that have led to this group's moniker as the *generación decapitada*. This melancholia is perhaps best communicated by Ernesto Noboa y Caamaño's "Hastío" (Tedium):

Vivir de lo pasado por desprecio al presente	Living from the past, despising the present
mirar hacia el futuro con un hondo terror,	terrorized by a glimpse of the future
sentirse envenenado, sentirse indiferente	poisoned, indifferent
ante el mal de la vida y ante el bien del amor.	before the evil of life and the goodness of love.[24]

Despite their implicit castigation of Quito's landscape, Noboa and his fellow "decapitated" poets located the sentiment of paralysis and aporia as a continual characteristic of modern life with only a minimal spatial referent. However, the lone novel associated with this movement, José Rafael Bustamante's *Para matar el gusano* (1913), evokes and subverts the positivist paradigms established by Mera, Andrade, and Martínez to create a cartography of *decapitado* ennui. Published serially in *Letras,* the work revisits the constrictive idyllic paradigm of the liberal novels of the turn of the century yet echoes the *modernista* image of the city as a cage of lechery and debauchery.[25] Unlike its depiction in previous Ecuadorian novels, the countryside, in Bustamante's view, had lost its redemptive potential and instead had begun to conform to the incapacitating paralysis of the encroaching modern city.

Bustamante realizes this critique through spatially charged narratives interrogating the relationship between the metropolis and its hinterland. The first narrative concerns a love triangle between archetypes—the urban elite (Jorge), the poor youth (Roberto), and the simple country girl (Inés)—that contrasts urban decadence with pastoral purity. In a circuitous and predictable plot, the timid Roberto falls for Inés, who is in turn seduced by wealthy Jorge's vitality. Her first lover learns of her betrayal from a neighbor and then falls into a cycle of drink and desperation that eventually leads to his dissolution: he becomes a beggar living in the ironically titled Quebrada Jerusalén, the polluted ravine on the southern edge of the city.

Roberto attempts to escape Quito's clutches through a series of moves from one dwelling to another—dwellings that parallel his mental state, document the city's modernizing path, and reveal the class biases of municipal and state planning measures.[26] As a child, he and his mother, Rosa, live in a crumbling colonial in squalid San Marcos. Soon after he meets Jorge and Inés, Rosa moves to a modern home with a garden in the burgeoning middle-class neighborhood of La Tola on Quito's eastern edge. However, Roberto secretly longs to flee to the northern environs, by the Ejido or Alameda parks, with their captivating views, and he finds the perfect spot after his engagement—the high point of his life. The long hours he spends in the Ejido cannot stem his ensuing disintegration following Inés's betrayal and Rosa's death. In the last two chapters of the novel, we see him in a dark, stuffy bar surrounded by other lowlifes and, finally, on the southern back streets near the San Diego cemetery and in a cave in the Quebrada, where he lives. The description of the street on which he is crouching when he meets his final companion, a stray dog, exemplifies the equation between urban space and Roberto's spiritual state:

> The shifty and solitary alley rises, hides and disappears into the austere hill, fleeing from the mistreatment it has suffered as it exits the city to become a heap of dung and rubbish. A tired and repugnant corridor between the cemetery and two or three low and melancholic huts that are half paved with uneven cobblestones riddled with soapy water flowing from the nearby homes and half in dirt, weeds, trash and excrement. And there we see a man, a ghost, a specter that sleeps and dreams, grumbles and babbles, scratches his fleas and lice, sitting on the threshold of a closed door. For such a street, such a man.[27]

Like the alley, Roberto has been consumed by his fellow man, a hopeless ghost of his former self, trapped in a desperate cycle of filth and rubbish. A man defiled by his environment.

Bustamante, unlike his liberal forebears, interrogates the positivist paradigm by deploying signs of progress as signifiers of internal disruption at key points in the novel. One motive demonstrating this effort concerns the changing standards in public nocturnal lighting. For instance, while traditional candle-lit streets are remarked in early passages in the book, Roberto's encounter with a lurid kerosene lamp occurs just after he discovers the potential liaison between Inés and Jorge. Similarly, it is by the light of the new electric streetlamps years later that he glimpses her betrayal. A second example can be seen in the metaphor of modernization's vacuity. This theme dominates the closing pages of the book, when the old beggar Roberto happens upon his childhood home in San Marcos. Like so much of Quito, it has received a modernizing face-lift that conceals a completely unchanged interior. The *anciano* (old man) collapses before the realization that his happiest memories are of a despicable hovel that betrays the unscathed idyll, despite his lifelong turmoil and steady destruction.

This combination of the liberal image of Quito as backwater with a critique of modernization's uneven reach is both the cause and result of Bustamante's essentially nostalgic understanding of the contemporary world. Yet this is not a nostalgia that seeks to restore a past world but instead uses Roberto's search to comment upon the uneven results of progress. Indeed, Bustamante's interrogation notes more than the decadence of modernity. His protagonist's true flaw is his idealism, identified as an anachronism in contemporary *quiteño* society, for Roberto is no *vecino* of this dystopic city or of the modern world.

Bustamante's despairing condemnation, while reflective of the broader *modernista* antipathy to positivist models, also anticipated two future trends in literary portraiture of the capital. The first, largely restricted to the 1920s, would explore a hedonistic and surrealist cityscape rooted in the grotesque descriptions of Roberto's final days. This critique originated within a cadre of vanguardists associated with two reviews—*Caricatura* (1919–1922) and *Hélice* (1926)—that echoed and reconsidered the Dadaist and surrealist trends then in vogue in Europe. Authors such as Alberto Coloma Silva, Pablo Palacio, and Humberto Salvador crafted a vision of a banal city oscillating between its perpetual insularity and a desire for cosmopolitan centrality, a representation supported by the disjointed structure of their writings. The work of the latter two writers dovetailed with intense social criticism, a characteristic typical of the *indigenista* and socialist critiques of Ecuadorian social relations of the 1930s.

Vanguard Dreams

As noted previously, the centennial of the Battle of Pichincha in 1922 propelled the reconstruction of Quito under the aegis of the Junta del Centenario. Besides establishing new services and erecting statuary and markers of a heroic sensibility, the junta also sought to rehabilitate the image of the colonial city center as a harmonious antecedent for the Liberal modernization program. Isaac Barrera, chosen to be junta coordinator in part because of his induction into the Sociedad Ecuatoriana de Estudios Históricos Americanos due to his well-respected biography of nineteenth-century liberal Vicente Rocafuerte, elaborated this argument in his introductory essay to the commemorative volume celebrating the centennial. Barrera's essay echoes his literary repudiation of contemporary society by idealizing the city's baroque glory as the harbinger of a contemporary renaissance.[28] Barrera's call reverberated throughout the Liberal academy, and a vogue for tributes to Quito's halcyon days emerged thereafter.

The most consequential early panegyrics are the writings of the diplomat and genealogist Cristóbal Gangotena y Jijón and the nostalgist Alejandro Andrade Coello, who for long time held a post at the Instituto Nacional Mejía. Gangotena's *Al margen de la historia* (1924) collects colonial picaresque adventures encountered during his genealogical studies. The tales feature a quaint, idyllic city of priests and caballeros whose quietude is interrupted momentarily by the appearance of a rogue or fool, as is often the case in folkloric tales. Despite the sometimes bawdy humor of several pieces that are reminiscent of the lively sketches of coastal culture popularized the previous decade by José

Antonio Campos in Guayaquil, in Gangotena's Quito, the rambunctious antics come to a close, order is restored, and the idyll endures.[29] For example, in "La virgen de la empanada," Gangotena relates the story of a colonial official with a mania for the occult who discovers an image of the Virgin Mary in a spot of lard on the wrapper of his empanada one morning. His amused neighbors encourage his devotion to the miracle—which is placed in a venerated urn—until finally a prankster burns the rotting parchment and restores order.[30]

Whereas Gangotena firmly located the idyllic city in the colonial past, the guided tours compiled by his liberal colleague Alejandro Andrade Coello and published regularly in *El Comercio* as "Crónicas de Quito" offer a window onto the past from the perspective of the contemporary city. In these vignettes, Andrade ambulates through the old center until a "chance" encounter with a site of memory initiates a digression to document the historical importance of monumental churches, to recite a colorful legend, or to explore a personal memory. These reminiscences become more common in his later columns, as do a series of ludic characters from "the old Quito, gone and never to return."[31] As in Gangotena's writings, these rogues—a one-man band, a blind *aguador* (water carrier) who answered insults in verse, a cross-dressing mestizo who deceived the city's well-to-do into entrusting their daughters to his care—not only decorate a bleak landscape but also provide an essential social function by helping the city to overcome regret with laughter.[32]

One of the crucial elements of these chronicles concerns their setting, which focuses on the picturesque neighborhoods of the colonial center. Public spaces such as the Plaza San Francisco and the Plaza de la Independencia appear as markers of heroism and civility, while streets such as the infamous La Ronda, home of many nineteenth-century poets, become those enchanting, "badly paved streets, narrow and dark, but rich in memories."[33] Unlike in Barrera's holistic centennial essay, these chronicles purge the newer districts that serve as foils to the worthy structures of the *centro*. Thus, architecture and tradition form a unified front against modernization. Indeed, in Andrade's account of Quito's colonial churches, he even imagines the unspeakable pains of previous generations ("recóndito dolor de nuestros abuelos") witnessing the disappearance of the artistic relics of ancient Quito.[34]

Whereas the Liberal cause had at one time garnered the support of Quito's radical fringe, these stale nostalgic pieces frustrated a new generation of vanguardists who considered Quito's sanctification to be an absurdity. Their critique found expression in an expanding culture of independently produced literary magazines. As Humberto Robles has argued, these new reviews represented a national phenomenon but were particularly active in Quito, Loja, Cuenca, and Guayaquil due to the universities in those areas. In Quito, the Escuela de Bellas Artes also proved an incubator for avant-garde art students inspired by the birth of modernist trends in Europe, the United States, and, increasingly, Mexico. Far

Fig. 6.1. Guillermo Latorre, "Nuestros historiógrafos. Sr. de Gangotena de Cristóbal de Jijón de—ExCónsul en Vladivostok," *Caricatura* 2:57 (February 29, 1920). Courtesy Banco Central del Ecuador.

from simply communicating foreign movements, however, these collectives developed a critical art, caricature, and satire that interrogated the ongoing liberal hegemony with an increasingly radical vanguardist position.[35]

The first of these new collectives coalesced around a satirical review named *Caricatura,* which was founded by art students in 1918 and would prove popular enough with the city's progressive fringe to appear monthly for the next three years. Its popularity stemmed not only from its attention to reporting current literary and artistic trends but also its lampooning of local notables, as in Guill-

ermo Latorre's portrait of Cristóbal Gangotena (fig. 6.1).[36] Besides these carica-
tures, the magazine included a series of incisive parodies by Alberto Coloma
Silva, an art student at the Escuela de Bellas Artes who would prove a direct
influence on future iterations of the phantasmagorical chronotope.

Coloma's primary literary contribution to the magazine consisted of a column titled "Crónicas de Quito," written under the pseudonym Ramiro de Sylva,
that appeared before he won a scholarship to study painting in France and Spain
in 1920.[37] These chronicles turn the universal ethos into an internal critique as
Don Ramiro lampoons the pretensions of an isolated Andean hamlet despite
its universal desires. Coloma's inaugural column, for instance, features Don
Ramiro's doomed search for amusement in a fundamentally mundane cityscape
considered poetic by insufferable romantics unaware of contemporary conditions. Indeed, Coloma's alter ego encounters a preening *hombre de talento* (an
intellectual or bohemian), whose pomposity brings a chuckle to the chronicler
as he realizes that the man's risible visage is as absurd as his own.[38] In a later
column, Don Ramiro explores the city streets searching for some newsworthy
scandal, perhaps a crime. Instead, he finds little of note, only priests gesticu-
lating with their cigarettes, a fitting at the tailor's, and a friend's car splashing
through a pothole. At home, faced with the blank page, he laments the need to
invent the grotesque in order to satisfy his own and the public's yearning for the
sensational.[39] Similar jocularity appears in a piece under the byline of Henry
Nick (most likely also Coloma) that scoffs at the Junta del Centenario's attempts
to fill in potholes by emphasizing the potent sunshine of the Shyri capital that
dries the pooled rainwater better than any paving efforts could.[40]

Coloma and his *Caricatura* collaborators largely avoided explicit political
posturing. The trauma of the 1922 Guayaquil massacre and the triumphant 1925
Julian Revolution, however, recast the struggle over Quito's idyllic landscape as
part of a national and international class conflict. After Coloma moved to Europe to study painting, a new collective sought an appropriate response. Led by
essayist Raúl Andrade and *indigenista* painter Camilo Egas, the cohort included
Caricatura veterans Carlos Andrade (Kanela) and Guillermo Latorre, the poet
Gonzalo Escudero, and a young law student recently arrived from Loja named
Pablo Palacio, who would become one of the foremost Ecuadorian authors of the
twentieth century.[41]

Propelled by Egas, the collective began publishing a new review named *Hélice* in 1926. The publication engaged the implosion launched by Tristan Tzara's
Dadaist proclamations but, instead of abandoning art altogether, sought to find
a new formal language to critique the European fascination with exotic indigeneity that Egas had begun exploring during an earlier sojourn in the City of
Light.[42] As Escudero put it in the opening editorial to the first issue, "We under-
stand that the Art is the alchemy of the improbability, because if the Art was
true, the artistic expression would not exist." *Modernismo* was dead; instead,

the editors sought "cosmopolitanism, adventurousness, authenticity."[43] Michele Greet has underscored the political nature of this call. In particular, she cites the importance of Egas's indigenist revolutionary impulse, which not only antici-pated José Carlos Mariátegui's call for recasting the international class struggle in Andean terms but also represented one of the first continental acknowledg-ments of the radical artistic innovations Diego Rivera was spearheading in Mexico. Despite these innovations, the *quiteño* public proved indifferent to the journal and largely ignored the exhibits in Egas's gallery, a situation that led him to leave Ecuador and relocate to New York, where he would become a leading faculty member of the New School for Social Research.[44]

Hélice folded following Egas's departure, yet the alternative modernism it had espoused proved formative for two of the most innovative authors of twentieth-century Ecuadorian literature: Loja-born Pablo Palacio and Guaya-quil native Humberto Salvador. Their experiments in the late 1920s reworked the trope of Quito as phantasmagorical site by exploding the generic frame-works of the liberal and *modernista* novels of denunciation to incorporate a sur-realist ethos with an attendant awareness of social conditions.

Palacio began this process in his contributions to later issues of *Hélice,* which included "Un hombre muerto a puntapies" and "El antropófago," each of which would be reproduced in his 1927 collection, also named *Un hombre muerto a pun-tapies.*[45] The title piece, often cited as the quintessential Palacio tale, begins with the narrator encountering a newspaper account of a *vicioso* (a delinquent) found dead the night before, apparently after being kicked to death. Fascinated by the implausibility and horror of the incident, the narrator traverses the city trying to learn more about the vice-ridden corpse. After visiting the police station—where he learns the man's surname (Ramírez) and receives two photographs (in which Ramírez is shown to have had a large nose)—he returns to his armchair à la Sherlock Holmes to reconstruct the crime. The narrator proceeds by lu-dicrous induction to conclude that the subject's name was Octavio (due to his large nose, supposedly a characteristic of the Roman emperor Octavian), that Ramírez was a foreigner (who ever heard of a *quiteño* named Octavio?), and that his vice was homosexuality, which had led to the attempted rape of a passing boy (no rationale). The *puntapies* (kicks) came from the lad's father, whose powerful blows culminate in murder.

The grotesque hedonism of this tale tests the limits imposed by the regu-lated idyll, which is abandoned as a fundamental characteristic of the city. In-stead, Palacio reveals a Quito dominated by the fluctuation of a rootless and surreal landscape indebted to the Rabelaisian carnivalesque. "El antropófago" indeed provides homage to Rabelais, as the cannibal on display in a museum shares Gargantua's fate of having spent an extra two months in the womb.[46] While at first horrified, the student narrator soon excuses the cannibal having bitten his wife's breast and bitten the face of their young son due to his father having been a butcher. As Bakhtin has noted of the ribaldry of the folkloric

Fig. 6.2. Guillermo Latorre, cover for Pablo Palacio's novel *Débora* (1927). Courtesy Library of Congress.

humor that drove Rabelais, in Palacio, gluttony looms ever present and there are only "cheerful deaths."[47]

Palacio's surrealist abstraction reached its pinnacle in his cubistic 1927 novel *Débora,* which incorporates greater attention to social conditions inflected by his burgeoning investment in socialism.[48] The novel presents a fragmented account of a day in the life of a superfluous man known only as the Teniente, or Lieutenant. The book demands a new formal conception of the city as it satirizes the nostalgic circuits of an Andrade Coello or Gangotena. Instead of romantic tales of yore, the Teniente's stroll reveals a vicious landscape where progress is under attack by the excuses of the reactionary *gemebundos* (howlers). There is no point

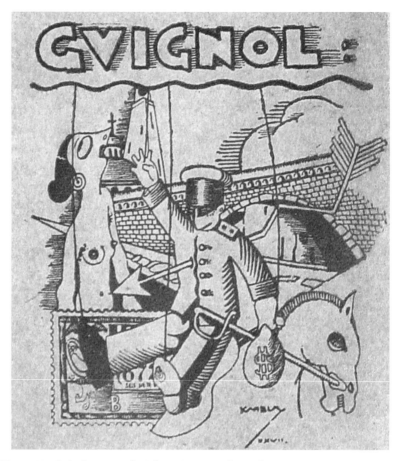

Fig. 6.3. Kanela, back cover art for *Débora*. Courtesy Library of Congress.

to such romanticism, considering the terrifying state of the poor. And even when memory does intrude, it is of a dystopic moment, far removed from the picturesque and frivolous, that causes the Teniente to retreat into his dreams.

The first edition of *Débora* paired Palacio's hallucinatory prose with prints by his comrades from *Hélice*, Guillermo Latorre and Kanela, which introduced the Teniente's Janus-faced world. The cover featured Latorre's vision (fig. 6.2), which centers on the disembodied military figure whose face nuzzles into a woman's thigh, just below her naked buttocks. Slices of the city form his coat, from La Ronda's picturesque homes to the mountains above. Other images from the story shuffle about him, including money, stamps, boots, and the number 57, his address. On the back cover is Kanela's interpretation of the story (fig. 6.3). Now the Teniente appears as the marionette Guignol, a popular nineteenth-century French puppet show and also the tongue-in-cheek namesake for the

Grand-Guignol, a French theater of horror stories that began appearing during the 1920s.[49] The clownish figure pierced by a bent arrow carries a moneybag and a sword that harnesses a hobbyhorse. A naked woman again accompanies the soldier, this time arising from a stamp as if she were a jack-in-the-box. A church spire and stone bridge represent traditional architecture while a molar (Guignol's creator Laurent Mourguet at one point pulled teeth for a living) acts the part of a cumulous cloud.

Palacio's novel merges these two visions of this character—kaleidoscopic cityscape and carnivalesque puppet—in a fractured stream of consciousness developed in three sections. The first and third focus on the characters of an anonymous city that has been denied riches and is frustrated by sexual urges. Here, the Teniente is alone with rambling thoughts that course through the routine tasks of a bureaucrat and become both a lengthy rumination on poverty and a rambling riff on what one could do with a million sucres. The monologue ends with the vapid conclusion that life as a millionaire would be comfortable, wouldn't it?[50] The book's final pages return to the forlorn frustrations of love as the Lieutenant consorts with women he finds unsatisfying, including a prostitute and his landlady's homely daughter. An imaginary muse, the Débora of the title, finally appears in the novel's closing page, where we also learn that the soldier has died, absurdly, from a paper cut. As Elizabeth Coonrod Martínez has pointed out, the Teniente's inability to reach his own mystical creation mirrors the novelist's frustration with a character that refuses to come to life and a plot in which we are forewarned that nothing will happen.[51]

These desultory ruminations bookend a parody of the romantic stroll through Quito's living museum of colonial grandeur that owes much to the counter-cartographies of Andrade, Bustamante, and Coloma.[52] A panoramic view from the hilly neighborhood of San Marcos—already home to Roberto Andrade's Pacho Villamar and Bustamante's Roberto—inspires a digression on the hunger of its thousands of impoverished dwellers rather than the ennui of the romantic chronicle. Palacio quickly drops this critique when another anonymous lieutenant (Teniente B) interrupts the protagonist to impart an asinine tale of having been interrupted in flagrante delicto by his lover's husband the day before. Together, the two officers visit La Ronda, famed muse of nostalgic poets, and they find it under assault from "El Relleno," that is, the infilling of the old brooks that once traversed the city. Palacio avoids common sentimentalism and instead censures these nostalgics for their elevation of the smell of urine above the asphalt of progress: "Truthfully, a crooked and narrow street that does not allow passage to a bus may be picturesque, it may be enchanting due to its urine smell, it may give an illusion of transitioning, from one moment to the next, between the rounds of night owls. But asphalt is newer and there exclaims the force of thousands of men."[53] This castigation of the nostalgic continues once the Teniente—finally alone again—cruises the drunkenness of El Placer before passing to the slums of the Barrios Bajos. There, he stands transfixed before a long flight of steps that triggers a memory of the door above; it opens onto a room of filth and muck where he once satisfied his carnal lust, and all the while he is reflecting on the trap that the scene represents for the children he hears in the next room, as from the slums come only thieves and prostitutes. With this memory, his paralysis disappears, he returns home, he wraps his mind around the earlier seduction of his landlady's daughter, who may or may not be pregnant, and finally begins a dream of frustrated love.[54] The novel abruptly ends.

Débora's radical rethinking of the colonial cityscape recalls the frustrations of Roberto's search to escape Quito's confines in Bustamante's *Para matar el gusano,* yet it painstakingly avoids letting the reader identify with the cause of the protagonist. Indeed, there is no lasting cause, romantic impulse, or even desire; the Teniente's supposed muse never appears, and one encounters his thoughts merely as a means to survive a contaminated environment. This is no nihilistic representation per se, as Palacio situates the source of this conflict in the social relations represented by the nightmarish tour through the *centro*—a stance in concert with his burgeoning socialist philosophy. He would later expand this consideration in his last novel, *Vida del ahorcado* (1932), which condemns the bourgeois impulse by tracing the tentacles of its violence against humanity and nature. A trial of the bourgeois by the violated forest, nature itself, frames the conflict even as it foreshadows the possibility of reconciliation in an alternate social web.[55]

A complement to Palacio's pessimism can be found in the similarly fantastical experiments of his socialist colleague, Humberto Salvador. Born in Guayaquil in 1909, Salvador migrated to Quito following the loss of his parents when he was a young child. He studied literature at the Mejía, where he also began writing fiction strongly influenced by the French "maestros" such as Stendhal, Flaubert, Gide, and Balzac.[56] His first stories appeared in 1925 in *Claridad,* the semi-official magazine of the Julian government, and were followed by contributions to the radical student review *Llamaradda* after he began studying law at the Universidad Central in 1927. Modern drama, particularly Pirandello's *Six Characters in Search of an Author* (1921), both inspired his production of prize-winning plays, published as far afield as Argentina, and also heavily influenced the stories collected in *Ajedrez* and his novel *En la ciudad he perdido una novela* (both published in 1929). Expanding Palacio's earlier critique, Salvador's writings illustrate a frenetic and fragmented Quito dominated by pulsating encounters between modernity's recklessness and the frustrating endurance of tradition.

His early works—he would later try his hand at social realism—represent the first local acceptance of the paradoxical impulses of modern life. An obsession with psychological deviance tinged with clinical curiosity pervades these pieces, a scenario that Wilfrido Corral has linked to Salvador's own studies in Freudian theory.[57] A tale like "El amante de las manos," for instance, recalls Palacio's "El antropófago," given its eventual devolution into a ritualistic devouring of a lover's hands. Salvador, however, painstakingly recreates the steps of this deterioration into madness, avoiding the dependence on the sudden revelation typical of Palacio's narrative. The potential intrusion of insanity into a quotidian moment appears again in "La navaja," in which a narrator, bored with the mundane discussions in the barbershop, daydreams that his barber metamorphoses into a homicidal maniac. This fantasy appears ludicrous ("¡Caramba! ¿Realidad? No; ilusión"), but it is also addictive.[58] The bohemian narrator follows the thought to its finish—a hallucination of his own death—attracted by a horror laced with uncertainty.

Salvador, moreover, attributes a modern sensibility to technology that ruptures the veneer of tradition and quietude that obscures the stifling forces of capitalism. The barber's clock in "La navaja," for instance, belongs to a consortium of contemporary timepieces sensitive to the avant-garde's disgust with a Fordist mentality: "They do not resign themselves to the vulgarity of being exact."[59] In "Las linternas de los autos," the city's nightlife is described from the perspective of a car's headlights, those "*ojos de la noche*" that observe depravity under darkness, from prostitution to theft and murder. As witness simultaneously to bourgeois excess and modernity's "*escenarios movibles*" (movable stages) life has no secrets for the "*sabia linterna*" (wise lantern).

The trope of lucid personification returns in Salvador's best-known treatment of the fantastical city, his 1929 novel *En la ciudad he perdido una novela*. In this work, which focuses on a fictional author's attempt to create characters that refuse his autocratic ministrations, Quito's neighborhoods, salons, cinemas, and tramlines appear as archetypal personalities, which he terms *subpersonajes*. For Salvador's narrator, these "subcharacters" conspire with the city to obfuscate the spaces identified with main players such as the refined Josefina and the nihilist Carlos, a process that hides these characters' individuality from the authorial hunt. Salvador's narrator laments this situation in his description of his elusive muse, Victoria: "I'll begin by locating her. Locating a person in the classic city of San Francisco de Quito proves more difficult, even, than divining a friend's cards during a high-stakes game of chance. She escapes. In order to catch up, one must desperately run through the streets. Fortunately, the paved roads are less painful than the sidewalk; however, when one reaches cobblestones the chase becomes dolorous. You must quit. The character thus escapes and not even the Devil could find her."[60] In this passage, Salvador deconstructs several of the usual visions of idyllic Quito, which obscures its characters by virtue of its own evasive yet classic character. Jaundiced reality intrudes for the pursuer as he traipses across the city streets, where the asphalt's yield provides pyrrhic relief for an author encumbered by a rigid cobblestone not even the devil himself could weather.

The quest is compulsive, and so the author searches for Victoria's home, turning now to the popular neighborhood of El Tejar, lamentably yet another "*barrio lleno de piedras*" (barrio full of stones) on Pichincha's upper slopes. In a spot riddled in legend and memory, Salvador retreats for an instant into the loyal transcription of an old-fashioned chronicler. However, he rejects the anodyne for malicious witches, a widow possessed by a devil, and a multitude of dwarfs whose spirits only recently capitulated to the assault of electricity that appeared with the suddenness of an Apache's attack in an American western.[61] And yet tradition holds fast, held tightly by *"casas coloniales, madres del pecado"* (colonial houses, mothers of sin), including the neighborhood church, *"la señora del barrio,"* under whose shadow the locals drink flavors of the past such as *aguardiente* and *chicha de jora* (corn beer).

After El Tejar, the pace accelerates. The resurgent ghosts shield Victoria on her way to a salon, then disappear as she leaps into an automobile speeding toward the Edén cinema, where the slapstick films of Charlie Chaplin and Buster Keaton regale the faithful crowd. Inside the theater, we encounter the romantic malcontent Carlos, whom Victoria cannot stand, and so she vanishes again, giving way to a new muse: the wealthy Josefina. A resident of one of the luxurious chalets on the northern edges of town, Josefina gives the author even more trouble since she never walks anywhere, only taking trams and automobiles speeding past the Alameda and Ejido parks on her way to the impressionist canvas of her garden. Even her mansion, in its grand opulence where the windows are "frames for the cubist nude of voluptuousness" scoffs at the lowly artist.[62]

As the novel continues its episodic meandering through a crowd of new characters and subcharacters, the author eventually comes to realize the futility of his attempt at comprehensive knowledge. Quito cannot be understood through a single character, a single building, a single neighborhood. The capsule of the chronicle thus is revealed as presumptuous, for only in the collection of fragments can one bring the city to light. The realization is stark but promising for the vanguard, who alone understands this reality:

> Each neighborhood symbolizes a tendency. . . . Hallucinatory novels, with legendary aspects and classic prose, one finds in "El Tejar." The medieval in the cloisters of "Santo Domingo" or "San Diego." The perverse in "La Tola." The modern rests in the central streets, where automobiles are protagonists of all flings and all love stories. The romantic in the section of "La Alameda." And when one reaches the "Ejido" they become naturalists. Realism is hidden like a cat in any house. One can search for the vanguard in the city, throughout all its neighborhoods.[63]

Quito's attack on his novel thus stems from its very character as a modern city: a schizophrenic landscape whose essence cannot be known except by pastiche. The city thus hid within its paradox a Pirandellian character thwarting attempts to know its nature yet offering up tantalizing glimpses of clearly defined individual neighborhoods, whose very clarity is also illusory. Such a definition ruptured the conventional view of Quito as a site easily illumined by the insight of an expert narrator such as Gangotena, Andrade Coello, or even Palacio. According to Salvador, only the vanguard, with its ability to transcend essentializing definitions, can be found throughout the landscape.

The Social Realist Necropolis

Salvador's and Palacio's surrealistic writings raised the ire of their fellow Socialist Party members. A critical moment came in 1930, when a group of writers from Guayaquil published *Los que se van,* a collection of tales highlighting the brutality of life in the rolling hills of the coastal plateau. The book's coauthors, Demetrio Aguilera Malta, Joaquín Gallegos Lara, and Enrique Gil Gilbert, followed up its publication with calls for a socially conscious national literature. Gallegos Lara, in particular, embraced the task of exalting socialism in a series of essays published in 1931 and 1932 that formulated a comprehensive critique of recent avant-garde activity as a nativist extension of bourgeois mentality. He singled out Salvador's *En la ciudad he perdido una novela* as a trite example of formalism, instead advocating a literature featuring the nation's rural and urban poor. Manifestos abounded in the leftist press as editorial pages clamored to answer Gallegos's challenge, with even the "decadent" Salvador turning his back on his previous work.[64] This energy infused the intellectual elite and propelled a literary renaissance that yielded some of Ecuador's best-known fiction of the twentieth century, including Jorge Icaza's *indigenista* novel *Huasipungo* (1934), José de la Cuadra's forerunner to magical realism, *Los Sangurimas* (1934), and Demetrio Aguilera Malta's *Don Goyo* (1933). Their heroes included the oppressed Indian, the verbose and violent *montubio* (literally, a resident of the Andean foothills; figuratively, a country bumpkin), and the colloquial Afro-Ecuadorian.

These novels drew upon a lengthy intellectual history reaching back to Juan León Mera but were most immediately influenced by Loja attorney Pío Jaramillo Alvarado's exploration of pre-Columbian history. Jaramillo's *El indio ecuatoriano* (1922) simultaneously lauded a noble indigenous tradition going back to the legendary pre-Incaic Kingdom of Quito while arguing for a contemporary alliance between indigenous communities and the Socialist Party. Jaramillo's writings helped accelerate rural political activism and also fostered literary exploration of these ideas, beginning with Fernando Chaves's *Plata y bronce* (1927), whose emphasis on the corruption of priests and *hacendados* presaged the onset of social realism.[65] Most exponents of this new *indigenismo* located their writings in the countryside in order to demonstrate the exploitative relations of a no longer vacuous hinterland. This is not to say, however, that the city disappears from the social realist novel. Indeed, Federico Chalupa has commented on the import of the capital as the space "associated with the white elite" in no less a work than Icaza's *Huasipungo,* a scathing rebuke of life on an Andean hacienda and generally regarded as the foremost example of the indigenist movement. It is in Quito, however, that Don Alfonso Pereira brokers a deal with the gringo Mr. Chappy to build a highway through an indigenous community's small plots known as *huasipungos*. It is the city's scandalmongers whom Pereira flees upon learning of his daughter's illegitimate pregnancy. And from Quito comes the regiment that suppresses an indigenous insurrection in the work's climactic scene.[66]

The framework developed by Icaza and his colleagues echoed the vituperative castigation of the city typical of the polemical writing at the turn of the twentieth century as well as of contemporary sociological and psychological thought. Particularly influential in the Ecuadorian context were José Carlos Mariátegui's agrarian socialism, with its emphasis on the urban origins of rural poverty, along with the reformist pedagogy of the Mexican revolutionary government.[67] While *Hélice* had promulgated Rivera's work in 1926 to general indifference, the visit of Mexican educator Moises Sáenz in 1931, as part of a regional tour designed to investigate the conditions of South American indigenous groups, proved more influential. Sáenz's contacts with figures like Jaramillo Alvarado and Chaves influenced his encyclopedic *Sobre el indio ecuatoriano* (1933); its treatment of the hardships of rural life expanded Jaramillo's research and foreshadowed the advent of social realist literature.[68] Sáenz's call for a more responsible pedagogy and a comprehensive sociological study of the plight of the Ecuadorian Indian encouraged further academic study. Of particular relevance for the social realist novel were the studies of urban and periurban poverty conducted in the *suburbios* by Dr. Pablo Arturo Suárez of the Universidad Central in the early 1930s. Suárez's subsequent statistical and qualitative portrait of these slums published in 1934 provided a wealth of information mined by authors such as Icaza and Humberto Salvador as they created a denunciatory urban literature.[69]

The second integral element of works such as Icaza's *En las calles* (1935) and Salvador's socialist fiction was the incorporation of a Freudian concern with sexual deviance. For both authors, this inflection in their work stemmed partially from their university studies; Icaza had at one time been a medical student before turning to the theater, while Salvador's thesis, "Esquema sexual" (Universidad Central, 1933), represented the first comprehensive Spanish-language survey of the role of sexuality in contemporary psychological theory.[70] Salvador's studies of Freud, Jung, and Soviet theorist Alexandra Kollontai formed the basis for his portrayal of the social origins of sexual transgression in subsequent novels.[71] These referents also heavily influenced Icaza, particularly in his early drama, which emphasized the causal relationship between environment, sexual repression, and perversion.

Icaza's plays turn upon a sense of moral ambiguity stemming from the social conditions in which his characters exist—conditions in which violence results from environmental conditions rather than a person's existential choices. For example, "Como ellos quieren" (1930) examines the warping of the lust felt by Lucrecia, a young provincial girl studying in Quito, whose liaisons with a poor lover are curtailed by her father's family. Besotted by neurasthenia and an accompanying hysteric disorder, she bites her uncle's cheek and attempts to strangle her cousin before choosing the "independent" life of a prostitute.[72] Similarly, "¿Cuál es?" features an oedipal crisis as two brothers (Hijo 1 and Hijo 2) fantasize about killing their philandering drunk of a father whose exploits have caused their mother to contract a venereal disease. When he is finally murdered, neither brother is certain who inflicted the fatal knife wound, even as the members of the community (and their mother) remain certain it was Hijo 1 because he had publicly railed against the patriarch—yet another score for the *quiteño* gossips.[73]

Icaza partially abandons the ambiguity of these early experiments in the societal indictment of *Huasipungo,* where sex stands revealed as an abusive curse besotting the indigenous women of the Cuchitambo hacienda. A central sequence delineates the social origins of these conflicts by tracing the adventures of Don Alfonso Pereira. After being awakened from slumber by the shouts of his workers attempting to save the cripple Andrés Chiliquinga from stampeding cattle, Pereira rapes Chiliquinga's wife Cunshi, who is acting as wet nurse to his son. She is summarily returned to Chiliquinga's *choza* the following day, leading the cripple to wonder what may have occurred. Cunshi never speaks—after all, her attacker "was the boss, who could do what he would in his dominion." Pereira's lecherous escapades continue the next evening in drunken cavorting with the parish priest. Their carousing ends with first Pereira and then the cleric consorting with the housekeeper, Juana, who tellingly echoes Cunshi's exculpation of the master within a moral compass. As she puts it (in an internal monologue), sex with Pereira represents only a potential sin whereas, "with the priest, it wasn't a sin." Nevertheless, when her youngest son observes her return to her quarters, adjusting her blouse, his gaze fills her with the deepest shame.[74]

The violence against women presages the escalation of Pereira's oppression, which ultimately leads to a futile insurrection among the Indians of Cuchitambo that is suppressed by soldiers arriving from the capital. This event foreshadows the central conflicts of Icaza's next novel, *En las calles.*[75] Like its predecessor, this work features a domineering *hacendado*—Don Luis Antonio Urrestes—whose political and economic power straddles the urban and rural realms. The protagonists are two *cholos,* or mestizos, named Ramón Landeta and José Manuel Játiva, who flee the hamlet of Chaguarpata after Urrestes encroaches on their water rights. The novel follows their journey to Quito, where they join the toiling masses, Landeta as a porter at a factory owned, ironically, by Urrestes, and Játiva as a police officer. While Icaza demarcates the transformative experiences each suffers, the novel's climactic recounting of a riot reveals an enveloping and tragic social structure.

Icaza's treatment of Landeta's acculturation to the factory evokes his early drama as well as the liberal idyll. The *cholo* quickly gains the trust of his superiors for his faithful service. In the factory, he also meets the hardworking and comely Claudina, who supports her drunken father. In a nod to the theme of pastoral liberation in many early liberal novels, the two frequent the nearby eucalyptus forests, whose lumber feeds the smokestacks; these liaisons lead to Claudina's pregnancy and a confrontation with her father. Although she is able to withstand her father's inebriated wrath, the couple's joy ends when management forbids a unionization drive, which leads Claudina to join her coworkers in storming the factory. Landeta, still guarding the gates, lets her and a few others inside, and then the police confront the assembled crowd. He attempts to sneak them out the back door near a putrid knoll reeking of urine and feces guarded by a lone police officer. The guard hesitates when attacked by Landeta but then drives a bayonet into the *cholo's* breast. Only then does Landeta realize that his killer was none other than his former companion, José Manuel Játiva.

Játiva's killing of his *compadre* demarcates the fragmentation of the city and underscores an earlier appeal made by the strikers to the police citing their common mestizo ancestry—"*cholos mismo son!*" This appeal also reinforces Icaza's treatment of Játiva's schizophrenic alternation between his identities as the *cholo* from Chaguarpata and *policía número* 120. It is the cop who kills Landeta, but it was Játiva whose trigger finger hesitated when his friend had just emerged from the factory. The keeper of the peace smashes the butt of his rifle into the head of a pregnant Indian as his troop suppresses a rural uprising, but it is Játiva who recognizes her glassy eyes as those of his wife following her execution by Urrestes's minions for poaching corn. Finally, it is *policía número* 120 who stands next to *policía número* 132 as the latter collapses, shouting, "Me jodieron estos carajos," as they attempt to control a crowd protesting a rigged election. But it is Játiva who takes up the call for solidarity between police and workers until another anonymous soldier finally crushes the head of the "*escandaloso policía.*"[76]

The anguish of Játiva's and Landeta's experiences develops a macrospatial argument linking the city and the countryside. In it, the city no longer appears to be the exploiter of the countryside, as in *Huasipungo,* but instead functions as one part in an overarching system of exploitation. Other elements of the novel that help develop this leveling of difference between the urban and rural realms can be seen in Urrestes's constant presence in both spheres and the riot that closes the novel itself. Evoking the carnage of the Guerra de los Cuatro Días of 1932—the bloody street battle that resulted from the disqualification of the fascist presidential candidate Neptalí Bonifaz for having been born in Peru—the combat occurs as a result of a disputed election between Urrestes and another *hacendado,* Solano del Castillo.[77] The two spare no expense, rounding up able Indians and *cholos* from their haciendas to force an armed confrontation. Játiva's eventual awareness of the extent of this manipulation matters little, for the struggle must continue, and even Urrestes and Solano are only playing bit parts in a drama of systemic brutality.

Icaza also tackles the physical embodiment of the exploitative national dynamic on a microspatial level. Early in the novel, for example, the contingent from Chaguarpata encounters the massive Presidential Palace ("más grande que la casa de la hacienda," or larger than the hacienda house) before bedding down in Santo Domingo Plaza, the evocative description of which is worth quoting at length:

> At 10 PM, more or less, a tattered scrounger arrived, scratched his groin, head, and louse-ridden armpits before ringing some medals—saints, virgins, crosses—as well as a few amulets dangling off his chest, and then, in between curses and special prayers, he curled up into a ball of rags on the ground. A bit later a blind man accompanied by a shoeless boy appeared and did the same. Later there came an Indian—a public porter in disgrace—"Anyone can. Anyone. Even the native . . . " thought the troupe of villagers, dragging themselves slowly toward the miserable covering offered by the portico. It was a windy and cold night, but no worse than the hovels of the alpine moors. Luckily, they were already accustomed.[78]

The distinction between the palace's luxurious halls and the cold stone of the plaza recreates the social map of the city. The colonial center no longer serves a nostalgic role but instead demarcates centuries of exploitation. The squalid living quarters of the urban and rural poor, from Chaguarpata to La Tola to Chimbacalle, each contain the same bare floors and lack of amenities. For Icaza, this is the heart of the city, a point underscored by his striking choice to avoid the private sphere of the wealthy, who only appear in public sites such as the government palace, offices, and Urrestes's factory.

Icaza's dystopic vision rests on a spatial account of power evoking the liberal idyll infused with an indigenist-inflected attention to subaltern actors. A similar frame dominates the social realism of Humberto Salvador's three socialist novels of the 1930s—*Camarada* (1933), *Trabajadores* (1935), and *Noviembre* (1939). Despite Gallegos Lara's challenge, Salvador maintains the surreal landscapes, fragmented narratives, and an obsession with psychological trauma and sexual deviance that characterized his earlier works. Other elements include the sporadic inflection of an *indigenista* mysticism that recalls Mariátegui's project to develop a distinctly Andean socialism and a tendency to universalize Quito's particularities that links Salvador to the synechdochal chronotopical trends explored throughout this book.[79]

Each of Salvador's socialist novels explores a particular dimension of this iconoclastic aesthetic. The first of the three, *Camarada*, features interlocking episodes that develop a fragmented montage that shifts through time and space, providing only a conceptual map to anchor the reader.[80] This conceptual tool is provided by Salvador's fascination with both Marxism and sexual psychology, which had been the subject of his thesis, "Esquema sexual." *Camarada* thus provides episodic accounts of the violence of bourgeois sexual transgression that ultimately contrast with working-class fidelity and modesty.

Most of the novel centers on traumatic encounters that a young bureaucrat named Alberto has with three equally unattainable women. The first is his cousin Lucrecia, with whom he shared an illicit sexual experience as a child. The memory of this incident haunts him as he courts the frigid Gloria, herself tormented by the incestuous advances of her father and a series of enjoyable but forbidden lesbian experiences in boarding school.[81] Alberto finally meets a potential companion in the young proletarian Julia, whose parents are the only moral characters in the novel. Although the two young people do eventually kiss, Alberto refrains from pursuing a sexual relationship because "Julia is poor. She has no right to pleasure."[82] However, Julia too is implicated by bourgeois lechery when her boss attempts to seduce her on her lunch hour. When she refuses, she loses her job. Alberto, though, cannot help her because he falls victim to Depression downsizing. The novel ends as he begins to starve.

Salvador's next socialist novel, *Trabajadores* (1935), moves away from the formulaic proselytizing of *Camarada*. The novel abandons two-dimensional characterization and includes naturalistic portraits of proletarian life along with heightened attunement to the semiotics of urban space. These changes may be traced to Salvador's service in the Ministry of Social Welfare, a haven for socialist militants, which provided him with firsthand experience of the plight of the urban and rural poor.[83] He develops this through a refrain—*la vida sin vida* (lifeless life)—that provides an ontological framework exploring the denigration of the human spirit as a result of social exploitation.[84]

Salvador deploys this sociological analysis in three sections, the first and third of which discuss the emerging class consciousness of ten-year-old Gonzalo Gálvez as he and his family struggle to survive after his father, an army lieutenant, is severely beaten for his alleged involvement in a planned coup. The middle section fleshes out the social milieus in which the Gálvez family operates by presenting a series of scenes portraying daily life in their neighborhood. Throughout, Salvador reconsiders Quito as a liminal and fluid space that belies the intransigence of class exploitation and offers the potential for revolutionary possibility in young Gálvez.

A primary theme within *Trabajadores* concerns the lifeless existence of the marginal and disenfranchised. Salvador maps this trope upon a cityscape that resembles the fragmented vistas of *En la ciudad he perdido una novela* but without the whimsy of the earlier novel. In *Trabajadores,* instead of fluidity, motion is either arrested or signifies social decline. Thus, Lieutenant Gálvez transitions, always a bit later than he would like, from the military hospital to his crowded home to the spa town of Baños to the cemetery, each step furthering his decline. His sister Teresa migrates to Quito from the city of Ambato and is at one point faced with the possibility of traveling to Guayaquil at the request of a former lover who has found some mercantile success in the port. This potentially liberating journey recalls *Pacho Villamar* and Salvador Ramirez's tours to the coast, yet Teresa remains entrenched in a decrepit city due to the need to take care of her family.[85] Their continued financial erosion forces a shift from a moderately comfortable apartment in the central neighborhood of La Merced to tiny rooms in La Chilena—what Salvador refers to as "the last human nest of the city"—following Gálvez's loss of his pension.[86]

While the lack of freedom to travel where one wants or, conversely, being forced to move to less costly quarters are examples of how poverty limits potential in adult lives, the city slowly opens up to the young Gonzalo Gálvez, a narrator whose name we learn only in the closing pages of the novel. Gonzalo's journeys at the behest of his family introduce him to the class divides at society's core.[87] This knowledge is communicated via three journeys across the valley, which illuminate the urban fluidity characteristic of Salvador's earlier work and reveal a Marxist framework. The first of these journeys is at the behest of Gonzalo's aunt, Teresa, who sends him to visit the elite chalets near Avenida Colón, where the boy travels to beg for new clothes from the reputably generous Señor Pérez. Gonzalo longingly gazes at the trolley passing by, wishing that he did not need to trudge across the expanse of the city, only to find that the refined dandy awaiting him at journey's end has no interest in his supplications.[88] The second is a bus trip to Chimbacalle, where his father is about to board the train for Baños. An urchin lacking the fare is run over by a chauffeur anxious to press on. Finally, on a second trip to the northern chalets, this time near the Parque de Mayo (today's Ejido Park), Gonzalo tries to collect payment for a dress Teresa had made for a debutante. In the garden at the customer's home, he meets a girl his own age whose doll reminds him of his neighbor Beatriz, who cries at night for lack of food. Although the girl is touched by his tale, her father lets loose his dogs to drive away a boy he considers a truant, thus impeding Gonzalo's ability to collect the much-needed funds.

Gonzalo's journeys—collecting the payment for Teresa, caring for his father—reveal the nature of the city. It is a divided but intertwined space, as Salvador makes clear in an evocative passage that occurs just before Gonzalo's encounter with the young girl:

> My life was an irony—how ironic that a starved and ragged boy could enter homes saturated with luxurious comforts.
>
> It was a sensational discovery—next to the destitute Quito I knew existed another Quito—that of the powerful.
>
> These were two distinct cities that life's great sarcasm arranged close by. Two contradictory cities that were nevertheless interwoven, the one fused in the other.[89]

For Gonzalo, despite his tender age, the city that had frustrated Salvador's vanguard narrator a few years earlier has bared its essential paradox in which the interdependence of poverty and wealth is obvious. As Salvador makes clear, this knowledge comes with a price, as the innocence of youth is overwhelmed by the jaded irony of adolescence.

A secondary dehumanizing trope concerns male sexual depravity, which builds on Salvador's studies in sexual psychology and eugenics. For Salvador, traditional sexual mores evoke social injustice or personal frustration. He develops this indictment by presenting archetypal situations that pervert these frustrations. For example, while collecting Gálvez's pension, Teresa encounters a provincial schoolteacher named Laura who lost her job for refusing the advances of a government inspector. Gonzalo's sister Lola, on the other hand, takes up with the handsome son of a local shopkeeper, who abandons her after she becomes pregnant. Tellingly, her family's worries center on the arrival of a new mouth to feed, and family members counsel her to abort the fetus. She refuses.[90] Finally, Salvador explores the twisting course of lust by detailing their one-eyed brother Alfredo's passion for the comely Chabela, who refuses the grotesque *tuerto* (one-eyed man) as she recalls flamboyant romps with Gerardo, the dashing son of her employer. Alfredo's already substantial drinking accelerates amid his frustration, fueling lonely masturbation in a dark alley—"Esto es para los pobres!" (This is for the poor!).[91] Finally, he abandons the miserable courtship and attempts rape. Chabela fends him off by clubbing him on the head with a stone.

The emotional bankruptcy of adult men is contrasted with the experiences of young Gonzalo. After his father's release from prison, the boy endures entreaties for euthanasia and an attempted suicide before the military pension enables the invalid's transit to the southern spa of Baños, a small hamlet on the cusp between the sierra and the Amazon that is famous for its hot springs.[92] As in the novels of Andrade or Martínez, this parody of the liberating rural escapade proves equally pyrrhic following the father's return to Quito. In his dying breath, he calls to Gonzalo by name, identifying the boy for the first time and symbolically declaring his manhood. In the closing pages of the book, Gonzalo finally embraces his father's Marxism, replacing the national flag draped over the coffin with a red ribbon. This political awareness parallels a sexual awakening when Gonzalo kisses Beatriz for the first time and discovers that her mouth is "*una fruta maravillosa.*" This intimate and legitimate sexual encounter bolsters Salvador's broader claim that sexual liberation would accompany political deliverance. The book ends with its now mantric opening line: "We workers of the world will create the new humanity."[93]

Trabajadores integrates Salvador's fascination with the fluidity of modern identities into his political project. In his final socialist novel of the 1930s, *Noviembre* (1939), these tropes escape the contours of social realism with the reintroduction of the hallucinatory prose of *En la ciudad he perdido una novela.* Salvador deploys this renewed surrealism to redefine *indigenismo*'s mysticism in an effort that anticipates Orwell's *Animal Farm* (1945) amid a scathing indictment of the inner workings of government.[94]

The first third of the novel treats social climbers, focusing on the attempts by the young bureaucrat Alberto Andrade and a secretary named Marta Gangotena to ascend the political ladder. Andrade's primary skill is his sycophancy, whereas Marta employs her looks, though of course without sacrificing her "honor." Salvador contrasts their ability to navigate Quito's corrupt intrigue with the honorable designs of the socialist bureaucrat Hernán Navarro and his friend Jaime, who strive to resist the repressive Dictador, whose qualifications are limited to trading wisecracks with soldiers in the Plaza de la Independencia. While Alberto and Marta rise to the top of their professions, Jaime and Hernán suffer from the widening abuses of the despot and his henchman, Herr Heller, the German-born chief of police rumored to have trained with the Gestapo. The city slowly descends into a reign of terror, worsened by a failed military insurrection that leads to the death of a young poet named Jorge Aguirre, whose only crime was to climb the barricades in search of an ode.

The two-year presidency of the engineer Federico Páez, who rode a 1935 military coup to power, provided the primary inspiration for Salvador's novel *Noviembre.* Despite some initial legislation sympathetic to workers and the indigenous populations, Páez's inability to restrain the tumult of the Great Depression delegitimated his autocratic rule. The press, especially the leftist daily *El Día,* increasingly waged a war of words that led the Calderón regiment to stage an insurrection in November 1936, which indeed featured the death of a poet— the *guambra* (child) Zambrano—on whom Salvador's idealistic Jorge Aguirre was based. According to the American traveler Albert Franklin, Zambrano's death "gave transcendence" to the insurrection and proved a galvanizing force for the deepening opposition.[95] Páez turned increasingly authoritarian in ensuing months and indeed named a Nazi sympathizer to head the Quito police.[96] The expansion of state terror ultimately led the military to withdraw its support for the government. In October, the minister of defense, Alberto Enríquez, forced Páez's resignation and installed an interim government calling for a "renewal" of the progressive spirit.[97]

Noviembre's denouement loosely follows this narrative while introducing fantastical and mystical elements that Salvador deploys as symbols of Quito's innate spirit. These symbols begin to make their appearance with the poet's death, when Jorge Aguirre's lone shot inspires a cavalcade of bullets, accompanied by a chorus of "Down with intelligence and long live death!"—words that had been famously spoken by Falangist general Millán Astray to rebut the criticism of the great Spanish essayist and poet Miguel de Unamuno at the University of Salamanca in 1936.[98] Salvador frames the city's ensuing carnage as a crucifixion delivering a crown of thorns to the Andean capital.[99] This Christian image explodes into a surrealist ode following the battle, during which the fearful quiet haunts the young activist Hernán. He collapses while watching the Dictador distribute ministerial assignments and hallucinates that the leader gaily passes plates of bones and morsels of raw meat to a crowd of yapping and snarling dogs whose mouths intermittently resemble those of humans. He collapses before this delusion, which evokes the Rabelaisian grotesque that had fascinated the 1920s avant-garde while also anticipating the famous conclusion of Orwell's *Animal Farm,* in which it is impossible to differentiate between the revolutionary pigs and the capitalist men.[100]

The novel's final pages develop an image of Quito as a phantasmagorical skeleton populated by "ghosts appearing as living men as they have lost the qualities that bring mankind praise."[101] Again, Hernán hallucinates, this time seeing a visit by the dead poet, Jorge Aguirre, who compares his martyrdom to the attack on genius and creativity in fascist Europe. Aguirre's words awaken anonymous hordes of ghosts who clamor for the execution of government traitors and call for the Andes themselves to awaken, which they do. First Mount Pichincha opens its arms, followed by its siblings Chimborazo, Cayambe, and El Altar, sending a shudder through the earth and presaging the arrival a reborn Atahualpa, who delivers a speech claiming America for the workers of the world and calling for the resurrection of the ancient spirit of the city, slumbering all this time. At this climactic moment, Hernán awakes to find his friend Jaime telling him that it is all over. The military has deposed the Dictador and placed a new progressive government in his place. The city and nation are finally free.[102]

Within the generic constitutions of the novel of the phantasmagorical dystopia, *Noviembre* provides the first attempt to rehabilitate the city's image via the seismic intrusion of a primordial past rupturing historical colonialism to create a new future that is both local and universal. The novel's dizzying conclusion introduces an *indigenista* metaphor that, for all its potency, is framed as the hallucination of a starving man hopeful for the future but certainly not in his right mind—as evidenced by his earlier vision of the transmutation of potential ministers into howling dogs. This vision recalls the trial of humanity from Palacio's *Vida del ahorcado* but serves a different point—that of rehabilitating the soul of a city long slumbering yet potentially ripe for change and renewal.[103] As such, it can be compared to the progressive spirit of the liberal idyll despite its ironic sensibility. After all, while animate mountains and dead Incas do not build the society of the future, Hernán awakes from his own dreams to gaze upon a city bathed in resplendent sunlight, a sight that is "a symphony of light and color . . . beautiful, ardent, and voluptuous."[104] The idyll has finally been transgressed and transformed.

The Chronotope of an Anti-Modern City

In the early twentieth century, the historic Iberian evocation of the civilizing force of urbanity encountered a new lineage of denunciations and castigations of city life. The potential liberation offered by rural climes did appear alongside this critique; however, the authors proclaiming the barbarism of city life were not pastoral nostalgists. The urban is laced with the rural and heavily implicated in its terror, even in the writings of an Andrade or Bustamante whose idealized countrysides are more prominent. These works thus deconstruct the counter-cartography offered by Juan León Mera in *Cumandá,* arguing vociferously against the capital's "traditional" society, which becomes a banal absurdity masking the social reality they hope to illuminate.

One of the critical elements of these poetics of denunciation concerns an ironic approach to the positivist paradigm that verges on the postmodern. While there is a broad embrace of social justice and progress offered in opposition to Quito's retrograde *gemebundos,* these novels attempt to illustrate the coexistence of the modern and the traditional in an increasingly dialogical fashion. By exploding the perceived disjuncture between the future and the past, these authors offer a conceit of the city as a simulacrum.[105] Although operating from distinct politics, this framework builds upon Juan León Mera's counter-cartographic vision of national development, wherein progress is turned on its head in a country going the wrong way. Andrade's and Martínez's naturalist melodramas layer liberal polemic upon this essentially dystopian vision while Bustamante, Salvador, Icaza, and Palacio each interrogate the paradigm of progress itself.

The futile attempts to *know* the Pirandellian and phantasmagorical city owe much to contemporary literary experimentation, especially the currents of *modernismo,* surrealism, Dadaism, and socialist realism. They also stem, however, from the particular milieu of Quito, in which the modern and the traditional maintained an incessant tango, as well as from the peculiar biographical circumstances of the authors themselves. From Mera to Palacio, Bustamante to Salvador, a provincial upbringing inflects the critique of the insular idyll while highlighting the possibility (and difficulty) of its transgressing. It is worth noting that Mera and Martínez both hailed from Ambato, Palacio from Loja, and Salvador from Guayaquil. Even Bustamante and Icaza spent many of their formative years on family haciendas in Pifo and Latacunga, despite having been born in the city. These authors' displacement as migrants qualifies their fictional constitution of Quito as a closed community. As David Sibley has noted, in such a "strongly classified space," intruders must be shunned.[106] The denunciation of this insularity as a phantasmagorical construction masking social tension thus comes with an intimate familiarity based not only in ideological study but also in life experience. This was not their city, and their estrangement is projected onto the cityscape they depict.

The relationship between the city and its hinterland both locally and nationally formed a critical component of the character of these novels and stories. However, in spite of the political ties that did exist between urban intellectuals and indigenous communities, these works cannot claim to directly represent the latter's perspective. Indeed, even the most widely known *indigenista,* Jorge Icaza, demonstrates a rootedness in urban discourse that demonstrates cleavages between the city and its hinterland. However, this observation belies the direct engagement with the urban economy by indigenous communities. Moreover, it also obscures the degree to which indigenous communities—in particular the commune of Santa Clara de San Millán—themselves manipulated history, and especially genealogy, as insiders aware of the leverage of historicity within the city's modernizing present.

Chapter 7

Santa Clara de San Millán
The Politics of Indigenous Genealogy

In July 1940, a group of indigenous *comuneros* from the town of Santa Clara de San Millán on Quito's outskirts petitioned Ecuador's minister of social welfare to form an alternate cabildo. This communiqué criticized the current leadership, charging that the body constituted an elite oligarchy, or *gamonal,* a term usually reserved for landed and agroexport oligarchy. The petition claimed further that the cabildo members had grown wealthy through their manipulation of the community's common lands. Of particular concern to the petitioners were urban properties that lay in the town's northern environs, which they charged the cabildo had distributed among themselves. In conclusion, the *comuneros* alleged that those who were unable to gain the favor of the cabildo for access, such as the elderly or the deaf, were forced to beg in order to survive.[1]

Pedro Pablo Tumipamba and Francisco Tumipamba, scions of a leading clan, presented the petition. These two brothers had long hoped to join the cabildo's membership, only to be thwarted by their father, long-standing legal representative José Federico Tumipamba, who claimed they were still too young. Earlier attempts to appeal his decision, both to the cabildo and the ministry, had ended in failure, precipitating this new strategy of petitioning with support from the marginalized factions, a tactic that sought to exploit fissures in the *comuna*.[2] For the impoverished and elderly, the pastures and plots of the traditional communal lands represented sustainability for ancestral practices besieged by the expanding city. For local entrepreneur Feliciano Simbaña, on the other hand, common lands provided a resource for the growing network of rental properties; he was thus trading on the very forces of change that threatened his fellow community members. National politics also played a part. As Pedro Pablo and Francisco Tumipamba would have well known, the Ministry of Social Welfare was dominated by socialist intellectuals inclined to support a crusade against a *gamonal*.[3]

Whereas his sons had adopted the language of class exploitation in their bid to form an alternate cabildo, José Federico Tumipamba issued a response that deployed decades of experience crafting land histories and local genealogies. In his response, he defended a set of statutes drafted in 1910 that guaranteed the community's autonomy despite the official prohibition of collective land-holdings in the mid-nineteenth century. These thirty-year-old codes afforded the elder Tumipamba a means of challenging the alternate cabildo's legitimacy, particularly after his brother-in-law, José Gabriel Collahuaso, joined its ranks. Because Collahuaso had been born in the town of Sangolquí in Quito's south-eastern environs, Tumipamba could claim that his participation in the body contradicted a requirement that cabildo membership be hereditary. This argument not only conveniently disregarded Collahuaso's longtime role as cabildo president but also inherently challenged the juridical primacy of the 1937 Ley de Comunas, which carried no such genealogical requirements for membership. Such a stipulation, however, *did* exist in Santa Clara's earlier regulations and had also been debated at the congressional level on various occasions during the 1920s and 1930s.[4] Tumipamba's manipulation of parallel legal codes, along with a second argument he made regarding procedural irregularities in the constitution of the alternate cabildo, ultimately prevailed. Soon after, however, he reached an arrangement with his sons, who finally achieved their desire to join the traditional governing council, having aptly demonstrated precocious political power.[5]

The 1940 conflict in Santa Clara demarcates several political forces at play within this indigenous community during the early twentieth century. These include generational clashes, economic opportunism, and the manipulation of local histories and genealogies when dealing with both state and internal conflicts. Each of these phenomena lay intertwined within three historical threads.

The first thread concerns the critical contestation between the state, the landowning elite, and indigenous communities over control of autonomous *ejidos* (common pastures) in the town's environs. The origins of this strife lay in the colonial era but intensified periodically during the nineteenth century. Santa Clara offered consistent challenges to these machinations, often using a strategy common among indigenous populations: underscoring their historic ties to the region and defending colonial land titles. This defensive tactic, however, existed in dynamic tension with the interdependent economic relations the community enjoyed with the expanding metropolis. The second line of inquiry in this chapter concerns the development of the periurban economy. Santa Clara's incursions into Quito's real estate market, especially following the inception of the Mariscal Sucre suburb in its backyard in the 1920s, demonstrate that a significant indigenous minority profited from the transformations occasioned by urban expansion and land speculation during the twentieth century.[6] The third theme concerns the community's articulation of microhistories of land use and community genealogy within what Joanne Rappaport has termed a "universal perspective" referencing national and international phenomena with direct bearing on local circumstances.[7] The manipulation of Liberal and Socialist Party rhetoric and sympathies played a critical aspect in this endeavor.

A growing body of work seeks to reconsider the relationship of indigenous groups to the state in the Andes. Scholars have long held that the process of nation-building during the nineteenth century significantly reduced indigenous participation in local governance by limiting the reach of traditional prerogatives. In the Ecuadorian case, for example, Andrés Guerrero has observed that the Liberal state operated as a "ventriloquist" that systematically marginalized indigenous communities even when publicly operating in their interests.[8] The scholarship on Peru, particularly the work of Florencia Mallon and Mark Thurner, has challenged the efficacy of this program by positing that indigenous communities appropriated and manipulated the tenets of liberal republicanism to serve their interests.[9] Similar arguments regarding the participation of indigenous communities within the political sphere in Ecuador have been advanced by Federica Morelli, Aleezé Sattar, Erin O'Connor, and Galo Ramón, culminating in Marc Becker's tracing of active linkages between indigenous and leftist militants from the 1920s to the present.[10]

With the exception of Morelli's engagement with late colonial and early republican municipal politics, none of these studies addresses the plight of urban or periurban communities. The inhabitants of Santa Clara de San Millán, unlike Becker's communist allies from rural Cayambe or Sattar's millenarian insurrectionaries from Yaruquíes, came into daily contact with a very present state in which interstitial apertures for self-rule were minimal.[11] Access to urban markets and the mechanism of governance, however, also facilitated the exploitation of sociopolitical fault lines. The community's deployment of history ought therefore to be seen as a negotiating strategy, one that expanded political and entrepreneurial opportunities during the city's early modernization. Moreover, the interrogation of the cabildo's narrative illustrates the processes whereby even successful chronotopes continued to be challenged by alternate collectives seeking to make their own experience normative.

The Colonial City and "Its" *Corregimiento*

The communal legislation passed in 1937 re-imagined the guarantees afforded to tributary indigenous populations during the colonial period. These guarantees accompanied the pattern of settlement whereby insular Spanish cities were to be surrounded by subservient indigenous centers deployed through a vast hinterland, or *corregimiento*. The privileging of European urbanity within a system of domination had its counterpart in the access that sedentary populations had to the public lands known as *ejidos*. The cabildo administered these plots and parceled them out to not only Spanish *vecinos* but also those *pueblos de indios* that could demonstrate four generations of local kinship ties. In exchange, these populations of *originarios* promised to pay a biannual poll tax.

This system built upon long-standing Iberian practice and proved largely successful from an administrative standpoint. It not only established the political and economic supremacy of the Spanish cabildo but also invested the local indigenous nobility with a stake in its success because the upper echelons of Indian ranks were promised larger properties and privileges. While some groups of *originarios,* including those of Santa Clara de San Millán, vigorously protested the loss of local control over farmland, guaranteed access to arable land proved fundamental to maintaining a measure of autonomy.[12] Communities created elaborate family trees cementing their *originario* status, at times even exaggerating their lineage, as in the case of the Duchicela clan in the Riobamba region.[13] In contrast, *forasteros,* roving populations without ties to sedentary clans, met periodic persecution, and many attempted to join *originario* settlements. Such attempts not only expanded intraethnic tension but also increased competition for *ejido* plots. For example, incoming *forasteros* overran the Uyumbicho community south of Quito in the sixteeenth century, resulting in demographic pressures that led to near catastrophic deforestation and xenophobic clashes.[14]

In 1591, with the introduction of the *alcabala* (sales tax) into the Viceroyalty of Peru, *originario* status also provided a comparative advantage in the marketplace. The high rates *originarios* paid in tribute left them exempt from the new levies and in a prime position to collude with merchants from other ethnic groups seeking to evade the tax. Quito was no exception, with Indian market women known as *gateras* commonly acting as fronts for Spaniards introducing goods into the city's marketplaces. Over the course of the seventeenth century, these indigenous merchants systematically lobbied to expand the list of comestibles exempt from the *alcabala* as they expanded their importance in the regional black market, much to the chagrin of Audiencia officials and the mestizo and mulatto owners of small groceries or *pulperías*.[15]

The eighteenth century saw tax evasion spread across the Quito *corregimiento.* A series of plagues and the decline of the textile economy in the wake of Bourbon free trade policies pushed increasing numbers of tribute-paying Indians into the hacienda system, especially into the wealthy Jesuit concerns in the Chillo and Añaquito valleys.[16] These *originarios* conspired with large landowners to personally deliver bulk goods into the city and thus evade duties. *Gateras* also saw their business grow as smaller proprietors and urban farmers cultivating small plots known as *solares* turned to them to avoid arousing Audiencia suspicions.[17] An act establishing a Crown monopoly over the production of *aguardiente* in 1746, ostensibly to fund construction of a new royal palace, exacerbated this situation. Rural elites nurtured ties with local tax-farmers (who collected taxes for the Crown but were not employed by the Crown directly) to avoid levies on the drink's production while smaller producers supplied the informal distilleries installed beside the San Blas slaughterhouse on the northern edge of the city.[18]

The new measures also inspired two major urban riots that underscore the informal linkages between entrepreneurs and *originario* communities. The first was the aforementioned 1747 subaltern protest sparked by the arrival of Lima commissary Gregorio Ibáñez Cuevas. Besides symbolically branding Quito as a place of enslavement, like Egypt was for the Hebrews of the Bible, the protesters' retreat to the utopian Franciscan sanctuary of San Diego likely succeeded precisely because the *originario* township of La Magdalena, just beyond the limits of San Roque parish, smuggled foodstuffs to the rebels, again demonstrating the strong ties between the city and its environs. The second conflict developed during the administration of Viceroy Pedro Messía de la Cerda, who took office in 1760 at the height of the Seven Years' War (1756–1763).[19] Struck by the fact that Quito's revenues represented a third of those collected in the viceregal capital of Bogotá despite its similar population, Messía de la Cerda imposed direct control of the *alcabala* and the *aguardiente* monopoly in March 1764.[20] A year later, local viceregal representative Juan Díaz de Herrera instituted the reforms.

The transition to state control of the monopoly proceeded relatively smoothly, largely due to Díaz de Herrera's successful lobbying of elite producers. Active resistance erupted in late May, however, when he attempted to reform the *alcabala* and require the registration of *solares* in San Roque and San Sebastián, each being an ethnically mixed popular parish with strong ties to the Chillo and Turubamba valleys. Wild rumors circulated in both city and *corregimiento* that this reform would impose a radical new order eliminating *ejidos,* trebling tribute rates, and taxing newborns. On the evening of May 22, a largely plebeian crowd congregated in the Santa Barbara plaza and demolished the customs house in protest.[21] Neither the cabildo nor the elite answered the Audiencia's calls to suppress the riot, so it was several chaotic days before local Jesuits finally negotiated a settlement suspending the reforms and granting the rioters immunity from prosecution.

An uneasy calm fell over the city for the next few weeks, until June 23, on the eve of the festivities for the feast of San Juan Bautista, which coincided with the semiannual arrival of thousands of *corregimiento* Indians to pay their tributary obligations. *Corregidor* Sánchez Osorio, fearing a race riot, sent patrols to preemptively arrest potential troublemakers in San Roque and San Sebastián. These maneuvers backfired as hundreds gathered in both parishes in answer. Sánchez Osorio led a patrol to confront the crowds, against the advice of his subordinates, killing two en route, which led to full-scale rioting that targeted symbols of peninsular authority, such as the home of a Cádiz-born merchant and the Palace of the Audiencia, where 150 guards confronted a multiethnic force of perhaps 10,000. When unfounded rumors spread that 500 *corregimiento* Indians had joined the San Blas force, the authorities abandoned the palace and sought refuge in the city's monasteries.

The crowds celebrated their success with several days of sustained looting until local creoles grew anxious about the lack of authority. Aided by Jesuit intermediaries, the cabildo negotiated a truce on July 4; however, intermittent rioting and increased criminal activity continued throughout the year. *Alcabala* and tribute collection plummeted throughout the *corregimiento* as well. This situation persisted until the arrival of additional viceregal troops sent from Bogotá in early 1766.

Martin Minchom's demographic study of the riot notes that major altercations primarily involved inhabitants of the southern parishes of San Roque and San Sebastián, suggesting that the Audiencia leadership hoped to create an ethnic cleavage among the rioters by emphasizing the indigenous angle. Anthony McFarlane and Chad Black have each challenged this interpretation, highlighting the psychological role that *corregimiento* Indians played as members of the city's plebeian population. As even Minchom notes, the informal commercial ties between urban and rural subalterns fed the rumor mill prior to the riots, as attested by public notary Juan Mateo Navarrete's account of both verbal and written communications between Sangolquí and Quito.[22] Though impossible to quantify, the presence of three thousand *corregimiento* Indians ostensibly hoping to pay their tribute likely emboldened the city's plebeian population. Moreover, the erosion of tribute and *alcabala* revenue throughout the *corregimiento* the rest of the year suggests, at minimum, that the indigenous populations of the environs took advantage of the chaos to evade their obligations to pay the tribute tax.[23]

Like its 1747 predecessor, the Rebellion of the Barrios thus demarcates the interdependence of multiracial urban subalterns and the hinterland's indigenous population. It also illustrates the delicate balance of reciprocity and informality that had developed in the Quito region by the late eighteenth century. Imperial attempts to upset this dynamic in the name of the royal treasury proved unsuccessful, as would be made even more evident in the southern Andes during the Tupac Amaru and Tupac Katari uprisings in 1780–1781. As had already been the case in the Quito incidents, initial conflicts erupted as a result of the local *corregidor*'s inability to navigate the complex culture of reciprocity that had emerged over three centuries. The subsequent imperial decision to limit the *cor-*

regidor's autonomy by placing him under the jurisdiction of the local cabildo was intended to mitigate the potential for future insurrections. In the case of the city and *corregimiento* of Quito, the return to a system dominated by local networks and nepotism helped produce decades of peace not disturbed until the wars of independence, in which new alliances and factions developed.

Continuity and Crisis in the Postcolonial Commune

The Rebellion of the Barrios erupted during the initial attempts by the Bourbon state to centralize control over informal economic structures developed under the porous Habsburg administration. Increased surveillance proved adept at suppressing further urban insurrection—indeed, Quito was the only major Andean city not to undergo extreme upheaval following a 1778 directive to centralize tribute collection.[24] Minimizing rural anxiety and increasing the state's revenue required more subtle methods, however, which were successfully implemented by Audiencia president José García León y Pizarro (1778–1784). García León's administrative interventions invested greater powers in his office and forced the retirement of several judges who had resisted centralization during the 1760s. Equally important, however, was his cultivation of local indigenous leaders prior to enforcing the viceregal directive to transform the hitherto elected post of *gobernador de indios* into a state appointee. While Quito's caciques undoubtedly understood that this measure would limit the autonomy of smaller centers, the potential expansion of a community's resources was an attractive proposition for many ambitious leaders. With their support, García León transformed Quito into the Crown's most reliable revenue source and ultimately gained himself a seat on the prestigious Council of the Indies.[25]

The new regulations lessened hacienda and *obraje* control over indigenous labor. According to Federica Morelli, this change fueled an expanding labor market that increased the possibilities for peonage, which was a system that originally afforded financial mobility to individuals and groups seeking temporary employment before it evolved into a system characterized by perpetual indebtedness.[26] The discretionary income or tribute subsidies afforded by peonage increased the stake of *corregimiento* indigenous populations in the urban economy, which appears to have contributed to rural stability in the Quito environs despite frequent uprisings elsewhere in the Audiencia.[27] Minchom goes so far as to argue that faith in the docility of these communities may have fueled the Quito aristocracy's failed bid for independence in August 1809. Fear of a widespread rebellion undoubtedly influenced the Audiencia's representatives at the Cortes de Cádiz—Guayaquil natives José Mejía and José Joaquín de Olmedo—who roundly criticized peninsular liberals hoping to eradicate indigenous tribute in order to avoid needlessly aggravating Indian communities.[28] Although some Quito communities selectively embraced the establishment of a democratic franchise, most continued to provide tributary payments to the *gobernador de indios* to defend their common lands.[29] Similar resistance developed throughout the empire, leading to tribute's return following the restoration of Ferdinand VII in 1814.[30]

The question of tribute and its correlating sustenance of collective property rights continued to be a contentious issue facing the nascent republican state. Bolívar outlawed the practice in Colombia in 1821, yet implementation only gained traction in 1826. A new code passed that year sought to redistribute these lands via a three-tiered system in which the majority would be either kept in reserve as communal property or be distributed to individuals in a Jeffersonian bid to create a class of settled, propertied citizens. The remaining *"tierras baldíos"* (empty lands) would be sold at public auction. Indigenous communities opposed the law, with Indians from San Felipe marching into Latacunga, groups near Guamote and Pasto denying the law's applicability to their populations, and multiple cabildos simply ignoring the mandates altogether.[31] Stunned Liberal lawmakers restored tribute in 1828 along with its concomitant privileges under the euphemistic rubric of the *contribución personal.* The *gobernadores de indios* still collected the tribute tax, but new state officials known as *teniente politicos* adjudicated intracommunal conflicts and operated as a second line of surveillance. Limits on direct representation and the ongoing erosion of collective representation, especially following tribute's eradication once again, in 1857, allowed these agents to act as what Andrés Guerrero has termed "ventriloquists" communicating (and often distorting) indigenous concerns to the state.[32]

Guerrero's provocative thesis has been highly influential as an analytical tool for studying the discursive justification for the spread of centralized state power, but it has also been criticized for its lack of empirical evidence regarding state-indigenous interaction. Derek Williams, for instance, reads government intrusions into conflicts between Indians and local institutions such as municipalities, *hacendados,* and the Church as a bid for moral authority over quasi-independent regional actors rather than as a systematic attempt to disenfranchise indigenous communities.[33] Similarly, Aleezé Sattar's analysis of Chimborazo *comuneros* notes their savvy deployment of rhetoric designed to propel state intervention against local actors, taking advantage of the fault lines of a "bifurcated state" in which the Supreme Court in Quito proved particularly responsive to indigenous arguments.[34]

While a systematic review of the nineteenth-century juridical record in the Quito environs is beyond the scope of this chapter, existing research on the *corregimiento* suggests that a similar process ensued. Morelli, for example, cites an 1836 appellate court case whereby an indigenous community in the Machachi region on the southern edge of the *corregimiento* easily repelled the Quito municipality's attempt to parcel out common lands for a local school by referencing the 1828 restoration of tribute and its explicit defense of communal authority.[35]

A creative deployment of historical charters and manipulation of Sattar's "bifurcated state" thus proved instrumental for this Machachi community.

The cleavages between the Quito elite and the city magistrate are more clearly delineated in an 1835 dispute involving Santa Clara de San Millán. In this case, the magistrate upheld usufruct rights to trees, water, and paths through three plots on the upper slopes of Pichincha. The decision came despite the presentation of land titles to the plots by José María Tejada and Domingo del Mazo, the owners of the nearby haciendas of Pambachupa and Santa Clara. Although the court recognized that the lands technically belonged to Tejada and del Mazo, their only compensation for allowing indigenous access was three days of labor per annum, an arrangement that echoed both colonial precedent and republican laws.[36] Although this solution did not satisfy either party, the settlement lasted for almost two decades, until the passage of the 1854 Ley de Indigenas by the progressive Urbina government.

President José María Urbina's ambiguous statutes provided an opening for the community to request a reconsideration of the magistrate's decision. Urbina shared the liberal antipathy toward the feudal remnants of the colonial system, and his government simultaneously proved a strong patron of Ecuador's indigenous population, particularly those whose "freedom" remained assured by the autonomy afforded by collective landholdings.[37] The government also eased barriers to indigenous litigation by eliminating the system of tutelage whereby Indians were forced to rely on external legal representation, usually provided by the Church. This statute corresponded to a continuation of the liberal desire to establish equality before the law; however, it also maintained the right for collective litigation on the part of *comuneros.* The state adopted a similarly hybrid approach regarding landholding itself: while the law enabled the divestment of collective properties in deference to traditional liberalism, it did not mandate such action.

Derek Williams has noted that these circumstances may have ultimately accentuated indigenous agency by expanding the paternalist responsibilities of the state even during the landlord-friendly García Moreno government.[38] The renewal of the conflict between Santa Clara de San Millán and the del Mazo family bolsters this interpretation.[39] This dispute began soon after the new code's passage, when Domingo del Mazo's widow, Juana, reaffirmed her claim over the territories of Cataloma, Lomagorda, and Rosaspamba. The Superior Court, breaking with its prior practice, now accepted the countersuit levied by the community and began to consider the question in 1855. Pilar Pérez has noted in a recent history of forestry in Quito's environs that the community challenged del Mazo's titles by establishing an extended history of usufruct rights that predated the oldest deed (from 1641).[40] The key testimony involved a former parish priest, Juan Ferrín, who noted that Añaquito Indians had been granted water rights on the upper slopes of Pichincha immediately after the Conquest.[41] The

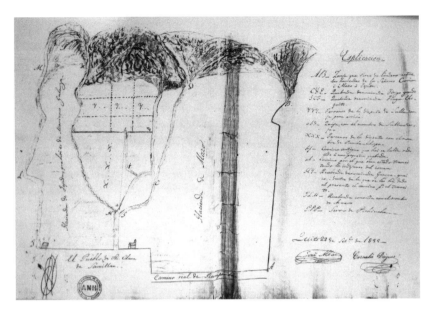

Fig. 7.1. Map of Rosaspamba, Cataloma, and Lomagorda. Courtesy Archivo Nacional de Historia, Quito.

more than thirty witnesses called by the community's defender, Pablo Antonio Salazar, also provided insight into the importance the properties played in the maintenance of Santa Clara's economic independence. Neighbors and business associates from as far afield as Machachi, a good day's journey by mule train, came to testify. Their statements portrayed a relatively prosperous and interconnected population whose timber and agricultural enterprises formed an integral part of the regional economy.

Faced with the prospect of rejecting the legitimacy of land titles or denigrating a local market force, Superior Court judge Pedro Fermín Cevallos—founding member of the Liberal Party and a well-known historian—postponed his decision by arguing that the references to various landmarks, streams, peaks, and roads crisscrossing the upper slopes of Pichincha remained imprecise. He therefore ordered a new measurement of the lands in question in order to establish their relation to the del Mazo hacienda and the town of Santa Clara de San Millán. The resulting map (fig. 7.1) not only acquainted the judge with the somewhat remote area under discussion but also provided del Mazo's attorney, Ramón Delgado, a spatial argument by highlighting the distance between the properties on the upper slopes of Pichincha and the Indian town along the royal road. Delgado's contention that indigenous communal lands would have been contiguous to settlements reflected contemporary considerations more than colonial precedence. Nevertheless, this interpretation satisfied Fermín Cevallos on the question of ownership, which was awarded to Juana del Mazo. However, the judge also maintained the state's patronage of indigenous communities by reaffirming the *comuna*'s usufruct rights as an economic necessity.

As in 1835, this arrangement suited neither party, which led to a third hearing at the Supreme Court beginning in July 1857. Both Delgado and Salazar presented radically different argumentation in this new chamber. Delgado's dismissive tone disappeared, replaced by a respectful series of depositions seeking to discredit the indigenous claim for usufruct rights. For example, when discussing a 1769 bill of sale, Delgado now emphasized that the hacienda enjoyed the yearly labor of five Indians from Santa Clara de San Millán, an obligation that designated a tributary relationship rather than the community's ownership of the property.[42] Moreover, he argued that the case represented a national imperative given that the community's attempt to supersede the legal title would establish a precedent that would denigrate the institution of private property nationwide. Salazar roundly criticized Delgado's arguments as just so much flowery language, but his own amounted to little more than a series of expositions regarding the "miserable" state of his clients, a traditional argument designed to appeal to the paternalist whims of the state.[43]

This argument may well have worked; however, the passage of the decree eliminating tribute on October 30, 1857, ended the primary justification for indigenous collective landownership. The justices, who had heard final arguments earlier that month, postponed a decision until the following March, a hiatus during which they appear to have ruminated on the implications of the new statute.[44] Their final sentence sidestepped the issue by upholding the previous judgments in a vague opinion that summarily ignored crucial details such as whether usufruct rights would continue to be enjoyed and the number of days the *comuna* would have to serve del Mazo. Even after Salazar attempted to clarify these matters, the court refused to answer, arguing that these were new issues not discussed during the trial. While this point denoted the delicate future of communal landholding, it ultimately benefited Santa Clara de San Millán, which enjoyed continued usufruct rights to the properties. Indeed, the group accelerated its lumber trade to such a degree that del Mazo's son-in-law, Manuel Chiriboga, would complain to the court anew a decade later. Despite his myriad attempts to label the community as a cancer frustrating "progress," the matter was again summarily dismissed.[45]

Santa Clara's tussle with del Mazo illuminates the ambivalent status of indigenous collective properties. Ultimately, neither the *comuna* nor the *hacendado* was able to consolidate unitary control over the lands in question despite a forty-year struggle. This failure resulted from the coexistence of conflicting notions of property under a fluid legal code where precedent was consistently ignored in legislation yet applied in the courtroom. As Santa Clara's denizens appear to have well understood, the recourse to colonial-era tactics such as the underscoring of customary usage and necessity continued to be clear justifications for the maintenance of usufruct rights even when titles were not held.

The case also illustrates the important role played by access to the central state apparatus. The community's rapid move to exploit the propitious circumstances engendered by the 1854 Ley de Indígenas suggests the existence of a feedback loop less developed in more isolated areas. Whereas Santa Clara managed to consolidate usufruct rights, rural areas across the country suffered a steady erosion in the number of similar plots due to the encroachment of the growing hacienda system. This was particularly the case in areas such as Chimborazo, where *hacendados* systematically carved up indigenous lands during the 1860s by exploiting not only intra-ethnic conflicts but also the potential to legally divest collective landholdings established the previous decade. By 1871, tensions had developed to such an extent that an insurrection of perhaps ten thousand souls erupted under the leadership of Fernando Daquilema of Yaruquíes in an ultimately fruitless gesture that encouraged militarization of the state presence.[46] Violence did not erupt on the Daquilema scale in other areas of the country; however, heavily indigenous zones like Cotopaxi and Imbabura also saw their share of localized clashes. The Quito region, however, remained quiet. As in the late colonial period, the city's proximity to power and the subsequent empowerment of the indigenous communities on its periphery may have had a hand in this situation.

The Laws of *Comunas*

The incompatibility of pseudo-colonial systems of territorial adjudication with liberal conceptions of property lay at the core of the conflicts regarding indigenous communal lands during the nineteenth century. The hybrid responses instituted by Urbina and maintained by García Moreno and subsequent administrations did not solve this ongoing tension. Only with the advent of the 1895 revolution did enough political clout accrue to the Liberal Party to reopen the argument about collective property ownership. As in the nineteenth century, the key issue concerned the juridical status of these populations and their holdings. While the elimination of tribute had theoretically removed the legal justification for *ejidos,* in practice, collective access to common lands continued unabated. Moreover, the juridical rights to collective representation enshrined in the 1854 law contradicted the essential guarantees of individual citizenship espoused by administrations bent on dragging the nation into the twentieth century.

A revival of the vitriolic assault on the indigenous character accompanied the state's new enthusiasm for eliminating debt peonage. This attitude echoed nineteenth-century criticism of the system's degrading effects on indigenous populations, more often than not emphasizing the incessant drunkenness of these indebted peons.[47] These accusations had a double purpose. On the one hand they elaborated a racial positivism indebted to Gobineau and Spengler, whose theories had spread throughout Latin America during the latter third of the nineteenth century. On the other hand, they bolstered the state's argument regarding the necessity of continued patronage of indigenous populations mired in permanent indebtedness through *concertaje.* As they had fifty years earlier, Liberals argued that this condition laid bare the immorality of the hacienda, and they again called for the dismantling of the peonage system. Numerous scholars have noted that this platform was intended to relocate indigenous labor to coastal cacao plantations.[48] However, until the eradication of *concertaje* in 1919, there were only minimal changes in everyday relations between the state, rural indigenous communities, and *hacendados.*

Liberals lamented this situation, but their internal squabbles postponed any action until after Alfaro's death in 1912. A new indigenous code, passed in 1913, promulgated the paternalist spirit of nineteenth-century liberalism by reaffirming protection for collective landownership while stipulating that the "quasi-contract of community" necessitated liaising with the state. The code inspired vitriolic responses. In an essay in the law review *Revista Forense,* for example, Loja attorney Darío Palacios argued that the code resurrected an institution that had been eradicated by piecemeal legislation passed in the last third of the nineteenth century. Palacios's critique resonated in a series of condemnations of the status quo by liberal lawmakers and bureaucrats.[49] One of the more adamant came from geographer Nicolás Martínez, who had just begun overseeing a railroad commission working to link Ambato with the Amazonian interior. His ensuing 1916 monograph on the province of Tungurahua's indigenous populations reconsidered the usual Liberal defense of the self-reliance and freedom experienced by these communities. Instead, he slammed the ferocity and separatism that had met his crew's attempts to survey *comunero* lands and advocated increased regulation.[50] The 1919 passage of the law outlawing *concertaje* encouraged congressional deputy Victor Manuel Peñaherrero to introduce a bill redefining communal ownership as a contract with minimal hereditary protections and well-established bureaucratic oversight. The stage was set for a systemic debate concerning the future of these properties. It was a debate that had emerged in concert with the flourishing of *indigenismo* during the 1920s and 1930s.

Ecuadorian *indigenismo* incorporated both aesthetics and politics, with its proponents attempting to negotiate a space for alternatives to Eurocentric paradigms. As in Mexico or Peru, the movement largely involved leftist intellectuals whose idealization of pre-Columbian life merged with a push for social egalitarianism and the creation of a transnational "Indoamerica" as a counterweight to the capitalist world. As discussed earlier, Jorge Icaza, Fernando Chávez, and Humberto Salvador translated this theory into an emphatic condemnation of the hacienda and its owners—the white urban elite. This framework echoed the political theory of the radical liberal Pío Jaramillo Alvarado, who considered the commune a potential corrective to the greed of the landowning class.[51]

In his early writings, including the influential *El indio ecuatoriano,* Jaramillo maintained that the communal experience of self-rule prepared indigenous populations for greater incorporation into the national community, thus echoing a standard liberal line.[52] His socialist leanings emerged after the 1925 Julian Revolution and inspired a critical response to Isidro Ayora's abandonment of the progressive spirit of the original government. This response resulted in Jaramillo's brief exile to Panama in 1926, after which he emerged as a figure bridging the liberal and socialist camps, particularly on the indigenous question. His writings increasingly invoked the necessity to transform the commune into a cooperative under the aegis of the state, a position influenced by the experimentation of the Mexican state and the writings of Peruvian socialist José Carlos Mariátegui. This argument crystallized in 1928 during a heated debate with conservative Alfonso Mora of Cuenca, who argued that the commune was a debilitated institution whose glory days during the colonial era had long since passed. Jaramillo countered that the independent *comunero* was a good worker, clean and industrious, whose protection would ultimately pay dividends in the liberation of the entire race. This hardline stance, with its concomitant vision of the state's enabling role, found favor in the newly formed Ministerio de Previsión Social (Ministry of Social Welfare), which would become a defender of collective rights in coming years.[53]

The ministry's position represented a tactical response to increased rural agitation during the 1920s, Jaramillo's altruistic rhetoric notwithstanding. Heavy inflation and food shortages during the postwar recession sparked labor conflicts across the country as well as violent repression, most infamously in the deaths of as many as a thousand cacao workers in a 1922 strike in Guayaquil.[54] Rural populations soon joined their urban counterparts in protesting both employer demands to do more work with no increase in pay and the growing price of necessities, at first with similarly unfortunate results. In 1923, for example, complaints by Indians regarding the workload on the Leito hacienda in Tungurahua province led to a military assault that left thirty-nine dead and twenty wounded. The Julian Revolution's call for greater social responsibility, however, emboldened both urban and rural activists in the later years of the decade, particularly following the 1926 founding of the Socialist Party of Ecuador (Partido Socialista del Ecuador, or PSE).

Indigenous groups formed one of the critical constituencies supporting the PSE in its early days. Of particular importance was the Sindicato de Trabajadores Campesinos de Juan Montalvo (Syndicate of Workers of Juan Montalvo), an indigenous union from the northern Pichincha county of Cayambe. Founded in January 1926 under the leadership of Jesús Gualavisí, the syndicate organized an invasion of formerly communal lands that had become part of the Changalá hacienda owned by Gabriel García Moreno's son, Gabriel García Alcázar. Although ultimately repelled by two government battalions the following month, the invasion and its notoriety brought overtures of solidarity from urban leftists such as Ricardo Paredes and Luis F. Chavez. Besides placing editorials in the proto-socialist reviews *La Antorcha* and *La Vanguardia,* intellectuals petitioned the government to nationalize the lands under dispute and included Gualavisí in the organizing congress of the Socialist Party that May. By November, the syndicate's renewed assault on the hacienda had a new battle cry: "Long live socialism!"[55]

The alliance between urban leftists and rural Indians alternated between paternalist frameworks and reciprocal relations. The editorials noted above echoed the rhetoric of indigenous assimilation and *mestizaje* that Jaramillo had borrowed from José Vasconcelos, Victor Raúl Haya de la Torre, and the racial positivist tradition more broadly. Marc Becker has posited, however, that sustained contact shifted the paternalist tenor of this encounter toward a more equitable one as indigenous goals altered the party's platform. Similarly, a cadre of indigenous activists adopted organizing strategies, such as labor stoppages, from their urban allies. Two Kayambi women, Dolores Cacuango and Tránsito Amaguaña, proved particularly adept at straddling the hacienda and the meeting hall, with Cacuango eventually joining the Central Committee of the Communist Party of Ecuador.[56] By the mid-1930s, their work had led to strikes across Cayambe as well the heavily indigenous provinces of Chimborazo and Cotopaxi, foreshadowing a potentially devastating conflagration along class and ethnic lines.

The Ministerio de Previsión Social accelerated its program to bolster support for indigenous communes at the same time that this unrest was developing. In 1931, the ministry cosponsored a study of the situation of the Ecuadorian Indian by Mexican pedagogue Moises Sáenz, who visited the heavily indigenous provinces of Imbabura, Pichincha, Chimborazo, and Cotopaxi. Sáenz's report echoed Jaramillo's earlier call for market-based land distribution to indigenous peoples; the latter had based his recommendation on what he called the people's traditional love for land as well as noticeable patterns of territorial accumulation among Indians with disposable income. Again, the communist overtones of pre-Columbian society served to legitimate this essentializing claim concerning indigenous behavior that, in classic liberal fashion, justified greater state patronage.[57] A proposal for a new land code stipulating greater ministry involvement in everyday governance—including division and divestment of communal lands—followed soon after Sáenz's visit. The proposal generated substantive opposition by both the Right and the Left as a result of its radical shift of power to the ministry, which led to the land division project being postponed multiple times over the next several years.

The ultimate passage of what would come to be known as the Ley de Comunas owed much to the political upheaval of the 1930s. The economic pains of the Great Depression convinced the military to depose President Isidro Ayora in August 1931, sparking two decades' turmoil during which the presidency operated on a revolving-door basis.[58] A critical moment occurred in 1932, when a disputed election fueled four days of bloody violence between the military and proto-fascist street gangs in Quito. Local institutions attempted to fill the void; however, minimal changes occurred in the everyday governance of rural indigenous populations. This situation changed only under the dictatorship of Federico Páez, the engineer whose administration operated with leftist support but became increasingly autocratic.

One of Páez's progressive decrees, delivered on July 30, 1937, formally reconstituted legal communal land under the aegis of the Ministerio de Previsión Social. New *comunas* established had to meet several criteria, such as a minimum population of fifty persons, a five-member cabildo to govern the *comuna*, regular minutes, elections, and an inventory of collective goods. The law codified support for common possession of property if it had been in possession of the community for thirty years—a provision that protected hacienda lands from expropriation or challenge. The law thus theoretically offered a potential response to rural unrest by bolstering indigenous landownership without undoing the status quo. Moreover, the law's stipulation that cabildos could purchase or divest common lands encouraged greater market engagement while the need to gather the support of both the membership and the ministry potentially limited intercommunal clashes. Finally, the statute called for the "betterment" of the group's moral, intellectual, and material situation.[59]

While the new legislation called for the establishment of *comunas* by the end of 1937, only twenty-five had been constituted by 1938, leading to an extension of the deadline. Ten times that number appeared in the following year, primarily in the Andean provinces of Chimborazo and Cotopaxi, where there was a long history of communal action. Pichincha, despite both the extensive activism of communities in Cayambe and its proximity to the capital, lagged behind. Becker has speculated that the activist past of indigenous groups in Cayambe moderated their enthusiasm for the new regulations, which they interpreted as meddling by the Ministerio de Previsión Social. Economic realities also hampered those communities that initially adopted the *comuna* structure. Absenteeism from *comuna* meetings in Azcásubi Alto in the southern part of the canton, for instance, increased due to the ministry's insistence on children attending distant state schools in keeping with the law's encouragement of local cultural progress. This position ignored economic reality, which made the extended journey to these schools a practical impossibility. With no funds or pedagogical training available for a local school, enthusiasm for the new regulations waned during the 1940s and afterward.[60]

Tight finances limited the reach of *comunas* in the Cayambe region, but Kim Clark has recently argued that the greater opportunities offered by proximity to the Quito marketplace fueled a desire for common lands in its environs. She particularly cites the example of peasants tied to the Tolóntag hacienda in the parish of Pintag to the east of the capital. Beginning in 1934, the resident *huasipungueros* had challenged leaseholder José Ignacio Izurieta for access to the hacienda's lands, and they garnered support from the populist president José María Velasco Ibarra until his ouster in August 1935. Land invasions followed in 1936, and, in the 1940s, *huasipungueros* petitioned that their committee be recognized as the council for an autonomous *comuna*. The petition stalled in the ministry as a result of the technical implausibility of such a move; as a group of peasants legally tied to a hacienda, the group was ineligible for such status. Inexplicably, at some point in the summer of 1944, the minister authorized its formation, ostensibly due to repeated petitioning. Although this may have been a clerical error—and was decried as such in internal communications—Clark posits that the decision may have been tied to Velasco Ibarra's return to power in the so-called Glorious Revolution of May 1944. She therefore highlights the benefits of selective engagement with the paternalist state, in which loyalty to a particular caudillo provided real political and economic gains.[61]

Although both Clark and Becker note the importance of local dynamics and the regional political economy, neither systematically engages the importance of proximity to the capital. Given Pintag's location not far from Quito, on the edge of the Chillo Valley—a longtime source of produce for the Quito market—the *huasipunguero* desire to gain control over productive lands suggests their consideration of urban trading possibilities. Indeed, the prosperity that the peasants of Tolóntag enjoyed by 1945 likely emerged from a decade of virtual control over profitable lands that enabled both sustainable agriculture and the marketing of their surplus.

Such activities had a long history within the city's environs, as previously noted. The twentieth-century expansion of Quito, however, both challenged traditional modes of production and offered alternate and often lucrative economic possibilities. Santa Clara de San Millán was one of the first populations to establish *comuna* status, and its decision to do so in 1938 built upon decades of entrepreneurial activity engaging the new opportunities afforded by the expanding city. This type of risk-taking activity was balanced by the security afforded by their common lands. The community's support for Eloy Alfaro and his lax policy on communal holdings during his struggle with Leonidas Plaza had paid dividends by 1911, at which point Santa Clara received official recognition as a semi-autonomous collective and likely regained its holdings on the upper reaches of Pichincha.[62] The leadership of the community zealously guarded its authority over these properties despite frequent attempts by disgruntled members to profit by the nebulous state of collective lands. The state's new regulations in 1938 thus represented a chance to formally regulate these internal conflicts, and the cabildo thus embraced these new laws. The cabildo selectively embraced economic diversification while maintaining strict control over both collective property and internal political hegemony. For both these endeavors, controlling the public status of historic narratives was critical and helped create a subaltern chronotope of urban indigenous autonomy.

The *Comuna's* Development through Genealogy

Santa Clara emerged from the nineteenth century as one of the wealthier indigenous communities in the Quito area. Its primary economic activities continued to be lumber, animal husbandry, and some artisanal production—particularly carpentry, as a result of the fine hardwoods on Pichincha's forested slopes. A few enterprising souls owned small shops specializing in dried goods and farming equipment. These businesses congregated along the Carretera del Norte—later renamed Carrera 18 de septiembre and now Avenida 10 de agosto—which remained the primary artery linking Quito with the breadbasket of the Añaquito plains. The shops catered to laborers from the haciendas of La Granja and El Batán and indigenous merchants from northern areas such as Rumipamba, Zámbiza, or Cotocollao. Some such customers stayed at the rooms rented out by Nicolás Conchambay, a respected elder whose home served as an informal community center. Friends, acquaintances, and especially kinfolk from across Añaquito gathered frequently to gossip, receive messages, conduct business, or even await trial.

Across the Carretera del Norte from Conchambay's house stood an imposing neoclassical mansion, a harbinger of change known as La Circasiana. The building belonged to Manuel Jijón, a doctor, artistocrat, and entrepreneur responsible for installing Quito's first electric works, in 1894. Somewhat whimsically named for his wife's Eastern European roots, the house provided a weekend and summer residence where the elegant couple and their young son, Jacinto, could escape the bustle of the city. The novelty of their presence inspired elaborate welcoming festivals from the indigenous community, including celebratory arches in an echo of colonial deference.[63] However, the Jijóns also pioneered a wider expanse of nouveau riche summer soujourns in Santa Clara's backyard following the 1908 completion of the Guayaquil-Quito railroad.[64] Sporting events followed at a rude track denoted the Hippodrome, located about a kilometer east of the Jijón house along the still unpaved Avenida Colón. Patrons of its horse races and polo and tennis matches included the fashionable dandies of Quito such as the Durini brothers and their friend Genaro Larrea. Others rented automobiles for day excursions along the dusty country roads, oblivious to existing indigenous communities.

Next came suburbanization projects by local and foreign speculators who sought to cash in on the growing fascination with the bucolic lifestyle. The Larrea family again took the lead by converting agricultural land west of Alameda Park into the Ciudadela Larrea in 1906. With the completion of a citywide tramline in 1914 that ended at the Avenida Colón, however, the possibility of a grander suburb in the hitherto rural enclave became more attractive. By 1917, the Anglo-French Syndicate had purchased a wide tract of land north of the Larrea development. They designated it the Ciudadela América, with streets named for the nations of the hemisphere. Prominent architects, such as the Durini and Russo brothers, pushed north of the old Ejido during the late 1910s, presaging the accelerated investment that followed the 1922 commemoration of the centennial of the Battle of Pichincha in the park. Over the next decade, the resulting Ciudadela Mariscal Sucre grew to abut the Avenida Colón, the Hippodrome, the Jijón mansion, and, of course, the *comuna* of Santa Clara de San Millán.

The juxtaposition of the traditional indigenous village and extravagant villas made for a striking contrast. Nowhere was this more evident than in the distinct material cultures of the two populations. For example, the sons of Elisa Criollo, matriarch of the powerful Tumipamba clan, inherited several deeds upon her death, along with a series of household items of limited value; these items included an old wooden box, a bolt to close windows, a bronze chocolate pot, an old leather case, a small cardboard jewelry box, an iron plate, another small wooden box, and a small wooden table.[65]

The relative simplicity of these goods stands in marked contrast to the extravagance of what their new neighbors possessed. The avant-gardist and (much) later secretary general of the Socialist Party, Enrique Terán, brought a Bechstein baby grand piano to his home in the Ciudadela Larrea, while Victor Iza imported French porcelain lavatories for his villa in the Mariscal. Those fixtures survived the journey from France, the haul up the mountains on the railroad, and transport from the train station at Chimbacalle, only to be smashed during installation, to his great chagrin.[66] These efforts paled in comparison to the integrated plan adopted for Enrique Freile Gangotena's villa, Quinta Miraflores. One approached the house through elaborate gardens containing two fountains, plaster statuary, and an arboretum with a small orange grove, a coconut palm, and other flowering trees. Marble stairs led up to the house itself, which contained twelve bedrooms and featured elements such as iron-adorned wooden banisters, mother-of-pearl doorhandles, and massive ceramic vases. A secondary, more intimate series of gardens adorned the interior, while servants' lodges and some cultivated lands lay beyond.[67]

Freile's particular indulgences carried risks during the volatile 1920s, when the country's economy fractured due to the decline of the cacao industry. The mortgage for his mansion was held by the Banco del Pichincha, a highland concern that first opened its doors in 1906 and became the primary bondholder for the new developments in the capital's northern environs. His payments on the 50,000-sucre mortgage totaled 2,775 sucres per annum over twenty-five years, a sum more than ten times the cost of renting a modest home near Santa Clara. Freile began having trouble making his payments and defaulted on other debts. In April 1926, for instance, he was involved in three separate litigations over relatively small sums that allowed his creditors to eye Miraflores itself. One of these involved a two-year-old loan from Manuel Zurita for 300 sucres. Although Freile had already paid 100, Zurita threatened to impound the deed for the entire property if he did not receive the amount due immediately. Needless to say, Freile rapidly raised the remaining funds so as not to lose his estate.[68] The other two cases concerned luxury items that also figured in the performance of prosperity, namely, Freile's tailored suits and the garage for his automobile. While he quickly paid the garage fees, it took more than two years for him to honor his debts to his tailor, Alejandro Reyes. When Freile finally made his payments, it was once again because Reyes threatened to impound the salon furniture proudly displayed at the Quinta, an unthinkable affrontery to his mise-en-scène.[69]

While Freile honored the debts on his mortgage and the relatively high-profile obligations to society figures, he was less considerate when entering into contracts with subaltern actors also seeking to engage the real estate market. One such example was Julio Mena, a small-time merchant who rented a *tienda* (store or a sort of apartment) from Hercilia García at the corner of 18 de septiembre and Colón. In December 1920, Mena entered into an ill-considered contract with Freile in which he offered fifty sucres to purchase a load of gravel sitting on the patio at the Freile family home on Plaza San Francisco, presumably materials left over from the construction of Miraflores. Having given a ten-sucre deposit, Mena bought a cart the following January from Luis de Toro of Latacunga and transported almost all of the stones to the north. However, Freile soon took Mena to court, as the latter had left the smaller stones on the patio and had not paid for the remainder of the load by January 19.[70] Mena then paid Freile and carted off the rest of the gravel, but he could not afford the court costs with which he was subsequently saddled. This shortfall led him to default on his cart payments, which prompted de Toro to sue him the following March.[71] As Mena tried to rectify *this* matter, he fell behind on rent, which led his landlady to start eviction proceedings in October 1922.[72] Although he appears to have been able to weather the storm that year, the matter was not completely resolved until 1925, when the landlady finally received the last of her rent payments, with Mena once again saddled with court costs. He was in effect the victim of a volatile marketplace.[73]

A more successful model can be seen among the Santa Clara community, which manipulated its properties to best take advantage of private and public planning schemes. One of the first and most successful attempts to do so came at the intiative of a carpenter named José Federico Tumipamba. Known locally as Federico, Tumipamba dominated the commune's affairs after being named its legal representative in 1911, though his father and then his brother-in-law officially served as cabildo presidents until the 1940s.[74] One of Tumipamba's first projects involved the growing market for Santa Clara lumber due to increased construction north of the city. He hoped to expand access to the communities' forests on Pichincha to meet this demand, but to do so would require building a new road, which the community could not afford. In 1917, Tumipamba therefore approached Enrique Chiriboga, heir to the neighboring Pambachupa hacienda, whose ancestors had attempted to eliminate the community's right to their properties on Pichincha. After months of discussion and multiple drafts of a contract, the indigenous *"vecinos de Benalcázar"* signed an agreement with Chiriboga to build a toll road, the profits of which would be shared equally between both parties. Under this contract, the *hacendado* provided all of the land that would be developed, thus securing the integrity of the community's holdings, while the Indians would provide the labor. Strikingly, the contract also included a clause acknowledging that the foreseen municipal expropriation of the road would terminate the deal, an extremely prescient measure given that the road led into what is still an underdeveloped sector of the mountain west of Avenida Vargas, today's Avenida América.[75]

Comuneros who carefully tracked municipal policies also were able to find new possibilities for individual investment. For instance, in 1925, several *comuneros,* including Nicolás Tipantocta and Feliciano Simbaña, divested themselves of titled properties at the edge of the La Granja hacienda near the Rumipamba River in anticipation of a crackdown by the Junta de Embellecimiento de la Ciudad on the common practice of maintaining grazing plots in what was technically street frontage.[76] Simbaña invested his proceeds in a new lot, closer to Avenida Colón, where he began to build a house in the late 1920s. Upon completing a rude structure in 1931, Simbaña leased the building to a man named Guillermo Jaramillo for five years, with the first two years' rent (552 sucres) delivered in advance. The last three years would then be paid at a reduced rate determined by how many improvements Jaramillo undertook during the interim. Two years later, Simbaña promptly evicted Jaramillo, despite the latter's having paneled, papered, and whitewashed four rooms, fixed several walls, built a new brick room, and painted the exterior. Jaramillo sued for breach of contract, yet the judge found that Simbaña had the right to evict his tenant, stipulating that the cost of materials be refunded. In other words, Simbaña managed to receive two years' rent and substantial improvements on his property at cost without having to pay for labor. He promptly leased the house again, at a substantially higher rate.[77]

The *comuneros'* divestiture of land parcels in 1925 required disciplined actions. Their careful strategy bears the imprint of Federico Tumipamba, whose efforts as de facto head of the community were intended to foster a collectivist spirit while advancing the community's economic growth. The toll road exploit in 1917 advanced this objective, as did Tumipamba's later organization of two *"bandas de soplo,"* or wind ensembles, that represented Santa Clara de San Millán when playing at citywide festivities, or *peñas.* Tumipamba eschewed the informal arrangement that such groups usually adopted and instead operated these bands as legally bound societies with contractual statutes. These included severe punishments for anyone who left the company. One who did leave was Julio Jaramillo, no relation to the famous Julio Jaramillo who was a *pasillo* singer from Guayaquil. When the band member Jaramillo contracted a lung ailment and had to cease participating, Tumipamba impounded his horn.[78] Missing a rehearsal carried a fee of one sucre, whereas an absence from a performance merited the steep charge of ten sucres.[79] Tumipamba slammed the few members who skipped multiple shows with lawsuits for breach of contract, even those like Santiago Llumipanta, who moved as far away as the Chillo Valley, still a good day's journey in the late 1920s.[80]

Tumipamba's activist governance accelerated in 1927 after the death of his father, Juan de Dios Tumipamba. Federico's brother-in-law, José Gabriel Collahuaso, replaced the elder Tumipamba as cabildo president. Over the next several years, the younger Tumipamba followed a stringent policy designed to more tightly control the operations of communal landholding and aver the cabildo's primacy as public representative and owner of these lands. He first asserted control over the crucial right to distribute plots. Under the traditional organization of the community, families farmed or administered sections of the communal lands over generations, which at times gave a false sense of ownership and led to thorny disputes regarding inheritance, particularly after marriages outside the community.

Such was the case of Nicolás Tipantocta and Fernanda Tipán, whose right to communal lands stemmed from Tipán's earlier marriage to the *comunero* Hilario Aiña. Upon the death of Tipán's former brother-in-law, Rafael Aiña, Tumipamba took control of the land Aiña had farmed and planted his own crops in 1927. Tipantocta challenged the legality of this action, petitioning the Ministry of Social Welfare in September 1930 for control of the family plot, called "Romerillos." Tipantocta specifically accused Tumipamba of theft and clearly regarded him as the instigator, at one point contrasting the situation to the administration of collective lands during the lifetime of Hilario Aiña. In a follow-up letter, Tipantocta not only maintained that Tumipamba inconvenienced multiple *comuneros* but also challenged his juridical status as a leader ("*jefe*") of the community.

Faced with the prospect of a direct challenge to its administration, the community closed ranks. A neighbor, Juan Chalco, testified that Miguel Aiña, son of Rafael Aiña, had rented the property to Federico Tumipamba. Moreover, Chalco held that he had never met Hilario Aiña and was unaware of any marriage with Tipán, who had never made any effort to cultivate Romerillos. Miguel Aiña himself subsequently confirmed that he had rented the lot to Tumipamba, effectively closing the matter.[81] The commissioner of labor, Alberto Batallas, found against the plaintiff, specifically citing a lack of proof regarding Tipán's nuptials with Aiña. Despite Tipantocta later presenting a marriage certificate, accompanied by further recriminations about Tumipamba's malevolent intentions, the case remained closed.[82]

The manipulation of the marriage record signified by Chalco and Aiña's testimony undercuts their critical statements regarding Tipán's right to benefit from Romerillos and calls into question the assertion that Tumipamba had rented the property. The case therefore suggests that community membership and usufruct rights remained pliable privileges meted out by the cabildo, at times justified by manipulation of the very state actors on its doorstep. This situation can be even more clearly demonstrated through another case played out between 1927 and 1930.

As in the Tipantocta-Tipán complaint, the key issue in this conflict concerned the sale of communal properties, in this case a lot that formed part of the Cataloma territory that had once been under the control of the Chiriboga family of the Pambachupa hacienda. However, this particular dispute embroiled various members of the Tumipamba family and culminated in a failed attempt by the council to deploy a fabricated history of land use to resolve the thorny conflict between Federico and his uncle, José Antonio Tumipamba. The conflict concerned a fallow plot controlled by Antonio Tumipamba, who had filed a questionable suit for entitlement in 1926. The following March he sold the plot for five hundred sucres to Pedro Camacho, an employee of the Legación Americana.[83] No immediate steps were taken to counter this move. However, when Federico's cousin Francisco Tumipamba sold an adjacent plot the following March, the cabildo sprang into action to stop a domino effect.

Internal politics may have influenced this extended delay. Antonio Tumipamba's brother Juan—Federico's father—was still president of the *comuna* in 1927 and probably discouraged legal proceedings. Juan's death that same year, however, caused a power vacuum that remained unfilled until José Gabriel Collahuaso, Federico Tumipamba's brother-in-law, was named president in 1928, despite his lack of hereditary membership in the *comuna*. Tumipamba remained as *procurador* but would ever after be referred to as Santa Clara's head or *jefe*. Francisco Tumipamba's sale of common lands would therefore have been seen as the first real test of the new power structure and was taken as such by the cabildo. At an emergency meeting on April 26, 1928, the cabildo resolved to petition the Ministry of Social Welfare to bar individual *comuneros* from selling the community's property (essentially presaging the 1937 Ley de Comunas) while also demanding restitution for the two lots in question.

The letters crafted by Collahuaso and Tumipamba clearly express fear of communal chaos while articulating a specific conceit regarding the historicity of the violation. Collahuaso's cover letter focuses on the illegality of the actions, noting that the seizure of the Aiña plot violated the first three articles of Santa Clara's statutes, a statement obviously intended to reify both the validity of the documents as well as the status of the collective holdings. In a telling phrase, Collahuaso highlights Antonio Tumipamba's neglect of "the sacred rights left by our aboriginal ancestors to conserve our lands as property of each and every one of the *comuneros*."[84] This clause not only alludes to traditional frameworks of legitimacy by referencing long-standing precedent but also highlights the stakes involved regarding individual and collective landownership. Federico Tumipamba's more elaborate letter echoes similar commonplaces. For instance,

he notes that the lands have been held "*desde tiempo immemorial*" (from time immemorial), a common phrase found in scores of colonial and ninteenth-century
petitions, while he also challenges Antonio and Francisco Tumipamba's honor
("*con estudiada mala fé*," with deliberate bad faith). He continues to alert the minister of the dangers of not acting, predicting "complete anarchy and disorder,"
which would occur as a result of the fact that "other unsuspecting *comuneros* will
follow the disloyal path the sales have wrought."[85]

The cabildo then sent copies of the men's letters to *El Comercio,* which published them on April 29, 1928.[86] This strategy traded upon the ongoing fear of
a widespread indigenous rebellion within city limits. Dating back to the 1765
Rebellion of the Barrios, the fear of major unrest had become more pronouncd
with the recent land invasions across Cayambe and other parts of the Andean
corridor. In what might be considered a performative move seeking to parlay
these concerns into support for their position, the cabildo followed the letters
with ritualistic violence of its own. Collahuaso, Tumipamba, and the rest of
the cabildo converged on Pedro Camacho, who had sped up the mountain after
reading the notice in *El Comercio,* and informed him that land he had bought
was communal property. After advising him to leave, they uprooted his alfalfa
crop.[87]

Camacho's connections at the Legación Americana enabled him to hire
an accomplished lawyer named Alejandro Cueva. Cueva's brief on his client's
behalf argued that the title Camacho held trumped any claim by the abstract
commune. A review of nineteenth-century legislation, particularly focusing on
the civil codes of 1873 and 1877, maintained that common landholding had been
outlawed. Cueva also took pains to directly assault the legitimacy of the commune itself, noting that the statute's assertion of the indivisibility of its property
directly countered the constitution's protection for private property. As such, he
maintained that Santa Clara could only be considered a fiction and even denied
that Antonio Tumipamba had ever belonged to the institution. As should be
clear, this reasoning followed the same line elaborated both by Domingo del
Mazo and Enrique Chiriboga in their mid-nineteenth-century attempt to take
control of Cataloma and Rosaspamba and by the standard contemporary liberal
arguments detailed above.

The commune responded by producing statutes whose approval by Eloy
Alfaro clearly demarcated their credentials. Sympathetic ears in the ministry, particularly those Socialist Party members already collaborating with indigenous populations elsewhere, called for an inspection to verify the extent
of the land under dispute. The subsequent report from the Teniente Político
highlighted the contiguity of both parcels with Santa Clara's land and called
for supporting the commune's petition. Antonio Tumipamba was ordered to
return the funds he had received from Camacho and place the land back into
the hands of the cabildo.

The *comuna's* strategy of simultaneous legal action, the manipulation of the public press, and ritualistic violence therefore appear to have worked, allowing the community to regain control over the property. Given their lack of trust in Antonio Tumipamba, the council members opted to hand the property over to Luís Tumipamba, another of Federico's nephews. Two years later, Antonio Tumipamba retaliated by petitioning the Ministerio de Previsión Social to return the land to his control and in the process properly reinstate him within the community. In his request for adjudication, he maintained that Federico Tumipamba operated as a tyrant, punishing him for the honest mistake he had made two years earlier as a result of ignorance of the law. Moreover, he accused Luís Tumipamba of having bribed Federico by paying twenty-two sucres for usufruct rights.[88]

Rather than resort to colonial precedent or affirm their status as indigenes needing the patronage of the state, Federico Tumipamba and José Gabriel Collahuaso presented themselves in their defense as law-abiding citizens following the will of an autonomous council operating with the full knowledge of the ministry. Federico particularly sought to diminish his own role in the altercation so as to counteract the charges of nepotism levied by his uncle. He noted that each step taken against both sellers in 1928 had been ordered by the cabildo with the full knowledge of the ministry. When pressed on the issue of whether José Antonio had been ousted from the community, Federico swore that he had merely informed his uncle about a verbal order from then-minister Pedro Pablo Egüez Baquerizo. Collahuaso echoed these precepts in his statement while also informing the new labor comissary, Alberto Batallas, that Luís Tumipamba had merely been paying his property taxes. Upon being subpoenaed to clear the matter, Luís Tumipamba confirmed that he had inherited the plot after the death of his father, also called Juan de Dios Tumipamba, in 1912. He also offered an elaborate history of the land's use, stating that first he had farmed it for four years befote renting the parcel to Federico Tumipamba for the next four. In 1920, he claimed to have let the lot to José Antonio Tumipamba for twelve years and had received it back when the community had taken charge of the land after ousting Pedro Camacho two years earlier.[89]

As would later be confirmed by Federico, this story was a complete fabrication and appeared as such to Batallas as well. Not only was there no earlier mention of Luís Tumipamba as the land's owner but the plausibility of Collahuaso's explanation for the twenty-two-sucre payment made little sense given the community's earlier tax obligations. In 1927, for instance, Santa Clara's property taxes totaled ninety-six sucres on lands valued at twenty-four thousand sucres, almost fifty times Camacho's purchase price of five hundred sucres.[90] Batallas thus sided with Antonio Tumipamba and decried Federico Tumipamba's autocratic rule while recommending his censure for the "*simulacro democrático*" enveloping Santa Clara. Faced with the possibility of further erosion of the community's territory, Federico approached his uncle to negotiate a private solution. Under this accord, the property would be divided into three parts: one for Antonio Tumipamba, one for the cabildo (administered, naturally, by Federico Tumipamba), and one for Luís Tumipamba. Three weeks later, Antonio signed an agreement that promised him control over the parcel "hasta cuando díos [tenga] queja alguna" (until God complains). Significantly, the right to sell the property remained rescinded and Cataloma's inviolability remained secure. Federico's prestige, however, had taken a hit, and his activities appear to have been curtailed over the next several years while less affluent commoners sought out Batallas's help with their own inheritance issues.[91]

The new legislation introduced in 1937, however, strengthened the cabildo's political position. Its primary responsibilities remained the administration of common property but now under much more formal guidelines. The council comprised five members in the traditionally bureaucratic posts of president, vice president, secretary, treasurer, and legal representative. These would be elected annually at a December gathering of the general membership during which census rolls would also be generated. Monthly contributions from members paid for the meetings of the cabildo, which was then charged with planning investments and divesting lands, if desired, while encouraging the "moral, intellectual, and material benefit of the community," a somewhat nebulous charge harkening back to the nineteenth-century *hacendado's* paternal responsibilities for his indigenous charges.[92] These meetings were private, and while, technically, the public could add items to the agenda, the requisite support of one-third of the cabildo's constituents proved difficult to gather in practice.[93]

The strengthened cabildo of Santa Clara de San Millán maintained a program of intensified infrastructural development over the next decade. New challenges appeared with the Banco del Pichincha's development of the bordering sector of the Pambachupa hacienda into the Ciudadela Pichincha, a project that led to an extended lawsuit concerning water rights. Rising land values again sparked interest in private divestment of land and internal political challenges, issues that underlay the 1940 constitution of an alternate cabildo spearheaded by Federico Tumipamba's two sons, as discussed earlier. These conflicts, which potentially threatened the sanctity of the community given the regional strength of the financial institution and the problem of legitimation, once again led the cabildo to deploy a multipronged strategy involving entrepreneurial savvy, intensive politicking, and an attention to fixing the narrative of community history. I have already mentioned Federico Tumipamba's backroom deal with his sons to increase their political participation in the cabildo; similar attention to coalition building appears to have curtailed the conflict with the bank as well. In this case, the impetus may have been a radical shift in national politics. The triumph of the Glorious Revolution in May 1944 brought populist leader José María Velasco Ibarra back to power in Ecuador with the support of numerous indigenous polities incorporated under the Federación Ecuatoriana de Indíos (FEI). This situation presented Santa Clara with a dilemma because the new president's brother, Pedro Velasco Ibarra, had overseen the Banco del

Pichincha during their recent conflicts over water rights. Federico Tumipamba, who had taken over as cabildo president during the 1940s, responded by sending a congratulatory letter to the new government and extending an invitation to the bank to collaborate on a new avenue bisecting its lands. Named for former president Isidro Ayora, the new street represented an acknowledgment of the benefits to expanding the arteries connecting Santa Clara's properties with the new Ciudadela Pichincha on its limits.[94]

Situating Santa Clara within historical narratives proved an important tool to these enterprises. While traditional formulas such as evocations of the "ancestral" importance of communal lands or references to ownership since "*tiempo inmemorial*" continued to appear in cabildo depositions, a new attention to mainstream history followed. This shift bespeaks an awareness of the legitimacy the community's extended legal existence afforded the Ministry of Social Welfare as well as its respect for particular forms of narrative and evidence. The new history-aware stance proved crucial to ongoing internal disputes, as can be seen in a truncated clash between Federico and his nephew Luís Tumipamba that erupted in March 1938, just months after the commune's official formation. This dispute began when Federico chopped down eucalyptus saplings along a wall each man owned as part of the subdivision of the Cataloma property wrested from José Antonio Tumipamba a decade earlier. Rather than simply diagram the borders, Federico instead provided a thirty-year narrative of the parcel's adminstration. The detailed discussion of the conflict with Antonio Tumipamba and the subsequent partition delegitimated Luís Tumipamba's case by highlighting his more recent claim to the property. Federico furthered his assault upon his opponent's trustworthiness by noting that Luís Tumipamba had exaggerated the degree of the violation by stating that an entire "forest" had been destroyed. This recourse to historical and factual accuracy appealed to the bureaucracy, and the story was confirmed after a truncated survey by the Teniente Político.[95]

History also proved critical in the development of shifting alliances with the state, whose protection would prove invaluable as internal and external conflicts raged. The person who appears to have taken the initiative in this area was José Gabriel Collahuaso, whose status as a cabildo president was bolstered by his simultaneous activities as an *albañil,* or master builder. These deployments of historicity took many forms, depending on the audience he sought to cultivate. Alongside the defense of the cabildo genealogical narrative, Collahuaso engaged multiple bureaucratic organizations, all the while framing the experience of himself and his community within a "national" historical narrative.

Two particularly striking incidents occurred during the Great Depression. Paradoxically, each appears to have engaged separate state polities. The first coincided with the quadricentennial of the death of Atahualpa in 1533. Collahuaso, in conjunction with other master *albañiles,* collaborated with the conservative municipality to erect a monument to Atahualpa at the summit of the Panecillo.

Collahuaso and his cohort marched to the Panecillo to lay the cornerstone on August 28, 1933. There, he delivered a speech framing the monument as an act of contrition for the republic's previous lack of commitment to the slain Incan leader and to his heirs, the "*raza indígena.*"[96]

Mercedes Prieto reads his subsequent plea for a racial unity tempered by each community's Christian faith as indicative of a conservative underpinning of the entire event, a thesis bolstered by the participation of the Centro Católico de Obreros in the celebration. Moreover, that same year the municipality oversaw a plethora of sanitized commemorations of Atahualpa, including athletic events and romantic poetry declamations.[97] However, the long-standing relationship of Collahuaso and the Santa Clara cabildo with the Ministerio de Previsión Social suggests intimate familiarity with the socialist *indigenista* idea of Atahualpa as an alternate founding father. Moreover, Collahuaso and his fellow masons also levied a call for an eight-hour workday, which was a central goal of the Socialist Party. These observations suggest that Collahuaso deployed his knowledge of multiple constructions of indigenous and national history in order to secure broader socioeconomic gains, addressing both the conservative municipality and the socialist ministry at once.

A similar attempt to take advantage of historically inflected considerations of legitimacy can be seen in the strategy Collahuaso initiated when faced with the prospect of an alternate cabildo in 1940. In his communications with the ministry, the cabildo president interrogated the dissenting faction's understanding of the community's statutes and requested that these be distributed to the membership. Significantly, Collahuaso justified this relatively expensive request by reminding the minister of the great prestige of Santa Clara, which stemmed from "its strong organization and [its heritage as] one of the first to receive juridical status in Ecuador during the last days of the government of General Eloy Alfaro, precursor of modern legislation protecting peasant communities"[98]

Collahuaso's formulation is striking. Not only does he underscore the efficacy (and therefore legitimacy) of the cabildo's governing practices but he also identifies the cabildo's origins with a hero of radical liberalism—Eloy Alfaro, who is highlighted as the precursor of the contemporary social legislation defending peasant communities. These statements tie Santa Clara, its cabildo, its statutes, and its economic activities to a macronarrative of social reform. This linkage exists not only in the reference to Alfaro but also in the manipulation of coded language, such as the identification of Santa Clara de San Millán with a peasant community rather than an indigenous commune. While "peasant community" is a misnomer for what was actually a mixed population of agricultural workers, lumber merchants, artisans, and small-scale real estate speculators, the use of the epithet served its purpose: to legitimize the cabildo in the eyes of the socialist bureaucrats of the Ministry of Social Welfare. As such, it ensured the community's ongoing place within an urban fabric that increasingly turned its back on traditional modes of production and socialization.

The Chronotope of Genealogical Power

In commemoration of the centennial of Quito's declaration of independence, local photographer José Domingo Laso produced the city's first mass-distributed tourist viewbook in 1909.[99] The volume's images emphasized the capital's colonial monumentality, commercial infrastructure, and modern elements. In the introduction, Laso also proudly noted his efforts to alter the cityscape by removing undesirable elements that detracted from the modern and progressive character he hoped to convey. A number of images show the result of Laso's alterations; for example, images of public plazas contain evidence of clumsy erasures. Although it is impossible to identify the erased elements without the photographic negatives, Angel Emilio Hidalgo and Maria Elena Bedoya have posited that they most likely represent indigenous peoples, images of whom are conspicuously absent from the book.[100] If so, Laso's "modern" Quito translates into a simple racial caricature: a city bereft of Indians. Two years later, however, Santa Clara de San Millán received public acknowledgment as an autonomous community existing within city limits.

The contemporaneity of these two events speaks to a broader dynamic within the history of urban indigenous polities. Laso's portrait echoes both racial positivism and the policy of rural segregation of the indigenous that has formed part of the Ecuadorian landscape since colonial times. My gloss of the urban and periurban indigenous suggests that such a situation rarely existed in reality. Santa Clara's de facto and de jure control over common lands, despite Liberal antipathy toward corporate privileges, well illustrates this tendency. It also points to the frequency with which an urban Indian population straddled economic, social, and cultural worlds. I have argued that, in nineteenth-century depositions, the community sought to accentuate its economic importance to the city. Once armed with state-affirmed legal title to these properties, the community's leadership selectively expanded its role in the shifting modern economy, diversifying traditional practices such as animal husbandry, forestry, and artisanal production to include some real estate speculation and infrastructural development. These changes unsettled many *comuneros* and lay at the heart of the juridical conflicts of the late 1920s and 1930s. Federico Tumipamba's autocratic entrepreneurialism, coupled with the writing and rewriting of land histories and community genealogies, responded to this situation and afforded the community the means to weather the economic trials of the Great Depression and to do so with relative success.[101]

In conceiving of the role that narratives of the past played in the community's development, it is useful to consider Joanne Rappaport's concept of a "universal perspective." In her study of historical interpretation among the Nasa people of the Colombian Andes, Rappaport highlights the relationship between native myth/genealogies and indigenous interaction with the state, contending that communities successfully involved in national politics tend to relate local mythologies to a universal perspective. She is referring to "an understanding of the interrelationships between historical process in an array of communications, as well as a clear image of the major developments in the dominant society that have bearing on local history and political process." She asserts that histories coded with signifiers directed to or evocative of mainstream points of reference are particularly likely to arise at moments when "broad-based organization" is needed; she is referring in particular to the widespread coordination of resistance to the Colombian state's attempts to wrest control of *resguardos* (vacant lands) from indigenous populations.[102]

The *comuneros* of Santa Clara de San Millán never codified their interpretation of local history in the form of a book, as occurred among the Nasa. However, their need for sustained collaboration to cement the economic benefits of collective landownership did indeed dovetail with a deepening sophistication of historical interpretation. In the nineteenth century, the community demonstrated an understanding of the variegated nature of the state juridical system in its attempt to counter the legal titles to Cataloma, Lomagorda, and Rosaspamba held by the del Mazos. Even though the community failed to gain titles to these properties, their appeals to have customary exploitation rights to these properties passed muster at the local level and cemented usufruct rights in the Supreme Court. Although the historical record remains unclear as to precisely how these lands returned to the Santa Clara *comuneros'* control, their attention to national politics and support of Eloy Alfaro likely played a role. Certainly, by the Depression era, the cabildo elite had internalized the necessity of framing legal and economic enterprises within a discursive matrix that linked Santa Clara to Liberal and Socialist party reformism.

This articulation developed slowly in the course of a series of internal struggles over landownership occasioned partly by the developing real estate market in the region. The central player in this process was undoubtedly José Federico Tumipamba, whose authority derived partly from an ability to maneuver between state, *comuna,* and the monied classes and partly from control over family and land genealogies. The rank-and-file commune membership increasingly challenged his oversight of this historical record during the late 1920s and 1930s, precisely at the moment when increasing real estate values bumped against declining agricultural revenue and minimal opportunities for alternate forms of employment. During this period, Tumipamba gradually strengthened his ties to the Ministry of Social Welfare and, in the process, codified a narrative that firmly located the commune within the sociopolitical struggles that concomitantly enveloped the rural Andes. This narrative took the form of performative gestures such as the destruction of Pedro Camacho's crops, which evoked Cayambe's agrarian unions, as well as the increasing adoption of coded terminology facilitated by the bureaucrats overseeing communal affairs, reaching its apex following the establishment of formal regulations in 1937.

The commune of Santa Clara de San Millán continues to exist. During the past half century its ties to an agricultural economy have continued to erode and its membership has largely moved away from the area just north of the Mariscal, where most of its members lived at the start of the twentieth century. However, it continues to control the properties atop the mountain and has recently reentered public discourse concerning the city's responsibilities to its indigenous populations. As in the era discussed in this chapter, the community has not shied away from petitioning for the maintenance of its water rights, this time threatened by Quito's *teleférico,* a gondola that takes tourists from the city to the summit of Pichincha. Moreover, the community continues to strengthen ties to progressive activist groups, such as Quito Para Todos and Alianza País. Not only have these groups provided pro bono support for the community's current endeavors but they have also promulgated the group's expanded vision of its historical ties to the Quito valley. Among their proposals for the development of a memorial landscape dedicated to illuminating the social tensions of previous centuries is a plaque located at the intersection of Colón and 10 de agosto avenues identifying the land as the former property of the Comuna de Santa Clara de San Millán. Should such an enterprise come to fruition, the corner would thus house both a monument to preservation, enshrined in Jacinto Jijón's former residence—where the Municipal Archives and the Fondo de Salvamento reside—and an antimonument to a periurban population still articulating its claim to a central node in the urban fabric.

Postscript

In 1935, a minor bureaucrat named Alfonso García Muñoz began publishing a column in the Quito daily *El Comercio* titled "Estampas de mi ciudad." These affectionate chronicles featured a wily figure known as Don Evaristo Corral y Chancleta. Don Evaristo was a *chulla*, or prototypical urban mestizo, who combined the detachment and critical gaze of a Baudelarian *flâneur* with the tragicomic sensibility of Chaplin's Little Tramp. Over the next nine years, García Muñoz collaborated with comic actor Ernesto Albán on dramatic adaptations of the *estampas*, until the Glorious Revolution of 1944 sent him into exile along with several other members of the Arroyo del Rio administration. García Muñoz resided in Bogotá the rest of his life, even refusing to return to Quito in 1994 for a municipal festival celebrating his unique cultural importance.[1] Albán, however, continued to perform the skits that made him famous and even scripted a few *estampas* of his own. Others adopted the popular form—by 1949, only eight of the thirty-six *estampas* Albán performed were García Muñoz originals.[2] The repertoire expanded in the second half of the century to include films and television specials, until Albán's death in 1984. Ten years later, the city government made a mascot of Don Evaristo, using a cartoon likeness with his trademark bowler hat and bushy mustache to advertise programs such as litter collection and cultural events. Today, the Teatro Variedades has been renamed in honor of the comic actor, and revivals of his classic performances occur regularly. His daughter has even established a YouTube channel dedicated to his work.[3]

The popularity of this artful *chulla* stems from his ethos: a picaresque rogue traipsing through the public square. This figure had, in fact, a unique chronotopical gaze defined by his breezy ambivalence to the trappings of modern life. In his study of the chronotope, Bakhtin reminds us that the figure of the rogue, fool, or clown originated within the carnivalesque entertainments of the classical and medieval worlds. Besides subverting the monotony of everyday life, these characters "create around themselves their own special little world, their own chronotope," which inverts and interrogates the conventions of polite society through carnivalesque inversion. As such, rogues can critique a culture through laughter and irony and in the process bare its peculiarities, foibles, and hierarchies.[4]

Don Evaristo serves this function precisely as he turns the tables on the figures of his contemporary city, from *chapitas* (police officers), to *traperos* (street vendors) to Alameda Park's statue of Simón Bolívar, whom Evaristo imagines must be eternally bored because he can never dismount his steed (*brioso corcel*). A favorite victim of Evaristo, especially of his skills as an amateur pickpocket, is an obtuse *gringo* who foolishly employs him as a tour guide and receives in return a flurry of misinformation amid a series of hijinks. El Gringo ends up in scrapes like a Carnival water fight, from which the two emerge drenched but victorious after successfully storming a townhouse.

These satirical portraits are rich in detail and interwoven with the sites, traditions, and encounters common to García Muñoz's modernizing city. And yet they seem to escape the staid conventions of both positivist and nostalgic discourses. The plucky Don Evaristo acknowledges the dialogical nature of the surveyed city, where hypocrisy and contradiction abound and life is at once modern and traditional, formal and burlesque. This playful approach to time and space and to social markers gives the *estampas* their particular flavor. For example, upon passing beneath the sixteenth-century Arco de la Reina, Don Evaristo muses, "I would have liked to contemplate this Arch in earlier times, before the arrival of electric light. I figure it would have been a special place for romantic liaisons, gangster ambushes, and stabs in the back. Today, civilization, with its powerful 'osrams,' deflowers the dark, impeding the shadows to cover love, theft, and murder."[5] This ironic view of electric lighting—as hindrance to romance, robbery, and murder—undercuts the glow of modernization as manifested by powerful Osram-brand lightbulbs. Yet Evaristo is not sentimental. His contemplation of the arch during its heyday inspires a self-consciously anachronistic portrait in which contemporary characters, such as the gangsters of American cinema, have intruded on the age of the cloak and dagger. Fusing Quito's contemporary existence with its past embeds his tale within a permeable historical matrix with a global purview encompassing both popular and high culture.

Asserting the inseparable juxtaposition of the modern and the traditional has been associated with a postmodern sensibility but is also integral to traditional positivist frameworks.[6] *Quiteños* from across social, racial, and political divides acknowledged these contradictions. However, disagreement existed as to the currency of a given "past," "present," or "future." I have demarcated a series of constellations of accepted and repudiated narratives adopted by specific groups and shaped by their chronotopical organization. Although influenced by historic alliances of a political or socioeconomic nature, these boundaries proved distinctly porous. These heuristically developed chronotopes gathered into their orbit a series of utterances associated with authors and audiences often separated in time and space. As Bakhtin notes, in the "world represented in the work," a dialogical process envelops these "real world" actors:

> The work and the world represented in it enter the real world and enrich it, and the real world enters the work and its world as part of the process of its creation, as well as part of its subsequent life, in a continual renewing of the work through the creative perception of listeners and readers. Of course this process of exchange is itself chronotopic: it occurs first and foremost in the historically developing social world, but without ever losing contact with changing historical space. We might even speak of a special *creative* chronotope inside which this exchange between work and life occurs, and which constitutes the distinctive life of the work.[7]

Thus, society and its stories mutually constitute one another. A culture's chronotopes prove generative in both a literary and a social sense, indelibly marking the world from which they originate as they are encountered, re-encountered, and renewed by authors and audiences. By extension, those engaging a conversation that stretches across time and space join a group of what might be termed chronotopical producers.

With García Muñoz's *estampas,* dialogism stems from the polyvalence of multiple chronotopes inflected by an extended history of refraction and renewal that continues to the present. This history begins with García Muñoz himself, whose writings owe a debt to a lengthy tradition of satirical sketches articulating an ironic sensibility known as *sal quiteña.* This epithet originated in nineteenth-century feuilletons and has also been associated with the *tradiciones* of Hispanist Cristóbal Gangotena or the Dadaist ennui of Alberto Coloma Silva.[8] With the *estampas,* however, this *sal* passed from the page to the boards to television and the Internet—at each stage altered and rewritten by multiple authors and audiences. This process of destruction and renewal feeds the genre and perpetuates the chronotope. Tracing the publics and producers implicated in the development of the *estampa*—nineteenth-century humorists, García Muñoz, Ernesto

Albán, the urban mestizo, Mexican film studios, gringo businessmen, and even contemporary social networking sites—thus provides sociological insight into the historical development of the city's image, politics, and sociocultural configurations.

Mapping the tangled development of such discourses in Quito's history has been the central project of this book. Of particular interest is a series of iterations that took shape during the early twentieth century, when the city outgrew its colonial era limits. The narrative coordinates emphasized here responded to the dominant chronotope of the day—a technocratic, *positivist* vision of modernization, one that had global resonance yet garnered support locally from the Liberal Party that ran the government. These responses rarely critiqued "progress." Rather, they tended to advocate soft defiance of Liberal positivism by substituting a historical framework that highlighted *their* experiences and *their* city. They created new histories that strategically embraced and rejected local traditions, always with an eye toward situating the particular constellation of actors at the center of regional, national, and global currents. As the presence of such "historicist" narratives proliferated, the political and economic benefits of identification with such a chronotope expanded. And so the minor chronotope of Quito's historicity, reframed as an indicator of global leadership building upon colonial and some nineteenth-century discourses, expanded into a genre-defining trope of local affirmation whose enduring iterations continue to mark the city's politics, image, and economy.[9]

This declaration of world historical leadership was not unique to Quito. As discussed earlier, one of the goals of Latin American intellectual output during the early twentieth century was to (re)assert relevance despite increasing marginalization on the global scene. State-backed enterprises designed to showcase urban modernity formed a critical component of the proclamation of national progress, as has been demonstrated by the multiple studies of *fin-de-siglo* monumental urban planning in the region's major capitals. Elites, the state, and intellectuals in Buenos Aires, Rio de Janeiro, or Mexico City deployed historicist architecture, allegorical constructions of sanitized pre-Columbian populations, and mythscapes celebrating the pantheon of nationalist heroes in an effort to declare their city's membership in an exclusive club—what we today call global cities. Despite the difference in scale, a similar impulse underlay Quito's prolific inversion of global positivist paradigms across political, cultural, socioeconomic, and racial divides. Indeed, considering how and why such an insular city gave rise to this maelstrom of chronotopic histories has been a central question of this study.

As discussed at the outset of this book, this process occurred against a backdrop of intensifying regional competition in nineteenth- and twentieth-century Ecuador. This struggle originated in the colonial period, when citizenship in the Iberian tradition based national or universal identity on membership in a local group of *vecinos.* Echoes of this structure exist within the attempts to articulate a national consciousness during the nineteenth and early twentieth centuries, remarking the continued reliance upon the local as a symbol for the national. Attesting to Quito's global historical import became even more important as regional strife intensified during the second half of the nineteenth century, especially following the Liberal Revolution in 1895. The proclivity to situate urban identities within tiered teleologies tied to origin ought to be considered a function of these tensions.

Subsequent discussion diagrammed the internal logic of six crucial chronotopes developed during the early twentieth century. The first step in each chapter concerned identifying precursors, which in most cases required reorienting the analytical framework toward the colonial period. Such was the case with the search for institutional autonomy on the part of the municipality or the defense of common lands pursued by the Comuna de Santa Clara de San Millán. The city's cartographers and Hispanists also celebrated particular colonial moments during which Quito had arguably transcended its relative provinciality to become a site of world historical importance. Meanwhile, the Durinis and the city's dystopians highlighted Quito's provinciality (as if history had stood still) with an eye toward asserting their own claim to be cosmopolitan modernists.

Crafting a chronotope with validity in the modern city, however, depended upon refracting these originary tropes, moments, or sites so as to focus on the particular social group deploying them in the present. The process of articulation involved a substantial period of time during which a plurality of actors reconfigured extended traditions, vocabularies, and associations. This germination did not follow a straightforward teleological path, despite the assertions of its inventive interlocutors. The case of the canonical Hispanist celebration of Quito's messianic global role can serve as a case in point. Despite an extended history, with precursors in the millenarian visions of the colonial period, a hostile diplomatic climate impeded the chronotope's development through most of the nineteenth century. The revival associated with the Academia Nacional de Historia and the conservative municipalities of the 1930s crystallized a new set of actors desiring to recapture local, national, and international prominence. They succeeded in fashioning a unique holiday celebrating the city's Spanish heritage, yet even *Seis de diciembre* escaped their sociopolitical designs during its popularization in the second half of the twentieth century. This history suggests that despite generic convention, chronotopes remained contingent upon the social milieu in which they emerged or reemerged. Emphasizing these contexts, and particularly the upheaval of Quito's *fin-de-siglo,* has been central to the analysis throughout this study.

Chronotopes born during times of extreme flux can be imagined as especially resilient. Their plasticity enables them to serve as mutable frames for myriad goals, sometimes associated with several constituencies but often tied to the shifting circumstances of a particular population. Among the collectives discussed in this book, perhaps the manipulation demonstrated by the Durini family or the *comuna* of Santa Clara de San Millán most directly illustrates this point. Both groups frequently spun their history (both discursively and spatially) to adapt to shifting social, political, economic, or cultural circumstances. The Durinis could construct a building that went from being an expression of elite sophistication to a declaration of a hybrid Andean vernacular depending on the moment and the audience. Federico Tumipamba and José Gabriel Collahuaso pivoted between performances of deferential or defiant indigeneity while articulating an Alfarista, proto-socialist, or neo-Incaic identity. The polyphony of these iterations at times threatened to devolve into absurdity; however, the generic framework offered a mask of stability and consistency. In the case of the Durinis, this façade concerned their identity as cosmopolitan interlocutors; in the case of Santa Clara, the autonomous commune, with its traditional leaders proudly at the helm, provided a central leitmotif.

This nimble manipulation of history reflected an entrepreneurial appropriation of the past common not only to Santa Clara and the Durinis but also to institutional actors. The various institutions benefited from additional state support yet achieved this support only because of their ability to craft a chronotopical framework that afforded them legitimacy and enabled them to reach political as well as economic goals. Such was the case of the Hispanist gaze of the National Academy of History, which reconsidered the intellectual tradition of Iberian exceptionalism while articulating a special millenarian role for Quito. Similarly, the municipal council and the military's cartographers refracted colonial administrative structures and the city and nation's unique role in the development of geographic science to carve out new spaces for commercial and political enterprise. Finessing the past and identifying places and sites infused with it therefore provided not only a legitimizing frame but also concrete financial and social benefits.

The elasticity of a given chronotope also opened it to the charge of hypocrisy, which fueled a counter-cartographic series of coordinates underscoring the phantasmagorical attributes of the idyllic Quito. The poetics of denunciation advanced by Quito's detractors highlighted the city's estrangement from the course of global history. Spatial metaphors equating the national and global hinterland as a space of potential redemption transcended myriad stylistic attributes, from romanticism to surrealism. A sense of irony invigorated popular and literary works that put forth negative views of Quito and the nation, beginning with critical interrogation of a positivist spirit in the works of Mera or Bustamante but becoming a palpable source of satirical wit in Palacio's formal experiments or Salvador's absurdist gestures. Laughter's potential to invert social hierarchies enlivened the chronotope and accentuated its potential to chastise the solipsistic flavor of the city's intellectual climate.

The criticism inherent within the phantasmagorical chronotope highlights the possibility of refraction and alteration of a given chronotope once it entered the public sphere. Indeed, such dialogism increased as the narratives discussed in this book encountered each other in cacophonous counterpoint. Moreover, the second half of the twentieth century saw an expansion in the number of readers, listeners, and viewers as the public sphere expanded. These public actors increasingly harnessed the narratives for their own purposes, in the process popularizing discourses previously limited to elite actors. Thus, the celebration of Spanish Quito inaugurated by the Hispanist municipality became a popular celebration while the notion of the city's geographical centrality blurred into tourist kitsch at Mitad del Mundo.

Despite their limits, these chronotopes have proved resilient. As was the case during the early twentieth century, their contemporary dynamism grows out of the depth of the narrative tradition that frames each configuration of space-time. Aware of global trends, the actors developing the modern city's chronotopes sought layers of meaning within local customs. The chronotopes' potency also derived from the celebration of emblematic sites within the city that served as anchors of narrative signification. This process of creating a three-dimensional cartography of allusion took multiple forms, including depiction in literature, historical preservation, construction, illumination, monuments, and imagination. Certain locations, such as the Panecillo, Alameda Park, or the city's environs, enjoyed the attentions of competing actors and proved to be pliable.

Above all, these layered histories provided their respective authors and the public with a means to navigate the changing city. By establishing points of continuity between the past and the future, they fixed an interpretation of a rapidly shifting landscape. The modern stood revealed as unique and homegrown, and Quito found its place on a map of national and global currents. Thus, the upheaval of modernity translated into something knowable and autochthonous. And their city was established at the center of the world.

Notes

Prelude

1. Centro de medios independientes, Ecuador, "Kito Anti-Taurino," http://ecuador
.indymedia.org/es/2002/12/1206.shtml (accessed February 21, 2008).

2. Eric Hobsbawm and Terence Ranger, eds., *The Invention of Tradition* (Cambridge:
Cambridge University Press, 1983).

3. For recent studies of these phenomena in Latin America, see Mauricio Tenorio
Trillo, "1910 Mexico City: Space and Nation in the City of the Centenario," *Journal of
Latin American Studies* 28:1 (February 1996): 75–104; Adrian Gorelik, *La grilla y el parque:
espacio público y cultura urbana en Buenos Aires, 1887–1936* (Buenos Aires: Universidad
Nacional de Quilmes, 1998); Mark Overmyer-Velázquez, *Visions of the Emerald City:
Modernity, Tradition, and the Formation of Porfirian Oaxaca, Mexico* (Durham, NC: Duke
University Press, 2006).

4. M. M. Bakhtin, "Forms of Time and Chronotope in the Novel: Notes toward a
Historical Poetics," in M. M. Bakhtin, *The Dialogic Imagination,* ed. Michael Holquist,
trans. Caryl Emerson and Michael Holquist (Austin: University of Texas Press, 1981),

84–85. See also Nele Bemong et al., eds., *Bakhtin's Theory of the Literary Chronotope: Reflections, Applications, Perspectives* (Ghent, Belgium: Academia Press, 2010).

5. Maurice Halbwachs, *The Collective Memory,* trans. Francis J. Ditter Jr. and Vida Yazdi Ditter (New York: Harper & Row, 1980). See also Pierre Nora, ed., *Realms of Memory: Rethinking the French Past,* 3 vols. (New York: Columbia University Press, 1996–1998); and Svetlana Boym, *The Future of Nostalgia* (New York: Basic Books, 2001).

6. Bakhtin distinguishes between major and minor chronotopes: minor chronotopes are motivic in nature while major chronotopes are generic, that is, genre-producing. Bakhtin, "Forms of Time." See also Jay Ladin, "Fleshing Out the Chronotope," in *Critical Essays on Mikhail Bakhtin,* ed. Caryl Emerson (New York: G. K. Hall, 1999), 212–36; and Nele Bemong and Pieter Borghart, "Bakhtin's Theory of the Literary Chronotope: Reflections, Applications, Perspectives," in *Bakthin's Theory,* ed. Bemong et al., 7–8.

7. On metahistory, see Hayden V. White, *Metahistory: The Historical Imagination in Nineteenth-Century Europe* (Baltimore: Johns Hopkins University Press, 1973).

8. On *vecindad* and early modern citizenship, see Tamar Herzog, *Defining Nations: Immigrants and Citizens in Early Modern Spain and Spanish America* (New Haven: Yale University Press, 2003).

9. A. Kim Clark, *The Redemptive Work: Railway and Nation in Ecuador, 1895–1930* (Wilmington, DE: Scholarly Resources, 1998).

10. See Lucas Achig, *El proceso urbano de Quito: ensayo de interpretación* (Quito: Centro de Investigaciones; CIUDAD, 1983); Fernando Carrión, *Quito: crisis y política urbana* (Quito: CIUDAD; Editorial El Conejo, 1987); and Manuel Castells, *City, Class, and Power,* trans. E. Lebas (New York: St. Martin's Press, 1978).

11. Milton Luna Tamayo, *Historia y conciencia popular: el artesanado de Quito, economia, organización, y vida cotidiana, 1890–1930* (Quito: Corporación Editora Nacional, 1989); Guillermo Bustos, "Quito en la transición: actores colectivos e identidades culturales urbanas (1920–1950)," in *Enfoques y estudios históricos: Quito a través de la historia,* by Paul Aguilar et al. (Quito: Editorial Fraga, 1992), 163–88; Manuel Espinosa Apolo, *Mestizaje, cholificación y blanqueamiento en Quito primera mitad del siglo XXI* (Quito: Universidad Andina Simón Bolívar Ecuador, Abya-Yala, Corporación Editora Nacional, 2003).

12. Eduardo Kingman Garcés, *La ciudad y los otros, Quito 1860–1940: higienismo, ornato y policía* (Quito: FLACSO, 2006).

13. See, e.g., Jeffrey D. Needell, *A Tropical Belle Epoque: Elite Culture and Society in Turn-of-the-Century Rio de Janeiro* (Cambridge: Cambridge University Press, 1987); Teresa A. Meade, *"Civilizing" Rio: Reform and Resistance in a Brazilian City, 1889–1930* (University Park: Pennsylvania State University Press, 1997); and, to a lesser degree, John Lear, *Workers, Neighbors, and Citizens: The Revolution in Mexico City* (Lincoln: University of Nebraska Press, 2001).

14. Jorge Hardoy, ed., *Urbanization in Latin America: Approaches and Issues* (Garden City, NY: Anchor Books, 1975); Jorge Hardoy and Richard Morse, eds., *Rethinking the Latin American City* (Washington, DC: Woodrow Wilson Center Press; Baltimore: Johns

Hopkins University Press, 1993); and Richard Morse, *New World Soundings: Culture and Ideology in the Americas* (Baltimore: Johns Hopkins University Press, 1989).

15. Tenorio Trillo, "1910 Mexico City"; Marisol de la Cadena, *Indigenous Mestizos: The Politics of Race and Culture in Cuzco, Peru, 1919–1991* (Durham, NC: Duke University Press, 2000); Overmyer-Velázquez, *Visions of the Emerald City.*

16. Luis Roniger, "Global Immersion: Latin America and Its Multiple Modernities," in *Globality and Multiple Modernities: Comparative North American and Latin American Perspectives,* ed. Luis Roniger and Carlos H. Waisman (Brighton, UK: Sussex Academic Press, 2002), 79–105.

Chapter 1. The Politics and Poetics of Regionalism

1. The phrase "denial of coevalness" is associated with Johannes Fabian's analysis of distinction created within anthropological studies between the Western scientist and the "other," whose primitive nature separates it from belonging to the same era of progress and development. Walter Mignolo has appropriated this terminology in his call for "a denial of the denial of coevalness," with regard to the Western project of colonization in the Americas from the sixteenth century onward. My appropriation acknowledges these implicit criticisms of the Western imperial project while simultaneously considering the economic benefits of selectively engaging with modes of appropriating the past as a tradable commodity. See Johannes Fabian, *Time and the Other: How Anthropology Makes Its Object* (New York: Columbia University Press, 1983); and Walter Mignolo, *The Darker Side of the Renaissance: Literacy, Territoriality, and Colonization,* 2nd ed. (Ann Arbor: University of Michigan Press, 2003), xi–xii.

2. Herzog, *Defining Nations.* For the continued relevance of the construction of a transnational, reflexive notion of postcolonial citizenship, see Antonio Annino, "El Jano bifronte: los pueblos y los orígenes del liberalismo en México," in *Crisis, reforma y revolución: Mexico; historias de fin de siglo,* ed. Leticia Reina and Elisa Servín (Mexico City: Taurus, Consejo Nacional para la Cultura y las Artes, Instituto Nacional de Antropología e Historia, 2002), 209–51; and Roniger, "Global Immersion."

3. Richard L. Kagan, with Fernando Marías, *Urban Images in the Hispanic World, 1493–1793* (New Haven: Yale University Press, 2000).

4. Kim Gauderman, *Women's Lives in Colonial Quito: Gender, Law, and Economy in Spanish America* (Austin: University of Texas Press, 2003), 4.

5. John Leddy Phelan, *The Kingdom of Quito in the Seventeenth Century: Bureaucratic Politics in the Spanish Empire* (Madison: University of Wisconsin Press, 1967), 49.

6. Bernard Lavallé, *Quito y la crisis de la alcabala 1580–1600* (Quito: IFEA, Corporación Editora Nacional, 1997).

7. Kris Lane, *Quito 1599: City and Colony in Transition* (Albuquerque: University of New Mexico Press, 2002), 178–80.

8. One of the most extensive analyses of the emergence of the *quiteño* market can be found in Gauderman, *Women's Lives.* See also Lane, *Quito 1599,* chaps. 3 and 5.

9. Susan V. Webster, *Arquitectura y empresa en el Quito colonial: José Jaime Ortiz, Alarife Mayor* (Quito: Abya-Yala, 2002), 49.

10. See Lane, *Quito 1599*, xi–xiii. See also Thomas B. F. Cummins and William B. Taylor, "The Mulatto Gentlemen of Esmeraldas, Ecuador," in *Colonial Spanish America: A Documentary History*, ed. Kenneth Mills and William B. Taylor (Wilmington, DE: Scholarly Resources, 1998), 147–49.

11. The most comprehensive study of Quito's sculpture remains Gabrielle G. Palmer's *Sculpture in the Kingdom of Quito* (Albuquerque: University of New Mexico Press, 1987).

12. Carmen Fernández-Salvador, "Images and Memory: The Construction of Collective Identities in Seventeenth-Century Quito" (PhD diss., University of Chicago, 2005), esp. chap. 3.

13. The origins of the controversy lay in Isaac Newton's gravitational theories, which predicted that the Earth could not be a pure sphere but would instead be elliptical.

14. For recent scholarship considering La Condamine's European views of the exotic American landscape, see Neil Safier, *Measuring the New World: Enlightenment Science and South America* (Chicago: University of Chicago Press, 2008); Deborah Poole, *Vision, Race, and Modernity: A Visual Economy of the Andean Image World* (Princeton: Princeton University Press, 1997); and Jorge Cañizares-Esguerra, "Postcolonialism *avant la lettre*? Travelers and Clerics in Eighteenth-Century Colonial Spanish America," in *After Spanish Rule: Postcolonial Predicaments of the Americas*, ed. Mark Thurner and Andrés Guerrero (Durham, NC: Duke University Press, 2003), 89–109.

15. Extensive scholarly analysis of the Rebellion of the Barrios began to appear around 1990. Scholars have alternately characterized the rebellion as an anticipation of the southern Andean strife of the 1780s, as a moment of great racial tension, as a moment of subaltern racial harmony, and as predominantly urban or involving significant participation from the *corregimiento*. For more on the uprising, see Kenneth J. Andrien, "Economic Crisis, Taxes, and the Quito Insurrection of 1765," *Past and Present* 129 (November 1990): 104–31; Anthony McFarlane, "The 'Rebellion of the Barrios': Urban Insurrection in Bourbon Quito," *Hispanic American Historical Review* 69:2 (May 1989): 283–330; and Martin Minchom, *The People of Quito, 1690–1810: Change and Unrest in the Underclass* (Boulder, CO: Westview Press, 1994).

16. A concise discussion of Espejo's use of satirical prose can be found in Julie Greer Johnson, *Satire in Colonial Spanish America: Turning the New World Upside Down* (Austin: University of Texas Press, 1993). See also Reinaldo Mino, *Eugenio Espejo y la defensa de los indios* (Quito: Sistema Nacional de Bibliotecas, 1995); and *Visión actual de Eugenio Espejo* (Quito: Fundación Eugenio Espejo/Fundación Friedrich Naumann, 1988).

17. On Rocafuerte and the Cortes de Cádiz, see works by Jaime E. Rodriguez O.: *The Emergence of Spanish America: Vicente Rocafuerte and Spanish Americanism, 1808–1832* (Berkeley: University of California Press, 1975); and *The Independence of Spanish America* (Cambridge: Cambridge University Press, 1998).

18. Marie-Danielle Demalas and Yves Saint-Geours elaborate on Cuenca's role as an intellectual and political arbiter in their work *Jerusalen y Babilonia: religión y política*

en el Ecuador, 1780–1880, trans. Carmen Garatea Yuri (Quito: Corporación Editora Nacional, 1988), 32. For the population of its district and relative importance in the early nineteenth century, see Julio Carpio Vintimilla, *La evolución urbana de Cuenca en el siglo XIX* (Cuenca: Universidad de Cuenca [IDIS], 1983), esp. 75–83.

19. Mark J. von Achen, *King of the Night: Juan José Flores and Ecuador, 1824–1864* (Berkeley: Univeristy of California Press, 1989).

20. Rafael Quintero and Erika Silva, *Ecuador: una nación en ciernes,* 3rd ed. (Quito: Abya-Yala, 1998), 74.

21. Unlike the other cities, Loja did not contend to be the center of a new national government. Not having the wealth or position from which to form an independent state, *lojanos* called for a federal system with more provincial autonomy.

22. Quintero and Silva, *Ecuador,* 82. Quintero and Silva's analysis of the installation of a neo-Iberian state evokes similar arguments concerning the continuity of administrative structures, commented upon most concisely by François-Xavier Guerra in *Modernidades e independencias: ensayos sobre las revoluciones hispánicas* (Madrid: Editorial MAPFRE, 1992), albeit at a temporal distance of some decades.

23. Derek Williams, "Negotiating the State: National Utopias and Local Politics in Ecuador, 1845–75" (PhD diss., State University of New York at Stony Brook, 2001).

24. Jean Paul Deler, "Estructuración y consolidación del área central (1830–1942)," in Jean Paul Deler, Nelson Gómez, and Michel Portais, *El manejo del espacio en el Ecuador: etapas claves* (Quito: Centro Ecuatoriano de Investigación Geográfica, 1983), 187–91.

25. Ricardo D. Salvatore and Carlos Aguirre, "The Birth of the Penitentiary in Latin America: Toward an Interpretive Social History of Prisons," in *The Birth of the Penitentiary in Latin America: Essays on Criminology, Prison Reform, and Social Control, 1830–1940,* ed. Ricardo D. Salvatore and Carlos Aguirre (Austin: University of Texas Press, 1996), 11.

26. Alexandra Kennedy Troya and Alfonso Ortiz Crespo, "Continuismo colonial y cosmopolitismo en la arquitectura y el arte decimonónico ecuatoriano," in *Nueva historia del Ecuador,* vol. 8, *Época republicana II,* ed. Enrique Ayala Mora (Quito: Corporación Editora Nacional/grijalbo, 1990), 124–31.

27. See Williams, "Negotiating the State."

28. The number of children attending school in the countryside rose from 13,459 in 1867 to 32,000 by 1875. See Enrique Ayala, "Gabriel García Moreno y la gestación del estado nacional en el Ecuador," *Cultura* 4:10 (May–August 1981): 163.

29. On souvenirs, see Blanca Muratorio, "Nación, identidad y etnicidad: imágenes de los indios ecuatorianos y sus imagineros a fines del siglo XIX," in *Imágenes e imagineros: representaciones de los indígenas ecuatorianos, siglos XIX y XX,* ed. Blanca Muratorio (Quito: FLACSO, 1994), 150.

30. For an introduction to Montalvo, see Roberto Agramonte, *La filosofía de Montalvo* (Quito: Banco Central del Ecuador, 1992). See also Arturo Andrés Roig, *Pensamiento social de Juan Montalvo: sus lecciones al pueblo* (Quito: Editorial Tercer Mundo, 1984). A selection of his writings can be found in Galo René Pérez, ed., *Montalvo* (Quito: Banco Central, 1985).

31. García Moreno is the most frequently studied individual in Ecuadorian history. His dramatic death captured the imagination of conservatives not only in Ecuador but across the world, and his martyrdom became a favorite subject, inspiring countless biographies, tributes, and historical dramas in Europe and the rest of South America, particularly during the *fin-de-siglo*. See, e.g., Agustine Berthe, *García Moreno: les héros martyr* (Paris: Retaux-Bray, 1890); M. T. Joséfa, *García Moreno, président de la république de l'Equateur* (Paris, 1892); Giacinto Simonato, *"Dio non muore!" García Moreno, drama storico in 4 atti* (Milan: G. Daviero, 1933); Manuel Galvéz, *Vida de don Gabriel García Moreno* (Buenos Aires: Editorial Difusión, 1942). A strong contemporary biography is Peter V. N. Henderson, *Gabriel García Moreno and Conservative State Formation in the Andes* (Austin: University of Texas Press, 2008).

32. Native Ecuadorian cacao could grow only in the rather deep topsoil found near the many rivers that cross the coastal plains. The new variety, cacao Benezuela, on the other hand, could grow without difficulty in drier, hilly areas. Nonetheless, it was a weaker species and less resistant to disease, a factor that ultimately served to decimate a large portion of the crops of the late 1910s. See Lois Crawford de Roberts, *El Ecuador en la época cacaotera: respuestas locales al auge y colapso en el ciclo monoexportador,* trans. Erika Silva and Rafael Quintero (Quito: Editorial Universitaria, 1980), 49–54, 165–70.

33. The most extensive study on the cacao period is still Lois Crawford de Roberts's *El Ecuador en la época cacaotera,* which presents an analysis of cacao growth patterns, Ecuador's role in international markets, and the fortunes of the Guayaquil cacao elite. Andrés Guerrero's *Los oligarcas del cacao: ensayo sobre la acumulación originaria en el Ecuador; hacendados cacaoteros, banqueros exportadores y comerciantes en Guayaquil (1890–1910)* (Quito: El Conejo, 1980) elaborates a Marxist critique of the accumulation of wealth in the industry's development. Guayaquil's development in the late nineteenth and early twentieth centuries has been well covered by Ronn F. Pineo, *Social and Economic Reform in Ecuador: Life and Work in Guayaquil* (Gainesville: University Press of Florida, 1996). Pineo stresses the importance of both the city's monoculture dependency and regionalism to Guayaquil's *fin-de-siglo* labor and economic history.

34. For more on Juan León Mera, see Xavier Michelena, *Juán León Mera: antología esencial* (Quito: Banco Central/Abya-Yala, 1994); and Julio Pazos Barrera, ed., *Juan León Mera: una vision actual* (Quito: Corporación Editora Nacional, 1995). The term *serrano* refers to inhabitants of the Andean section of Ecuador.

35. Remigio Crespo Toral, "Modesto Espinosa, Semblanza," in *Biblioteca ecuatoriana mínima: prosistas de la república* (Puebla, Mexico: Editorial J. M. Cajica Jr., 1960), 439–46. See also José Modesto Espinosa, *Obras completas,* vol. 1, *Artículos de costumbres* (Freiburg, Germany: B. Herder, 1899).

36. The similarity of the work of Guerrero and Fuentes was the subject of an exhibition, "Quito-Lima: Siglo XIX," held at the Centro Cultural Metropolitano in Quito, October 23–November 14, 2002.

37. Claudio Malo González, "Histos en la plástica cuencana del siglo XX," in *De la inocencia a la libertad: arte cuencano del siglo XX,* ed. Andrés Abad Marchán (Cuenca: Banco Central del Ecuador, 1998), 47–49.

38. Crawford de Roberts, *Ecuador en la época cacaotera,* 66–67.

39. Muratorio, "Nación, identidad y etnicidad," 164–67.

40. Japan and China were at war in 1894, and although Chile wanted to sell a warship to Japan, a pact of neutrality prevented the sale. The Ecuadorian consul in New York, when approached to broker the deal, agreed to attempt to persuade the national government to purchase the ship from Chile, sail it to Japan under the Ecuadorian flag, and then sell it to Japan. The disclosure of such an unpatriotic use of the national standard led to widespread furor.

41. Rafael Quintero and Erika Silva follow Cuenca's role in the shift in national politics in their article, "La crisis nacional general de 1895," *Cultura* 4:11 (September–December 1981): 106–7.

42. The most extensive account of the Liberal Revolution is Enrique Ayala Mora's *Historia de la revolución liberal ecuatoriana* (Quito: Corporación Editora Nacional, 1994).

43. Indeed, González Suárez was the only bishop left in the country after Archbishop Ordóñez died in 1906. See Santiago Castillo Illingworth, *La iglesia y la revolución liberal: las relaciones de la iglesia y el estado en la época del liberalismo* (Quito: Ediciones del Banco Central del Ecuador, 1995), 252–321, on the bishop's efforts to rebuild church institutions.

44. Deler, "Estructuración y consolidación," 177.

45. Clark, *Redemptive Work,* 109; Dirección Nacional de Estadística, *Ecuador en cifras, 1938–1942* (Quito: Imprenta del Ministerio de Hacienda, 1944), 288.

46. Deler, "Estructuración y consolidación," 213.

47. Jean Paul Deler, *Ecuador: del espacio al estado nacional* (Quito: Banco Central del Ecuador, 1987), 184.

48. Clark, *Redemptive Work.*

49. Edwing Guerrero Blum, *Instituto Nacional Mejía: historia y proyección; ciento seis años de educación laica y democrática* (Quito: E. Guerrero Blum, 2003.)

50. Linda Alexander Rodríguez, *The Search for Public Policy: Regional Politics and Government Finances in Ecuador, 1830–1940* (Berkeley: University of California Press, 1985), 95.

51. The devaluation of the sucre devastated the purchasing power of workers but helped the cacao elite, who were able to get cheap labor at home and still sell their product at high prices abroad. See Crawford de Roberts, *Ecuador en la época cacaotera,* 157.

52. Tenguel's decline represents a typical case: it was eventually abandoned as a cacao plantation, but in the 1930s the United Fruit Company converted it to banana cultivation. See Steve Striffler, *In the Shadows of State and Capital: The United Fruit Company, Popular Struggle, and Agrarian Restructuring in Ecuador, 1900–1995* (Durham, NC: Duke University Press, 2002), 24–28.

53. On both the expanding market and public health, see Pineo, *Social and Economic Reform in Ecuador,* esp. chap. 7.

54. It is difficult to arrive at exact population figures given that census data are limited. During the time period of this study, the only years for which reliable census data are available are 1906 and 1922.

55. Clark, *Redemptive Work,* 120.

56. Eduardo Kingman has pointed out the importance of Quito's directories as a measure of the growth of consolidated concerns. See Eduardo Kingman Garcés, "Quito, vida social y modificaciones urbanas," in *Enfoques y estudios históricos,* ed. Aguilar et al., 149. He points out that the five largest tailors in the city employed 121 journeymen while the next nineteen had only 149.

57. The formation of the society has been well documented in histories of Ecuadorian labor organization. See Manuel Chiriboga Alvear, *Resumen histórico de la Sociedad "Artística e Industrial del Pichincha,"* 1892–1917 (Quito: Encuadernación Nacionales, 1917).

58. Milton Luna Tamayo, "Orígenes del movimiento obrero de la sierra ecuatoriana: el Centro Obrero Católico," *Cultura* 9:26 (September–December 1986): 286–93.

59. Between 1914 and 1920, prices for basic foodstuffs rose dramatically. For example, sugar prices rose 200 percent, flour prices increased 110 percent, potatoes doubled in price, and the price of lard jumped 95 percent. See Alexei Páez Cordero, *Los orígenes de la izquierda ecuatoriana* (Quito: Abya-Yala, 2001), 91.

60. For an introduction to Ecuadorian labor history, see Patricio Ycaza, *Historia del movimiento obrero ecuatoriano: de su génesis al Frente Popular* (Quito: CEDIME, 1984); and Páez Cordero, *Orígenes de la izquierda ecuatoriana.* The 1922 massacre is treated in Pineo, *Social and Economic Reform in Ecuador,* which also provides a context for the event by considering the process of urbanization and development in the port city. For firsthand accounts, see Jorge Carrera Andrade, *El volcán y el colibrí: autobiografía* (Quito: Corporación Editora Nacional, 1989); and J. Alejo Capelo, *El crimen del 15 de noviembre de 1922* (Guayaquil: Litografía e Impr. de la Universidad de Guayaquil; Librería y distribuidora Continental, 1983).

61. On the Julian Revolution, see Juan J. Paz y Miño Cepeda, *Revolución juliana: nación, ejército y bancocracia* (Quito: Abya-Yala, 2000).

62. See Rodríguez, *Search for Public Policy,* chap.5, on the Kemmerer mission and the Central Bank. See also Paul W. Drake, *The Money Doctor in the Andes: The Kemmerer Missions, 1923–1933* (Durham, NC: Duke University Press, 1989), 125–74.

63. See Valeria Coronel, "A Revolution in Stages: Subaltern Politics, Nation-State Formation, and the Origins of Social Rights in Ecuador, 1834–1943" (PhD diss., New York University, 2011).

64. The *tradición* features a detailed discussion of a historical event, often interrupted with a short contextual essay. For more on Palma, see one of the many collections of his *tradiciones* as well as Isabelle Tauzin Castellanos, *Las tradiciones peruanas de Ricardo Palma: claves de una coherencia* (Lima: Universidad Ricardo Palma, 1999); or Estuardo Núñez, *Ricardo Palma escritor continental: tras las huellas de Palma en Hispanoamérica* (Lima: Banco Central de Reserva del Perú, 1998).

65. Although the *crónica* or chronicle originated in newspapers, most of these authors published collected editions. See Alejandro Andrade Coello, *Motivos nacionales (crónicas quiteñas),* vol. 2 (Quito: Imprenta de la Escuela de Artes y Oficios, 1927); José Antonio Campos, *Cosas de mi tierra* (Guayaquil: Imprenta Garay, 1929); Alejandro An-

drade Coello, *Del Quito antiguo* (Quito: Imprenta "Ecuador," 1935); Modesto Chavez Franco, *Crónicas del Guayaquil antiguo* (Guayaquil: Imprenta Municipal, 1930); Cristóbal Gangotena y Jijón, *Al margen de la historia: leyendas de frailes, pícaros y caballeros* (Quito: Imprenta Nacional, 1924); J. Gabriel Pino Roca, *Leyendas, tradiciones y páginas de historia de Guayaquil* (Guayaquil: Editorial Jouvin, 1930).

Chapter 2. Mapping the Center of the World

Epigraph: "Con el estudio de la Geografía los pueblos se animan, se despiertan, se desarrollan y mueven progresivamente, porque ella sola constituye hoy la ciencia de la vida: la elevación de miras, como suele decirse, y el provecho pecuniario ¿qué son sino frutos reales del conocimiento exacto de todo cuanto vemos y observamos en la superficie de cualquier territorio de nuestro planeta?" Luis G. Tufiño, *Servido Geográfico del Ejercito Ecuatoriano y la única base práctica en los estudios de la facultad de cienrias (proyecto)* (Quito: Imprenta y Encuadernación Nacionales, 1911), 2.

1. J. B. Harley, *The New Nature of Maps: Essays in the History of Cartography,* ed. Paul Laxton (Baltimore: Johns Hopkins University Press, 2001). Besides seminal essays such as "Silences and Secrecy: The Hidden Agenda of Cartography in Early Modern Europe," "Maps, Knowledge, and Power," and "Deconstructing the Map," the collection also includes J. H. Andrews's critique of Harley's methodology. For a consideration of Harley's (mis)use of Foucaldian and Derridean concepts of textuality, see Barbara Belyea, "Images of Power: Derrida, Foucault, Harley," *Cartographica* 29:2 (summer 1992): 1–9.

2. See Denis Wood with John Fels, *The Power of Maps* (New York: Guilford Press, 1992); and Denis Wood and John Fels, *The Natures of Maps: Cartographic Constructions of the Natural World* (Chicago: University of Chicago Press, 2008). See also Denis E. Cosgrove, ed., *Mappings* (London: Reaktion Books, 2001); and Emanuela Casti, *Reality as Representation: The Semiotics of Cartography* (Bergamo, Italy: Bergamo University Press–Sestante, 2000). An ongoing debate on the deconstruction of cartography can be found in the University of Toronto's eminent journal *Cartographica,* particularly the essays in the special issues of spring 1993 ("Introducing Cultural and Social Cartography") and autumn–winter 1998 ("Cartography and Statecraft").

3. John Pickles, *A History of Spaces: Cartographic Reason, Mapping, and the Geo-Coded World* (London: New York: Routledge, 2004).

4. Raymond B. Craib, *Cartographic Mexico: A History of State Fixations and Fugitive Landscapes* (Durham, NC: Duke University Press, 2004). See also Jordana Dym and Karl Offen, eds., *Mapping Latin America: A Cartographic Reader* (Chicago: University of Chicago Press, 2011).

5. Kagan, with Marías, *Urban Images of the Hispanic World.*

6. Barbara Mundy, *The Mapping of New Spain: Indigenous Cartography and the Maps of the* Relaciones Geográficas (Chicago: University of Chicago Press, 1996).

7. The omniscient "God's-eye view" of planar projections has been treated elo-

quently in Pickles, *History of Spaces*. For the encounter between European and Andean cosmographic views, see Mignolo, *Darker Side of the Renaissance*, chaps. 5–6.

8. Brading has analyzed the development of a sense of differentiation between creole and peninsular Spanish citizens that began soon after colonization and deepened as Spanish culture became more rooted in the American landscape. See D. A. Brading, *The First America: The Spanish Monarchy, Creole Patriots, and the Liberal State, 1492–1867* (Cambridge: Cambridge University Press, 1991). A synthesis of these arguments can be found in D. A. Brading, "Patriotism and the Nation in Colonial Spanish America," in *Constructing Collective Identities & Shaping Public Spheres: Latin American Paths*, ed. Luis Roniger and Mario Sznajder (Brighton, UK: Sussex Academic Press, 1998), 13–45.

9. Kagan, with Marías, *Urban Images in the Hispanic World*, 129–31.

10. See Phelan, *Kingdom of Quito*, 177–95, on Mariana de Jesus.

11. Fernández-Salvador, "Images and Memory," esp. chap. 3.

12. Pedro de Mercado, *Historia de la Provincia del Nuevo Reino y Quito de la Compañía de Jesus*, vol. 3 (Bogotá: Biblioteca de la Provincia de Colombia, 1957).

13. On Cantuña's chapel and the socioreligious significance of this somewhat apocryphal figure, see Susan Verdi Webster, "The Devil and the Dolorosa: History and Legend in Quito's Capilla de Cantuña," *The Americas* 67:1 (July 2010): 1–30.

14. See Fernández-Salvador, "Images and Memory," chap. 3, esp. 157–77.

15. See Safier, *Measuring the New World*; and Brading, *First America*, 422–28.

16. La Condamine's orientalizing vision has been treated by numerous scholars. See Safier, *Measuring the New World*; Poole, *Vision, Race, and Modernity*; and Cañizares-Esguerra, "Postcolonialism *avant la lettre?*"

17. On Humboldt's time in Ecuador, see Segundo E. Moreno Yañez, *Alexander von Humboldt: diarios de viaje en la Audiencia de Quito*, trans. Christiana Borchat de Moreno (Quito: Occidental Exploration and Production, 2005). See also Mary Louise Pratt, *Imperial Eyes: Travel Writing and Transculturation*, 2nd ed. (New York: Routledge, 2008); and Laura Dassow Walls, *The Passage to Cosmos: Alexander von Humboldt and the Shaping of America* (Chicago: University of Chicago Press, 2009).

18. On Quito during the Colombian period, see María Susana Vela Witt, *El Departamento del Sur en la Gran Colombia, 1822–1830* (Quito: Abya-Yala, 1999). The relevant laws can be found in *Cuerpo de leyes de la República de Colombia* (Caracas: Valentin Espinal, 1840).

19. See Francisco Miranda Ribadeneira, *La primera escuela politécnica del Ecuador: estudio histórico e interpretación* (Quito: Ediciones Feso, 1972); and Jorge Gómez R., *Las misiones pedagógicas alemanas y la educación en el Ecuador* (Quito: Abya-Yala, 1993). A firsthand account can be found in J. Gualberto Pérez, *Recuerdo histórico de la Escuela Politécnica de Quito* (Quito: Tip. Prensa Católica, 1921).

20. Teodoro Wolf, *Geográfica y geología del Ecuador* (Leipzig: F. A. Brockhaus, 1892), 4.

21. Pérez, *Recuerdo histórico*, 8.

22. Even though he was one of the most important architects and cartographers of his day, no biographical study of Pérez exists. The most detailed information on his formative years can be found in Miranda Ribadeneira, *La primera escuela*, esp. 56, 109–14,

352–53. A somewhat fanciful portrait of his ironic sense of humor can be found in Andrade Coello, *Del Quito antiguo.*

23. *El Municipio* 3:36 (October 10, 1887): n.p.

24. Ibid. The original quotation is "la oposición de la mayor parte de los dueños de
casa, que no permitían, se tomasen las medidas."

25. *El Municipio* 3:37 (October 28, 1887): n.p.

26. *El Municipio* 5:78 (October 30, 1889): n.p.; 13:67 (December 31, 1897): 532–33.

27. For an introduction to the literature on this topic, see Hobsbawm and Ranger,
Invention of Tradition; and Nora, *Realms of Memory.*

28. On cartographic commodification, see Catherine Delano-Smith, "The Map
as Commodity," in *Approaches and Challenges in a Worldwide History of Cartography,* ed.
David Woodward, Catherine Delano-Smith, and Cordell D. K. Yee (Barcelona: Institut Cartogràfic de Catalunya, 2000). See also James R. Akerman, "Twentieth-Century
American Road Maps and the Making of a National Motorized Space," in *Cartographies
of Travel and Navigation,* ed. James R. Akerman (Chicago: University of Chicago Press,
2006), 151–206.

29. On Peru, see de la Cadena, *Indigenous Mestizos;* and Poole, *Vision, Race, and Modernity.* For Mexico, see Magali M. Carrera, "From Royal Subject to Citizen: The Territory of the Body in Eighteenth- and Nineteenth-Century Mexican Visual Practices,"
in *Images of Power: Iconography, Culture and the State in Latin America,* ed. Jens Andermann and William Rowe (New York: Berghahn Books, 2005), 17–35; Craib, *Cartographic
Mexico;* and Mauricio Tenorio Trillo, *Mexico at the World's Fairs: Crafting a Modern
Nation* (Berkeley: University of California Press, 1996). For a comparative example, see
Zeynep Çelik, *Displaying the Orient: Architecture of Islam at Nineteenth-Century World's
Fairs* (Berkeley: University of California Press, 1992).

30. Betty Salazar Ponce, "De hija a hermana . . . ," in *Ecuador-España: historia y perspectiva,* ed. María Elena Porras and Pedro Calvo-Sotelo (Quito: Embajada de España,
2001), 152. See also *La République de l'Équateur et sa participation à la Exposition Universelle
de 1900* (Paris: Imprimerie du "Correo de Paris," 1900).

31. Brooke Larson, *Trials of Nation Making: Liberalism, Race, and Ethnicity in the Andes, 1810–1910* (Cambridge: Cambridge University Press, 2004), 138–39.

32. Diario de Avisos, *El Ecuador en Chicago* (New York: A. E. Chasmar, 1894).

33. Higley primarily worked for American businesses across Latin America, eventually settling in Peru. See H. G. Higley, *Map of the Mosquito Shore, Nicaragua, Central
America* (New York: G. W. and C. B. Colton & Co., 1894); and H. G. Higley, *Plano pan-
orámico de la ciudad de Guayaquil* (Guayaquil, 1899).

34. Walter William Ristow, *American Maps and Mapmakers: Commerical Cartography
in the Nineteenth Century* (Detroit: Wayne State University Press, 1985).

35. *Mission du Service Géographique de l'Armée pour la mesure d'un arc de méridien équatorial en Amérique du Sud sous le controle scientifique de l'Académie des Sciences, 1899–1906,*
multiple vols. (Paris: Gauthier-Villars, 1910–1922).

36. Vacas Galindo's conception of the history of Ecuadorian territoriality is summarized in his first book, *La integridad territorial del Ecuador* (Quito: Tipografía y en-

cuadernación Salesiana, 1905). See also *Manifesto de la Junta Patriótica Nacional* (Quito: Imprenta y encuadernación nacionales, 1910). For more about the history of the study of territorial rights, see Adam Szászdi, "The Historiography of the Republic of Ecuador," *Hispanic American Historical Review* 44:4 (November 1964): 537–43.

37. "Acta de la primera Junta preparatoria," *Boletín de la Sociedad Geográfica de Quito* 1:1 (1911): 66–67; "El Registro Civil," *Boletín de la Sociedad Geográfica de Quito* 1:1 (1911): 74–75; "La Región Oriental," *Boletín de la Sociedad Geográfica de Quito* 1:1 (1911): 77–78.

38. Luis G. Tufiño, *Servicio Geográfico del Ejercito Ecuatoriano y la única base práctica en los estudios de la facultad de ciencias (proyecto)* (Quito: Imprenta y Encuadernación Nacionales, 1911), 1–4, 16–26.

39. "Informe del Secretario General de la Sociedad Geográfica de Quito, Señor Francisco Talbot, presentado al finalizar el primer año social de 1910 a 1911," *Boletín de la Sociedad Geográfica de Quito* 1:1 (1911): 92–98.

40. Tenorio notes the lack of destruction in the planning of the Porfirian capital, which stands in stark constrast to the Western European example. Instead, he describes the expansion of the city as a process of colonizing the environs and underscores the particularly racist imagination behind the plan and its discrediting of the existing inhabitants, that is, peasants. See Tenorio Trillo, "1910 Mexico City," 86.

41. Carrera Andrade, *El volcán y el colibrí,* 21–22.

42. Archivo Nacional del Ecuador (hereafter ANE): Civiles, 1° El Sagrario XXVIII (July 28, 1909).

43. Jose D. Laso, *Quito a la vista* (Quito: J. D. Laso and J. R. Cruz, 1911); and *Quito a la vista, segunda entrega* (Quito: J. D. Laso and J. R.Cruz, 1912).

44. Angel Emilio Hidalgo and María Elena Bedoya, "Guayaquil y Quito: la imagen deseada, 1910–1930," *Boletín de la Biblioteca Municipal de Guayaquil* 87 (2003): 169–79.

45. Humberto Peña Orejuela, *Guia de Bolsillo de Quito* (Quito: Talleres Tipográficos Nacionales, 1920). Subsequent editions appeared throughout the 1920s and 1930s, with the last coming out in 1940.

46. J. Enrique Ribadeneira and Luis Cornelio Diaz V., *Cien años de legislación militar, 1830–1930* (Quito: Editorial Gutenberg, 1930), 27.

47. Froilán Holguín Balcázar, *Plano comercial de Quito* (Quito, 1920). For more on Holguín's life, see Froilán Holguín Balcázar, *Mi capricho de hacerme hombre* (Guayaquil: Editorial Senefelder, 1936), esp. 15–22, where he details his first journey to Guayaquil.

48. *Gaceta Municipal* 10:94 (February 4, 1922): 11–12.

49. This ordinance also echoes the similar performance of gratitude displayed by the municipality when presenting Gualberto Pérez with a medal upon its acceptance of his map of the city in 1888.

50. For more on the 1922 celebrations, see Ernesto Capello, "The City as Anachronism: Remembering Quito in the Liberal Era" (MA thesis, University of Texas at Austin, 2001), 63–72.

51. See Luís T. Paz y Miño, *Apuntaciones para una geografía urbana de Quito* (Mexico City: Instituto Panamericano de Geografía e Historia, 1960); *Guía para la historia de*

la cartografía ecuatoriana: Primera Exposición Geográfica nacional (Quito: Imprenta del Ministerio del Tesoro, 1948).

52. *El Instituto Geográfico Militar a través de la historia* (Quito: Instituto Geográfico Militar, 2002), 31–32, 42–47.

53. Ibid., 47–55.

54. See *Plano de la ciudad de Quito levantado por el Servicio Geográfico Militar y obsequiado al muy I. Concejo Municipal* (Quito: Servicio Geográfico Militar, 1932), also reproduced in *El Instituto Geográfico Militar,* 55.

55. *Plano de la ciudad de Quito hecho para actividad* (Quito: Fotolitografía Editorial Chimborazo, 1931).

56. *El Instituto Geográfico Militar,* 59.

57. Holguín also crafted views of Guayaquil and Cuenca during the same year.

58. "Informe del Secretario General de la Sociedad Geográfica de Quito."

59. A. I. Chiriboga N. and Georges Perrier, *Las misiones científicas francesas en el Ecuador: 1735–1744; 1899–1906* (Quito: Imprenta Nacional, 1936), esp. iii–ix.

60. Humberto Vera H., *Equator: History and Geography of the Equatorial Monument,* trans. Adriana Vera S. (Quito: Ediciones Ecuador, 1990), 19–20.

Chapter 3. Hispanismo

Epigraph: Julio [Giulio] Aristíde Sartorio, "La ciudad de Quito es un Joyero," *Alas,* December 1934, 21. Sartorio was an Italian painter who visited Quito in 1924. The original text reads, "La ciudad de Quito es un joyero precioso y germen espiritual, testigo de los lazos que unen al Ecuador con la latinidad renaciente. Quito, sin arte gótico, que nació para el futuro, no se deje defraudar jamás por la presionante modernidad y conserve para el porvenir puro de la América Latina la forma y el alma con el cual nació."

1. Extensive discussions of Quito's primitive services can be found in the travelogues of Ernest Charton, Ida Pfeiffer, Albert Franklin, and others. For a summary, see Jill Fitzell, "Teorizando la diferencia en los Andes del Ecuador: viajeros europeos, la ciencia del exotismo y las imágenes de los indios," in *Imágenes e imagineros: representaciones de los indígenas ecuatorianos, siglos XIX y XX,* ed. Blanca Juratorio (Quito: FLACSO, 1994). See also Poole, *Vision, Race, and Modernity.*

2. The classic work on the Spanish contribution to Hispanism is Frederick Pike's *Hispanismo, 1898–1936: Spanish Conservatives and Liberals and Their Relations with Spanish America* (South Bend, IN: University of Notre Dame Press, 1971), while an overview of activities designed to foster communication can be found in Isidro Sepúlveda Muñoz, "Medio siglo de asociacionismo americanista español 1885–1936," in *Espacio, Tiempo y Forma* 4 (1991): 271–290. An excellent discussion of the multifaceted nature of Spanish intellectual production during the *fin-de-siglo* can be found in Javier Varela's *La novela en España: los intelectuales y el problema español* (Madrid: Taurus, 1999). Christopher Schmidt-Nowara has provided a new framework for understanding Spanish imperial

policy in the nineteenth-century Caribbean through the lens of national history writing in *The Conquest of History: Spanish Colonialism and National Histories in the Nineteenth Century* (Pittsburgh: University of Pittsburgh Press, 2006). For Mexican Hispanism, see Ricardo Pérez Montfort, *Hispanismo y Falange: los sueños imperiales de la derecha española* (Mexico City: Fondo de Cultura Económica, 1992). A full-length study of Ecuadorian Hispanism has yet to be developed. An introductory sketch can be found in Guillermo Bustos, "El Hispanismo en el Ecuador," in *Ecuador-España*, ed. Porras and Calvo-Sotelo. See also Ernesto Capello, "Hispanismo casero: la invención del Quito hispano," in *Procesos: revista ecuatoriana de historia* 20 (fall 2003–spring 2004); and Guillermo Bustos, "La hispanización de la memoria pública en el cuarto centenario de fundación de Quito," in *Etnicidad y poder en los países andinos,* ed. Christian Büschges, Guillermo Bustos, and Olaf Kaltmeier (Quito: Corporación Editora Nacional, 2007), 111–34.

3. On the ethnic composition of the city center, see Carrión, *Quito: crisis y política urbana;* Kingman Garcés, *La ciudad y los otros;* and Espinosa Apolo, *Mestizaje.*

4. Cañizares-Esguerra presents an intriguing analysis of European images of the barbaric American wilderness in his comparison of Spanish and Puritan attitudes toward a landscape peopled with demons and satanic forces. See Jorge Cañizares-Esguerra, *Puritan Conquistadors: Iberianizing the Atlantic, 1550–1700* (Stanford, CA: Stanford University Press, 2006). Other extensive discussions of this religious and cultural encounter include Brading, *First America;* Patricia Seed, *Ceremonies of Possession in Europe's Conquest of the New World, 1492–1640* (Cambridge: Cambridge University Press, 1995); Serge Gruzinski, *Images at War: Mexico from Columbus to Blade Runner (1492–2019),* trans. Heather MacLean (Durham, NC: Duke University Press, 2001); Richard Morse, "Cities as People," in *Rethinking the Latin American City,* ed. Morse and Hardoy, 3–19; and John Leddy Phelan, *The Millennial Kingdom of the Franciscans in the New World* (Berkeley: University of California Press, 1970).

5. See Kenneth R. Mills, *Idolatry and Its Enemies: Colonial Andean Religion and Extirpation, 1640–1750* (Princeton: Princeton University Press, 1997).

6. José Joaquín Olmedo, *Obra poética* (Quito: Editorial Casa de la Cultura Ecuatoriana, 1971), 78.

7. Although the indigenous coerced labor system known as the *mita* was repealed during the Cortes, Olmedo's were some of the earliest pleas for its abolition, which were met with skepticism. For more on his time in Cádiz, see Luis Andrade Reimers, *Olmedo: el estadista* (Quito: Editorial Ediguias, 1993), 48–50.

8. For example, consider Huayna Capac's opening speech: "¡Guerra al usurpador! — ¿Qué le debemos? / ¿luces, costumbres, religión o leyes . . . ? / ¡Si ellos fueron estúpidos, viciosos, / feroces y por fin supersticiosos! / ¿Qué religión? ¡la de Jesús? . . . ¡Blasfemos! / Sangre, plomo veloz, cadenas fueron / Los sacramentos santos que trajeron. / ¡Oh religión! ¡oh fuente pura y santa / de amor y de consuelo para el hombre! / ¡cuántos males se hicieron en tu nombre!" Olmedo, *Obra poética,* 165.

9. Rodríguez, *Emergence of Spanish America.*

10. A clear summary of the events surrounding Flores's attempted mission can be

found in Jorge W. Villacres Moscoso, *Historia diplomática de la República del Ecuador* (Guayaquil: Imprenta de la Universidad de Guayaquil, 1971), 2:222–51. For a more in-depth analysis of Flores's political career and predilection toward monarchism in the 1840s, see Mark J. Van Aken, *King of the Night: Juan José Flores and Ecuador, 1824–1864* (Berkeley: University of California Press, 1989).

11. Aimer Granados García, "Congresos e intelectuales en los inicios de un proyecto y de una conciencia continental latinoamericana, 1826–1860," in *Construcción de las identidades latinoamericanas: ensayos de historia intelectual (siglos XIX y XX)*, ed. Aimer Granados García and Carlos Marichal (Mexico City: El Colegio de México, Centro de Estudios Históricos, 2004).

12. Alonso Zamora Vicente, *La Real Academia Española* (Madrid: Espasa Calpe, S.A., 1999), 345.

13. Pike, *Hispanismo, 1898–1936*, 33.

14. Zamora, *La Real Academia*, 345–48.

15. For more on Unión Iberoamericano, see Muñoz, "Medio siglo," 273–78; and Varela, *La novela en España*. Ecuador's contribution to the 1892 quadricentennial exposition is treated in Salazar, "De hija a hermana," in *Ecuador-España*, ed. Porras and Calvo-Sotelo, 156–59.

16. On regionalism and transcendent national histories, see Josep Maria Fradera, *Cultura nacional en una societat dividida: patriotisme i cultura a Catalunya (1838–1868)* (Barcelona: Curial, 1992). See also Varela, *La novela en España*; and Schmidt-Nowara, *Conquest of History*.

17. Pike, *Hispanismo, 1898–1936*, 67–68.

18. In the original, "fruto valioso del esfuerzo civilizador y cristiano de la raza hispana." Quoted in Ascensión Martínez Riaza, "El Perú y España durante el oncenio: el hispanismo en el discurso oficial y en las manifestaciones simbólicas (1919–1930)," *Historica* 18:2 (December 1994): 349.

19. The exposition had been planned since 1905 and was initially meant to be a world's fair, but it was scaled down to just Spanish America by 1908 and later expanded to include the "other" Iberia, that is, Portugal and Brazil. A variety of factors, largely economic, kept the exposition on the drawing board for another two decades. There were plazas dedicated to Spain and another to the Americas, which housed the colonial art exhibit. National palaces existed for all the Spanish American republics. See Eduardo Rodriguez Bernal, *Historia de la Exposición Ibero-Americana de Sevilla de 1929* (Seville: Ayuntamiento de Sevilla, 1994); and Tenorio Trillo, *Mexico at the World's Fairs*, 220–40. For a discussion of the exposition as a catalyst for anti-Spanish sentiment, see Pérez Montfort, *Hispanismo y Falange*, 61–64.

20. Raanan Rein, "Francoist Spain and Latin America, 1936–1953," in *Fascism Outside Europe: The European Impulse against Domestic Conditions in the Diffusion of Global Fascism*, ed. Stein Ugelvik Larsen (Boulder, CO: Social Science Monographs, 2001); Nicolás Cárdenas and Mauricio Tenorio, "Mexico 1920s-1940s: Revolutionary Government, Reactionary Politcs," in *Fascism Outside Europe*, ed. Larsen; Pérez Montfort, *Hispanismo y Falange*.

21. The growing number of these studies also found resonance in Latin America. For example, the Spanish scholar M. Romera Navarro published a book in 1917 detailing the history and growth of North American Hispanist studies. See M. Romera Navarro, *El hispanismo en Norte-América: exposición y crítica de su aspecto literario* (Madrid: Renacimiento, 1917).

22. In the early work *Our America,* for instance, he conceives of the new American man as being characterized by multiplicity and creativity. However, he soon began to find even more creativity south of the border. For a good discussion of this aspect of his thought, and the transition to Hispanophilia, see Ricardo Fernández Borchart, *Waldo Frank: un puente entre las dos Américas* (Coruña, Spain: Universidade da Coruña, 1997), 22–37.

23. Despite Frank's contribution to the widening of the American audience for Latin American literature, Irene Rostagno notes that his literary sympathy with the classical authors of the nineteenth and early twentieth century and consequent disdain for the more avant-garde writings of the early *vanguardia* "reinforced the prevailing notion of Latin American literature as provincial, local color writing." Irene Rostagno, *Searching for Recognition: The Promotion of Latin American Literature in the United States* (Westport, CT: Greenwood Press, 1997), 15. Although Rostagno is correct, Frank's regard for the romantic tradition should be viewed as an outgrowth of a strong tradition of *hispanistas* revering provincial life for its own sake, from Clarín to Güiraldes to Gálvez, and not merely as a reactionary attitude toward contemporary literature.

24. Jeane Delaney, "The Discovery of Spain: The Hispanismo of Manuel Gálvez," in *Bridging the Atlantic: Toward a Reassessment of Iberian and Latin American Cultural Ties,* ed. Marina Pérez de Mendiola (Albany: State University of New York Press, 1996), 74–79.

25. See "A los escritores ecuatorianos," *Unión Iberoamericana,* February 10, 1888, 16, about the library; and "La Unión Iberoamericana," *Unión Iberoamericana,* January 1, 1888, 4, about their vision of regional conflicts. See "Tratado de comercio entre España y el Ecuador," *Unión Iberoamericana,* March 15, 1888, 22–23, concerning the group's efforts toward securing the treaty. See "Tratados suscritos entre el Ecuador y España, 1840–2001," in *Ecuador-España,* ed. Porras and Calvo-Sotelo, 250, regarding the signing of the protocol to secure such a treaty.

26. Good studies of González Suárez include Enrique Ayala Mora, "Introducción," in *Federico González Suárez: la polémica sobre el estado laico,* ed. Enrique Ayala Mora (Quito: Corporación Editora Nacional, 1980); and Castillo Illingworth, *La iglesia y la revolución liberal.*

27. See Marcelino Menéndez Pelayo, *Epistolario,* multiple vols. (Madrid: Fundación Universitaria Española, 1981–1989), esp. 6:215, 343; 7:289, 335; and 19:293, 541.

28. See Varela, *La novela en España,* 31, for a discussion of how Menéndez Pelayo inherited these values from his early teachers, especially Joaquim Rubió, and also 50–54, for a greater explication of Menéndez Pelayo's providential philosophy. For González Suárez, see Gabriel Cevallos García, *La historia en el Ecuador,* in *Reflexiones sobre la his-*

toria del Ecuador, primera parte (Quito: Ediciones del Banco Central del Ecuador, 1987), 188–89.

29. As he put it in the introduction to the *Historia general,* "La historia, como enseñanza moral, es una verdadera ciencia, que tiene un objeto nobilísimo, cual es hacer palpar á los hombres el gobierno de la Providencia divina en las sociedades humanas." See Federico González Suárez, *Historia general de la República del Ecuador* (rpt., Quito: Edit. Casa de la Cultura Ecuatoriana, 1969), 1:22.

30. González Suárez, *Historia general,* 1:25.

31. His only discussion of independence came in various speeches and pamphlets scattered throughout the era. In these, he stressed that the organic growth of the Ecuadorian nation led to a necessary separation from Spain, thus downplaying the abruptness of the break. For a good example of these ideas, see "Discurso pronunciado el día 10 de agosto de 1881 en la Catedral de Quito," in Federico González Suárez, *Obras oratorias* (Quito: AYMESA, 1992), 193–211.

32. González Suárez, *Historia general,* 1:1049–102.

33. Federico González Suárez, *Historia general de la República del Ecuador,* vol. 2 (rpt., Quito: Edit. Casa de la Cultura Ecuatoriana, 1970). The key passages are in chap. 10 of Tomo IV.

34. Reginaldo M. Duranti, *La veracidad del Señor Doctor Don Federico González Suárez en orden a ciertos hechos referidos en el Tomo IV de su Historia general* (Santo Domingo: privately printed, 1894), v, 37–43. See also Pedro Schumacher, *Teocrada o demoniocracia? Cristo o Lucifer? Quién vencera? Quién como Dios!* 2nd ed. (Freiburg, Germany: B. Herder, 1897).

35. See "Defensa de mi criterio histórico," in González Suárez, *Historia general,* vol. 3.

36. "De la actitud que conviene a los católicos seglares en el Ecuador en las circunstancias presentes" (1908), in *Homenaje del Comité Central a la memoria del Excmo. Y Rvdmo. Sr. Dr. Dn. Federico González Suárez, Meritisimo Arzobispo de Quito en el primer centenario de su nacimiento* (Quito: Imprenta de la Universidad Central, 1944).

37. Luna Tamayo, "Orígenes del movimiento obrero," 289–92.

38. Szászdi, "Historiography of the Republic," 514–15.

39. Jacinto Jijón y Caamaño, "Examen crítico de la veracidad de la *Historia del Reino de Quito* del P. Juan de Velasco de la Compañía de Jesús," in *Boletín de la Sociedad Ecuatoriana de Estudios Históricos Américanos* 1:1 (June–July 1919): 33–63. See also Pío Jaramillo Alvarado, *El indio ecuatoriano,* 3rd ed. (Quito: Talleres Gráficos del Estado, 1936); Szászdi, "Historiography of the Republic," 506–11.

40. Jacinto Jijón y Caamaño, *Política conservadora,* vol. 1 (Riobamba: La Buena Prensa del Chimborazo, 1929), 128–29.

41. Ibid., 1:147.

42. Julio Tobar Donoso, *Catolicismo social* (Quito: Editorial Ecuatoriana, 1936); *García Moreno y la instrucción pública* (Quito: Editorial Ecuatoriana, 1940); *Las relaciones en-*

tre la iglesia y el estado Ecuatoriano: resumen histórico (Quito: Editorial Ecuatoriana, 1938); *Monografías históricas* (Quito: Editorial Ecuatoriana, 1938).

43. Isaac Barrera, *Relación de las fiestas del primer centenario de la batalla de Pichincha, 1822–1922* (Quito: Talleres Tipográficos Nacionales, 1922).

44. Archivo Gangotena Jijón, Quito (hereafter AGJ), 07-04, Notas 1 (G) Varios años, Quito, Currículo vitae; AGJ/Q, 08-18, Epist. 1 Varios Siglo XX, June 10, 1929.

45. Gangotena y Jijón, *Al margen de la historia*. See also Ernesto Capello, "City, Chronicle, Chronotope: Re-Constructing and Writing Old Quito," *Journal of Latin American Urban Studies* 6 (fall 2004): 41–43.

46. González Suárez, *Historia general,* vol. 3, 401–2.

47. No biography of Navarro exists, but useful sketches can be found in Centro de Estudios Pedagógicos e Hispanoamericanos de Panama, *Summary of Ten Lectures on Ecuadorian Art by José Gabriel Navarro* (Panamá: Centro de Estudios, 1935); and in Jorge Salvador Lara's contribution to José Gabriel Navarro, *Estudios históricos* (Quito: Grupo Aymesa, 1995).

48. For example, see José Gabriel Navarro, *La escultura en el Ecuador (siglos XVI al XVIII)* (Madrid: Real Academia de Bellas Artes de San Fernando, 1929), esp. 4, or his essay on the works included in the 1930 Madrid exhibition devoted to Spanish art in the Indies. See Sociedad Española de Amigos del Arte, *Aportación al estudio de la cultura española en las Indias: catálogo general ilustrado de la Exposición* (Madrid: ESPASA-CALPE, 1930).

49. Sociedad Española, *Aportación al estudio de la cultura española,* 61–62.

50. Susan Webster has noted substantial indigenous influence on the decorative aspects of many of Quito's main churches, especially in the seventeenth- and eighteenth-century temples like El Sagrario, Guápulo, and La Compañía. She argues that this arose from the fact that Spanish overseers paid less attention to façade and columnar decoration. See Webster, *Arquitectura y empres,* 49.

51. Schmidt-Nowara, *Conquest of History,* 130–60, esp. 134–35, 150–54.

52. The original reads "edificios espléndidos, conventos e iglesias de rara magnificencia, cuadros y estatuas, mobiliario civil y religioso en cantidad formidable, joyas de delicada orfebrería, etc. . . . era un testigo mudo que abonaba en [la defensa de España]." José Gabriel Navarro, "El Estado Actual de los Estudios Históricos en el Ecuador y su importancia para la historia de España," in Navarro, *Estudio históricos,* 47.

53. José Gabriel Navarro, "El municipio de América durante la asistencia de España," in Navarro, *Estudios históricos,* 177–82.

54. The original quotations are "la unión de los Quiteños en el culto al pasado" and "Quito se perpetuará por su peregrina belleza en la devoción del extranjero curioso y será siempre un centro de turismo." José Gabriel Navarro, "De cómo Quito sería siempre un centro de turismo," *El comercio,* August 11, 1926, 3.

55. Juan de Dios Navas E. and Julio Tobar Donoso, *Discursos de ingreso y recepción en la Academia Nacional de Historia el 6 de enero de 1927* (Quito: Tipográfica de la "Prensa Católica," 1927), 41–42.

56. See Capello, "City as Anachronism," 52–72.

57. *Gaceta municipal,* 16:40 (June 30, 1931): 468–70.

58. José Rumazo González, "Las fundaciones de Santiago y San Francisco de Quito," *Gaceta municipal* 17:49 (March 31, 1932): n.p.

59. *Gaceta municipal,* 19:71 (January 31, 1934): 23.

60. *Gaceta municipal* 19:73 (March 31, 1934): 111–4.

61. See Ernesto Capello, "Arquivo: Jacinto Jijón y Caamaño, 'La fecha de fundación de Quito,'" *Brújula* 5:1 (December 2006): 37–43, concerning the controversy over the date of the city's founding. See also Bustos, "La hispanización," 113–16.

62. The original reads "la fundación de la ciudad de Quito ha de considerarse como la iniciación y aún el establecimiento de la nacionalidad ecuatoriana." "Solemnizase el cuarto centenario de la fundación de Quito," *El comercio,* August 28, 1934, 16.

63. A summary of the month's events can be found in "Programa de festejos acordados por el Concejo municipal en conmemoración del IV centenario de fundación española d' Quito," *El comercio,* December 6, 1934, 3–5. For a further description of the art exhibit, see Rosaura E. Galarza H., "Exposición Artística de los Conventos de Quito," *Alas,* December 1934, 52–53.

64. With the exception of two volumes in the late 1930s devoted to González Suárez, whose strong historiographical association with Hispanism has already been noted, the series has reproduced data only from Quito's colonial period. The two volumes on González Suárez were Nicolas Jiménez's biography, published in 1936, and González Suárez's *Defensa de mi criterio histórico* (1937).

65. See *Gaceta municipal* 19:77 (August 28, 1934).

66. Besides the focus on the colonial era, the selection of photographs included portraits of many of the contributors to the volume but no other representation of Quito's modern ways.

67. Only a portrait of the eighteenth-century critic of the crown, Eugenio Espejo, represents any form of independence sentiment.

68. *Gaceta municipal* 19:79 (October–December 1934): 264.

69. José Gabriel Navarro, "Quito," *El comercio,* December 6, 1934, 3–7.

70. "Así como la ciudad tiene dos aspectos, el uno colonial, que se observa de preferencia en el corazón de la urbe, en las zonas centrales y otro, el moderno que sonríe especialmente en las ciudadelas y se extiende por el norte de Quito, cabe considerar, dentro de las mismas calles, lugares, lo que fue la ciudad antigua y cual es su característica actual." "Los grabados d'este número," *El comercio,* December 6, 1934, 10.

71. "Quito Cuadricentenario, cuatro estilos arquitectónicos," *El comercio,* December 6, 1934, 16.

72. Bustos, "La hispanización," 126–28.

73. Ibid., 116.

74. See Jacinto Jijón y Caamaño, *Sebastián de Benalcázar,* 3 vols. (Quito: Corporación de Estudios y Publicaciones, 1983). Only the first volume was published in 1936. Jijón had not yet completed the third and final volume when he died in 1950.

75. "El Ilustre Municipio de Quito ha creado la 'Orden de Caballeros de Quito,'" *El comercio,* November 15, 1942, 17.

76. There is an ironic nature to this statue's history, as it was erected on May 24, that is, the anniversary of Quito's liberation from the Spanish. See Gonzalo Zaldumbide, "Sebastián de Benalcázar," in Zaldumbide, *Significado de España en América, ensayos* (Quito: Letramía, 2002), 115–29.

77. The institute's Web site can be accessed at http://iech.tripod.com.

78. Carlos Jaramillo Abarca, "Quito, 468 años de historia," *El comercio,* December 7, 2002, A5.

79. "Ecuador/Quito," LOC/PP, NYWTS-Subj/Geog.

80. Benjamín Gento Sanz, *Guia del turista en la iglesia y convento de San Francisco de Quito* (Quito: Imprenta Americana, 1940).

81. *Gaceta municipal* 26:97 (August 10, 1940): 7.

82. J. M. González de Valcárcel, *Restauración monumental y "puesta en valor" de las ciudades americanas (Architectural Conservation and Enhancement of Historic Towns in America)* (Barcelona: Editorial Blume, 1977).

Chapter 4. Governance and the Sovereign Cabildo

1. The original quote is "esta capital ha sido muy desatendida." "Carlos Freire Z. al Presidente del Concejo," *El municipio* 12:1 (December 20, 1895): 1–2.

2. Achig, *El proceso urbano de Quito;* Carrión, *Quito: crisis y política urbana.*

3. Kingman Garcés, *La ciudad y los otros.*

4. de la Cadena, *Indigenous Mestizos;* Overmyer-Velázquez, *Visions of the Emerald City.*

5. See Herzog, *Defining Nations,* for a genealogy of kinship networks across the Quito region.

6. On cabildo politics, see Pilar Ponce Leiva, *Certeza ante la incertidumbre: élite y cabildo de Quito en el siglo XVII* (Quito: Abya-Yala, 1998), esp. 364–74, 430–31. See also Minchom, *People of Quito,* 35–37, on the cabildo's participation in the local elite's encroachment on indigenous common lands in the eighteenth century.

7. Federica Morelli, "Las reformas en Quito: la redistribución del poder y la consolidación de la jurisdicción municipal (1765–1809)," in *Jahrbuch für Geschichte von Staat, Wirtschaft und Gessellschaft Lateinamerikas,* no. 34 (1997): 193–206.

8. Enrique Ayala Mora, "El municipio en el siglo XIX," in *ProcesoS: revista ecuatoriana de historia,* no. 1 (1991): 72. For a discussion of the role of the municipality in and after independence, see Federica Morelli, *Territorio o nazione: riforma e dissoluzione dello spazio imperiale in Ecuador, 1765–1830* (Soveria Mannelli, Italy: Rubbetino Editore, 2001), chap. 5. This situation was not unique to Quito, as has been noted in Guerra, *Modernidad e independencias.*

9. Ayala Mora, "El municipio," 80–81.

10. "Ley de régimen municipal – 1878," in *Colección de leyes, ordenanzas y contratos* (Guayaquil: Imprenta Americana, 1890), 24–27.

11. Ibid., 28.

12. See Pineo, *Social and Economic Reform,* chap. 4.

13. See Kingman Garcés, *La ciudad y los otros*.

14. "Varios asuntos," *El municipio* 3:30 (July 15, 1887): n.p.

15. "Decreto Legislativo," *El municipio* 6:98 (January 17, 1891): n.p.

16. "Actas," *El municipio* 2:24 (February 23, 1887): n.p.

17. "Ordenanzas," *El municipio* 9:145 (May 27, 1893): 3–4.

18. "Actas," *El municipio* 9:150 (August 29, 1893): 6.

19. "Actas," *El municipio* 10:175 (December 7, 1894): 8.

20. "Solicitud presentada por los dueños de las fábricas de jabón para que no se lleve á efecto la ordenanza aludida," *El municipio* 9:134 (January 13, 1893): 4–5.

21. "Informe de Manuel Jijón B., 9 enero 1900," *El municipio* 16:118 (February 28, 1900): 984.

22. Taxes on liquor introduced into the city were lower than those on liquor produced within the city. Advocates for the *aguardiente* producers of these two regions were able to defeat the measure, claiming that it would lead to double taxation. See "Actas," *El municipio* 2:23 (January 15, 1887): n.p.

23. As Paz y Miño put it, "se ve que se compone de las dos palabras siguientes: trans que significa mas allá, y vía camino. Tranvía es, pues, un camino que no reconoce límites." See "Actas – 9 febrero 1889," *El municipio* 5:70 (May 24, 1889): n.p.

24. "Informe del Jefe Político," *El municipio* 5:68 (April 27, 1889): n.p.

25. Members of the Concejo Municipal elected the council's president for a period of six months. Andrade Marín received only a single vote, presumably his own, in the 1890 election. "Acta de Instalación," *El municipio* 4:64 (February 12, 1889): n.p.

26. "Ordenanza," *El municipio* 6:97 (December 30, 1890): n.p. This included S/.3,000 for the marketplace, S/.1,696 to pay for the importation of a manual handcart from the United States as the first step in constructing urban trams, another S/.1,000 for debts, and S/.2,000 for public lighting.

27. As of 1883, the firm of Vinuesa and Ontaneda was to be given preferential treatment in the installation of electric lighting. Their outrageous cost and lack of efficiency in contacting the municipality about changes led the council to complain that they represented an obstacle to progress. This led to pleas to eliminate the firm's privileged bargaining position. See, e.g., "Varios asuntos," *El municipio* 3:30 (July 15, 1887): n.p.

28. "Actas – 6 julio 1887," *El municipio* 3:34 (September 10, 1887): n.p.

29. Dietz was the premier U.S. manufacturer of kerosene lamps throughout the nineteenth and twentieth centuries. See Robert Erwin Dietz, *A Leaf from the Past* (New York: R. E. Dietz Company, 1913).

30. For the transition from candle to gas to electrical lighting, see Wolfgang Schivelbusch, *Disenchanted Night: The Industrialization of Light in the Nineteenth Century*, trans. Angela Davies (Berkeley: University of California Press, 1988), 50–69.

31. The original reads "Nuestro pueblo es pobre y no hay que molestarle con ese lujo de contribuciones. Más tarde, cuando el invento esté perfeccionado, de suyo se ha de venir á nuestro suelo, sin necesidad de lanzarnos al campo de las conjeturas." "Actas – 5 julio 1888," *El municipio* 4:54 (August 10, 1888), n.p.

32. "Actas – 5 julio 1888," n.p.

33. "Ordenanza – Abril 26, 1892," *El municipio* 8:122 (May 5, 1892): n.p.

34. "Informe del Jefe Político al Concejo Cantonal de Quito – 1894," *El municipio* 10:161 (February 28, 1894): 8.

35. Linda Rodríguez has described the impact of Liberal fiscal decentralization on national finances, noting its long-term negative effects, which resulted from wasteful spending and the stagnation of many projects due to a lack of effective oversight. Although Rodríguez points out the importance of local interests in shaping this policy, she does not identify the degree to which this policy bolstered municipal power throughout the country. See Rodríguez, *Search for Public Policy*, 88–117.

36. See Clark, *Redemptive Work*.

37. "Plaza de mercado," *El municipio* 13:45 (May 18, 1897): 353.

38. See the issues of *El municipio* from 12:1 (December 20, 1895) to 12:5 (January 17, 1896) for these changes. An additional attempt to alter the volume number from twelve to one appeared in the January 17, 1896, edition, a change that did not stick.

39. "Variedades," *El municipio* 12:12 (March 14, 1896): 73.

40. For Pérez, see "Patriotismo," *El municipio* 12:7 (January 31, 1896): 33–34. For Naranjo, see "Variedades," *El municipio* 12:12 (March 14, 1896): 73.

41. "Ordenanza," *El municipio* 12:4 (January 10, 1896): 13.

42. "Actas – 15 April 1896," *El municipio* 12:17 (May 13, 1896): 111.

43. "Oficio de RE Patiño a Eloy Alfaro, 19 septiembre 1896," *El municipio* 12:26 (October 3, 1896): 183; "Actas – 26 noviembre 1896," *El municipio* 12:32 (December 12, 1896): 236–37.

44. "Plaza de Mercado," *El municipio* 13:45 (May 18, 1897): 352.

45. "Ordenanza para vender terrenos municipales," *El municipio* 13:56 (September 17, 1897): 431–34.

46. Mario Vásconez, Andrea Carrión, Ana María Goetschel, and Nancy Sánchez, *Breve historia de los servicios en la ciudad de Quito* (Quito: CIUDAD, 1997), 51–53.

47. "Ordenanza," *El municipio* 13:51 (August 14, 1897): 395–96.

48. The *empedrado* or cobblestone paving of the street unit was described by Vidal Enríquez Ante in "Informe del Jefe Político," *El municipio* 13:67 (December 13, 1897): 533. The tax for street cleaning was passed February 21, 1899, though it had been discussed since late 1898. It actually shrank the official vision of the *centro* by pushing the western boundary one block farther east, to Carrera Cuenca, and the northern boundary one block farther south, to Carrera Manabí. See "Ordenanza de impuestos a predios urbanos," *El municipio* 15:99 (March 9, 1899): 819–20.

49. The contract for arc lighting was signed with local industrialists who had been the first to successfully create public lighting in the city, including Manuel Jijón Larrea (father of Jacinto Jijón y Caamaño) and Julio Urrutia. Joined by Victor Gangotena, they signed a contract with the municipality in late 1899. Progress proceeded so slowly that the *concejo* regularly complained about the contractors' inefficiency through mid-1900, yet renewed efforts after the threat of retaliation appear to have led to reports of progress in November 1901 and February 1902. See "Contrato," *El municipio* 15:112 (October 25, 1899): 931.

50. "Contrato sobre tranvías eléctricos," *El municipio* 20:201 (October 5, 1904): 1689–91.

51. "Actas – 28 mayo 1906," *El municipio* 22:255 (June 26, 1906): 170–72.

52. "Ordenanzas," *El municipio* 20:196 (August 13, 1904): 1649–52.

53. See Kingman Garcés, *La ciudad y los otros,* esp. chap. 6, "Los primeros higienistas y el cuidado de la ciudad," in which Kingman analyzes the use of the municipal police for street cleaning and public health advocates' discursive creation of an unhealthy city desperately needing reform. See also Kingman Garcés, "Quito, vida social y modificaciones."

54. "Actas – 29 octubre 1905," *El municipio* 21:231 (November 1905): 1933.

55. Clark, *Redemptive Work,* 147–54.

56. For more on Andrade Marín's work that year, see Karine Peyronnie and René de Maximy, *Quito inattendu: Le Centre Historique en devenir* (Paris: CNRS Éditions, 2002), 54–62.

57. "Oficio de Feliciano Checa a Ministerio del Interior," in *El municipio* 22:262 (September 6, 1906): 228.

58. República del Ecuador, *Decreto Supremo de 31 de octubre de 1907 ordenando una gran exposición nacional en Quito para el 10 de agosto de 1909* (Quito: Imprenta Nacional, 1907).

59. Eloy Alfaro, *Mensaje del Presidente de la República al Poder Legislativo sobre Exposición Nacional* (Quito: Imprenta Nacional, 1908), 5.

60. See Tenorio Triollo, "1910 Mexico City"; and Adrián Gorelik and Graciela Silvestri, "The Past as the Future: A Reactive Utopía in Buenos Aires," in *The Latin American Cultural Studies Reader,* ed. Ana Del Sarto, Alicia Ríos, and Abril Trigo (Durham, NC: Duke University Press, 2004), 427–40.

61. María Antonieta Vasquez Hahn, *El Palacio de la Exposición, 1909–1989* (Quito: CNPCC and Casa de la Cultura Ecuatoriana, 1989), 39–46.

62. "Ordenanza – 3 enero 1910," *Gaceta municipal* 1:1 (January 29, 1910): 2–3.

63. "Actas – 29 December 1909," *Gaceta municipal* 1:3 (February 12, 1910): 30. This measure diverges from the previously discussed plan to begin levying *aguardiente* taxes in Santa Prisca.

64. "Contrato para construcción de tranvías eléctricas," *Gaceta municipal* 1:3 (February 12, 1910): 41–44.

65. "Ordenanza," *Gaceta municipal* 1:5 (February 1910): 50.

66. ANE: Protocolos, Notaria 1, 546:247 (August 6, 1913).

67. "Sesión de inauguración del Concejo Municipal de 1916 y 1917 (20 de diciembre de 1915)," *Gaceta municipal* 7:63 (January 1916): 795–815, esp. 810–15.

68. Isaac Barrera, *Relación de las fiestas del primer centenario de la batalla de Pichincha, 1822–1922* (Quito: Talleres Tipográficos Nacionales, 1922), 111–21.

69. The area described is north of today's Avenida Patria and bounded on the west and east by the streets 10 de agosto and 6 de diciembre, respectively—the beginning of the Mariscal Sucre neighborhood.

70. "Transacción – El Supremo Gobierno del Ecuador v. The Anglo French Pacific Sindicate Limited," *Gaceta municipal* 12:10 (February 8, 1925): 176–80.

71. "Decretos Legislativos – 1," *Gaceta municipal* 11:8 (November 30, 1925): 135–36.

72. Barrera, *Relación de las fiestas del primer centenario*, 74–76.

73. Manuel J. Calle, *Leyendas del tiempo heroico: episodios de la guerra de la independencia* (Guayaquil: Imp. de "El Telégrafo," 1905), 229–31.

74. "Se dispone que la 'Junta del Centenario de la Batalla de Pichincha' y la 'Junta Patriótica del Centenario,' se denominen, en lo sucesivo, 'Junta de Embellecimiento de Quito' y 'Junta de Mejoras y Obras Públicas de Guayaquil,' respectivamente, y se establecen nuevas rentas para la Junta en primer término citada," in Municipalidad de Guayaquil, *Colección de leyes, decretos, ordenanzas, resoluciones y contratos, correspondientes a esta municipalidad y correspondientes al año de 1922* (Guayaquil: Imprenta Municipal, 1923), 30–32, microfilm, New York Public Library.

75. Paz y Miño Cepeda, *Revolución juliana*, 41–43.

76. "Decretos Legislativos – 3," *Gaceta municipal* 11:8 (November 30, 1925): 136–37.

77. "Decretos de la Junta de Gobierno Provisional – No. 31," *Gaceta municipal* 12:10 (February 8, 1926): 180–85.

78. "Subvensión del Gobierno a la Municipalidad de Quito," *Gaceta municipal* 23:91 (December 31, 1938): 5–6.

79. The most comprehensive biography of this enigmatic figure is Héctor Coral Patiño's *Isidro Ayora* (Quito: Abrapalabra Editores, 1995).

80. Drake, *Money Doctor*.

81. República del Ecuador, *Ley de régimen municipal* (Guayaquil: Imprenta y Talleres Municipales, 1929), vii–xv.

82. The key article of the party platform was no. 15, which called for "libertad y autonomía de los Municipios, sin perjuicio de la vigilancia del Poder central." Jijón y Caamaño, *Política conservadora*, 2:177.

83. Adolfo Posada, *El régimen municipal de la ciudad moderna* (Madrid: Librería General de Victoriano Suárez, 1916). See also Adolfo Posada, *Escritos municipalistas y de la vida local* (Madrid: Instituto de Estudios de Administración Local, 1979).

84. Luna Tamayo, "Orígenes del movimiento obrero," 289–92.

85. Jijón y Caamaño, *Política conservadora*, 2:187.

86. Ibid., 1:122–23.

87. "Necesidad de mantener la ley de autonomía municipal," *Gaceta municipal* 16:38 (April 30, 1931), 265–67.

88. Ana María Goetschel, "Hegemonía y sociedad (Quito: 1930–1950)," in *Ciudades de los Andes: visión histórica y contemporánea*, ed. Eduardo Kingman Garcés (Quito: CIUDAD, 1992), esp. 319–24, 340–42.

89. Quoted in Kingman Garcés, *La ciudad y los otros*, 299.

90. A. Kim Clark, "Race, 'Culture,' and Mestizaje: The Statistical Construction of the Ecuadorian Nation, 1930–1950," *Journal of Historical Sociology* 11:2 (June 1998): 189. See also Kingman Garcés, *La ciudad y los otros*, 309–25, on Suárez's efforts to promote hygiene.

91. Lucía Simonelli, "Jacinto Jijón y Caamaño y el Barrio Obrero," *TRAMA* 55 (1991): 39.

92. Ibid., 40.

93. "A propósito de las Casas para Obreros," *Gaceta municipal* 19:75 (May 31, 1934): 201–2. See also Simonelli, "Jacinto Jijón," 40–42.

94. "Comunicación del Concejo Provincial de Pichincha, relacionada con la queja del Sr. Damián Miranda, a propósito de la Ordenanza sobre urbanización de los terrenos del Jockey Club," in *Gaceta municipal* 16:43 (September 30, 1931): 111–14.

95. "Resolución de la Corte Suprema, a propósito de la Ordenanza que autoriza formar un nuevo barrio, en terrenos del Jockey Club," *Gaceta municipal* 17:52 (June 30, 1932): 211–13.

96. "Una resolución de la Corte Suprema de Justicia acerca de los nuevos barrios," in ibid., 205–7.

97. Daniel Zamudio, "Sobre el urbanismo moderno," *Gaceta municipal* 19:72 (February 28, 1934): 71–81; Emilio Harth-Terre, "Asteriscos urbanos," *Gaceta municipal* 21:80 (September 30, 1936): 139–51.

98. J. Benítez, "Urbanización de ciudades," *Gaceta municipal* 23:87 (January 31, 1938): 99–111.

99. "Comunicaciones Oficiales," *Gaceta municipal* 23:91 (December 31, 1938): 3–5.

100. "Invítase al Sr. Armando Acosta y Lara, Decano de la facultad de Arquitectura Urbanística de la ciudad de Montevideo, para que, en compañía del Director del Plan Regulador de la misma ciudad, don Américo Ricaldoni, visite la ciudad de Quito," *Gaceta municipal* 23:93 (August 10, 1939): 40–41.

101. "Informe que el ingeniero uruguayo Sr. Armando Acosta y Lara, eleva al Concejo, exponiendo sus ideas respecto a la urbanización de la ciudad," *Gaceta municipal* 23:94 (November 10, 1939): 89–94. The Garden City movement, pioneered by the English utopian planner Ebenezer Howard, held that cities ought to reintegrate nature to mitigate the harshness of industrial spaces. See Ebenezer Howard, *Garden Cities of Tomorrow* (London: Swan Sonnenschein, 1902); and also Hall, *Cities of Tomorrow,* esp. chap. 4.

102. The municipal report and the relevant articles in the local press are reprinted in *Gaceta municipal* 23:94 (November 10, 1939). See in particular the municipal rejection of the project "La urbanización de la Ciudad y la derogatoria del Decreto de 4 de agosto de 1938," in ibid., i–vi, and *El Comercio*'s first article on the subject, "Senado aprueba proyecto perjudicial a las aspiraciones de esta ciudad – Trata de privar al Concejo del derecho de parcelar," in ibid., 9.

103. Walter Domingo D., "Entrevista a Guillermo Jones Odriozola sobre el Plan Regulador de Quito de 1942–1944," *TRAMA* 56 (January 1992): 34–41, esp. 35–36.

104. Guillermo Jones Odriozola, "Nociones urbanísticas y su relación con la ciudad de San Francisco de Quito," *Gaceta municipal* 27:102 (January 30, 1942): 98–107.

105. For example, Carrión, *Quito: crisis y política urbana;* Kingman Garcés, *La ciudad y los otros;* or Alfredo Lozano Castro, *Quito: ciudad milenaria, forma y símbolo* (Quito: Ediciones Abya-Yala, 1991).

106. The 1941 congress deserves a more extensive study of its own. Its minutes and

accords can be found in *Primero Congreso de Municipalidades del Ecuador: actas, acuerdos y resoluciones* (Quito: Imprenta Municipal, 1942).

107. The Rio summit's mandate to create hemispheric solidarity in the wake of the Japanese invasion of Pearl Harbor marginalized Tobar's mission. Several years later, the national government attempted to rescind its agreement to the treaty, declaring it null. Maps of Ecuador produced in the country thus continued to include the pre-1941 boundaries up until the late twentieth century, after a renewal of the armed conflict in 1996. A final peace accord was signed in 1998 under which Ecuador received access to the Amazon. For a summary of the conflict, see Enrique Ayala Mora, *Breve historia del conflicto Ecuador-Peru* (Quito: CDS, 1995).

108. *Velasquismo* as the epitome of Ecuadorian populism has been the subject of a number of studies. One of the best recent studies, which focuses on the mixed population that placed the demagogue in power so many times, is Carlos de la Torre Espinosa, *La seducción velasquista* (Quito: Libri Mundi/Grosse Luemern, FLACSO, 1997).

109. Municipio del Distrito Metropolitano de Quito, *Plan General de Desarrollo Territorial del Distrito Metropolitano de Quito, Memoria Técnica, 2006–2010* (Quito: Imprenta Municipal, 2006), 24.

Chapter 5. The Durini Cosmopolis

1. Pedro M. Durini R., tape-recorded interview by author, September 12, 2003, Quito; Museo de la Ciudad, Durini Collection (hereafter MC/D): Planos, Dibujos y Acuarelas, 212.

2. Carl E. Schorske, *Fin-de-Siècle Vienna: Politics and Culture* (New York: Vintage Books, 1981), 131–46. On architecture as the "embodiment of history," see Donald J. Olsen, *The City as a Work of Art: London, Paris, Vienna* (New Haven: Yale University Press, 1986), esp. 295–311. See also M. Christine Boyer, *The City of Collective Memory: Its Historical Imagery and Architectural Entertainments* (Cambridge, MA: MIT Press, 1996).

3. Kirsten Shultz, *Tropical Versailles: Empire, Monarchy, and the Portuguese Royal Court in Rio de Janeiro, 1808–1821* (New York: Routledge, 2001).

4. Tenorio Trillo, "1910 Mexico City." See also Meade, *"Civilizing" Rio*; Gorelik, *La grilla y el parque*; Needell, *Tropical Belle Epoque*; and Celina Borges Lemos, "The Modernization of Brazilian Urban Space as a Political Symbol of the Republic," trans. Elizabeth A. Jackson, *Journal of Decorative and Propaganda Arts* 21 (1995): 219–37.

5. Hardoy and Morse, *Rethinking the Latin American City*.

6. Marina Waisman, "Introduction," in *Latin American Architecture: Six Voices*, ed. Malcolm Quantrill (College Station: Texas A&M University Press, 2000), 5.

7. Roberto Segre, *América Latino, fin de milenio: raíces y perspectivas de su arquitectura* (Havana: Editorial Arte y Literatura, 1999), 72.

8. Carlos Maldonado, "La arquitectura de Quito en la época republicana," in *Quito: una visión histórica de su arquitectura* (Quito: I. Municipio de Quito–Junta de Andalucía, 1993), 137.

9. Gabriela Caicedo, "Entre la plaza San Francisco de Quito y la Piazza San Marco de Venecia," *TRAMA* 80 (2002): 36–39.

10. Kennedy Troya and Ortiz Crespo, "Continuismo colonial," 126–27.

11. Paúl Aguilar, *Quito: arquitectura y modernidad, 1850–1950* (Quito: Museo Municipal Alberto Mena Caamaño, 1995), 19.

12. *El municipio* 6:92 (July 17, 1890): n.p.

13. One element of the problems surrounding the project concerned Minghetti's expulsion from the country during the anticlerical fervor of the revolution's early days. See Alfonso Cevallos Romero and Pedro M. Durini, *Ecuador universal: visión desconocida de una etapa de la arquitectura ecuatoriana* (Quito: P. M. Durini R., 1990), 15–16.

14. Evelia Peralta, *Quito: guía arquitectónica* (Quito: I. Municipio de Quito–Junta de Andalucía, 1991), 73.

15. Brüning's extensive career forms an alternative pathway to the analysis provided in this chapter. Instead of having to search for patronage, as did the Durinis, he secured a place as primary architect for the Catholic Church, a position that allowed him to refashion the temples of the country, in particular a range of prominent structures such as the basilica in the resort town of Baños and the Quinche church, home of the famous Virgin of Quinche. For more on his work, see Alfonso Cevallos Romero, *Arte, diseño y arquitectura en el Ecuador: la obra del Padre Brüning, 1899–1938* (Quito: Museos del Banco Central del Ecuador/Abya-Yala, 1994).

16. Pedro M. Durini R., interview by author. In Ecuadorian parlance, the foreign architects (and artists) who settled in the country are regularly referred to with Hispanized names. Hence, Thomas Reed becomes Tomás Reed, Franz Schmidt becomes Francisco Schmidt, and so forth. Information is not available about all of these designers' appellations, and, as a result, I have chosen to use the Hispanized versions.

17. On consumption in Peru, see Paul Gootenberg, *Imagining Development: Economic Ideas in Peru's "Fictitious Prosperity" of Guano, 1840–1880* (Berkeley: University of California Press, 1993).

18. Astrid Fischel, *El Teatro Nacional de Costa Rica: su historia* (San José, Costa Rica: Editorial Teatro Nacional, 1992).

19. "Actas," *El municipio* 19:177 (March 14, 1903): 1493.

20. Lorenzo Durini to Pedro Durini, July 30, 1903, MC/D: Cartas y Correspondencia, 12:3; Pedro M. Durini R., interview by author.

21. Caicedo, "Entre la plaza San Francisco de Quito y la Piazza San Marco de Venecia." See also Maldonado, "La arquitectura de Quito," 137.

22. *El municipio* 6:92 (July 17, 1890): n.p. Eduardo Kingman correctly identifies this as the first attempt to regulate ornament in Quito but mistakenly identifies it as having been passed in 1880. See Kingman Garcés, *La ciudad y los otros,* 264.

23. Lorenzo Durini to Máximo Fernández, July 30, 1903; Lorenzo Durini to Pedro Durini, July 30, 1903, both in MC/D: Cartas y Correspondencia, 12:1–2 and 12:3–5, respectively.

24. Lorenzo Durini to Juan Durini, September 7, 1903, MC/D: Cartas y Correspondencia, 12:31.

25. Lorenzo Durini to Juan Durini, September 22, 1903, MC/D: Cartas y Correspondencia, 12:51.

26. Pedro M. Durini R., interview by author.

27. Lorenzo Durini to Máximo Fernández, July 30, 1903, MC/D: Cartas y Correspondencia, 12:2.

28. Lorenzo Durini to Francisco Durini, October 4, 1903; Lorenzo Durini to Juan Durini, September 7, 1903, both in MC/D: Cartas y Correspondencia, 12:73 and 12:33, respectively.

29. Cevallos Romero and Durini, *Ecuador universal*, 16.

30. "Contrato del Comité Diez de Agosto con Lorenzo Durini," *El municipio* 20:197 (September 7, 1904).

31. Pedro M. Durini R., interview by author.

32. Cevallos Romero and Durini, *Ecuador universal*, 150–51.

33. Lorenzo Durini to Francisco Durini C., July 23, 1906, MC/D: Cartas y Correspondencia, 32:16.

34. Pedro M. Durini R., interview by author.

35. Cevallos Romero and Durini, *Ecuador universal*, 141.

36. MC/D: Cartas y Correspondencia, 6. This copybook includes an inventory of the store as well as a log of daily transactions.

37. Contrato, MC/D: Cartas y Correspondencia, 37:135–38.

38. Mario Canessa Oneto, *100 años de historia del tenis ecuatoriano* (Guayaquil: Poligráfica C.A., 2000), 19–20. It is now known as the Quito Tennis and Golf Club. See also Cevallos Romero and Durini, *Ecuador universal*, 141.

39. Pedro Durini to Francisco Durini, January 16, 1907, MC/D: Cartas y Correspondencia, 22: 111; Cevallos Romero and Durini, *Ecuador universal*, 36. Genaro Larrea would later be one of Francisco's witnesses at his wedding in 1908 to Rosa Palacios. See Elsa Susana Morales Moreno, Alicia Verónica Oña Velasco, and María Verónica Padrón Cosíos, "Análisis histórico de la obra arquitectónica del Arq. Francisco Durini Cáceres en la ciudad de Quito" (BFA thesis, Universidad Central del Ecuador, 2001), 11.

40. Pedro Durini to Francisco Durini, January 16, 1907, both in MC/D: Cartas y Correspondencia, 22:111 and 22:112, respectively.

41. Cevallos Romero and Durini, *Ecuador universal*, 36–38.

42. MC/D: Cartas y Correspondencia, 10.

43. Froli had originally been commissioned to help with this work, but when Francisco took over the business after Lorenzo's death, he passed the contract to Capurro in part because of Froli's history of delays. Cevallos Romero and Durini, *Ecuador universal*, 55.

44. Francisco Durini to Pietro Capurro, May 1, 1907, May 2, 1907, both in MC/D: Cartas y Correspondencia, 34:84–90 and 34:109, respectively; Cevallos and Durini, *Ecuador universal*, 152–56. Capurro would again collaborate with Durini many years later on works such as the Gonzalo Cordova mausoleum (1930). See Cevallos Romero and Durini, *Ecuador universal*, 91.

45. Morales Moreno, Oña Velasco, and Padrón Círculo Militar, "Análisis histórico de la obra arquitectónica del Arq. Francisco Durini," 11; Aguilar, *Quito: arquitectura y modernidad*, 46–47.

46. This dual training was a common trend among students in Milan. See Richard A. Etlin, *Modernism in Italian Architecture, 1890–1940* (Cambridge, MA: MIT Press, 1991), 9. Durini's studies are mentioned in Lorenzo Durini to Juan Durini, September 9, 1903, MC/D: Cartas y Correspondencia, 11:30–34.

47. "Oficios," *El municipio* 22:241 (March 10, 1906): 53–54.

48. "Actas," *El municipio* 23:295 (December 26, 1907): 395–97.

49. "Actas," *El municipio* 23:297 (December 31, 1907): 415; Pedro M. Durini R., interview by author.

50. MC/D: Cartas y Correspondencia, 23:7, 10–11, 13, 40, 79–80, 88–89, 94, 99, 114–15.

51. Cevallos Romero and Durini, *Ecuador universal,* 155.

52. On this period in Milanese architecture, see Etlin, *Modernism in Italian Architecture.*

53. MC/D: Libros de Consulta 4; Revistas 3, 7.

54. Valerie Fraser, *Building the New World: Studies in the Modern Architecture of Latin America, 1930–1960* (London: Verso, 2000), 44–46.

55. Pedro M. Durini R., interview by author. The plans and Trier's designs are housed at the Museo de la Ciudad. See MC/D: Planos y Dibujos, 29:145–47. See also Aguilar, *Quito: arquitectura y modernidad,* 46–47; and Cevallos Romero and Durini, *Ecuador universal,* 153–54.

56. Aguilar, *Quito: arquitectura y modernidad,* 45; Cevallos Romero and Durini, *Ecuador universal,* 118–22; MC/D: Fotografías 75.

57. Aguilar, *Quito: arquitectura y modernidad,* 46–47. See also Espinosa Apolo, *Mestizaje;* and Kingman Garcés, *La ciudad y los otros.*

58. Ludwig Bemelmans, *The Donkey Within* (New York: Viking Press, 1941), 46–47.

59. Camilla Fojas notes in her study on cosmopolitanism among Latin American *modernista* authors that the engagement of characteristics from other places afforded the possibility to transgress gender/sexual norms, which could be seen in a literary form appropriating and reconstructing a barrage of foreign styles. See Camilla Fojas, *Cosmopolitanism in the Americas* (West Lafayette, IN: Purdue University Press, 2005), esp. 131–37.

60. A number of these sample items have been preserved in the Durini collection at the Museo de la Ciudad (MC/D) in the Revistas and the Libros de Consulta series.

61. MC/D: Revistas 9, 1.

62. MC/D: Libros de Consulta 2a; MC/D: Revistas 6; Pedro M. Durini R., interview by author. See also MC/D: Planos, Dibujos, e Acuarelas.

63. Aguilar, *Quito: arquitectura y modernidad,* 50–51.

64. Pedro M. Durini R., interview by author.

65. Fraser, *Building the New World,* 15.

Chapter 6. A Phantasmagoric Dystopia

1. No full biographical study of Calle exists at this writing, though there have been several short works examining the life of the illustrious journalist. The best are by far Alejandro Andrade Coello's *Manuel J. Calle, orientaciones periodísticas* (Quito: Imprenta "Ecuador," 1919), which appeared soon after Calle's death, and Diego Araujo's introductory essay to the collection *Un forzado de las letras: antología de Manuel J. Calle* (Quito: Ediciones del Banco Central del Ecuador, 1998).

2. Manuel J. Calle, "La semana," *Revista de Quito* 7 (February 16, 1898): 229–30.

3. Bakhtin, "Forms of Time," 247–48.

4. Minchom, *People of Quito.*

5. This paragraph is based largely on Minchom, *People of Quito,* 215–20. See also Federico González Suárez, *Historia general de la República del Ecuador,* vol. 5 (Quito: Imprenta del Clero, 1901), 172–85.

6. Ruth Hill, "The Roots of Revolt in Late Viceregal Quito: Eugenio de Espejo between Adam Smith and St. Rose," *Bulletin of Spanish Studies* 86:7–8 (2009): 146.

7. On Espejo's satires, see Johnson, *Satire in Colonial Spanish America,* 139–54.

8. See Ricardo Padrón, "*Cumandá* and the Cartographers: Nationalism and Form in Juan León Mera," *Annals of Scholarship* 12:3–4 (1998): esp. 226–27. See also Fernando Balseca, "En busca de nuevas regiones: la nación y la narrativa ecuatoriana," in *Crítica literaria ecuatoriana: antología,* ed. Gabriela Pólit Dueñas (Quito: FLACSO, 2001).

9. See Clark, *Redemptive Work.*

10. Johnson, *Satire in Colonial Spanish America,* 143–52.

11. Ana María Goetschel, *Educación de las mujeres, maestras y esferas públicas: Quito en la primera mitad del siglo XX* (Quito: FLACSO Sede Ecuador–Abya-Yala, 2007), 75–108.

12. Andrés Guerrero, *La semántica de la dominación: el concertaje de indios* (Quito: Ediciones Libri Mundi, 1991).

13. Francine Masiello, "Melodrama, Sex, and Nation in Latin America's *Fin de Siglo*," in *Theoretical Debates in Spanish American Literature,* ed. David William Foster and Daniel Altamiranda (New York: Garland Publishing, 1997), 181–90. See also Donald L. Shaw, *A Companion to Modern Spanish American Fiction* (London: Tamesis, 2002), 24.

14. The original text reads "bolsiconas desgreñadas; un viejecillo de ruin apariencia; pilluelos que iban silbando y . . . dos chullalevas con levitones largos y raídos, botas torcidas y viejas, sombreros que habían conocido muchas cabezas." Roberto Andrade, *Pacho Villamar* (1900; rpt., Quito: Clásicos Ariel, n.d.), 20–21.

15. Luís A. Martínez, *A la costa* (1904; rpt., Quito: Clásicos Ariel).

16. Masiello, "Melodrama, Sex, and Nation," 188.

17. Balseca has underscored Mariana's place within a trend of eroticizing Afro-Ecuadorians in twentieth-century Ecuadorian narrative. See Balseca, "En busca de nuevas regiones," 154.

18. Luís A. Martínez Holguín, *Andinismo, arte y literature* (Quito: Abya-Yala; Nuevos Horizontes, 1994).

19. Enrique Ayala Mora, *Historia de la revolución liberal ecuatoriana* (Quito: Corporación Editora Nacional, 1994); Clark, *Redemptive Work.*

20. Although vastly skewed toward the cold war era, the only overview of twentieth-century student activism in Ecuador remains Patricio Ycaza's *Movimiento estudiantil: ¿para dónde camina?* (Quito: Centro de Educación Popular, 1989).

21. See Chiriboga Alvear, *Resumen histórico;* and Luna Tamayo, "Orígines del movimiento obrero."

22. For an overview of this moment, see Ycaza, *Movimiento estudiantil,* 10–11. An extended account, including memorial testimonials, can be found in Aurelio Davila, *El 25 de abril de 1907: recuerdos históricos* (Guayaquil: "Popular," 1909).

23. Cathy L. Jrade, *Modernismo, Modernity, and the Development of Spanish American Literature* (Austin: University of Texas Press, 1998), 19. See also Angel Rama, *La ciudad letrada* (Hanover, NH: Ediciones del Norte, 1984); and Julio Ramos, *Desencuentros de la modernidad en América Latina: literatura y política en el siglo XIX* (Mexico City: Fondo de Cultura Económica, 1989). Each work has also appeared in English translation.

24. Ernesto Noboa Caamaño, "Hastío," in *Otros modernistas* (Quito: Ariel, n.d.), 52. The most comprehensive study of the movement spawned by the *generación decapitada* is Gladys Valencia Sala, *El círculo modernista ecuatoriana: crítica y poesía* (Quito: Universidad Andina, Abya-Yala, 2007). See also Raúl Andrade, "Retablo de una generación decapitada," in *El perfil de la quimera: siete ensayos literarios* (Quito: Casa de la Cultura Ecuatoriana, 1951), 65–105; Henri Michaux, *Ecuador: A Travel Journal,* trans. Robin Magowan (Seattle: University of Washington Press, 1970), esp. 61–64; and Isaac J. Barrera, *Del vivir: reflexiones de juventud* (Quito: Editorial Ecuatoriana, 1972), esp. 42, where he disdains bohemianism as *"el enemigo del talento."*

25. Although it appeared for the first time in *Letras,* Bustamante's novel was not published independently until 1935, when the Fernández firm, Editorial L. I. Fernández, finally brought the book to the greater public's attention. This move formed part of the company's tendency to publish the growing number of works by Quito's avant-garde, a policy encouraged by Jorge Fernández, the son of the firm's owner, himself a member of the *vanguardia* and the author of a number of short stories and a novel about the early Liberal years. Citations will be taken from the reprint edition: José Rafael Bustamante, *Para matar el gusano* (1913; rpt., Quito: Editorial Casa de la Cultura Ecuatoriana, 1960).

26. See Carrión, *Quito: crisis y política urbana;* Espinosa Apolo, *Mestizaje;* and esp. Kingman Garcés, *La ciudad y los otros.*

27. The original text reads, "La callejuela, esquiva y solitaria, sube, se esconde y desaparece por entre la áspera loma, cual si huyera del maltrato que las gentes le hacen sufrir, convirtiéndola en muladar y basurero allá abajo, en la ciudad, de donde arranca. Triste y repugnante callejuela entre el cementerio y dos o tres casucas bajas y melancólicas, mitad empedrada con piedras desiguales y toscas por las que se escurre agua jabonosa que sale de las casas, mitad tierra con desmedrados hierbajos, basura

y excrementos. Y en ella un hombre, un fantasma, un espectro que dormita y sueña, rezonga y balbuce, se rasca y se espulga, sentado en el umbral de una puerta cerrada. Para tal calle, tal hombre." Bustamante, *Para matar el gusano*, 241.

28. See Barrera, *Relación de las fiestas del primer centenario*, 26–30. See also Isaac J. Barrera, *Estudios sobre modernismo literario: publicado en el* Diario El Comercio *1 Enero 1910 – 10 de Abril 1910* (Quito: Casa de la Cultura Ecuatoriana, 1971), for Barrera's early defense of the precepts of *modernismo*.

29. Campos, who wrote under the pseudonym "Jack the Ripper," published sketches of a coastal life filled with conflict, violence, and mayhem—a fascinating counterpoint to the pious idyll more common in Quito. For instance, while Gangotena's priests and aristocrats ultimately uphold standards of honor and humility, Campos depicts friars whose sermons explain why crabs walk backward. See José Antonio Campos, *Linterna mágica* (Guayaquil and Quito: Ariel, n.d.); and also Campos, *Cosas de mi tierra.*

30. Gangotena y Jijón, *Al margen de la historia*, 201–8.

31. The original reads "el viejo Quito, que se va para no volver." Andrade Coello, *Motivos nacionales*, 2:277.

32. As he put it in the tale of the *aguador*, "A medida que las costumbres se modifican y los años transcurren, trastornando, como castillo de naipes, la dulce y vieja ingenuidad, dejamos de ver, en la querida y tradicional Quito, ciertos tipos familiares y pintorescos que van desapareciendo . . . y que hasta resultaban decorativos para la ciudad . . . [y quienes] . . . convierten, tal vez inconscientemente, en ludibrio hasta lo que es digno de lástima." Andrade Coello, *Del Quito antiguo*, 89.

33. The original reads "callejas mal pavimentadas, estrechas y oscuras, pero ricas en memorias del pasado." Andrade Coello, *Del Quito antiguo*, 48.

34. Andrade Coello, *Motivos nacionales*, 211–13. Sentiments like these also indicate the influence of *hispanista* tenets in the chronicle of the old city.

35. Humberto E. Robles, *La noción de vanguardia en el Ecuador: recepción - trayectoria – documentos. 1918–1934* (Guayaquil: Casa de la Cultura Ecuatoriana "Benjamín Carrión," Nucleo del Guayas, 1989). Robles's introductory essay is reprinted as "La noción de vanguardia en el Ecuador: recepción y trayectoria (1918–1934)," in *Crítica literaria ecuatoriana*, ed. Pólit Dueñas, 223–49.

36. See ibid., 227–31.

37. For a biographical sketch on Coloma, see Rodolfo Pérez Pimentel's online biographical dictionary, http://www.diccionariobiograficoecuador.com.

38. Ramiro de Sylva, "Crónicas de Quito, " *Caricatura* 1:4 (January 1, 1919): n.p.

39. This sentiment is expressed clearly in the following passage: "Y el cronista sigue recordando todo lo que ha visto. Todo es insignificante y despiadadamente sencillo. . . . No encuentra interesante ninguno de los motivos que ha observado. Nadie los leería. . . . Y el público de una ciudad en la que nunca sucede nada, quiere algo . . . algo . . . que no sea lo de todos los días. . . . Bueno. Entonces el cronista inventa, inventa disparates, locuras, absurdos. . . . ¡Y ésta es talvez su voluptuosidad del periodista . . . !" Ramiro de Sylva, "Crónicas de Quito," *Caricatura* 2:45 (December 7, 1919): 6–7.

40. Henry Nick, "Crónicas de Quito," *Caricatura* 1:7 (January 26, 1919): 9.

41. Although Palacio's work was long ignored after he was ostracized from the literary establishment following the turn toward social realism in the early 1930s, there has been a major revalorization of his writings since the 1980s. Numerous editions of his collected works have appeared, as well as a series of articles recasting his work as some of the most daring and important writing to have appeared in Ecuador. Citations from Palacio's works are from Pablo Palacio, *Obras completas,* ed. María del Carmen Fernández (Quito: Libresa, 1997). For an introduction to the recent criticism on Palacio's writings, see esp. María del Carmen Fernández, *El realismo abierto de Pablo Palacio en la encrucijada de los 30* (Quito: Ediciones Libri Mundi/Enrique Grosse-Luemern, 1991), as well as her introduction to the edition of his collected works cited above. For a comparison of Palacio and Salvador that focuses on their combative relationships with fellow socialists and their distinct uses of psychoanalysis, see Wilfrido H. Corral, "Humberto Salvador y Pablo Palacio: política literaria y psicoanálisis en la Sudamérica de los treinta," in *Crítica literaria ecuatoriana,* ed. Pólit Dueñas. For a review of avant-garde literature during the era, see Robles, "La noción de vanguardia."

42. Raúl Andrade in particular would later refer to the importance that the Dadaist movement had in his conception of how to organize the magazine. See Fernández, *El realismo abierto,* 56–57. On Egas's time in Paris, see Michele Greet, *Beyond National Identity: Pictorial Indigenism as a Modernist Strategy in Andean Art, 1920–1960* (University Park: Pennsylvania State University Press, 2009), esp. 38–48. On Egas's earlier exoticist painting, see Trinidad Pérez, "Exoticism, Alterity, and the Ecuadorean Elite: The Work of Camilo Egas," in *Images of Power,* ed. Andermann and Rowe, 111–21.

43. The original text reads, "comprendemos que el Arte es la alquimia de la inverosimilitud, porque si el Arte fuera la verdad, la expresión artística no existiría" and "cosmopolitismo, audacia, autenticidad." Gonzalo Escudero, "Hélice," *Hélice* 1:1 (April 26, 1926): 1.

44. Greet, *Beyond National Identity,* 64–84.

45. Pablo Palacio, "Un hombre muerto a puntapiés," in Palacio, *Obras completas,* 91–102; Palacio, "El antropófago," in ibid., 103–11.

46. Fernández notes this similarity; see Palacio, *Obras completas,* 107n2. This story anticipates Oswald de Andrade's "Anthropophagite Manifesto" both in spirit and in the use of cannibalism as a metaphor.

47. Bakhtin, "Forms of Time," 196. Bakhtin conceives of the carnivalesque as a moment of inversion in which traditional social relations can be subverted or overcome. For an expanded account of the importance of Carnival, see Mikhail Bakhtin, *Rabelais and His World,* trans. Hélène Iswolsky (Bloomington: Indiana University Press, 1984).

48. Like several of his fellow contributors to *Hélice,* Palacio joined the Socialist Party following Egas's departure and would become one of its central militants during the 1930s.

49. On Guignol, see http://amisdeguignol.free.fr/ (accessed November 25, 2010). See also Richard J. Hand and Michael Wilson, *Grand-Guignol: The French Theatre of Horror* (Exeter, UK: University of Exeter Press, 2002).

50. Pablo Palacio, *Débora,* in *Obras completas,* 178–81.

51. Elizabeth Coonrod Martínez, *Before the Boom: Latin American Revolutionary Novels of the 1920s* (Lanham, MD: University Press of America, 2001), 72–88.

52. This text paragraph refers to Palacio, *Débora*, in *Obras completas*, 182–93.

53. The original text reads, "En verdad, puede ser muy pintoresco el que una calle sea torcida y estrecha hasta no dar paso a un omnibús; puede ser encantadora por su olor a orinas, pude dar la ilusión de que transitará, de un momento a otro, la ronda de trasnochados. Pero está más nuevo el asfalto y grita allí la fuerza de miles de hombres." Palacio, *Débora*, in *Obras completas*, 190.

54. Coonrod Martínez, *Before the Boom*, 85–86. See also Fernández's editorial note in Palacio, *Obras completas*, 207n1.

55. Pablo Palacio, *Vida del ahorcado*, in *Obras completas*, 209–73.

56. José Otero, "Humberto Salvador: el hombre, sus temas y su creación" (PhD diss., University of New Mexico, 1970), 11–15.

57. See Corral, "Humberto Salvador y Pablo Palacio."

58. Humberto Salvador, *Ajedrez* (Quito: Escuela de Artes y Oficios, 1929), 12.

59. "No se resignan a la vulgaridad de ser exactos." Ibid., 12.

60. The original text reads, "Empezaré por localizarla. Es más difícil que adivinar una carta al compañero, en la entusiasta partida en la que se apuesta mucho, localizar a una persona en la clásica ciudad de San Francisco de Quito. Ella se nos escapa y para alcanzarla, tenemos que correr desesperadamente a través de las calles. Por fortuna, la carrera es menos penosa en el pavimento; pero, cuando llegamos a las calles empedradas, la persecución se vuelve dolorosa. Hay que renunciar a ella. El personaje se nos escapa y ni el demonio puede encontrarla." Humberto Salvador, *En la ciudad he perdido una novela,* with an introduction by María del Carmen Fernández (1929; rpt., Quito: Editorial Libresa, 1996), 91.

61. Salvador, *En la ciudad,* 93–94. María del Carmen Fernández has noted that the reference to the Apache compares modernity's sudden force to the attacks perpetrated by Apaches in many westerns of the era. Ibid., 94n1. Apaches indeed appear throughout the novel as symbols of barbarity, which presents an ironic contrast to the oft-lamented fate of the Ecuadorian Indian.

62. The original reads, "marcos para el desnudo cubista de la voluptuosidad." Salvador, *En la ciudad,* 133.

63. The original text reads, "Cada barrio simboliza una tendencia. . . . Novelas alucinadas, con corte de leyenda y prosa clásica, hay que encontrarlas en 'El Tejar.' Medioevales, en los claustros de 'Santo Domingo' o en 'San Diego.' Perversos, en el barrio de 'La Tola.' Modernas, en las calles centrales, donde los autos son protagonistas de todos los amoríos y de todos los amores. Románticas, en la sección de 'La Alameda.' Al llegar al 'Ejido,' se vuelven naturalistas. El realismo se esconde como un gato en cualquiera de las casas.

"La vanguardia se puede buscarla en la ciudad, a través de todos los barrios." Salvador, *En la ciudad,* 219–20.

64. Robles, *La noción de vanguardia,* 55–69.

65. See Marc Becker, *Indians and Leftists in the Making of Ecuador's Modern Indigenous Movements* (Durham, NC: Duke University Press, 2008).

66. Federico A. Chalupa, "The Ecuadorian City and Modernity: Jorge Icaza's Quito," in *The Image of the City in Literature, Media, and Society,* ed. Will Wright and Steven Kaplan (Pueblo: Colorado State University–Pueblo, 2003), esp. 150–51.

67. José Carlos Mariátegui, *Siete ensayos de interpretación de la realidad peruana* (Lima, 1928; rpt., Montevideo: Biblioteca de Marcha, 1970), 171–80.

68. Moises Sáenz, *Sobre el indio ecuatoriano y su incorporación al medio nacional* (Mexico City: Publicaciones de la Secretaria de Educación Pública, 1933), xi–xiii.

69. See Pablo Arturo Suárez, *Contribución al estudio de las realidades entre las clases obreras y campesinas* (Quito: Imprenta de la Universidad Central, 1934), as well as A. Kim Clark, "Race, 'Culture,' and Mestizaje: The Statistical Construction of the Ecuadorian Nation, 1930–1950," *Journal of Historical Sociology* 11:2 (June 1998): 185–211, esp. 188–93.

70. Ricardo Descalzi, *Historia critica del teatro ecuatoriano,* 6 vols. (Quito: Editorial Casa de la Cultura Ecuatoriana, 1968), 3:741–43, 788–90. See also Corral, "Humberto Salvador y Pablo Palacio," 297–99.

71. Salvador's thesis was soon published. See Humberto Salvador, *Esquema sexual* (Quito: Imprenta Nacional, 1934). On Ecuador's burgeoning feminist movement during this era, see Goetschel, *Educación de las mujeres;* and Ana María Goetschel, ed., *Orígenes del feminismo en el Ecuador: antología* (Quito: CONAMU; FLACSO; Municipio del Distrito Metropolitano de Quito; UNIFEM, 2006), 153–218.

72. "Como ellos quieren," in Jorge Icaza, *¿Cuál es? Sin sentido* (Quito: Su Librería, 1979).

73. "¿Cuál es? " in Icaza, *¿Cuál es? Sin sentido.*

74. The original quotes are "era el amo, que todo lo puede en la comarca" and "con el cura no era pecado." Jorge Icaza, *Huasipungo* (1934; rpt., Quito: Ediciones Libresa, 1983), 123 and 137, respectively.

75. Jorge Icaza, *En las calles* (1935; rpt., Quito: Editorial El Conejo, 1985).

76. Ibid., 210.

77. After Bonifaz's disqualification by Congress, armed bands from both the Right and Left marauded in the streets for weeks until an insurrection in a nearby military garrison led to four days of brutal fighting throughout the city in August 1932.

78. The original text reads, "A las diez, poco más o menos, llegó la figura haraposa de un pordiosero, se rascó las ingles, la cabeza y los sobacos piojosos, hizo sonar unas medallas—santos, vírgenes, cruces—y unos cuantos amuletos que llevada colgados en el pecho, y, entre carajos y oraciones de su especialidad, se acurrucó como un ovillo de trapos en el suelo. Más tarde apareció e hizo lo mismo que el mendigo un ciego con un muchacho descalzo. Luego llegó un indio—cargador público en desgracia— 'Cualquiera puede. Cualquiera puede, pes. Hasta el natural . . .' pensó la tropa de huasipungueros arrastrándose lentamente hasta el abrigo miserable del soportal. La noche fue ventosa y fría, más igual o peor que en la choza del páramo. Felizmente ellos estaban acostumbrados." Icaza, *En las calles,* 20.

79. As a result, Salvador would still be criticized for not focusing enough on the exploited rural Indian, as was the case in a review of *Noviembre* penned by Panamanian Víctor Hugo Escala in 1942; see also Otero, "Humberto Salvador," 46–48. There have been many studies of radical aesthetics in the interwar years; see esp. Beatriz Sarlo, *Una modernidad periférica: Buenos Aires, 1920 y 1930* (Buenos Aires: Ediciones Nueva Visión, 1988); Nicola Miller, *In the Shadow of the State: Intellectuals and the Quest for National Identity in Twentieth-Century Spanish America* (London: Verso, 1999); David Craven, *Art and Revolution in Latin America, 1910–1990* (New Haven: Yale University Press, 2002), chap. 2; and Fraser, *Building the New World,* regarding the establishment of an alternative modernism and the dialogical relationship between global and local politics of modern art and literature.

80. Humberto Salvador, *Camarada* (Quito: Talleres Tipográficas Nacionales, 1933).

81. Salvador's attitudes toward homosexuality are somewhat obtuse. As Wilfrido Corral has noted, Salvador condemns homosexuality as a societal evil in *Esquema sexual;* however, he simultaneously develops an extensive discussion of the aesthetic inspiration of homosexual encounters, dropping names as illustrious as Homer, Plato, Zola, Balzac, and Romain Rolland. See Corral, "Humberto Salvador y Pablo Palacio," 297–99; and Salvador, *Esquema sexual,* 251–55.

82. The original text reads, "Julia es pobre. No tiene derecho al placer." Salvador, *Camarada,* 183.

83. On the ministry's impact, see Valeria Coronel, "Orígenes de una Democracia Corporativa: estrategias para la ciudadanización del campesinado indígena, partidos políticos y reforma territorial en Ecuador (1925–1944)," in *Historia social urbana: espacios y flujos,* ed. Eduardo Kingman Garcés (Quito: FLACSO–Ministerio de Cultura, 2009), 323–64.

84. Otero uses this terminology, taken from Salvador, to describe the seemingly endless parade of beggars, prostitutes, lost bureaucrats, social climbers, and so forth, that pervade his novels. See Otero, "Humberto Salvador," chap. 6, "La vida sin vida."

85. Humberto Salvador, *Trabajadores* (1935; rpt., Quito: Editorial El Conejo, 1985), 78–82.

86. The original text reads, "el último nido humano de la ciudad." Ibid., 11. These words appear on the opening page of the novel, along with an embrace of the situation by the narrator. Despite his brave front, the situation is untenable for all who live there. Again, the influence of environment is paramount.

87. Salvador, *Trabajadores,* 100.

88. Ibid., 58–59.

89. The original text reads, "La vida fué conmigo irónica. Porque realmente era una ironía sangrienta el hecho de que un muchacho hambriento y andrajoso como yo, entrara a casas saturadas de lujo y comodidades.

"Hice un descubrimiento sensacional: el de que, junto al Quito desvalido que yo conocía, había 'otro' Quito: el de los poderosos.

"Eran dos ciudades distintas, que por un sarcasmo de la vida, estaban muy cerca la una de la otra. Dos ciudades contradictorias, y sin embargo, entrecruzadas, fusionadas la una en la otra." Salvador, *Trabajadores,* 161–62.

90. Ibid., 71–75. This stance echoes Salvador's support for abortion rights as well as voluntary sterilization, positions connected to his discussion of eugenics in *Esquema sexual,* 200–204, 296. For more on Latin American attitudes toward eugenics as social planning, see Nancy Stepan, *"The Hour of Eugenics": Race, Gender, and Nation in Latin America* (Ithaca, NY: Cornell University Press, 1991).

91. Salvador, *Trabajadores,* 112.

92. Salvador would later dedicate *La fuenta clara* to Baños's virtues.

93. The original text reads, "Los trabajadores de todos los países crearemos la nueva humanidad." Salvador, *Trabajadores,* 191 (both quotations).

94. Humberto Salvador, *Noviembre* (Quito: Editorial L. I. Fernández, 1939).

95. Albert E. Franklin, *Ecuador: Portrait of a People* (New York: Doubleday Doran, 1944), 292–96.

96. Páez's legislation includes the Ley de Comunas (Law of Communes) and a new labor code, each passed in 1937.

97. For more on Páez, see Enrique Ayala Mora, *Nueva historia,* vol. 10; and Marc Becker, "Comunas and Indigenous Protest in Cayambe, Ecuador," *The Americas* 55:4 (April 1999): 536–37.

98. The original text reads, "¡Abajo la inteligencia y viva la muerte!" Salvador, *Noviembre,* 260.

99. Ibid., 267–68.

100. Ibid., 356–61.

101. The original text reads, "fantasmas con apariencia de hombres vivos, porque han perdido las cualidades que enaltecen a la humanidad." Ibid., 377.

102. Ibid., 377–79.

103. See Palacio, *Vida del ahorcado,* in *Obras completas,* 243–46.

104. The original text reads, "una sinfonia de luz y color . . . bella, ardiente, y voluptuosa." Salvador, *Noviembre,* 379.

105. On the question of historical periodization and the relationship between the modern and traditional in Latin American literature and cultural studies, see Adam Sharman, *Tradition and Modernity in Spanish American Literature: From Darío to Carpentier* (New York: Palgrave Macmillan, 2006), 11–14.

106. David Sibley, "Outsiders in Society and Space," in *Inventing Places: Studies in Cultural Geography,* ed. Kay Anderson and Fay Gale (Melbourne: Longman Chesire, 1992), 115.

Chapter 7. Santa Clara de San Millán

1. Petition to ministry, received July 6, 1940, in Sistema Nacional de Archivos–Ministerio de Trabajo y Recursos Humanos, Sección Tierras (hereafter SNA-MTRH/Tierras), Box 179, Folder 13 (January–February 1940).

2. Subsequent paperwork contained in ibid.

3. Becker, *Indians and Leftists;* Coronel, "Revolution in Stages."

4. On the various statutes, see Mercedes Prieto, *Liberalismo y temor: imaginando los sujetos indígenas en el Ecuador postcolonial, 1895–1950* (Quito: FLACSO, 2004). On the *comuna,* see SNA-MTRH/Tierras 191:5.

5. Membership rolls from the early 1940s can be found in SNA-MTRH/Tierras 191:5.

6. Studies of indigenous entrepreneurialism during the colonial era include Jeremy Baskes, *Indians, Merchants, and Markets: A Reinterpretation of the Repartimiento and Spanish-Indian Economic Relations in Colonial Oaxaca, 1750–1821* (Stanford: Stanford University Press, 2005); Gauderman, *Women's Lives;* and Camilla Townsend, *Tales of Two Cities: Race and Economic Culture in Early Republican North and South America; Guayaquil, Ecuador, and Baltimore, Maryland* (Austin: University of Texas Press, 2000).

7. Joanne Rappaport, *The Politics of Memory: Native Historical Interpretation in the Colombian Andes,* 2nd ed. (Durham, NC: Duke University Press, 1998), 24.

8. Andrés Guerrero, "The Construction of a Ventriloquist's Image: Liberal Discourse and the 'Miserable Indian Race' in Late 19th-Century Ecuador," *Journal of Latin American Studies* 29:3 (October 1997): 555–90.

9. Florencia Mallon, *Peasant and Nation: The Making of Postcolonial Mexico and Peru* (Berkeley and Los Angeles: University of California Press, 1995); Mark Thurner, *From Two Republics to One Divided: Contradictions of Postcolonial Nationmaking in Andean Peru* (Durham, NC: Duke University Press, 1997).

10. Becker, *Indians and Leftists;* Morelli, *Territorio o nazione;* Aleezé Sattar, "An Unresolved Inheritance: Postcolonial State Formation and Indigenous Communities in Chimborazo, Ecuador, 1820–1875" (PhD diss., New School University, 2001); Erin O'Connor, *Gender, Indian, Nation: The Contradictions of Making Ecuador, 1830–1925* (Tucson: University of Arizona Press, 2007); Galo Ramón, *La resistencia andina: Cayambe, 1500–1800* (Quito: Centro Andino de Acción Popular, 1987). Also see A. Kim Clark and Marc Becker, eds., *Highland Indians and the State in Modern Ecuador* (Pittsburgh: University of Pittsburgh Press, 2007).

11. Kingman Garcés, *La ciudad y los otros,* esp. chaps. 3 and 5.

12. As late as the seventeenth century, Santa Clara continued protesting the expropriation of its lands for the expansion of the city. Rosemarie Terán Najas, "Censos, capellanías y elites, siglo XVII," *ProcesoS: Revista ecuatoriana de historia* 1 (1991): 23–48.

13. Karen Viera Powers, *Andean Journeys: Migration, Ethnogenesis, and State in Colonial Quito* (Albuquerque: University of New Mexico Press, 1995); and Powers, "A Battle of Wills: Inventing Chiefly Legitimacy in the Colonial North Andes," in *Dead Giveaways: Indigenous Testaments of Colonial Mesoamerica and the Andes,* ed. Susan Kellogg and Matthew Restall (Salt Lake City: University of Utah Press, 1998), 183–213.

14. Karen Viera Powers, "Land Concentration and Environmental Degradation: Town Council Records on Deforestation in Uyumbicho (Quito, 1553–96)," in *Colonial Lives: Documents on Latin American History, 1550–1850,* ed. Richard Boyer and Geoffrey Spurling (Oxford: Oxford University Press, 2000), 11–17.

15. Gauderman, *Women's Lives*, 98–106.

16. Kenneth Andrien, *The Kingdom of Quito, 1690–1830: The State and Regional Development* (Cambridge: Cambridge University Press, 1995), 81–84. See also Nicholas P. Cushner, *Farm and Factory: The Jesuits and the Development of Agrarian Capitalism in Colonial Quito, 1600–1767* (Albany: State University of New York Press, 1982).

17. Gauderman, *Women's Lives*, 106–12.

18. Andrien, "Economic Crisis," 199–201. See also Chad Black, "Between Prescription and Practice: Governance, Legal Culture, and Gender in Quito, 1765–1830" (PhD diss., University of New Mexico, 2006), 44.

19. Nationalist Ecuadorian historians have treated this uprising as an avatar of independence. The first such historian was Juan de Velasco, writing as early as 1789, and the trend continued with authors such as Federico González Suárez, Oscar Efrén Reyes, and Carlos de la Torre. More recent scholarship emphasizes its place within Atlantic insurrection, beginning with French historian Joseph Pérez in *Los movimientos precursores de la emancipación en Hispanoamérica* (Madrid: Alhambra, 1977). Anthony J. McFarlane expands attention to local political culture in "The 'Rebellion of the Barrios': Urban Insurrection in Bourbon Quito," *Hispanic American Historical Review* 69:2 (May 1989): 283–330. Andrien, "Economic Crisis," presents a detailed analysis of local and regional economics that interrogated previous assumptions regarding the rebellion's place within eighteenth-century tax rebellions, while Martin Minchom's *People of Quito* focuses on the socio-demographic background of the rebellion. Most recently, Chad Black has located the uprising within shifting considerations of governance in "Between Prescription and Practice." My treatment of the 1747 millenarian insurrection that follows builds upon Minchom's treatment in *People of Quito*.

20. The tensions actually began that January, when Audiencia lawyer Don Melchor Ribadeneyra outbid Don Pedro Guerrero to take control of the administration of the monopoly. Since Ribadeneyra's plans included multiple centralizing measures, such as the building of an independent royal distillery, local elites and merchants protested the move, leading the Audiencia to eventually choose Guerrero's bid. See Black, "Between Prescription and Practice," 44–48. McFarlane argues that Ribadeneyra acted as a front, not for viceregal authorities but instead for competing mercantile interests from the northern city of Ibarra. McFarlane, "'Rebellion of the Barrios,'" 287–88.

21. McFarlane, "'Rebellion of the Barrios,'" 305. Estimates of crowd size range from a low of three thousand or four thousand to a high of sixteen thousand to eighteen thousand.

22. Minchom, *People of Quito*, 229.

23. McFarlane, "'Rebellion of the Barrios,'" 312–14.

24. The lone call for rebellion in Quito was a truncated affair in which the drums struck by haberdasher Francisco Xavier de la Cruz of San Sebastián to rally the faithful only managed to alert a passing patrol. See Minchom, *People of Quito*, 233–34.

25. Black, "Between Prescription and Practice," 86–89.

26. Morelli, *Territorio o nazione*, 226.

27. For a comprehensive narrative of eighteenth- and nineteenth-century indig-

enous uprisings, see Segundo E. Moreno Yáñez, *Sublevaciones indígenas en la Audiencia de Quito: desde comienzos del siglo XVIII hasta finales de la colonia,* 4th ed. (Quito: Ediciones de la Pontificia Universidad Católica del Ecuador, 1995).

28. Minchom, *People of Quito,* 241.

29. Morelli, *Territorio o nazione,* 234–39; Federica Morelli, "Un neo-sincretismo político: representación política y sociedad indígena durante el primer liberalismo hispanoamericano; el caso de la Audiencia de Quito (1813–1850)," in *Muchas Hispanoaméricas: antropología, historia y enfoques culturales en los estudios latinoamericanistas,* ed. T. Krüggeler and U. Mücke (Madrid: Iberoamericana, 2001), 164.

30. See Alberto Flores Galindo, *Buscando un Inca: identidad y utopia en los Andes* (Lima: Instituto de Apoyo Agrario, 1987), which was later published in translation: Alberto Flores Galindo, *In Search of an Inca: Identity and Utopia in the Andes,* ed. and trans. Carlos Aguirre, Charles F. Walker, and Willie Hiatt (New York: Cambridge University Press, 2010). See also Charles F. Walker, *Smoldering Ashes: Cuzco and the Creation of Republican Peru, 1780–1840* (Durham, NC: Duke University Press, 1999); and Thurner, *From Two Republics to One Divided.*

31. Morelli, *Territorio o nazione,* 244–47.

32. See Andrés Guerrero, "Curagas y tenientes políticos: la ley de la costumbre y la ley del estado (Otavalo 1830–1875)," in *Estudios y debates* 2 (December 1989): 321–66; Guerrero, "Construction of a Ventriloquist's Image"; and Guerrero, "The Administration of Dominated Populations under a Regime of Customary Citizenship: The Case of Postcolonial Ecuador," trans. Mark Thurner, in *After Spanish Rule,* ed. Guerrero and Thurner, 272–309.

33. Derek Williams, "Administering the Otavalan Indian and Centralizing Governance in Ecuador, 1851–1875," in *Highland Indians and the State,* ed. Clark and Becker, 54–55.

34. Aleezé Sattar, "¿Indígena o Ciudadano? Republican Laws and Highland Indian Communities in Ecuador, 1820–1857," in *Highland Indians and the State,* ed. Clark and Becker, 22–36.

35. Morelli, *Territorio o nazione,* 254–57.

36. On this legal history, see Sattar, "Unresolved Inheritance," 261–62.

37. Urbina's policies particularly targeted further growth in the population of *conciertos,* or debt peons beholden to the hacienda, a strategy that echoed eighteenth-century liberal theory and the politics of figures like Bolívar and San Martín, whose dreams of transforming Indian communities into a class of yeoman farmers was a definite influence upon Urbina. See Derek Williams, "Popular Liberalism and Indian Servitude: The Making and Unmaking of Ecuador's Antilandlord State, 1845–1868," *Hispanic American Historical Review* 83:4 (November 2003): 700–710.

38. Williams, "Popular Liberalism," 731–33.

39. This discussion is based largely on two court cases before the Superior Court of Quito and the Supreme Court of Ecuador, records of which are found in the Archivo Nacional del Ecuador. See ANE, Indígenas, 175:29 (1857), "Civiles entre los indígenas de

Sta Clara de Sanmillan y la Sra Juana del Maso por terrenos, aguas, y servidumbres"; and ANE, Indígenas, 176:5 (1858), "Causa seguida entre loa Sra Juna del Mazo y el comun de indígenas de Santa Clara de Sanmillan sobre terrenos."

40. Pilar Pérez, "Cuando los montes se vuelven carbon: la transformación de los paisajes en los alrededores de Quito, 1860–1940" (MA thesis, FLACSO-Ecuador, n.d.), 69.

41. ANE, Indígenas, 175:29 (1857), 2, 11.

42. ANE, Indígenas, 176:5 (1858), 15.

43. Sattar, "Unresolved Inheritance," chap. 3, esp. 116–17, 127–31.

44. The last communication prior to the law's passage came on October 12, 1857, from Delgado. Between this time and mid-February, no written or oral communications appear in the court record, which suggests the officials' need to take stock of the juridical impact of the new law.

45. Pérez, "Cuando los montes se vuelven carbon," 68–78.

46. Sattar has provided the most extensive analysis of the Daquilema uprising's ties to the socioeconomic struggles of the mid-nineteenth century. See Sattar, "Unresolved Inheritance," 316–57.

47. Milton Luna Tamayo, ¿Modernización? Ambigua experiencia en el Ecuador: industriales y fiesta popular (Quito: IADEP, 1993), 76–77.

48. See Deler, Ecuador: del espacio al estado nacional; and Guerrero, La semántica de la dominación.

49. Prieto, Liberalismo y temor, 136.

50. Ibid., 135.

51. For more on Jaramillo and his place within the international indigenista movement, see José Antonio Lucero, Struggles of Voice: The Politics of Indigenous Representation in the Andes (Pittsburgh: University of Pittsburgh Press, 2008), 70–73. See also Rebecca Earle, The Return of the Native: Indians and Myth-Making in Spanish America, 1810–1930 (Durham, NC: Duke University Press, 2007), esp. chap. 7; and de la Cadena, Indigenous Mestizos.

52. Jaramillo, El indio ecuatoriano.

53. Prieto, Liberalismo y temor, 140–41. See also Lucero, Struggles of Voice, 70–72.

54. Pineo, Social and Economic Reform, chap. 8. See also Capelo, El crimen del 15 de noviembre de 1922.

55. Marc Becker, "Indigenous Communists and Urban Intellectuals in Cayambe, Ecuador (1926–1944)," International Review of Social History 49, supp. (2004): 41–48.

56. Becker, Indians and Leftists, 25–32. The Socialist Party was renamed the Communist Party in 1931.

57. Sáenz, Sobre el indio ecuatoriano, 93–124.

58. Carlos Arroyo del Rio came close to finishing a term but was deposed in his last months by the 1944 Glorious Revolution that was engineered by José María Velasco Ibarra with support from the Federación Ecuatoriana de Indíos and various center-left groups.

59. "Ley de Organización y Régimen de las Comunas," in Républica del Ecuador,

Registro Oficial 2:55 (August 6, 1937): 1517–19. See also Becker, "Comunas and Indigenous Protest," 531–59; Lucero, *Struggles of Voice,* 70–72; and Victor A. Gonzáles S., *Las tierras comunales en el Ecuador* (Guayaquil: Casa de la Cultura Ecuatoriana, Núcleo del Guayas, 1982), 66–70.

60. Becker, "Comunas and Indigenous Protest," 540–46.

61. A. Kim Clark, "Shifting Paternalism in Indian-State Relations, 1895–1950," in *Highland Indians and the State,* ed. Clark and Becker, 98–103.

62. It is unclear precisely at what point it regained its holdings on the upper reaches of Pichincha, but, by 1928, the community once again controlled Rosaspamba and Cataloma, two of the disputed territories. See SNA-MTRH/Tierras, 191:5.

63. Kingman Garcés, *La ciudad y los otros,* 155.

64. Carrera Andrade, *El volcán y el colibrí,* 21–22.

65. ANE: Parroquiales, 1º Benalcázar I (November 29, 1919).

66. ANE: Parroquiales, 1º Benalcázar II (November 13, 1922); ANE: Parroquiales, 1º Benalcázar III (November 24, 1922).

67. ANE: Parroquiales, 1º Benalcázar V (February 17, 1926).

68. Ibid.

69. ANE: Parroquiales, 1º Benalcázar V (April 8, 1926); 1º Benalcázar VI (May 6, 1928).

70. ANE: Parroquiales, 1º Benalcázar I (January 12, 1921).

71. ANE: Parroquiales, 1º Benalcázar II (March 28, 1922).

72. ANE: Parroquiales, 1º Benalcázar II (October 5, 1922).

73. ANE: Parroquiales, 1º Benalcázar IV (January 14, 1925).

74. SNA-MTRH/Tierras 191:5 (May 7, 1930).

75. ANE: Protocolos, Notaria 1º, 549:334.v (May 28, 1917); 549:404 (June 26, 1917).

76. ANE: Parroquiales, 1º Benalcázar IV (April 23, 1925).

77. ANE: Parroquiales, 1º Benalcázar VI (April 24, 1933).

78. ANE: Parroquiales, 1º Benalcázar II (October 28, 1922).

79. ANE: Protocolos, Notaria 3º, 193:761 (March 28, 1926).

80. ANE: Parroquiales, 1º Benalcázar VI (November 18, 1926).

81. SNA-MTRH/Tierras 191:5 (September 20, 1930–October 8, 1930).

82. Nicolás Tipantocta to Ministro del Interior, SNA-MTRH/Tierras 191:5 (March 25, 1931).

83. Documentation of the saga summarized in the text can be found in a series of depositions and peitions included in SNA-MTRH/Tierras 191:5 (April 26, 1928–June 25, 1930) as well as in summary form in a letter José Federico Tumipamba crafted years later, found in SNA-MTRH/Tierras 179:13.

84. The original text reads, "los sagrados derechos que nos legaron nuestros antepasados aborígenes en orden a la conservación de las tierras de propiedad de todos y cada uno de los comuneros." José Gabriel Collahuaso to Ministro de Previsión Social, SNA-MTRH/Tierras 191:5 (April 26, 1928).

85. The original text reads, "*la completa anarquía y desorden,*" and "otros incautos comuneros también seguirán camino de los desleales que han hecho las ventas." Fed-

erico Tumipamba to Ministro de Previsión Social, SNA-MTRH/Tierras 191:5 (April 26, 1928).

86. Pedro Camacho to Ministro de Previsión Social, SNA-MTRH/Tierras 191:5 (May 3, 1928).

87. Ibid.

88. José Antonio Tumipamba to Ministro de Previsión Social, SNA-MTRH/ Tierras 191:5 (May 2, 1930). See also SNA-MTRH/Tierras 179:13.

89. Luís Tumipamba Deposition, SNA-MTRH/Tierras 191:5 (May 30, 1930).

90. Contribución sobre predios rústicos, SNA-MTRH/Tierras 191:5 (October 25, 1927).

91. Juan Alberto Tumipamba to Ministro de lo Interior, SNA-MTRH/Tierras 191:5 (January 24, 1931).

92. Williams, "Popular Liberalism," 728–29.

93. "Ley de Organización y Régimen de las Comunas," 1518–19.

94. SNA-MTRH/Tierras 191:5.

95. SNA-MTRH/Tierras 179:13.

96. "El IV Centenario de Atahualpa," *El comercio,* August 21, 1933; "Programa de la Sociedad de Albañiles," *El comercio,* August 28, 1933.

97. Mercedes Prieto, "Los indios y la nación: historias y memorias en disputa," in *Celebraciones centenarias y negociaciones por la nación ecuatorianas* (Quito: FLACSO, 2010).

98. The original text reads, "su buena organización y, entre otras cosas, por ser una de las primeras que obtuvo personería jurídica en el Ecuador, en los últimos días del Gobierno del señor General Eloy Alfaro, precursor que fue de la moderna legislación protectora a las comunidades campesinas." José Gabriel Collahuaso to Ministro de Previsión Social, SNA-MTRH/Tierras 191:5 (July 12, 1940).

99. José Domingo Laso, *Quito a la vista* (Quito: J. D. Laso and J. R. Cruz, 1911).

100. Hidalgo and Bedoya, "Guayaquil y Quito," 169–79.

101. This success stands in contrast to the experiences of other subaltern populations in the city's environs. See Ernesto Capello, "City Fragments: Space and Nostalgia in Modernizing Quito, 1885–1942" (PhD diss., University of Texas at Austin, 2005), 170–82, esp. 178–82.

102. Rappaport, *Politics of Memory,* 24.

Postscript

1. For a biographical sketch of García Muñoz, see César Augusto Alarcón Costa, *Diccionario biográfico ecuatoriano* (Quito: FED/Editorial Raices, 2000), 502–3.

2. Ernesto Alban Mosquera, *Estampas quiteñas* (Quito: Editorial "Fray Jodoco Ricke," 1949). For a short history of the development of the *estampa* as a theatrical form, see Descalzi, *Historia crítica del teatro ecuatoriano,* 3:986–1017.

3. http://www.youtube.com/user/ruthximena#play/uploads (accessed September 1, 2009).

4. Bakhtin, "Forms of Time," 159–60. See also Bakhtin, *Rabelais.*

5. The original text reads, "Hubiera deseado contemplar ese Arco antiguamente, antes del advenimiento de la luz eléctrica. Figúrome que habrá sido sitio especial para citas amorosas, emboscadas de 'ganster' y puñaladas a mansalva. Ahora, la civilización, con sus 'osrams' potentes, desflora la oscuridad impidiendo que en las sombras se ame, se robe y se asesine." Alfonso García Muñoz, *Estampas de mi ciudad* (Quito: Imprenta Nacional, 1936), 125. Osram was and is an American brand of lightbulbs.

6. Adam Sharman has made this point with regard to *modernismo*'s development. See Sharman, *Tradition and Modernity in Spanish American Literature,* esp. chap. 4.

7. Bakhtin, "Forms of Time," 254. This argument has a strong association with the Heideggerian conception of the work of art, within which the figure of the preserver is considered paramount to the ongoing existence of the "world" set up by the work. See "Origin of the Work of Art," in Martin Heidegger, *Poetry, Language, Thought* (New York: Harper & Row, 1971), 66–68.

8. I treat this subject in Capello, "City Fragments," chap. 8.

9. On major and minor chronotopes, see Bakhtin, "Forms of Time"; Ladin, "Fleshing Out the Chronotope"; and Bemong and Borghart, "Bakhtin's Theory of the Literary Chronotope," in *Bakhtin's Theory,* ed. Bemong et al., 7–8.

Selected Bibliography

Archival Collections

Quito

AGJ	Archivo Gangotena Jijón
AHBC/Q	Archivo Histórico del Banco Central del Ecuador
	Colección Fotográfica; Fondo Jijón y Caamaño
AHM	Archivo Histórico Metropolitano
ANE	Archivo Nacional del Ecuador
	Casas; Civiles; Criminales; Indígenas; Mapoteca; Protocolos; Parroquiales
BCBCE	Biblioteca Cultural del Banco Central del Ecuador
	Fondo Jijón y Caamaño
BEAEP	Biblioteca Ecuatoriano "Aurelio Espinosa Pólit"
	Hojas Volantes; Mapoteca
MC/D	Museo de la Ciudad, Colección Durini

SNA-MTRH   Sistema Nacional de Archivos–Ministerio de Trabajo y
       Recursos Humanos
       Tierras

United States

LOC/GM   Library of Congress, Geography & Map Division
LOC/PP   Library of Congress, Prints & Photographs Division
NYPL   New York Public Library
       Colección de leyes, decretos, ordenanzas, resoluciones y
         contratos, concernientes a esta municipalidad [Guayaquil],
         1890–1926; Map Collection

Newspapers and Magazines

Alas (Quito), 1934–1935
América (Quito), 1925–1942
Bagatelas: Revista quincenal festiva (Quito), 1922
Boletín de la Exposición (Quito), 1909
Boletín de Obras Públicas (Quito), 1943
Boletín de la Sociedad Geográfica de Quito (Quito), 1911
Boletín de Sociedad de Técnicos y Constructores (Quito), October 1926
Boletín Semanal Universidad Popular "Llamarada" (Quito), 1930
Caricatura (Quito), 1921–1924, 1950
Claridad (Quito), 1925
El comercio (Quito), selected months, 1906–1944
El debate (Quito), selected months, 1939–1944
El día (Quito), selected months, 1925–1942
La era moderna (Quito), 1911
Gaceta municipal (Quito), 1910–1943
La guitarra (Quito), 1888
Hélice (Quito), 1926
Letras (Quito), 1912–1918
El municipio (Quito), 1885–1908
El obrero (Quito), 1933–1934
Registro civil (Quito), selected months, 1900–1942
Registro municipal (Quito), 1909
Revista de Quito (Quito), 1898
Rieles (Quito), 1929–1931
Semana gráfica (Guayaquil), 1934
Unión iberoamericana (Quito), 1888
Vanguardia (Quito), 1931

Primary Sources

Alban Mosquera, Ernesto. *Estampas quiteñas.* Quito: Editorial "Fray Jodoco Ricke," 1949.

Alfaro, Eloy. *Mensaje del Presidente de la República al Poder Legislativo sobre Exposición Nacional.* Quito: Imprenta Nacional, 1908.

Andrade, Raúl. "Retablo de una generación decapitada." In *El perfil de la quimera: siete ensayos literarios,* 65–105. Quito: Casa de la Cultura Ecuatoriana, 1951.

Andrade, Roberto. *Pacho Villamar.* 1900. Reprint, Quito: Clásicos Ariel, n.d.

———. *¿Quién mató a García Moreno?*: autobiografía de un perseguido. Quito: Abya-Yala, 1994.

———. *¡Sangre! ¿Quién la derramó? (historia de los últimos crímenes cometidos en la nación del Ecuador).* Quito: El Quiteño Libre, 1912.

———. *Seis de agosto o sea muerte de García Moreno.* Portoviejo, Ecuador: Oficina Tipográfica del Colegio "Olmedo," 1896.

Andrade Coello, Alejandro. *Del Quito antiguo.* Quito: Imprenta "Ecuador," 1935.

———. *Manuel J. Calle, orientaciones periodísticas.* Quito: Imprenta "Ecuador," 1919.

———. *Motivos nacionales (crónicas quiteñas).* Vol. 2. Quito: Imprenta de la Escuela de Artes y Oficios, 1927.

Barrera, Isaac. *Del vivir: reflexiones de juventud.* Quito: Editorial Ecuatoriana, 1972.

———. *Estudios sobre modernismo literario: publicado en el Diario El Comercio 1 Enero 1910 – 10 de Abril 1910.* Quito: Casa de la Cultura Ecuatoriana, 1971.

———. *Relación de las fiestas del primer centenario de la batalla de Pichincha, 1822–1922.* Quito: Talleres Tipográficos Nacionales, 1922.

Baudelaire, Charles. "The Painter of Modern Life." In *The Painter of Modern Life and Other Essays,* by Charles Baudelaire, translated and edited by Jonathan Mayne, 1–40. London: Phaidon Press, 1964.

Bemelmans, Ludwig. *The Donkey Within.* New York: Viking Press, 1941.

Borja, Arturo, Humberto Fierro, and Ernesto Noboa Caamaño. *Otros modernistas.* Quito: Ariel, n.d.

Bustamante, José Rafael. *Para matar el gusano.* 1913. Reprint, Quito: Editorial Casa de la Cultura Ecuatoriana, 1960.

Calle, Manuel J. *Un forzado de las letras: antología de Manuel J. Calle.* Edited by Diego Araujo. Quito: Ediciones del Banco Central del Ecuador, 1998.

———. *Leyendas del tiempo heroico: episodios de la guerra de la independencia.* Guayaquil: Imp. de "El Telégrafo," 1905.

Campos, José Antonio. *Cosas de mi tierra.* Guayaquil: Imprenta Garay, 1929.

———. *Linterna mágica.* Guayaquil and Quito: Ariel, n.d.

Capelo, J. Alejo. *El crimen del 15 de noviembre de 1922.* Guayaquil: Litografía e Impr. de la Universidad de Guayaquil; Librería y distribuidora Continental, 1983.

Carrera Andrade, Jorge. *El volcán y el colibrí: autobiografía.* Quito: Corporación Editora Nacional, 1989.

Centro de Estudios Pedagógicos e Hispanoamericanos de Panamá. *Summary of Ten Lectures on Ecuadorian Art by José Gabriel Navarro*. Panama City: Centro de Estudios, 1935.

Chiriboga Alvear, Manuel. *Resumen histórico de la Sociedad "Artística e Industrial del Pichincha," 1892–1917*. Quito: Encuadernación Nacionales, 1917.

Chiriboga N., A. I., and Georges Perrier. *Las misiones científicas francesas en el Ecuador: 1735–1744; 1899–1906*. Quito: Imprenta Nacional, 1936.

Compañía "Guía del Ecuador." *El Ecuador, Guía comercial, agrícola e industrial de la república*. Guayaquil: E. Rodenas, 1909.

Cuerpo de leyes de la República de Colombia. Caracas: Valentin Espinal, 1840.

Davila, Aurelio. *El 25 de abril de 1907: recuerdos históricos*. Guayaquil: "Popular," 1909.

Diario de Avisos. *El Ecuador en Chicago*. New York: A. E. Chasmar, 1894.

Dietz, Robert Erwin. *A Leaf from the Past*. New York: R. E. Dietz Company, 1913.

Espinosa, José Modesto. *Obras completas*. Vol. 1, *Artículos de costumbres*. Freiburg, Germany: B. Herder, 1899.

Franklin, Albert B. *Ecuador: Portrait of a People*. Garden City, NY: Doubleday, Doran, 1943.

Gangotena y Jijón, Cristóbal. *Al margen de la historia: leyendas de frailes, pícaros y caballeros*. Quito: Imprenta Nacional, 1924.

García Muñoz, Alfonso. *Estampas de mi ciudad*. Quito: Imprenta Nacional, 1936.

———. *Estampas de mi ciudad*. Vol. 2. Quito: Imprenta de Educación, 1937.

———. *Estampas de mi ciudad*. Vol. 3. Quito: Ediciones Patria, 1941.

Gento Sanz, Benjamín. *Guia del turista en la iglesia y convento de San Francisco de Quito*. Quito: Imprenta Americana, 1940.

González Suárez, Federico. *Carta del Ilmo. y Rmo. Sr. Dr. D. Federico González Suárez, Obispo de Ibarra, á su Vicario General, explicada por el mismo autor*. Quito: Tip. de la Escuela de Artes y Oficios, 1900.

———. *Historia general de la República del Ecuador*. 7 vols. 1890–1903. Reprinted in 3 vols. Quito: Edit. Casa de la Cultura Ecuatoriana, 1969–1971.

———. *Memorias íntimas*. Quito: Editorial Gutenberg, 1931.

———. *Obras oratorias*. Quito: AYMESA, 1992.

Gran guía de la República del Ecuador, S.A. Quito: Tip. Fernández, 1936.

Holguín Balcázar, Froilán. *Mi capricho de hacerme hombre*. Guayaquil: Editorial Senefelder, 1936.

Icaza, Jorge. *Cholos*. 1937. Reprint, Quito: Libresa, 1993.

———. *¿Cuál es? Sin sentido*. Quito: Su Librería, 1979.

———. *En las calles*. 1935. Reprint, Quito: Editorial El Conejo, 1985.

———. *Huasipungo*. 1934. Reprint, Quito: Libresa, 1983.

Jaramillo Alvarado, Pio. *El indio ecuatoriano*. 3rd ed. Quito: Talleres Gráficos del Estado, 1936.

———. "El nuevo Tahuantinsuyo." *América* 11 (1936): 153–58.

———. *Estudios históricos*. Quito: Editorial Artes Gráficas, 1934.

Jijón y Caamaño, Jacinto. "La ecuatorianidad." In *Estudios básicos sobre la nacionalidad ecuatoriana,* 105–46. Quito: Centro de Estudios Históricos del Ejercito, 1998.

———. *Influencia de Quito en la emancipación del continente americano: la independencia (1809–1824).* Quito: Imprenta de la Universidad Central, 1924.

———. *Política conservadora.* Vol. 1. Riobamba: La Buena Prensa del Chimborazo, 1929.

———. *Política conservadora.* Vol. 2. Quito, 1934.

———. *Sebastián de Benalcázar.* 3 vols. 1936–1950. Reprint, Quito: Corporación de Estudios y Publicaciones, 1983.

Manifiesto de la Junta Patriótica Nacional. Quito: Imprenta y encuadernación nacionales, 1910.

Mariátegui, José Carlos. *Siete ensayos de interpretación de la realidad peruana.* Lima, 1928. Reprint, Montevideo: Biblioteca de Marcha, 1970.

Martínez, Luís A. *A la costa.* 1904. Reprint, Quito: Clásicos Ariel, n.d.

———. *Andinismo, arte y literatura.* Quito: Abya-Yala–Nuevos Horizontes, 1994.

Menéndez Pelayo, Marcelino. *Espistolario.* Multiple vols. Madrid: Fundación Universitaria Española, 1981–1989.

Mera, Juan León. *Juan León Mera: antología esencial,* edited by Xavier Michelena. Quito: Banco Central/Abya-Yala, 1994.

Mercado, Pedro de. *Historia de la Provincia del Nuevo Reino y Quito de la Compañía de Jesus,* vol. 3. Bogotá: Biblioteca de la Provincia de Colombia, 1957.

Michaux, Henri. *Ecuador: A Travel Journal.* Translated by Robin Magowan. Seattle: University of Washington Press, 1970.

Mission du Service Géographique de l'Armée pour la mesure d'un arc de méridien équatorial en Amérique du Sud sous le controle scientifique de l'Académie des Sciences, 1899–1906. Multiple vols. Paris: Gauthier-Villars, 1910–1922.

Monografía ilustrada de la provincia de Pichincha. Quito, 1922.

Montalvo, Juán. *Montalvo.* Edited by Galo René Pérez. Quito: Banco Central, 1985.

Navarro, José Gabriel. *Contribuciones a la historia del arte en el Ecuador. Vol. 2, El arte en las fundaciones mercedarias la Basílica y el convento de la Merced: la iglesia y el convento de la recolección del Tejar.* Quito: Talleres Gráficos de Educación, 1939.

———. *La escultura en el Ecuador (siglos XVI al XVIII).* Madrid: Real Academia de Bellas Artes de San Fernando, 1929.

———. *Estudios históricos.* Quito: Grupo Aymesa, 1995.

———. *La Iglesia de la Compañía en Quito.* Madrid: Antonio Marzo, 1930.

Navas E., Juan de Dios, and Julio Tobar Donoso. *Discursos de ingreso y recepción en la Academia Nacional de Historia el 6 de enero de 1927.* Quito: Tipográfica de la "Prensa Católica," 1927.

Olmedo, José Joaquín. *Obra poética.* Quito: Editorial Casa de la Cultura Ecuatoriana, 1971.

Palacio, Pablo. *Obras completas,* edited by María del Carmen Fernández. Quito: Libresa, 1997.

Peña Orejuela, Humberto. *Guia de Bolsillo de Quito.* Quito: Talleres Tipográficos Nacionales, 1920.

Pérez, J. Gualberto. *Recuerdo histórico de la Escuela Politécnica de Quito.* Quito: Tip. Prensa Católica, 1921.

Pérez Montfort, Ricardo. *Hispanismo y Falange: los sueños imperiales de la derecha española.* Mexico City: Fondo de Cultura Económica, 1992.

Posada, Adolfo. *Escritos municipalistas y de la vida local.* Madrid: Instituto de Estudios de Administración Local, 1979.

——. *El régimen municipal de la ciudad moderna.* Madrid: Librería General de Victoriano Suárez, 1916.

Primer Congreso de Municipalidades del Ecuador: actas, acuerdos y resoluciones. Quito: Imprenta Municipal 1942.

República del Ecuador. *Decreto Supremo de 31 de octubre de 1907 ordenando una gran exposición nacional en Quito para el 10 de agosto de 1909.* Quito: Imprenta Nacional, 1907.

——. *Ley de régimen municipal.* Guayaquil: Imprenta y talleres municipales, 1929.

La République de l'Équateur et sa participation a la Exposition Universelle de 1900. Paris: Imprimerie du "Correo de Paris," 1900.

Ribadeneira, J. Enrique, and Luis Cornelio Diaz V. *Cien años de legislación militar, 1830–1930.* Quito: Editorial Gutenberg, 1930.

Salvador, Humberto. *Ajedrez.* Quito: Escuela de Artes y Oficios, 1929.

——. *Camarada.* Quito: Talleres Tipográficas Nacionales, 1933.

——. *En la ciudad he perdido una novela.* Introduction by María del Carmen Fernández. 1929. Reprint, Quito: Editorial Libresa, 1996.

——. *Esquema sexual.* Quito: Imprenta Nacional, 1934.

——. *La novela interrumpida.* Quito: Editorial Quito, 1942.

——. *Noviembre.* Quito: Editorial L. I. Fernández, 1939.

——. *Trabajadores.* 1935. Reprint, Quito: Editorial El Conejo, 1985.

Schumacher, Pedro. *Teocracia o demoniocracia? Cristo o Lucifer? Quién vencera? Quién como Dios!* 2nd ed. Freiburg, Germany: B. Herder, 1897.

Sociedad Española de Amigos del Arte. *Aportación al estudio de la cultura española en las Indias: catálogo general ilustrado de la Exposición.* Madrid: ESPASA-CALPE, 1930.

Suárez, Pablo Arturo. *Contribución al estudio de las realidades entre las clases obreras y campesinas.* Quito: Imprenta de la Universidad Central, 1934.

Tobar Donoso, Julio. *Catolicismo social.* Quito: Editorial Ecuatoriana, 1936.

——. *García Moreno y la instrucción pública.* Quito: Editorial Ecuatoriana, 1940.

——. *Las relaciones entre la iglesia y el estado ecuatoriano: resumen histórico.* Quito: Editorial Ecuatoriana, 1938.

——. *Monografías históricas.* Quito: Editorial Ecuatoriana, 1938.

Tufiño, Luis G. *Servicio Geográfico del Ejercito Ecuatoriano y la única base práctica en los estudios de la facultad de ciencias (proyecto).* Quito: Imprenta y Encuadernación Nacionales, 1911.

Vacas Galindo, Enrique. *La integridad territorial del Ecuador.* Quito: Tipografía y encuadernación Salesiana, 1905.

Wolf, Teodoro. *Geográfica y geología del Ecuador.* Leipzig: F. A. Brockhaus, 1892.

Zaldumbide, Gonzalo. *Significado de España en América, ensayos.* Quito: Letramía, 2002.

Secondary Sources

Achig, Lucas. *El proceso urbano de Quito: ensayo de interpretación.* Quito: Centro de Investigaciones; CIUDAD, 1983.

Adoum, Jorge Enrique. *La gran literatura ecuatoriana del 30.* Quito: Editorial El Conejo, 1984.

Agramonte, Roberto. *La filosofía de Montalvo.* Quito: Banco Central del Ecuador, 1992.

Aguilar, Paúl. *Quito: arquitectura y modernidad, 1850–1950.* Quito. Museo Municipal Alberto Mena Caamaño, 1995.

Akerman, James R. "Twentieth-Century American Road Maps and the Making of a National Motorized Space." In *Cartographies of Travel and Navigation,* edited by James R. Akerman, 151–206. Chicago: University of Chicago Press, 2006.

Andermann, Jens, and William Rowe, eds. *Images of Power: Iconography, Culture and the State in Latin America.* New York: Berghahn Books, 2005.

Andrien, Kenneth. "Economic Crisis, Taxes, and the Quito Insurrection of 1765." *Past and Present* 129 (November 1990): 104–31.

———. *The Kingdom of Quito, 1690–1830: The State and Regional Development.* Cambridge: Cambridge University Press, 1995.

Annino, Antonio. "El Jano bifronte: los pueblos y los orígenes del liberalismo en México." In *Crisis, reforma y revolución: Mexico; historias de fin de siglo,* edited by Leticia Reina and Elisa Servín, 209–51. Mexico City: Taurus, Consejo Nacional para la Cultura y las Artes, Instituto Nacional de Antropología e Historia, 2002.

Ayala Mora, Enrique. *Breve historia del conflicto Ecuador-Peru.* Quito: CDS, 1995.

———. "Gabriel García Moreno y la gestación del estado nacional en el Ecuador." *Cultura* 4:10 (May–August 1981): 141–74.

———. *Historia de la revolución liberal ecuatoriana.* Quito: Corporación Editora Nacional, 1994.

———. "Introducción." In *Federico González Suárez: la polémica sobre el estado laico,* by Federico González Suárez. Edited by Enrique Ayala Mora. Quito: Corporación Editora Nacional, 1980.

———. "El municipio en el siglo XIX." *ProcesoS: revista ecuatoriana de historia* 1 (1991): 69–86.

Ayala Mora, Enrique, ed. *Nueva historia del Ecuador.* Vol. 9, *Epoca republicana III: cacao, capitalismo, y Revolución Liberal.* Quito: Corporación Editora Nacional, 1983.

———. *Nueva historia del Ecuador.* Vol. 10, *Epoca republicana IV: el Ecuador entre los años veinte y los sesenta.* Quito: Corporación Editora Nacional, 1983.

Bakhtin, M. M. *The Dialogic Imagination.* Edited by Michael Holquist. Translated by Caryl Emerson and Michael Holquist. Austin: University of Texas Press, 1981.

———. *Rabelais and His World.* Translated by Hélène Iswolsky. Bloomington: Indiana University Press, 1984.

Balseca, Fernando. "En busca de nuevas regions: la nación y la narrativa ecuatoriana." In *Crítica de la literatura ecuatoriana: hacia el nuevo siglo,* edited by Gabriela Pólit Dueñas, 141–55. Quito: FLACSO, 2001.

Baskes, Jeremy. *Indians, Merchants, and Markets: A Reinterpretation of the Repartimiento and Spanish-Indian Economic Relations in Colonial Oaxaca, 1750–1821.* Stanford: Stanford University Press, 2005.

Becker, Marc. "Comunas and Indigenous Protest in Cayambe, Ecuador." *The Americas* 55:4 (April 1999): 531–59.

———. *Indians and Leftists in the Making of Ecuador's Modern Indigenous Movements.* Durham, NC: Duke University Press, 2008.

———. "Indigenous Communists and Urban Intellectuals in Cayambe, Ecuador (1926–1944)." *International Review of Social History* 49, supp. (2004): 41–64.

Bell, Duncan S. A. "Mythscapes: Memory, Mythology, and National Identity." *British Journal of Sociology* 54:1 (March 2003): 63–81.

Belyea, Barbara. "Images of Power: Derrida, Foucault, Harley." *Cartographica* 29:2 (summer 1992): 1–9.

Bemong, Nele, Pieter Borghart, Michel De Dobbeleer, Kristoffel Demoen, Koen De Temmerman, and Bart Keunen, eds. *Bakhtin's Theory of the Literary Chronotope: Reflections, Applications, Perspectives.* Ghent, Belgium: Academia Press, 2010.

Benavides Sólis, Jorge. *La arquitectura del siglo XX en Quito.* Quito: Banco Central del Ecuador, 1995.

Black, Chad. "Between Prescription and Practice: Governance, Legal Culture, and Gender in Quito, 1765–1830." PhD dissertation, University of New Mexico, 2006.

Borges Lemos, Celina. "The Modernization of Brazilian Urban Space as a Political Symbol of the Republic." Translated by Elizabeth A. Jackson. *Journal of Decorative and Propaganda Arts* 21 (1995): 219–37.

Boyer, M. Christine. *The City of Collective Memory: Its Historical Imagery and Architectural Entertainments.* Cambridge, MA: MIT Press, 1994.

Boym, Svetlana. *The Future of Nostalgia.* New York: Basic Books, 2001.

Brading, D. A. *The First America: The Spanish Monarchy, Creole Patriots, and the Liberal State, 1492–1867.* Cambridge: Cambridge University Press, 1991.

Bustos, Guillermo. "La hispanización de la memoria pública en el cuarto centenario de fundación de Quito." In *Etnicidad y poder en los países andinos,* edited by Christian Büschges, Guillermo Bustos, and Olaf Kaltmeier, 111–34. Quito: Corporación Editora Nacional, 2007.

———. "Quito en la transición: Actores colectivos e identidades culturales urbanas (1920–1950)." In *Enfoques y estudios históricos: Quito a través de la historia,* 163–88. Quito: Editorial Fraga, 1992.

Caicedo, Gabriela. "Entre la plaza San Francisco de Quito y la Piazza San Marco de Venecia." *TRAMA* 80 (2002): 36–39.

Canessa Oneto, Mario. *100 años de historia del tenis ecuatoriano.* Guayaquil: Poligráfica C.A., 2000.

Cañizares-Esguerra, Jorge. *Puritan Conquistadors: Iberianizing the Atlantic, 1550–1700.* Stanford: Stanford University Press, 2006.

Capello, Ernesto. "Arquivo: Jacinto Jijón y Caamaño, 'La fecha de fundación de Quito.'" *Brújula* 5:1 (December 2006): 37–43.

———. "The City as Anachronism: Remembering Quito in the Liberal Era." MA thesis, University of Texas at Austin, 2001.

———. "City, Chronicle, Chronotope: Re-Constructing and Writing Old Quito." *Journal of Latin American Urban Studies* 6 (fall 2004): 37–56.

———. "City Fragments: Space and Nostalgia in Modernizing Quito, 1885–1942." PhD dissertation, University of Texas at Austin, 2005.

———. "Hispanismo casero: la invención del Quito hispano." *ProcesoS: revista ecuatoriana de historia* 20 (fall 2003–spring 2004): 55–77.

———. "Imaging Old Quito: The Postcolonial City as Universal Nostalgia." *City: Analysis of Urban Trends, Culture, Theory, Policy, Action* 10:2 (July 2006): 125–47.

Carpio Vintimilla, Julio. *La evolución urbana de Cuenca en el siglo XIX.* Cuenca: Universidad de Cuenca (IDIS), 1983.

Carrión, Fernando. *Quito: crisis y política urbana.* Quito: CIUDAD; Editorial El Conejo, 1987.

Castells, Manuel. *City, Class, and Power.* Translated by E. Lebas. New York: St. Martin's Press, 1978.

———. *The City and the Grassroots.* Berkeley: University of California, 1983.

Casti, Emanuela. *Reality as Representation: The Semiotics of Cartography.* Bergamo, Italy: Bergamo University Press–Sestante, 2000.

Castillo Illingworth, Santiago. *La iglesia y la revolución liberal: las relaciones de la iglesia y el estado en la época del liberalismo.* Quito: Ediciones del Banco Central del Ecuador, 1995.

Çelik, Zeynep. *Displaying the Orient: Architecture of Islam at Nineteenth-Century World's Fairs.* Berkeley: University of California Press, 1992.

Cevallos García, Gabriel. *La historia en el Ecuador.* In *Reflexiones sobre la historia del Ecuador, primera parte,* 55–217. Quito: Ediciones del Banco Central del Ecuador, 1987.

Cevallos Romero, Alfonso. *Arte, diseño y arquitectura en el Ecuador: la obra del Padre Brüning, 1899–1938.* Quito: Museos del Banco Central del Ecuador/Abya-Yala, 1994.

———, and Pedro M. Durini R. *Ecuador universal: visión desconocida de una etapa de la arquitectura ecuatoriana.* Quito: P. M. Durini R., 1990.

Chalupa, Federico A. "The Ecuadorian City and Modernity: Jorge Icaza's Quito." In *The Image of the City in Literature, Media, and Society,* edited by Will Wright and Steven Kaplan, 149–53. Pueblo: Colorado State University–Pueblo, 2003.

Clark, A. Kim. "Indians, the State and Law: Public Works and the Struggle to Control Labor in Liberal Ecuador." *Journal of Historical Sociology* 7:1 (March 1994): 49–72.

———. "La medida de la diferencia: las imágenes indigenistas de los indios serranos en el Ecuador (1920–1940)." In *Ecuador racista: imágenes e identidades,* edited by Emma Cervone and Fredy Rivera, 111–26. Quito: FLACSO Ecuador, 1999.

———. "Race, 'Culture,' and Mestizaje: The Statistical Construction of the Ecuadorian Nation, 1930–1950." *Journal of Historical Sociology* 11:2 (June 1998): 185–211.

———. *The Redemptive Work: Railway and Nation in Ecuador, 1895–1930.* Wilmington, DE: Scholarly Resources, 1998.

———, and Marc Becker, eds. *Highland Indians and the State in Modern Ecuador.* Pittsburgh: University of Pittsburgh Press, 2007.

Cobo Barona, Mario. *Luis A. Martínez: el arte de vivir y de morir.* Quito: Autosierra, 2003.

Coral Patiño, Héctor. *Isidro Ayora.* Quito: Abrapalabra Editores, 1995.

Corral, Wilfrido H. "Humberto Salvador y Pablo Palacio: política literaria y psicoanálisis en la Sudamérica de los treinta." In *Crítica literaria ecuatoriana: hacia un nuevo siglo,* edited by Gabriela Pólit Dueñas, 251–306. Quito: FLACSO Ecuador, 2001.

Coronel, Valeria. "Orígenes de una Democracia Corporativa: estrategias para la ciudadanización del campesinado indígena, partidos políticos y reforma territorial en Ecuador (1925–1944)." In *Historia social urbana: espacios y flujos,* edited by Eduardo Kingman Garcés, 323–64. Quito: FLACSO–Ministerio de Cultura, 2009.

———. "A Revolution in Stages: Subaltern Politics, Nation-State Formation, and the Origins of Social Rights in Ecuador, 1834–1943." PhD dissertation, New York University, 2011.

Cosgrove, Denis E., ed. *Mappings.* London: Reaktion Books, 2001.

Craib, Raymond B. *Cartographic Mexico: A History of State Fixations and Fugitive Landscapes.* Durham, NC: Duke University Press, 2004.

———. "Cartography and Power in the Conquest and Creation of New Spain." *Latin American Research Review* 35:1 (2000): 7–36.

Crawford de Roberts, Lois. *El Ecuador en la época cacaotera: respuestas locales al auge y colapso en el ciclo monoexportador.* Translated by Erika Silva and Rafael Quintero. Quito: Editorial Universitaria, 1980.

Crespo Toral, Remigio. "Modesto Espinosa, Semblanza." In *Biblioteca ecuatoriana mínima: prosistas de la república,* 439–46. Puebla, Mexico: Editorial J. M. Cajica Jr., 1960.

Cushner, Nicholas P. *Farm and Factory: The Jesuits and the Development of Agrarian Capitalism in Colonial Quito, 1600–1767.* Albany: State University of New York Press, 1982.

de la Cadena, Marisol. *Indigenous Mestizos: The Politics of Race and Culture in Cuzco, Peru, 1919–1991.* Durham, NC: Duke University Press, 2000.

Delaney, Jeane. "The Discovery of Spain: The Hispanismo of Manuel Gálvez." In *Bridging the Atlantic: Toward a Reassessment of Iberian and Latin American Cultural Ties,* edited by Marina Pérez de Mendiola, 71–82. Albany: State University of New York Press, 1996.

de la Torre Espinosa, Carlos. *La seducción velasquista.* Quito: Libri Mundi/Grosse Luemern, FLACSO, 1997.

Deler, Jean Paul. *Ecuador: del espacio al estado nacional.* Quito: Banco Central del Ecuador, 1987.

———, Nelson Gómez, and Michel Portais. *El manejo del espacio en el Ecuador: etapas claves.* Quito: Centro Ecuatoriano de Investigación Geográfica, 1983.

Demalas, Marie-Danielle, and Yves Saint-Geours. *Jerusalén y Babilonia: religión y política en el Ecuador, 1780–1880.* Translated by Carmen Garatea Yuri. Quito: Corporación Editora Nacional, 1988.

Descalzi, Ricardo. *Historia crítica del teatro ecuatoriano.* 6 vols. Quito: Editorial Casa de la Cultura Ecuatoriana, 1968.

Domingo D., Walter. "Entrevista a Guillermo Jones Odriozola sobre el Plan Regulador de Quito de 1942–1944." *TRAMA* 56 (January 1992): 34–41.

Drake, Paul W. *The Money Doctor in the Andes: The Kemmerer Missions, 1923–1933.* Durham, NC: Duke University Press, 1989.

Dym, Jordana, and Karl Offen, eds. *Mapping Latin America: A Cartographic Reader.* Chicago: University of Chicago Press, 2011.

Earle, Rebecca. *The Return of the Native: Indians and Myth-Making in Spanish America, 1810–1930.* Durham, NC: Duke University Press, 2007.

Espinosa Apolo, Manuel. *Mestizaje, cholificación y blanqueamiento en Quito primera mitad del siglo XX.* Quito: Universidad Andina Simón Bolívar Ecuador; Abya-Yala; Corporación Editora Nacional, 2003.

Etlin, Richard A. *Modernism in Italian Architecture, 1890–1940.* Cambridge, MA: MIT Press, 1991.

Fabian, Johannes. *Time and the Other: How Anthropology Makes Its Object.* New York: Columbia University Press, 1983.

Fernández Borchart, Ricardo. *Waldo Frank: un puente entre las dos Américas.* Coruña, Spain: Universidade da Coruña, 1997.

Fernández, María del Carmen. *El realismo abierto de Pablo Palacio en la encrucijada de los 30.* Quito: Ediciones Libri Mundi/Enrique Grosse-Luemern, 1991.

———. "Estudio Introductorio." In *En la ciudad he perdido una novela,* by Humberto Salvador. Quito: Editorial Libresa, 1996.

Fernández-Salvador, Carmen. "Images and Memory: The Construction of Collective Identities in Seventeenth-Century Quito." PhD dissertation, University of Chicago, 2005.

———, and Alfredo Costales. *Arte colonial quiteño: renovado enfoque y nuevos actores.* Quito: FONSAL, 2007.

Fischel, Astrid. *El Teatro Nacional de Costa Rica: su historia.* San José, Costa Rica: Editorial Teatro Nacional, 1992.

Fojas, Camilla. *Cosmopolitanism in the Americas.* West Lafayette, IN: Purdue University Press, 2005.

Foster, David William, and Daniel Altamiranda, eds. *Theoretical Debates in Spanish American Literature.* New York: Garland Publishing, 1997.

Fradera, Josep Maria. *Cultura nacional en una societat dividida: patriotisme i cultura a Catalunya (1838–1868).* Barcelona: Curial, 1992.

Galvéz, Manuel. *Vida de don Gabriel García Moreno.* Buenos Aires: Editorial Difusión, 1942.

Gauderman, Kim. *Women's Lives in Colonial Quito: Gender, Law, and Economy in Spanish America.* Austin: University of Texas Press, 2003.

Goetschel, Ana María. *Educación de las mujeres, maestras y esferas públicas: Quito en la primera mitad del siglo XX.* Quito: FLACSO Sede Ecuador–Abya-Yala, 2007.

———. "Hegemonía y sociedad (Quito: 1930–1950)." In *Ciudades de los Andes: visión histórica y contemporánea,* ed. Eduardo Kingman Garcés, 319–47. Quito: CIUDAD, 1992.

———, ed. *Orígenes del feminismo en el Ecuador: antología.* Quito: CONAMU; FLACSO; Municipio del Distrito Metropolitano de Quito; UNIFEM, 2006.

Gómez, Nelson. *La misión geodésica y la cultura de Quito.* Quito: Ediguias, 1987.

———. *Quito y su desarrollo urbano.* Quito: Editorial Camino, 1980.

Gómez R., Jorge. *Las misiones pedagógicas alemanas y la educación en el Ecuador.* Quito: Abya-Yala 1993.

González de Valcárcel, J. M. *Restauración monumental y "puesta en valor" de las ciudades americanas* (Architectural Conservation and Enhancement of Historic Towns in America). Barcelona: Editorial Blume, 1977.

Gootenberg, Paul. *Imagining Development: Economic Ideas in Peru's "Fictitious Prosperity" of Guano, 1840–1880.* Berkeley: University of California Press, 1993.

Gorelik, Adrián. *La grilla y el parque: espacio público y cultura urbana en Buenos Aires, 1887–1936.* Buenos Aires: Universidad Nacional de Quilmes, 1998.

———, and Graciela Silvestri. "The Past as the Future: A Reactive Utopía in Buenos Aires." In *The Latin American Cultural Studies Reader,* edited by Ana Del Sarto, Alicia Ríos, and Abril Trigo, 427–40. Durham, NC: Duke University Press, 2004.

Granados García, Aimer, and Carlos Marichal, eds. *Construcción de las identidades latinoamericanas: ensayos de historia intelectual (siglos XIX y XX).* Mexico City: El Colegio de México, Centro de Estudios Históricos, 2004.

Greet, Michele. *Beyond National Identity: Pictorial Indigenism as a Modernist Strategy in Andean Art, 1920–1960.* University Park: Pennsylvania State University Press, 2009.

Gruzinski, Serge. *Images at War: Mexico from Columbus to Blade Runner (1492–2019).* Translated by Heather MacLean. Durham, NC: Duke University Press, 2001.

Guerra, François-Xavier. *Modernidades e independencias: ensayos sobre las revoluciones hispánicas.* Madrid: Editorial MAPFRE, 1992.

Guerrero, Andrés. "The Construction of a Ventriloquist's Image: Liberal Discourse and the 'Miserable Indian Race' in Late 19th-Century Ecuador." *Journal of Latin American Studies* 29:3 (October 1997): 555–90.

———. "Curagas y tenientes políticos: la ley de la costumbre y la ley del estado (Otavalo 1830–1875)." *Estudios y debates* 2 (December 1989): 321–66.

———. *Los oligarcas del cacao: ensayo sobre la acumulación originaria en el Ecuador; hacendados, cacaoteros, banqueros exportadores y comerciantes en Guayaquil (1890–1910).* Quito: El Conejo, 1980.

————. *La semántica de la dominación: el concertaje de indios.* Quito: Ediciones Libri Mundi, 1991.

Guerrero Blum, Edwing. *Instituto Nacional Mejía: historia y proyección; ciento seis años de educación laica y democrática.* Quito: E. Guerrero Blum, 2003.

Halbwachs, Maurice. *The Collective Memory.* Translated by Francis J. Ditter Jr. and Vida Yazdi Ditter. New York: Harper & Row, 1980.

Hand, Richard J., and Michael Wilson. *Grand-Guignol: The French Theatre of Horror.* Exeter, UK: University of Exeter Press, 2002.

Hardoy, Jorge, ed. *Urbanization in Latin America: Approaches and Issues.* Garden City, NY: Anchor Books, 1975.

————, and Richard Morse, eds. *Rethinking the Latin American City.* Washington, DC: Woodrow Wilson Center Press; Baltimore: Johns Hopkins University Press, 1993.

Harley, J. B. *The New Nature of Maps: Essays in the History of Cartography,* edited by Paul Laxton. Baltimore: Johns Hopkins University Press, 2001.

Harvey, David. *The Condition of Postmodernity: An Enquiry into the Origins of Cultural Change.* Oxford: Blackwell Press, 1989.

Heidegger, Martin. *Poetry, Language, Thought.* New York: Harper & Row, 1971.

Henderson, Peter V. N. *Gabriel García Moreno and Conservative State Formation in the Andes.* Austin: University of Texas Press, 2008.

Herzog, Tamar. *Defining Nations: Immigrants and Citizens in Early Modern Spain and Spanish America.* New Haven: Yale University Press, 2003.

Hidalgo, Angel Emilio, and María Elena Bedoya. "Guayaquil y Quito: la imagen deseada, 1910–1930." *Boletín de la Biblioteca Municipal de Guayaquil* 87 (2003): 169–79.

Hobsbawm, Eric, and Terence Ranger, eds. *The Invention of Tradition.* Cambridge: Cambridge University Press, 1983.

El Instituto Geográfico Militar a través de la historia. Quito: Instituto Geográfico Militar, 2002.

Johnson, Julie Greer. *Satire in Colonial Spanish America: Turning the New World Upside Down.* Austin: University of Texas Press, 1993.

Joséfa, M. T. *García Moreno, président de la république de l'Equateur.* Paris, 1892.

Jrade, Cathy L. *Modernismo, Modernity, and the Development of Spanish American Literature.* Austin: University of Texas Press, 1998.

Kagan, Richard L., with Fernando Marías. *Urban Images of the Hispanic World, 1493–1793.* New Haven: Yale University Press, 2000.

Kennedy Troya, Alexandra, and Alfonso Ortiz Crespo. "Continuismo colonial y cosmopolitismo en la arquitectura y el arte decimonónico ecuatoriano." In *Nueva historia del Ecuador.* Vol. 8, *Época republicana II,* edited by Enrique Ayala Mora and Gonzalo Ortiz, 115–39. Quito: Corporación Editora Nacional/grijalbo, 1990.

Kingman Garcés, Eduardo. *La ciudad y los otros, Quito 1860–1940: higienismo, ornato y policía.* Quito: FLACSO, 2006.

————. "Quito y el siglo naciente." *Cultura: Revista del Banco Central del Ecuador* 8:24c (January–April 1986): 871–75.

————. "Quito, vida social y modificaciones urbanas." In *Enfoques y estudios históricos: Quito a través de la historia*, 129–52. Quito: Editorial Fraga, 1992.

————, and Ana María Goetschel. "Quito: las ideas de orden y progreso y las nuevas extirpaciones culturales." In *Enfoques y estudios históricos: Quito a través de la historia*, 153–62. Quito: Editorial Fraga, 1992.

Ladin, Jay. "Fleshing Out the Chronotope." In *Critical Essays on Mikhail Bakhtin*, edited by Caryl Emerson, 212–36. New York: G. K. Hall, 1999.

Lane, Kris. *Quito 1599: City and Colony in Transition*. Albuquerque: University of New Mexico Press, 2002.

Larsen, Stein Ugelvik, ed. *Fascism Outside Europe: The European Impulse against Domestic Conditions in the Diffusion of Global Fascism*. Boulder, CO: Social Science Monographs, 2001.

Lavallé, Bernard. *Quito y la crisis de la alcabala 1580–1600*. Quito: IFEA, Corporación Editora Nacional, 1997.

Lear, John. *Workers, Neighbors, and Citizens: The Revolution in Mexico City*. Lincoln: University of Nebraska Press, 2001.

Lozano Castro, Alfredo. *Quito: ciudad milenaria, forma y símbolo*. Quito: Ediciones Abya-Yala, 1991.

Lucero, José Antonio. *Struggles of Voice: The Politics of Indigenous Representation in the Andes*. Pittsburgh: University of Pittsburgh Press, 2008.

Luna Tamayo, Milton. *Historia y conciencia popular: el artesanado en Quito, economía, organización, y vida cotidiana, 1890–1930*. Quito: Corporación Editora Nacional, 1989.

————. "Orígenes del movimiento obrero de la sierra ecuatoriana: el Centro Obrero Católico." *Cultura* 9:26 (September–December 1986): 285–315.

MacCormack, Sabine. *Religion in the Andes: Vision and Imagination in Early Colonial Peru*. Princeton: Princeton University Press, 1991.

Maldonado, Carlos. "La arquitectura de Quito en la época republicana." In *Quito: una visión histórica de su arquitectura*, 137–52. Quito: I. Municipio de Quito–Junta de Andalucía, 1993.

————. *La arquitectura en Ecuador: estudio histórico*. Quito: Centro Audiovisual, 1982.

Malo González, Claudio. "Histos en la plástica cuencana del siglo XX." In *De la inocencia a la libertad: arte cuencano del siglo XX*, edited by Andrés Abad Marchán, 47–49. Cuenca: Banco Central del Ecuador, 1998.

Martínez, Elizabeth Coonrod. *Before the Boom: Latin American Revolutionary Novels of the 1920s*. Lanham, MD: University Press of America, 2001.

Martínez Riaza, Ascensión. "El Perú y España durante el oncenio: el hispanismo en el discurso oficial y en las manifestaciones simbólicas (1919–1930)." *Historica* 18:2 (December 1994): 335–82.

McFarlane, Anthony. "The 'Rebellion of the Barrios': Urban Insurrection in Bourbon Quito." *Hispanic American Historical Review* 69:2 (May 1989): 283–330.

Meade, Teresa A. *"Civilizing" Rio: Reform and Resistance in a Brazilian City, 1889–1930*. University Park: Pennsylvania State University Press, 1997.

Mignolo, Walter. *The Darker Side of the Renaissance: Literacy, Territoriality, and Colonization.* 2nd ed. Ann Arbor: University of Michigan Press, 2003.

Mills, Kenneth R. *Idolatry and Its Enemies: Colonial Andean Religion and Extirpation, 1640–1750.* Princeton: Princeton University Press, 1997.

Mills, Kenneth, and William B. Taylor, eds. *Colonial Spanish America: A Documentary History.* Wilmington, DE: Scholarly Resources, 1998.

Minchom, Martin. *The People of Quito, 1690–1810: Change and Unrest in the Underclass.* Boulder, CO: Westview Press, 1994.

Mino, Reinaldo. *Eugenio Espejo y la defensa de los indios.* Quito: Sistema Nacional de Bibliotecas, 1995.

———. *Visión actual de Eugenio Espejo.* Quito: Fundación Eugenio Espejo/Fundación Friedrich Naumann, 1988.

Miranda Ribadeneira, Francisco. *La primera escuela politécnica del Ecuador: estudio histórico e interpretación.* Quito: Ediciones Feso, 1972.

Morales Moreno, Elsa Susana, Alicia Verónica Oña Velasco, and María Verónica Padrón Cosíos. "Análisis histórico de la obra arquitectónica del Arq. Francisco Durini Cáceres en la ciudad de Quito." BFA thesis, Universidad Central del Ecuador, 2001.

Morelli, Federica. "Las reformas en Quito: la redistribución del poder y la consolidación de la jurisdicción municipal (1765–1809)." *Jahrbuch für Geschichte von Staat, Wirtschaft und Gessellschaft Lateinamerikas,* no. 34 (1997): 183–207.

———. *Territorio o nazione: riforma e dissoluzione dello spazio imperiale in Ecuador, 1765–1830.* Soveria Mannelli, Italy: Rubbetino Editore, 2001.

———. "Un neo-sincretismo político: representación política y sociedad indígena durante el primer liberalismo hispanoamericano; el caso de la Audiencia de Quito (1813–1850)." In *Muchas Hispanoaméricas: antropología, historia y enfoques culturales en los estudios latinoamericanistas,* edited by T. Krüggeler and U. Mücke, 151–65. Madrid: Iberoamericana, 2001.

Moreno Yañez, Segundo E. *Alexander von Humboldt: diarios de viaje en la Audiencia de Quito.* Translated by Christiana Borchat de Moreno. Quito: Occidental Exploration and Production, 2005.

———. *Sublevaciones indígenas en la Audiencia de Quito: desde comienzos del siglo XVIII hasta finales de la colonia.* 4th ed. Quito: Ediciones de la Pontificia Universidad Católica del Ecuador, 1995.

Morse, Richard M. *New World Soundings: Culture and Ideology in the Americas.* Baltimore: Johns Hopkins University Press, 1989.

———. "The Urban Development of Colonial Spanish America." In *The Cambridge History of Latin America.* Vol. 2, *Colonial Latin America,* edited by Leslie Bethell, 67–104. Cambridge: Cambridge University Press, 1984.

———, and Jorge E. Hardoy, eds. *Rethinking the Latin American City.* Washington, DC: Woodrow Wilson Center Press; Baltimore: Johns Hopkins University Press, 1993.

Mundy, Barbara E. *The Mapping of New Spain: Indigenous Cartography and the Maps of the Relaciones Geográficas.* Chicago: University of Chicago Press, 1996.

Muratorio, Blanca, ed. *Imágenes e imagineros: representaciones de los indígenas ecuatorianos, siglos XIX y XX.* Quito: FLACSO, 1994.

Needell, Jeffrey D. *A Tropical Belle Epoque: Elite Culture and Society in Turn-of-the-Century Rio de Janeiro.* Cambridge: Cambridge University Press, 1987.

Nora, Pierre, ed. *Realms of Memory: Rethinking the French Past.* Vol. 1, *Conflicts and Divisions.* Translated by Arthur Goldhammer. Edited by L. Kritzman. New York: Columbia University Press, 1996.

—————. *Realms of Memory: Rethinking the French Past.* Vol. 3, *Symbols.* Translated by Arthur Goldhammer. New York: Columbia University Press, 1998.

Nuñez, Estuardo. *Ricardo Palma Escritor Continental: Tras las huellas de Palma en Hispanoamérica.* Lima: Banco Central de Reserva del Perú, 1998.

Olsen, Donald J. *The City as a Work of Art: London, Paris, Vienna.* New Haven: Yale University Press, 1986.

Otero, José. "Humberto Salvador: el hombre, sus temas y su creación." PhD dissertation, University of New Mexico, 1970.

Overmyer-Velázquez, Mark. *Visions of the Emerald City: Modernity, Tradition, and the Formation of Porfirian Oaxaca, México.* Durham, NC: Duke University Press, 2006.

Padrón, Ricardo. "Cumandá and the Cartographers: Nationalism and Form in Juan León Mera." *Annals of Scholarship* 12:3–4 (1998): 217–34.

Páez Cordero, Alexei. *Los orígenes de la izquierda ecuatoriana.* Quito: Abya-Yala, 2001.

Palmer, Gabrielle G. *Sculpture in the Kingdom of Quito.* Albuquerque: University of New Mexico Press, 1987.

Pazos Barrera, Juan, ed. *Juan León Mera: una visión actual.* Quito: Corporación Editora Nacional, 1995.

Paz y Miño, Luis T. *Apuntaciones para una geografía urbana de Quito.* Mexico City: Instituto Panamericano de Geografía e Historia, 1960.

Paz y Miño Cepeda, Juan J. *Revolución juliana: nación, ejército y bancocracia.* Quito: Abya-Yala, 2000.

Peralta, Evelia. *Quito: guía arquitectónica.* Quito: I. Municipio de Quito–Junta de Andalucía, 1991.

Pérez, Pilar. "Cuando los montes se vuelven carbon: la transformación de los paisajes en los alrededores de Quito, 1860–1940." MA thesis, FLACSO-Ecuador, n.d.

Pérez, Trinidad. "La apropiación de lo indígena popular en el arte ecuatoriano del primer cuarto de siglo: Camilo Egas (1915–1923)." In *1 simposio de historia del arte: artes "académicas" y populares del Ecuador,* ed. Alexandra Kennedy Troya, 143–59. Quito: Abya-Yala/Paul Rivet 1995.

Peyronnie, Karine, and René de Maximy. *Quito inattendu: Le Centre Historique en devenir.* Paris: CNRS Éditions, 2002.

Phelan, John Leddy. *The Kingdom of Quito in the Seventeenth Century: Bureaucratic Politics in the Spanish Empire.* Madison: University of Wisconsin Press, 1967.

—————. *The Millennial Kingdom of the Franciscans in the New World.* Berkeley: University of California Press, 1970.

Piccato, Pablo. *City of Suspects: Crime in Mexico City, 1900–1931.* Durham, NC: Duke University Press, 2001.

Pickles, John. *A History of Spaces: Cartographic Reason, Mapping, and the Geo-Coded World.* London: Routledge, 2004.

Pike, Frederick. *Hispanismo, 1898–1936: Spanish Conservatives and Liberals and Their Relations with Spanish America.* South Bend, IN: University of Notre Dame Press, 1971.

Pineo, Ronn F. *Social and Economic Reform in Ecuador: Life and Work in Guayaquil.* Gainesville: University Press of Florida, 1996.

Pólit Dueñas, Gabriela, ed. *Crítica literaria ecuatoriana: antología.* Quito: FLACSO, 2001.

Ponce Leiva, Pilar. *Certeza ante la incertidumbre: élite y cabildo de Quito en el siglo XVII.* Quito: Abya-Yala, 1998.

Poole, Deborah. *Vision, Race, and Modernity: A Visual Economy of the Andean Image World.* Princeton: Princeton University Press, 1997.

Porras, María Elena, and Pedro Calvo-Sotelo, eds. *Ecuador-España: historia y perspectiva.* Quito: Embajada de España, 2001.

Powers, Karen Viera. *Andean Journeys: Migration, Ethnogenesis, and State in Colonial Quito.* Albuquerque: University of New Mexico Press, 1995.

———. "A Battle of Wills: Inventing Chiefly Legitimacy in the Colonial North Andes." In *Dead Giveaways: Indigenous Testaments of Colonial Mesoamerica and the Andes,* edited by Susan Kellogg and Matthew Restall, 183–213. Salt Lake City: University of Utah Press, 1998.

———. "Land Concentration and Environmental Degradation: Town Council Records on Deforestation in Uyumbicho (Quito, 1553–96)." In *Colonial Lives: Documents on Latin American History, 1550–1850,* edited by Richard Boyer and Geoffrey Spurling, 11–17. Oxford: Oxford University Press, 2000.

Pratt, Mary Louise. *Imperial Eyes: Travel Writing and Transculturation.* 2nd ed. New York: Routledge, 2008.

Prieto, Mercedes. *Liberalismo y temor: imaginando los sujetos indígenas en el Ecuador postcolonial, 1895–1950.* Quito: FLACSO, 2004.

———. "Los indios y la nación: historias y memorias en disputa." In *Celebraciones centenarias y negociaciones por la nación ecuatorianas,* edited by Mercedes Prieto and Valeria Coronel. Quito: FLACSO, 2010.

Quantrill, Malcolm, ed. *Latin American Architecture: Six Voices.* College Station: Texas A&M University Press, 2000.

Quintero, Rafael, and Erika Silva. "La crisis nacional general de 1895." *Cultura* 4:11 (September–December 1981): 93–107.

———. *Ecuador: una nación en ciernes.* 3rd ed. Quito: Abya-Yala, 1998.

Quito: una visión histórica de su arquitectura. Quito: TRAMA, 1993.

Rama, Angel. *La ciudad letrada.* Hanover, NH: Ediciones del Norte, 1984.

Ramos, Julio. *Desencuentros de la modernidad en América Latina: literatura y política en el siglo XIX.* Mexico City: Fondo de Cultura Económica, 1989.

Rappaport, Joanne. *The Politics of Memory: Native Historical Interpretation in the Colombian Andes.* 2nd ed. Durham, NC: Duke University Press, 1998.

Reimers, Luis Andrade. *Olmedo: el estadista.* Quito: Editorial Ediguias, 1993.

Ribadeneira, J. Enrique, and Luis Cornelio Diaz V. *Cien años de legislación militar, 1830–1930.* Quito: Editorial Gutenberg, 1930.

Ristow, Walter William. *American Maps and Mapmakers: Commercial Cartography in the Nineteenth Century.* Detroit: Wayne State University Press, 1985.

Robles, Humberto E. *La noción de vanguardia en el Ecuador: recepción - trayectoria – documentos. 1918–1934.* Guayaquil: Casa de la Cultura Ecuatoriana "Benjamín Carrión," Nucleo del Guayas, 1989.

Rodríguez, Linda Alexander. *The Search for Public Policy: Regional Politics and Government Finances in Ecuador, 1830–1940.* Berkeley: University of California Press, 1985.

Rodriguez Bernal, Eduardo. *Historia de la Exposición Ibero-Americana de Sevilla de 1929.* Seville: Ayuntamiento de Sevilla, 1994.

Rodríguez O., Jaime E. *The Emergence of Spanish America: Vicente Rocafuerte and Spanish Americanism, 1808–1832.* Berkeley: University of California Press, 1975.

———. *The Independence of Spanish America.* Cambridge: Cambridge University Press, 1998.

Roig, Arturo Andrés. *Pensamiento social de Juan Montalvo: sus lecciones al pueblo.* Quito: Editorial Tercer Mundo, 1984.

Romera Navarro, M. *El hispanismo en Norte-América: exposición y crítica de su aspecto literario.* Madrid: Renacimiento, 1917.

Roniger, Luis, and Carlos H. Waisman, eds. *Globality and Multiple Modernities: Comparative North American and Latin American Perspectives.* Brighton, UK: Sussex Academic Press, 2002.

Safier, Neil. *Measuring the New World: Enlightenment Science and South America.* Chicago: University of Chicago Press, 2008.

Salvatore, Ricardo D., and Carlos Aguirre, eds. *The Birth of the Penitentiary in Latin America: Essays on Criminology, Prison Reform, and Social Control, 1830–1940.* Austin: University of Texas Press, 1996.

Sarlo, Beatriz. *Una modernidad periférica: Buenos Aires, 1920 y 1930.* Buenos Aires: Ediciones Nueva Visión, 1988.

Sattar, Aleezé. "An Unresolved Inheritance: Postcolonial State Formation and Indigenous Communities in Chimborazo, Ecuador, 1820–1875." PhD dissertation, New School University, 2001.

Schivelbusch, Wolfgang. *Disenchanted Night: The Industrialization of Light in the Nineteenth Century.* Translated by Angela Davies. Berkeley: University of California Press, 1988.

Schmidt-Nowara, Christopher. *The Conquest of History: Spanish Colonialism and National Histories in the Nineteenth Century.* Pittsburgh: University of Pittsburgh Press, 2006.

Seed, Patricia. *Ceremonies of Possession in Europe's Conquest of the New World, 1492–1640.* Cambridge: Cambridge University Press, 1995.

Segre, Roberto. *América Latina, fin de milenio: raíces y perspectivas de su arquitectura*. Havana: Editorial Arte y Literatura, 1999.

Sepúlveda Muñoz, Isidro. "Medio siglo de asociacionismo americanista español 1885–1936." *Espacio, Tiempo y Forma* 4 (1991): 271–90.

Sharman, Adam. *Tradition and Modernity in Spanish American Literature: From Darío to Carpentier*. New York: Palgrave Macmillan, 2006.

Shaw, Donald L. *A Companion to Modern Spanish American Fiction*. London: Tamesis, 2002.

Shultz, Kirsten. *Tropical Versailles: Empire, Monarchy, and the Portuguese Royal Court in Rio de Janeiro, 1808–1821*. New York: Routledge, 2001.

Sibley, David. "Outsiders in Society and Space." In *Inventing Places: Studies in Cultural Geography*, edited by Kay Anderson and Fay Gale, 107–22. Melbourne: Longman Chesire, 1992.

Simonato, Giacinto. *"Dio non muore!" García Moreno, drama storico in 4 atti*. Milan: G. Daviero, 1933.

Simonelli, Lucía. "Jacinto Jijón y Caamaño y el Barrio Obrero." *TRAMA* 55 (1991): 37–43.

Stepan, Nancy. *"The Hour of Eugenics": Race, Gender, and Nation in Latin America*. Ithaca, NY: Cornell University Press, 1991.

Striffler, Steve. *In the Shadows of State and Capital: The United Fruit Company, Popular Struggle, and Agrarian Restructuring in Ecuador, 1900–1995*. Durham, NC: Duke University Press, 2002.

Szászdi, Adam. "The Historiography of the Republic of Ecuador." *Hispanic American Historical Review* 44:4 (November 1964): 503–50.

Tauzin Castellanos, Isabelle. *Las tradiciones peruanas de Ricardo Palma: claves de una coherencia*. Lima: Universidad Ricardo Palma, 1999.

Tenorio Trillo, Mauricio. *Argucias de la historia: siglo XIX, cultura y "América Latina."* Mexico City: Paidós, 1999.

———. *Mexico at the World's Fairs: Crafting a Modern Nation*. Berkeley: University of California Press, 1996.

———. "1910 Mexico City: Space and Nation in the City of the *Centenario*." *Journal of Latin American Studies* 28:1 (February 1996): 75–104.

Thurner, Mark, and Andres Guerrero, eds. *After Spanish Rule: Postcolonial Predicaments of the Americas*. Durham, NC: Duke University Press, 2003.

Valencia Sala, Gladys. *El círculo modernista ecuatoriana: crítica y poesía*. Quito: Universidad Andina; Abya-Yala, 2007.

Van Aken, Mark J. *King of the Night: Juan José Flores and Ecuador, 1824–1864*. Berkeley: University of California Press, 1989.

Varela, Javier. *La novela en España: los intelectuales y el problema español*. Madrid: Taurus, 1999.

Vásconez, Mario, Andrea Carrión, Ana María Goetschel, and Nancy Sánchez. *Breve historia de los servicios en la ciudad de Quito*. Quito: CIUDAD, 1997.

Vasquez Hahn, María Antonieta. *El Palacio de la Exposición, 1909–1989*. Quito: CNPCC/Casa de la Cultura Ecuatoriana, 1989.

Vela Witt, María Susana. *El Departamento del Sur en la Gran Colombia, 1822–1830*. Quito: Abya-Yala, 1999.

Vera H., Humberto. *Equator: History and Geography of the Equatorial Monument*. Translated by Adriana Vera S. Quito: Ediciones Ecuador, 1990.

Villacres Moscoso, Jorge W. *Historia diplomática de la República del Ecuador*. Vol. 2. Guayaquil: Imprenta de la Universidad de Guayaquil, 1971.

Walls, Laura Dassow. *The Passage to Cosmos: Alexander von Humboldt and the Shaping of America*. Chicago: University of Chicago Press, 2009.

Webster, Susan V. *Arquitectura y empresa en el Quito colonial: José Jaime Ortiz, Alarife Mayor*. Quito: Abya-Yala, 2002.

———. "The Devil and the Dolorosa: History and Legend in Quito's Capilla de Cantuña." *The Americas* 67:1 (July 2010): 1–30.

Williams, Derek. "Negotiating the State: National Utopias and Local Politics in Ecuador, 1845–75." PhD dissertation, State University of New York at Stony Brook, 2001.

———. "Popular Liberalism and Indian Servitude: The Making and Unmaking of Ecuador's Antilandlord State, 1845–1868." *Hispanic American Historical Review* 83:4 (November 2003): 697–733.

Wood, Denis, with John Fels. *The Power of Maps*. New York: Guilford Press, 1992.

Woodward, David, Catherine Delano-Smith, and Cordell D. K. Yee, eds. *Approaches and Challenges in a Worldwide History of Cartography*. Barcelona: Institut Cartogràfic de Catalunya, 2000.

Ycaza, Patricio. *Historia del movimiento obrero ecuatoriano: de su génesis al Frente Popular*. Quito: CEDIME, 1984.

———. *Movimiento estudiantil: ¿para dónde camina?* Quito: Centro de Educación Popular, 1989.

Zamora Vicente, Alonso. *La Real Academia Española*. Madrid: Espasa Calpe, S.A., 1999.

Index